Population, Ecology, and Social Evolution

World Anthropology

General Editor

SOL TAX

Patrons

CLAUDE LÉVI-STRAUSS
MARGARET MEAD
LAILA SHUKRY EL HAMAMSY
M. N. SRINIVAS

MOUTON PUBLISHERS · THE HAGUE · PARIS
DISTRIBUTED IN THE USA AND CANADA BY ALDINE, CHICAGO

Population, Ecology, and Social Evolution

Editor

STEVEN POLGAR

MOUTON PUBLISHERS · THE HAGUE · PARIS

DISTRIBUTED IN THE USA AND CANADA BY ALDINE, CHICAGO

General Editor's Preface

At the World Population Conference in Bucharest in 1974, delegates from the developing nations refused to accept as "the problem" the overproduction of people. They insisted that rates of population growth be treated in a broader socioeconomic context. This book provides for that task an anthropological perspective, discussing for the whole species, from its beginning, the what, when, how, and why of its increasing numbers. It does so in bio-medical, social, and historical perspective. Many of the critical discoveries recorded in this book are recent, some of them reported here for the first time. In his introductory essay, the editor puts together a consistent thesis based largely on new understandings from these recent data, and emphasizes the way in which his interpretations relate to other views expressed in the book. This work then is a major contribution inspired by an interaction and interchange of ideas among human scientists at the IXth International Congress of Anthropological and Ethnological Sciences.

Like most contemporary sciences, anthropology is a product of the European tradition. Some argue that it is a product of colonialism, with one small and self-interested part of the species dominating the study of the whole. If we are to understand the species, our science needs substantial input from scholars who represent a variety of the world's cultures. It was a deliberate purpose of the IXth International Congress of Anthropological and Ethnological Sciences to provide impetus in this direction. The *World Anthropology* volumes, therefore, offer a first glimpse of a human science in which members from all societies have played an active role. Each of the books is designed to be self-contained; each is an attempt to update its particular sector of scientific knowledge and is written by specialists from all parts of the world. Each volume should be read and reviewed individually as a separate volume on its own given subject. The set as a whole will indicate what changes are in store for anthropology as scholars from the developing countries join in studying the species of which we are all a part.

The IXth Congress was planned from the beginning not only to include as many of the scholars from every part of the world as possible, but also with a view toward the eventual publication of the papers in high-quality volumes. At previous Congresses scholars were invited to bring papers which were then read out loud. They were necessarily limited in length; many were only summarized; there was little time for discussion; and the sparse discussion could only be in one language. The IXth Congress was an experiment aimed at changing this. Papers were written with the intention of exchanging them before the Congress, particularly in extensive pre-Congress sessions; they were not intended to be read aloud at the Congress, that time being devoted to discussions — discussions which were simultaneously and professionally translated into five languages. The method for eliciting the papers was structured to make as representative a sample as was allowable when scholarly creativity — hence self-selection — was critically important. Scholars were asked both to propose papers of their own and to suggest topics for sessions of the Congress which they might edit into volumes. All were then informed of the suggestions and encouraged to re-think their own papers and the topics. The process, therefore, was a continuous one of feedback and exchange and it has continued to be so even after the Congress. The some two thousand papers comprising *World Anthropology* certainly then offer a substantial sample of world anthropology. It has been said that anthropology is at a turning point; if this is so, these volumes will be the historical direction-markers.

As might have been foreseen in the first post-colonial generation, the large majority of the Congress papers (82 percent) are the work of scholars identified with the industrialized world which fathered our traditional discipline and the institution of the Congress itself: Eastern Europe (15 percent); Western Europe (16 percent); North America (47 percent); Japan, South Africa, Australia, and New Zealand (4 percent). Only 18 percent of the papers are from developing areas: Africa (4 percent); Asia-Oceania (9 percent); Latin America (5 percent). Aside from the substantial representation from the U.S.S.R. and the nations of Eastern Euope, a significant difference between this corpus of written material and that of other Congresses is the addition of the large proportion of contributions from Africa, Asia, and Latin

America. "Only 18 percent" is two to four times as great a proportion as that of other Congresses; moreover, 18 percent of 2,000 papers is 360 papers, 10 times the number of "Third World" papers presented at previous Congresses. In fact, these 360 papers are more than the total of ALL papers published after the last International Congress of Anthropological and Ethnological Sciences which was held in the United States (Philadelphia, 1956). Even in the beautifully organized Tokyo Congress in 1968 less than a third as many members from developing nations, including those of Asia, participated.

The significance of the increase is not simply quantitative. The input of scholars from areas which have until recently been no more than subject matter for anthropology represents both feedback and also long-awaited theoretical contributions from the perspectives of very different cultural, social, and historical traditions. Many who attended the IXth Congress were convinced that anthropology would not be the same in the future. The fact that the next Congress (India, 1978) will be our first in the "Third World" may be symbolic of the change. Meanwhile, sober consideration of the present set of books will show how much, and just where and how, our discipline is being revolutionized.

This particular book, and its companion volume, *Population and social organization*, edited by Moni Nag, profited from a conference held in Oshkosh, Wisconsin, immediately prior to the Congress, where scholars gathered from all over the world to discuss the issues and prepare their presentation to the Congress. Here they also took the first steps toward anthropological participation in the United Nations Population Conference a year later in Bucharest. Combined or separately, these two volumes will certainly mark the beginning of "population anthropology" as a dynamic and important sub-discipline in its own right.

Chicago, Illinois　　　　　　　　　　　　　　　　　　　SOL TAX
February 14, 1975

Table of Contents

General Editor's Preface   v

Population, Evolution, and Theoretical Paradigms   1
   by *Steven Polgar*

Determination of the Size, Density, and Growth Rate of Hunting-
   Gathering Populations   27
   by *Fekri A. Hassan*

The Earliest Farming: Demography as Cause and Consequence   53
   by *Bennet Bronson*

Population Pressure and the Origins of Agriculture: An Archaeological Example From the Coast of Peru   79
   by *Mark N. Cohen*

Scarcity, the Factors of Production, and Social Evolution   123
   by *Michael J. Harner*

Population and Social Variation in Early Bronze Age Denmark:
   A Systemic Approach   139
   by *Klavs Randsborg*

Paleoecology, Paleodemography and Health   167
   by *J. Lawrence Angel*

Population Pressure, Land Tenure, and Agricultural Development
   in Southeastern Ghana   191
   by *G.K. Nukunya*

Group-Centered Behavior and Cultural Growth: A Summary of
   Ecology and Superstructures   219
   by *M. E. Sarmela*

Ethnocultural Development in External and Internal Isolates   227
  by *R. F. Its*

Social Evolution, Population, and Production   235
  by *James C. Faris*

Ecosystem Analogies in Cultural Ecology   273
  by *John W. Bennett*

Organizational Evolution from Mating Pairs to Trading Nations:
  Spontaneous and Competitive Striving with Interacting Individuals All Regulating Each Other   305
  by *F. L. W. Richardson*

Biographical Notes   337

Index of Names   341

Index of Subjects   347

Population, Evolution, and Theoretical Paradigms

STEVEN POLGAR

INTRODUCTION

Population anthropology seems to be emerging as a focussed area of investigation bringing together specialists from archeology, sociocultural anthropology, biological anthropology and applied anthropology. The monographs by Nag (1962), Stevenson (1968) and Acsádi and Nemeskéri (1970), the collections edited by Polgar (1971), Spooner (1972), Harrison and Boyce (1972) and Marshall and Polgar (i.p.), and the special issues of *Current Anthropology* (1972) and *World Archaeology* (1973) are illustrative of this trend. In addition to the present collection, Nag (i.p.) is editing another volume of papers presented at the IXth International Congress of Anthropological and Ethnological Sciences. While Nag's volume will be largely concerned with sociocultural and applied aspects of population studies, this one concentrates on historical and ecological perspectives.

The primary questions to be addressed in this book concern the role of population dynamics in evolutionary culture change. For example, is population change usually a consequence or a cause of other kinds of culture change? Are these relationships similar at different times and in different places, or is the role of population change highly variable? What are the relevant components of population dynamics for the culture historian? To what extent are population dynamics determined by biological factors as opposed to voluntary cultural influences? Should population growth among humans be regarded as a measure of evolutionary "success"?

To organize the various answers to these questions, I find it useful to employ the following simplified scheme for the major divisions of human evolution:

1. gathering-hunting bands;
2. unstratified food producers;
3. feudal societies; and
4. colonial and industrial societies.

In the first section of this paper I will briefly review the course of human evolution, emphasizing the demographic changes that might have been important. The second part of this introduction will consist of some comments on theories of causation and on the idea of evolution as "progress."

A few of the papers in this volume do not deal with population dynamics as a central issue; however, they do concern evolution and ecology, and since they were presented at the session of the Congress along with the rest, it was deemed appropriate to include them.

Finally, let me note that instead of merely introducing the papers in this volume I will take advantage of my position as editor to enter the debate and express my own views.

POPULATION AND EVOLUTIONARY TRANSITIONS

Hominization

Among pre-human primates, except for periods when given species expanded their range and their numbers, population was kept stationary by biological mechanisms (including species-specific patterns of intra- and inter-group social competition such as Richardson refers to in this volume). With hominization, certain physiological changes seem to have occurred which are highly relevant to population dynamics: first, ovulation changed from a seasonal to a monthly pattern; and second, lactation ceased to provide complete protection against fertilization. As a result of these changes, and perhaps of other factors such as the lengthening of the reproductive period and the possible lowering of mortality among the young under human patterns of parental care, a significantly increased potential for population growth developed. However, despite this potential to double the size of the group in each generation (Birdsell 1957), the rate of increase during the Pleistocene remained between 0.001 and 0.002 percent per year on the average (Hassan in this volume), which leads to the conclusion that voluntary cultural checks on natality appeared very early in human evolution. This position, set forth in more detail previously (Polgar 1972), and supported by Hassan, differs from Faris' views (in this volume). Faris also stresses the discontinuity between pre-human primates and humans, but for him the significant change is the ability of humans to create the subsistence necessary for an increasing population through "social production." He and I agree on the importance of human modes of production, and also that it is unlikely that infanticide and abortion were practiced as a deliberate population regulating "policy" by early food gatherers, but Faris does not consider the MAGNITUDE of potential population growth — as calculated by Birdsell, Deevey (1960), Hassan and myself — in the absence of consistently used birth spacing practices.

Human evolution in general during its first two million years was marked by a number of significant biological and cultural transformations, including the establishment of home bases for migratory bands, sexual division of labor in subsistence activities, incest rules, the transition through at least three successive species, periods of large game hunting, development of better tools, emergence of true language, and expansion into all continents. Compared to what happened later on, the environmental impact of gatherer-hunters was minor. Humans possibly contributed to the extinction of a number of large mammals, and their use of fire might have furthered the replacement of certain areas of forest by grasslands. Recent data on gathering-hunting societies seem to give considerable support to Sahlins' (1968) characterization of them as the "original affluent society" existing on a "low level of throughput," and to the general presumption that such societies lived under relatively homeostatic conditions in a way not much different from most other animal species. With this new understanding, so different from the earlier image of "savages" constantly exposed to hunger, cold, and early death, it becomes all the more puzzling (as pointed out by Bronson and by Cohen in this volume) why humanity should have embarked on the entirely different mode of existence involved in staple agriculture.

Transition to agriculture

There would be very little disagreement among anthropologists nowadays that the transition from gathering to food production was a gradual process, and also a very far-reaching one. Reliance on staple agriculture means that the human species is no longer an ordinary herbivore and carnivore, but after the large-scale domestication of plants and animals — with all that this implies for changing their genetic structure, where they will be found, how they grow and reproduce, and what other living organisms will be deliberately excluded from the areas utilized (Flannery 1965) — the entire ecosystem is radically altered. It is only with the inception of staple agriculture that we can characterize the human ecosystem as "contranatural," in the sense that Bennett (in this volume, following Odum 1969) describes the human use of the environment as one that reverses the usual process of ecological succession toward a "mature" system with low production per biomass. Since this trend arose only about 10,000 years ago, I would not think it is "inherent" in humankind in a species-specific way. Plants and other animals also have great POTENTIAL for population growth and consequent ecological disequilibration (in fact, the reproductive capacity of primates is quite low from this general perspective), but this is ordinarily checked by environmental, behavioral, and genetic regulation systems.

During several millennia preceding the changeover to agriculture, trends can be discerned toward the more intensive exploitation of smaller areas. Many prehistorians see a causative influence of late Pleistocene and early Post-Pleistocene climatic conditions on this phenomenon. Angel (in this volume) mentions this for Europe as well as the Eastern Mediterranean. Binford (1968) has proposed a model in which sedentism in some areas — dependent on more available acquatic resources and on migratory birds — established conditions for heterogeneity in population growth rates, which in turn created "tension zones"; incipient cultivation then developed in what at first were the less favored parts of such zones. Wright (1971) puts more emphasis once again on climatic factors, but follows Childe and Binford in assigning causative influence to population pressure. Following the theoretical model elaborated by the economist Boserup (1965), Smith and Young (1972) reason that increased sedentariness in Mesopotamia, coming after the period of warmer and wetter climatic conditions around 10,000 B.C. led to population growth as health was improved and the more settled mode of life permitted shorter spacing between children; they then hypothesize that this population growth continued beyond the carrying capacity of the environment, which in turn stimulated the development of agriculture. Cohen (this volume) also accepts the Boserup scheme in his analysis of the archeological sequence in the Ancón-Chillón region of Peru. He interprets his findings to indicate a gradual increase of population pressure on resources, leading to territorial expansion. the use of new sources of food, and eventually the adoption of agriculture. However, Smith and Young are unable to pinpoint specific sites where these preagricultural developments supposedly occurred, and Cohen is working in the absence of data from the main site of habitation — the river valley itself. With the exception of Binford, none of the above writers who are inclined to give a major causative role to population pressure in the origins of agriculture seem to have considered demographic processes in any detail; some do not even distinguish population growth as such from pressure upon resources due to high density. Hopefully the articles by Hassan, Bronson, and Angel in this volume will help to correct this situation.

Mesoamerica is the one area of agricultural origins to which the characterization of "settling in" in the Post-Pleistocene seems to apply the least.[1] As in the other regions where staple domestication started, which were also far from glacial boundaries, the change in climate was relatively small and occurred very gradually (MacNeish 1964). In valleys such as Tehuacán and Oaxaca there is some relatively predictable rainfall, whereas in coastal Peru reliance has to be primarily on rivers and subterranean sources of water. The main staple crop, maize, required considerable genetic modification before it could provide a major part of subsistence, whereas even the wild varieties of wheat and barley growing in Mesopotamia could furnish a great deal of food collected over a short period of time, and were more easily changed genetically (Flannery 1972). As a consequence, sedentism in Mesoamerica developed much more slowly and occurred considerably after the full domestication of maize, while in Mesopotamia and the Andes it preceded full-scale agriculture by perhaps as much as 2000 years (Flannery 1972). The development of technology — of both implements and facilities — was much more important in Mesopotamia and the Andes, while in Mesoamerica the primary emphasis apparently remained for a long time on the scheduling of activities, on being at the right place in the right season.

Explanations of the origin of agriculture based on population pressure, like the old "oasis" theory or "climatic shock," emphasize external "push" factors which drive gatherer-hunters towards agriculture out of necessity. Hypotheses to the effect that settled existence was less troublesome, that the output in food for a given amount of labor would be higher with agriculture than with collecting, or that the exploitation of different microenvironments and/or external trade encouraged the development of "surpluses" represent "pull" theories about the transition.

As many previous writers have pointed out, climatic change could not be a sufficient stimulus for the developments leading to the agricultural transition, since the warming and drying at the end of the Pleistocene was not a unique event, even if it had been sufficiently precipitous to affect

---

[1] I am grateful to Professor Donald L. Brockington of the University of North Carolina at Chapel Hill, Department of Anthropology, for a very helpful discussion of this topic. He is not responsible for any of the conclusions I have drawn here, however.

cultural processes. Increasing local population pressure is equally inadequate as a sufficient cause because (as Bronson notes in this volume)
it too might have occurred innumerable times before without leading to
reliance on domesticated staples. Among gatherers, furthermore, the
long-standing cultural means of reducing natality would probably be
intensified, to preserve the health of children or avoid intensified social
conflict, long before population came near the supporting capacity of the
environment, even if outmigration were blocked. Among the "causes"
of agricultural origins I would certainly include the attainment of a
higher level of human skills and technology by 20,000 B.C., a gradual
movement toward the exploitation of smaller units of terrain with longer
periods of occupancy in certain locales (including fishing spots in some
areas), and the intensification of exchange of different products (with a
concomitant production of some "surplus" for exchange). How these
various factors are invoked to explain the processes of cultural change,
relates to the kind of CAUSATIVE THEORY one espouses — a subject to
which I will turn in the next part of this essay.

It is important to distinguish the effect of population growth (or any
other factor) in the first transition to agriculture in a particular region
both from the effect of that factor in the adoption of staple agriculture by
neighboring groups, and from its effect on the intensification of agriculture
after it has been adopted. The introductory section of Cohen's paper (this
volume) refers to all three of these situations, but his empirical example
from Peru concerns one where staple agriculture is introduced from
elsewhere. He argues that knowledge about agriculture long antedates its
adoption, and that it was not until enough population pressure had built
up that the local transition took place. Cohen reports that squash, maize,
and other domesticated cultigens are not grown in the Ancón-Chillón
region for long periods (up to 2000 years or so) after the occurrence of
similar artifact horizons which link it with regions where these cultigens
were already grown. But do innovations in preparing stone tools necessarily "diffuse" at the same speed and along the same path as the complex
of behaviors involved in shifting from a collecting to a food producing
economy? I will not comment here further on the obscurity of the
"stimulus diffusion" concept, beyond metioning its problematic status. I
must, however, agree with Cohen that agriculture has expanded gradually
into much territory formerly occupied by gatherers, that in a competitive
situation gatherers will lose. But even in village agricultural systems I do
not see any "inherent" dynamic that leads to unremitting population
increase.

Finally, I want to remark on Cohen's estimates of the rate of population growth in the area he studied: from twenty-five to fifty people at around 10,000 B.C. to a maximum of 200 to 300 at the beginning of the first settled village agriculture period at 2500 B.C. — or an annual average growth rate of less than 0.01 percent; a rate between 0.4 and 0.7 percent in the following 750 years; a rate of around 0.1 percent between 1750 B.C. and A.D. 400; and then essentially no further growth until the Spanish conquest. These figures represent precisely the stepwise pattern to which Cohen objects in his introductory section! And the dramatic increase in the growth rate occurs AFTER the inception of agriculture (as he defines it), not before!

Transition to Feudalism

If the crux of the transition to staple agriculture is a fundamental change in ecological relationships, I think the corresponding central feature in the transition to feudalism is the change from reciprocal systems of exchange to major reliance on redistribution (cf. Polanyi 1957) and the associated development of power differentials between kin groups. This change in the POLITICAL-ECONOMIC system (for which I use "feudalism" for lack of anything better) is the essential element in the formation of states (which are primarily legal entities), in urbanization (a primarily geographic phenomenon), and in "civilization" (a primarily humanistic and ethnocentric concept).

Like hominization and the transition to agriculture, political-economic centralization has been a gradual process. Redistribution within the family, of course, developed among human gatherers; power differentials, as between adults and children and to a lesser extent between men and women, were also present already in preagricultural societies. Corporate kin groups jointly utilizing and having ownership rights in productive resources, however, do not become important until after the agricultural transition (see Harner 1970, Flannery 1972, Polgar 1973). Many early agricultural villages were probably composed of single lineages (Chang 1958). Within these lineages, the ethnographic evidence would indicate that older individuals have more power over a larger number of people than is the case among gathering-hunting bands. Between lineages, however, exchange relationships remain reciprocal and status relationships are egalitarian. On the basis of the archeological sequence in settlement patterns in the New World, Chang concludes that the single lineage stage was followed by multilineage and nonlineage patterns of village organization. The progression from intracommunity-localized multilineage to intercommunity-localized multilineage, and then to non-lineage societies, is accompanied by increasing political centralization. Flannery's review (1972) of the changes in the construction of dwellings in the Near East and Mesoamerica — from compounds with circular buildings to villages with square houses and increasingly with large "public buildings" — leads to similar conclusions about the early steps in the evolution of political organization toward feudalism.

The foregoing should not be taken to imply that I think there was a single, uniform pattern of evolution toward feudalism. There are important differences between "big men" and "chiefs" (Sahlins 1963), between temple administrators and warrior kings (Adams 1966), between "Mesopotamian careers" (Gearing 1961) and other paths to centralization. And there are societies which continued their development without a great deal of centralization of any kind. In some instances, a central position in a redistribution system — such as that of the Melanesian "big man" — is an achieved, non-hereditary role. In other cases, one lineage may have gained ascendancy over other lineages with which it had previously been related in an egalitarian exchange relationship, and become a "royal" descent group (cf. Mair 1964). Conquest states, slavery and class stratification are yet other significant developments which do not necessarily occur in a given sequence. At an advanced stage of political centralization, lineage organization is weakened — often by deliberate interference with juridical matters formerly considered the "private affairs" of the lineage (Y. A. Cohen 1969) — a development very probably reflected in the reappearance of "homestead"-type settlement patterns in the archeological sequences of Nuclear America (Chang 1958).

From the writings of Sir Henry Maine to present day anthropologists, questions of legitimate authority seem to have dominated the debates about the formation of the state. It seems to me, however, that it is less important to consider HOW DISPUTES ARE SETTLED than to ask WHICH SOCIAL UNIT HAS CONTROL OVER THE MAJOR PRODUCTIVE RESOURCES — or, as Faris puts it, over "social production." Thus, in a full-fledged feudal society the central power holders have ultimate control over the allocation of land. And if there are storehouses, large-scale irrigation works, government officials, armies, fortified towns, or long-distance traders, they too will be subject to control by the rulers.

My basic position about population and the transition to feudalism is that non-kin redistribution systems, at each step toward centralization of economic and political power, influenced the producers to create more of a "surplus" (cf. Orans 1966) — that the producers responded to this coercion by increasing the number of their children, i.e. their domestic labor power (cf. Polgar 1972, 1973), as well as intensifying their use of land.

The major factors that have been proposed by others as causes for the original emergence of "civilization" or urbanization include technology, sociopolitical organization, trade, warfare, and population growth and pressure. Recent discussions often refer to V. Gordon Childe as the main proponent of a purely technological explanation (e.g. Carneiro 1970, Smith and Young 1972, Cohen, this volume). Childe, in fact, changed his opinions over the years. But nowhere does he seem to have explained the "urban revolution" as he called it by a single cause — be it diffusion, technological development, or warfare. In *What happened in history*, for example, Childe emphasized both increasing conflict as population grew and expanded in late neolithic times, and the limitations of self-sufficient villages in the face of local natural calamities (1942:59–61). And about the subsequent transition to the "higher barbarism of the copper age" he writes:

The worst contradictions in the neolithic economy were transcended when farmers were persuaded or compelled to wring from the soil a surplus above their domestic requirements and when this surplus was made available to support new economic classes not directly engaged in producing their own food. The possibility of producing the requisite surplus was inherent in the very nature of the neolithic economy. Its realization, however, required additions to the stock of applied science at the disposal of barbarians as well as a modification in social and economic relations (1942:62).

Adams (1966, 1968) continues this multicausal approach, but gives less importance to technology, mentioning the presence of specialized micro-environments and subsistence pursuits in the areas where independent civilizations originated, and mechanisms of interzonal exchange and redistribution, and stresses the role of early cities as "nodes" in the appropriation and redistribution of agricultural surpluses, as well as administrators of the relations between specialized producers. Some of the contributors to this volume (particularly Bronson, Angel, Its, and Sarmela) also advocate multicausal explanations for evolutionary processes.

Among recent writers, Carneiro (1961, 1970), Boserup (1965), Harner (1970), Smith and Young (1972) and Cohen (this volume) have espoused population pressure as an initiating cause of political centralization and/or the intensification of agricultural production. Cross-sectional ethnographic comparisons indeed demonstrate a close correlation between population size and complexity of social organization (e.g. Naroll 1956, Carneiro 1967), and a study of population densities in Africa before

European dominance (Stevenson 1968) also confirms a direct relationship with feudal polities. But to test causal hypotheses one must look for evidence about the TEMPORAL SEQUENCE in which changes occur in the population-resource ratio, in political-economic centralization and in the patterns of subsistence. Archeological data clearly show that in the course of the transition to feudalism population GROWTH was substantial in areas such as Mesopotamia (Smith and Young 1972) and Mesoamerica (Sanders 1972). Evidence for the relationship between numbers of people and food production, i.e. degree of population PRESSURE, however, is much more difficult to assess. Agriculture was indeed intensified at some points, as shown by changes in pollen and tool types. From the summaries of archeological research like those of Sanders (1972) and Adams (1966), however, it can be concluded that the first appearance of the larger buildings indicating socio-political or religious centralization PREDATES or is contemporaneous with the upward inflection in the population growth curve in "Middle Formative" or equivalent periods, and is clearly earlier than large-scale irrigation.

The Danish Early Bronze Age findings reported by Randsborg (this volume) are quite relevant to this question. In one of the zones investigated there is a significantly greater number of graves than expected during Period III, as well as greater than average social differentiation. In the preceding horizon, it turns out, there is also somewhat greater status differentiation in this zone than in others but only the expected number of graves. Further investigation may well confirm this as an instance where political-economic centralization—perhaps at a point transitional between "big men" of the Melanesian type and hereditary nobles—stimulated population increase.

To return to some ethnographic analyses, Harner (1970) relied on cross-sectional comparisons, but he went beyond stating correlations and attempted to test alternative causative hypotheses. Plotting frequencies of societies at different levels of political complexity against relative reliance on hunting and gathering, he found a statistically significant distribution pattern which he interprets to confirm a model in which population pressure on resources is an antecedent to class stratification and the formation of states. Harner's results would be very damaging to my argument were it not for three points. First, as a substitute for a direct measure of population pressure he uses proportion of subsistence derived from hunting and gathering as opposed to fishing, animal husbandry, and agriculture. I think this is primarily an index of sedentism (complicated by pastoralists), which is by no means equivalent to population pressure. Second, he does not include a category for the "big man" type of political-economic centralization. Third, the data he uses from the *Ethnographic Atlas* are almost inevitably contaminated by the effects of colonialist domination (despite Murdock's selection procedures), a factor not randomly related to either sedentism or political and economic organization.

In his contribution to this volume, Harner contrasts social systemic demands for labor with demands for land. Making scarcity the cornerstone of his analysis, he seems to attribute to agriculturalists even in unstratified societies the same kind of capitalist psychology with unsatiable wants as Adam Smith had (cf. Orans 1966), adding only that services as well as goods are to be included. Harner goes on to describe the "big man" and the "chiefdom" phases of political-economic centralization, and associates the first with labor scarcity and the second with land scarcity. From there he moves to the early state, in which population pressure is even greater, and then discusses in a very stimulating way different types of warfare and technology. While Harner and I continue to disagree in fundamental ways, we now seem to be in accord on the point that population pressure on land did *not* cause the emergence of the "big man" system — the early stage of centralization where, in my view, a "surplus" might first have been extracted, and where population is first stimulated to grow beyond the "safe" level around 30 to 40 percent of the average annual SUPPORTING CAPACITY of the techno-environmental system.

Harner's approach is similar in some respects to that of Carneiro (1961, 1970). Carneiro's central idea is that "environmental circumscription" is a necessary condition for state formation since political centralization will follow upon population increase, leading to competition for land and warfare, in cases where defeated communities cannot or will not want to flee to a distant location. In contrasting the Amazon basin with the Peruvian coast, Carneiro (like many of the others discussed previously) ignores the magnitude of the human population growth potential, which could have filled the "vastnesses" of Amazonia in just a few centuries to a level as dense as the densest of the Peruvian valleys (cf. Bender 1971, for a more apt comparison between South American and West African tropical forest population dynamics). Carneiro makes a distinction between "coercive" and "voluntaristic" theories, which is somewhat like the "push" and "pull" factors I use. In emphasizing that independent village agriculturalists (or preagricultural fishing-gathering communities for that matter) will not voluntarily produce a surplus for someone else's benefit, despite their technological ability to do so, Carneiro and I both follow Childe, Pearson (1957), Orans (1966) and many other critics of liberal economic theory. Furthermore, I accept Carneiro's argument that political centralization tends to proceed faster when geographical barriers, ecological advantages, or population growth (following earlier stages of political centralization) create a "circumscribed" situation. In fact, this may be an opportune juncture to emphasize that I consider population growth and pressure to be important positive feedback stimuli to further steps toward centralization and warfare once the transition to feudalism has gotten under way.

But political centralization also creates countercurrents (cf. Sahlins 1963, for example) and urbanization leads to a deterioration in average health status (Polgar 1964; Angel, this volume), so the feudal period was notable for the rise and fall of empires and the ravages of great plagues. These conditions (or "contradictions" as many Marxists still call them if they haven't got rid of the Hegelian monkey on their backs — cf. Harris 1968) are substantially modified with the advent of colonialism and industrialization, the stage of evolution to which I will now turn.

Colonialism and Industrialization

Empires and plantations had their origins in the feudal period, and long-distance trade occurred even before agriculture. The particular combination of these elements into colonialism, beginning in sixteenth-century Europe, was conditioned by such technological improvements as fire-arms and ships that could sail on the high seas, and by the development of economic mercantilism. The desire to bypass intermediaries, to increase the profits from trade with the Far East, stimulated the technological improvements in ships. Outfitted with cannons and musket-bearing men, the European vessels soon established their superiority, not only along the coasts of Africa and the Americas but in the Indian Ocean and the Far East as well. The explorer-traders were followed by missionaries, garrisons to man forts, slavers, and colonial administrators.

The internal economic organization of Western Europe was significantly altered in the fifteenth and sixteenth centuries through the deliberate destruction of the local protectionism of towns by the state. Mercantilism involved the mobilization of national resources for "the purposes of power in foreign affairs" (Polanyi 1957: 65). But mercantilism transformed only capital into a marketable commodity; land and labor were not completely commercialized until the early nineteenth century when industrialization in England was already well under way (Polanyi 1957: 179ff). Despite wars and epidemics, the population of Europe grew quite substantially from 1650 to 1850, due in some significant part to the widespread adoption of potato cultivation (Langer 1963). And the proportion living in cities increased steadily, more through migration than natural increase. In England the combination of enclosure, the revised poor laws, and fluctuations in the economic success of foreign trade and manufacturing created a large "reserve army" of the unemployed, which in turn helped the final transformation of labor into a market commodity (Polanyi 1957: 91). As the upper class and the increasingly important middle class in Western Europe prospered, thanks to colonialism and industrialization, and as methods of birth control came into wider use and were improved, population growth levelled off in the late nineteenth and early twentieth centuries. The United States, the rest of Europe, and Japan followed suit as they became more urbanized, and upward mobility for large segments of the population became possible. Smaller families, however, had actually become common in some areas (including large sections of France) considerably in advance of these socioeconomic changes, for reasons that have yet to be satisfactorily explained (Coale 1969: Demeny 1968).

In the colonized areas, the main demographic impact of European penetration was a very severe decline in population, due to new diseases, the slave trade, and — with the introduction of firearms — aggravated warfare. Once the metropolitan powers achieved full domination, and shifted from conquest and pillage to the exploitation of the productive and purchasing powers of the colonized peoples, efforts were made to increase both the native and imported labor pools (cf. Polgar 1972; Faris this volume). Only in the last ten years, as the changed economic and political situation made the fast-growing population in the Third World less advantageous for the United States and Western Europe, has the tide turned to the encouragement of measures to slow the rate of increase.

In this era of nation states, population change thus became the object of deliberate national policies. Slavery and indenture were replaced by other measures encouraging immigration, and by public hygiene efforts, for the purpose of enlarging the size and productivity of the labor force. More recently, as the rapid growth of urban population (due both to the influx from the hinterland and to natural increase) exceeded labor requirements and overburdened the service sector, rural development and the building of new towns have become prominent issues in policy discussions. And family planning is now promoted in many countries as an instrument of "population control," instead of being genuinely offered to improve family health and welfare (Polgar i.p.).

The current situation, as we find ourselves at the beginning of a transition into post-industrial society, is also significant from the ecological point of view. Humans and their modification of the environment now affect the entire biosphere. Raw materials and pollutants are redistributed across the oceans and through the air, the limits in using fossil fuels and easily obtained minerals are within a calculable future, and the rate at which animal and plant species are becoming extinct is increasing. Richardson and Bennett, in their contributions to this book, echo the opinion of many commentators in seeing humanity on the brink of disaster. Both of them regard this as a result of characteristics somehow inherent in humanity in general. To me, however, this is not some kind of failure in self-regulation, but a much more specific consequence of the power imbalance favoring nation-states and industrial enterprises over communities and humankind as a whole. And the corresponding remedy I see is to eliminate these concentrations of power, rather than propagandizing a new ethos of ecological "naturalism" among the population at large.

THEORETICAL PARADIGMS

Causation

In attempting to explain culture change — whether on the scale of evolutionary transitions or of a more special, localized kind — it is tempting to look for some "prime movers" analogous to the FORCES of Newtonian physics. Population growth has been used as such an explanatory device in some recent theoretical models. Boserup (1965) has adopted an extreme position in this respect, considering population growth to be "autonomous" with respect to agricultural production; she thus reverses the more common idea that productivity is the independent variable and population change the dependent one. She associates this latter idea with Malthus, and an overriding purpose of her book is to argue against Malthusian views of economic change. Much as I applaud this objective, I believe that her influence on culture historians has been unfortunate to the extent that it has reinforced mechanical thinking in theory formulation. Indeed, the insistence by Cohen (this volume) that he does not consider population growth as an "independent" variable (and readers can judge by themselves to what extent his position is consistent in this regard) shows at least an awareness of this problem.

Carneiro's disagreement (1961, 1970) is not directed at Malthus but at environmental possibilism, and Harner (this volume) argues the formalist side against the substantivist one in economic anthropology. These last two authors, like Boserup, treat population growth as EXOGENOUS to their model of cultural dynamics, a position strongly attacked by Faris and Bronson (this volume) on theoretical grounds, and by Hassan (this volume) on the basis of empirical evidence.

Another external "force" which has a long history as a postulated cause of evolutionary change is climate, particularly in explanations of hominization and the transition to food production. Despite the renewed interest in this factor in connection with fluctuations in Southwest Asia around 10,000 to 8000 B.C. (Wright 1971), many prehistorians are now skeptical about climatic changes being an initial or sufficient cause for the origins of agriculture (see, for example, Bronson, this volume). There is still considerable debate, also, for and against the old idea that desiccation and the reduction of forests "pushed" some hominoids out into the open savanna and toward bipedalism.

Both population growth and climate may appeal to authors who think that culture change must eventually be traced back to noncultural causes. But in their attempt to counteract vitalism and other types of cultural idealist thinking, such authors commit the opposite error of "vulgar materialism" (cf. Faris' attack, in this volume, on those who overemphasize productive forces at the expense of productive relations, as well as his reference to Marx's statement that "every specified historical mode of production has its own specific laws of population, historically valid within its limits alone").

Some theories refer more to INTERNAL dynamics, such as inherent characteristics or "contradictions." The analogies evoked in these instances are not of something "pushing" from the outside, but of an unrelenting drive or some pressures building up inside the system, like steam in a cauldron which eventually might burst. Among the contributors to this book, Faris comes closest to evoking this kind of an image. While in his abstract discussion of evolutionary processes Faris allows for the interaction of internal and external factors, only internal forces are adduced to describe the end of European feudalism, for example, which "could simply not remain a viable and healthy mode of production — it could not maintain the same social relations and a change was necessitated as the contradictions became too great."

Bennett (this volume) also expresses dissatisfaction with the current state of anthropological thinking about evolutionary transitions. But his substitute, "A position with greater concern for policy would propose that there exists in human behavior a constant potential trend toward overexploitation of resources or pollution of the natural environment" does not, in my judgment, represent an advance in epistemology, whatever its heuristic value may be.

Multicausal theories are certainly more satisfactory than unicausal ones, particularly since none of the initiating factors proposed for explaining evolutionary transitions can be shown to have been operating only at the points in time and space when and where the changes from one stage to another took place. Given a relatively large number of factors, the probability of their occurring TOGETHER at one time and place could be small enough that such a model might serve quite adequately for theories of SINGLE origins. But neither the food producing nor the feudal transitions are now believed to have occurred only once, and some factors deemed important in one place have been found absent in others.

At least two more concepts need to be taken into consideration before we can have more satisfactory explanations. The first of these is familiar: the aggregation of prior changes, such as the achievement of fully bipedal locomotion before complex tool-making traditions can develop, or the end of feudal relations between lords and serfs before human labor can become a market commodity. This kind of threshold criteria, and what Faris (this volume) calls potentialities, however, have been quite troublesome in the past. On the one hand, they can easily become merely *ex post facto* arguments or definitional gimmicks (e.g. "civilization" arises when writing, monumental architecture and social stratification are present). Furthermore, many exceptions to proposed evolutionary sequences have been documented (e.g. staple agriculture before pottery in Peru, or political-economic centralization in the absence of food production among Indians of the Northwest coast of North America). But if care is taken to avoid circular reasoning, and if the thresholds may include some alternative conditions (EITHER A, OR B and C), this aspect of explanatory models can remain useful. After all, it seems clear that Neanderthals could not have experienced influenza pandemics, or independent villagers changed very much the carbon dioxide content of the ionosphere.

The second concept is quite new, at least in its more subtle formulation; I will call it the MARUYAMA MODEL OF MUTUAL CAUSAL PROCESSES. Maruyama (1963) has argued that theories of causation should include not only deviation-counteracting but also deviation-amplifying processes. Dumond (1972) has cited Maruyama in his discussion about expanding subsistence as a "choice" when a preagricultural group "perceives" a tendency for population to increase, and Bennett (this volume) refers to "typical human systems" — with increasing organization and a tendency to defer the costs of reversing ecological succession — as instances of positive feedback. But there is much more to Maruyama's model than positive feedback. To begin with, he combines deviation-amplifying processes with indeterminacy: "a small initial deviation, which is within the range of high probability, may develop into a deviation of very low probability (or more precisely, into a deviation which is very improbable within the framework of probabilistic unidirectional causality)." Furthermore, he gives examples of causal networks including more than two elements in which some connections have a positive sign (i.e. varying in a direct relationship to one-another) and others have a negative sign (i.e. varying inversely), and moreover some are unidirectional while others are mutually related. There is also a difference between Maruyama models and flowcharts — such as those of Cochran (1972) and Dumond (1972) — because the latter imply "decisions" while the former are not loaded down with that sometimes unnecessary or misleading psychomorphic implication.

Reliance on traditional explanatory models — whether unicausal or multicausal — fail in my opinion because they seek for overdeterminacy in retrodicting evolutionary events. Maruyama models by themselves may also lead us astray, however, because of their underdeterminacy ("the law of causality is now revised to state that similar conditions may result in dissimilar products," Maruyama 1963: 167). If we use a COMBINATION of probabilistic threshold statements and Maruyama models, I think we will come closer to explanations of cultural evolution and change which accord with the information we now have in hand. Some of the models of population dynamics among hunter-gatherers proposed by Hassan (this volume) and of the transition to staple agriculture by Bronson (this volume) are in fact not too different from this paradigm.

A highly tentative and sketchy "combination model" of the transition to feudalism, according to my analysis, would include some of the following propositions (1 to 3 being threshold factors, the remainder making up a mutually causative model):

1. "Pristine" political-economic centralization may arise in societies of food producers if: (a) they are organized into corporate lineages, when one lineage gains (through a series of medium-low probability "accidents") a strategic position *vis-à-vis* other lineages; or (b) they are not organized into corporate lineages, but there is a considerable degree of specialization between different communities in a region and certain other conditions (see below) obtain.

2. Such centralization may also originate among gatherer-hunters if they are located near the migration routes of a large supply of fish, and if they have developed techniques of catching and preserving large supplies of fish, and if trade with neighboring groups is already on a relatively

high level, and if vegetable foods are also abundant during a large part of the annual cycle.

3. Such centralization may also occur among nomadic pastoralists living in large areas of relatively flat land, if they are in contact with agriculturalists who are at least moderately centralized themselves.

4. The preservation and storage of foodstuffs (in granaries and the like, or "on the hoof") in excess of expected consumption in normal years is directly related to the fluctuation in crop yield due to climatic variables, insect damage, etc.

5. The exchange of some of this "disaster insurance surplus" between nearby communities will be directly related to the extent of ecological and technological differentiation among communities.

6. The greater the heterogeneity in geographical location, kin networks and age-sex distribution, the more certain groups (and individuals) will be in a relatively favored position to act as go-betweens in the exchange relationships described in proposition 5.

7. The more variability in resources available to minimal economic units (such as compounds or households) the greater the community sanctions developed to assure equitable distribution of goods between them.

8. There is low, but greater than zero probability that some individuals will escape or ignore the sanctions described in proposition 7 and take advantage of their fortuitously more favorable position (as described in proportion 6) to accumulate "goods" (i.e. objects and/or obligations from others).

9. Inhomogeneity in the accumulation of goods will be also directly associated with variations in the size of minimal economic units.

10. Variability in the size of minimal economic units (due to stochastic variations in births, deaths, interpersonal relationships between kin, "fortunes" and "misfortunes" influencing residential patterns, etc.) is kept within a relatively small range through the operation of optimal work team size, interpersonal conflict, regulation of reproduction, and optimal spatial arrangements of subsistence and domestic activities.

11. The size of the minimal economic unit will be mutually and directly related to the accumulation of goods such as described in propositions 7 and 8.

12. The frequency of raids between communities will be directly and mutually related to inhomogeneity in population density, and inversely and mutually related to the distance between communities.

13. There is an inverse mutual relationship between the exchange relations described in proposition 5 and the frequency of raids.

14. The more frequent raids are between communities the greater the probability that individuals will accumulate "goods" in the manner described in proposition 8.

15. The more individuals accumulate "goods" in the manner described in proposition 8, the more likely the development of political-economic centralization such as described in propositions 1, 2 and 3.

16. The more political-economic centralization develops the more pressure there will be on minimal economic units to increase their production/consumption ratio.

As I noted, this is a rather sketchy model, but nevertheless it is already much too complex to be adequately tested with archeological data alone. A similar model might be constructed for the intensification of agricultural production once political-economic centralization has begun — in other words an elaboration and extension of proposition 16. Nukunya's contribution (this volume) on southeastern Ghana refers to a community tied to a post-feudal market exchange system, but the questions raised concerning the high emigration from some communities as opposed to the development of a highly intensive cultivation pattern in an ecologically similar community might well be analyzed with the help of a Maruyama model.

Progress

As one reviews human history from the vantage point of hindsight it is very tempting to ask whether matters have improved or gotten worse. Thus, the past is typically glorified by old romantics, the future by young utopians, and the present by smug persons in their middle age. All of these are manifestations of "chronocentrism," that close cousin of ethnocentrism. The reader may well decide, after finishing this essay, that I myself am both a romantic AND a utopian! Several of the contributors to this book also regard evolution as enigmatic, that circumstances are getting both better AND worse at the same time. Moreover, positions taken with regard to population dynamics often seem to be quite diagnostic of an author's evaluation of human history in general.

Bennett's and Richardson's papers in this volume, as already mentioned, reiterate the current concerns about ecological destruction. They see human potentialities for creating havoc with the environment as an inherent quality, although Richardson appears to regard this as a recently activated capacity, a departure from the former "natural" state of balance between drive and restraint which came about with the rise of industrial-trading nations. Sarmela's paper also falls in the ambivalent group, with its description of "maximal social ecosystems" as more restrictive than "minimal social ecosystems," and yet, the former have higher productivity and an "increase of possibilities."

Nukunya and Faris (this volume) seem to be much closer to the progressivist position. Nukunya clearly regards the industry of the farmers in Anlo with approval, and sees them as better off than their neighboring communities whose population has increased much less as they migrated up and down the West African coast to work as fishermen. Faris appears to take it for granted that feudalism and capitalism were advances over previous stages of history, just as "social production" represents for him an advance over animals which had to restrict their numbers in order not to exceed the fixed potentials of their environment. Its (this volume) also regards a general progressive trend as a historical fact, but his interest focuses on the exceptions to this trend. Particularly interesting is his observation that "there would have been no progress without the communication of one people with another, and without the mutual exchange of experience." Lacking these stimuli, among cultural isolates "social development eventually became crippled and anachronistic." And — in a final methodological note — Its warns us against using such groups to reconstruct human evolution.

Population growth in organic evolution is commonly regarded as a sign (often as the main sign) of "adaptive success," in logical contrast to extinction which is tantamount to failure. In cultural evolution, the spread of a certain way of life — whether by multiplication of its original "carriers" or by diffusion to other peoples — has similarly been seen (by Westerners anyway) as a proof of its "superiority." One stage is said to be "superseded" by the next one — and not only when its archeological remains are closer to the surface! But our recent awareness of "over-population" and ecological problems has added to earlier doubts that "more" is inevitably "better." Odum's recommendation (1969) that mature successional stages in biotic communities are superior models for humans to imitate than the "young nature" of early succession with its low diversity, rapid nutrient cycling and high productivity per biomass, is characteristic of this new mood. The prospect of homo sapiens as the only herbivore on earth is as frightening to biologists as Aldous Huxley's *Brave New World* is to those who cherish cultural differences.

Malthus was not worried about ecology, and not even about the growth of the entire human population; his concern centered on the poor and on the possibility that the French revolution may spread to England. His theory on population growth was first and foremost an argument against the social reformers of his day. For his followers today, however, it is human population growth as such that has become "bad."

Boserup (1965) has attacked this position by trying to show that population growth is a stimulus to greater production and, as such, may well be considered "good." Her values become apparent when she writes, for example, of the replacement of long-fallow by multiple cropping: "in step with these changes, the Javanese peasant has been transformed from the careless idler of the old times, who has just to scratch the land to get food enough" (1965: 61), or of the numerically weak victims of slave raiders where "those left behind could easily find subsistence by means of long-fallow systems with the result that they were never able to break the vicious circle of sparse population, long-fallow agriculture, and low levels of civilization" (1965: 74). Carneiro (1961, 1970), Harner (1970, this volume), Smith and Young (1972) and Cohen (this volume) do not manifest such blatant symptoms of the Protestant Ethic — their use of such terms as "higher levels of development" and the like merely follows common anthropological usage, the pockmarks of that "childhood affliction" our science apparently caught in the early nineteenth century (Harris 1968: 37). The association between progressivism and a favorable view of population increase as a stimulus to "higher" things is common among Marxists too, as Faris' contribution to this book attests (despite his rejection of population growth as a necessary or sufficient cause of the major transitions and his negative judgment of the pronatalist effects of capitalism and imperialism).

Bennett and Richardson (this volume) regard not only ecological destruction but also the recent upswing in the rate of population increase with great alarm. Regaining a "natural balance" is for them an explicit objective. This is not necessarily a romantic goal or a conservative one, but as I struggle to reconcile my own concerns about ecological despoilation with my radicalism on issues of social justice, I appreciate how easily one can unwittingly serve the purposes of the Neo-Malthusian reactionaries (Polgar i.p.).

Yes, I agree with Bennett that objectivity in one's standards of inquiry and reportage does not require a pretension of value neutrality on evolution, culture change or any other phenomenon involving the human species. If such criteria as distributive justice, improved health, individual and cultural diversity, and safeguarding the ecological balance of our planet are chronocentric, I am willing to acknowledge such a bias.

So, let me state that I see the course of human evolution as enigmatic and curvilineal. In the transition from gatherer-hunters to independent village societies things got somewhat worse. The "original affluent society" (Sahlins 1968) was replaced by one in which people had to toil harder to ensure an uncertain harvest some months in the future. Men gained greater dominance over women, lineage elders over younger members of the group, and children were supposed to learn obedience more than resourcefulness. Perhaps the sickly received somewhat better care, but the frequency of disease probably increased a little rather than going down.

With the advent of feudalism, the human condition took a drastic turn for the worse, and not till just recently have we begun to challenge the unfortunate effects of political-economic centralization. Population growth in the feudal stage was often forced to reach (and sometimes exceed) the limits of supporting capacity, and urbanization led to five thousand years of one huge epidemic after another. Social stratification, war, slavery, and the subjugation of women are yet other characteristics of this miserable epoch. Certainly writing was invented, science had its beginnings and the arts flourished; but only a miniscule elite profited from these developments.

Colonialism and industrialism allowed a slightly larger segment of humanity to lead a better life, but at the cost of terrible repression, suffering and early death for the vast majority. Still, the new freedoms and comforts found in metropolitan societies have become a hope and an objective for the Third World. Participatory democracy, modern health care (including family planning), the attainment of equality by women, and opportunities for creative development of individual potential are conditions that need not be linked to the colossal waste and bureaucratic rigidity of contemporary industrial societies. Population growth will level off when opportunities for economic survival and advance are no longer tied to having four or five children per family. And the large enterprises which cause the squandering of resources and filthying of the environment can be forced to stop. But none of these positive outcomes are by any means certain. Identifying the real causes of our grave dangers is essential — and to do that it helps greatly to study the history of human ecology and population dynamics.

REFERENCES

ACSÁDI, GYORGY AND JANOS NEMESKÉRI
   1970   *History of human life span and mortality*. Budapest: Akadémiai Kiadó.
ADAMS, ROBERT MCC.
   1966   *The evolution of urban society*. Chicago: Aldine.

1968 "The natural history of urbanism," in *The fitness of man's environment*. Smithsonian Annual 2. New York: Harper Colophon.

BENDER, DONALD R.
1971 "Population and productivity in tropical forest bush fallow agriculture," in *Culture and population: a collection of current studies*. Edited by S. Polgar. Cambridge, Massachusetts: Schenkman.

BINFORD, LEWIS R.
1968 "Post-Pleistocene adaptations," in *New perspectives in archeology*. Edited by S. R. and L. R. Binford. Chicago: Aldine.

BIRDSELL, JOSEPH B.
1957 Some population problems involving Pleistocene man. *Cold Spring Harbor Symposia on Quantitative Biology* 22:47-69.

BOSERUP, ESTER
1965 *The conditions of agricultural growth*. Chicago: Aldine.

CARNEIRO, ROBERT L.
1961 "Slash and burn agriculture among the Kuikuru and its implications for cultural development in the Amazon Basin," in *The evolution of horticultural systems in native South America*. Edited by J. Wilbert. Caracas: Sociedad de Ciencias Naturales La Salle.
1967 On the relationship between size of population and complexity of social organization. *Southwestern Journal of Anthropology* 23:234-243.
1970 A theory of the origin of the state. *Science* 169:733-738.

CHANG, KWANG-CHIH
1958 Study of Neolithic social grouping: examples from the New World. *American Anthropologist* 60:298-334.

CHILDE, V. GORDON
1942 *What happened in history*. Harmondsworth: Pelican Books.

COALE, ANSLEY
1969 "The decline of fertility in Europe from the French Revolution to World War II," in *Fertility and family planning: a world view*. Edited by S. J. Behrman, L. Corsa, and R. Freedman. Ann Arbor: University of Michigan Press.

COCHRAN, ROGER
1972 Flowcharting in the study of population dynamics. *Medical Anthropology Newsletter* 3(3):6-8.

COHEN, YEHUDI A.
1969 Ends and means in political control: State organization and the punishment of adultery, incest and violation of celibacy. *American Anthropologist* 71:658-687.

CURRENT ANTHROPOLOGY
1972 *Anthropology and Population Problems* 13:203-267.

DEEVEY, EDWARD S.
1960 The human population. *Scientific American* 203:195-204.

DEMENY, PAUL
1968 Early fertility decline in Austria-Hungary, *Daedalus* 97:502-522.

DUMOND, DON E.
1972 "Population growth and political centralization," in *Population growth: anthropological implications*. Edited by B. Spooner. Cambridge, Massachusetts: MIT Press.

FLANNERY, KENT V.
   1965   The ecology of early food production in Mesopotamia. *Science* 147:
          1247–1256.
   1972   "The origins of the village as a settlement type in Mesoamerica and
          the Near East: a comparative study," in *Man, settlement and urbanism.*
          Edited by P. J. Ucko, R. Tringham, and G. W. Dimbleby. London:
          Duckworth.
GEARING, FRED O.
   1961   The rise of the Cherokee state as an instance in a class: the "Meso-
          potamian" career to statehood. *Bureau of American Ethnology
          Bulletin* 180:125–134.
HARNER, MICHAEL J.
   1970   Population pressure and the social evolution of agriculturalists.
          Southwestern Journal of Anthropology 26:67–86.
HARRIS, MARVIN
   1968   *The rise of anthropological theory.* New York: Crowell.
HARRISON, G. A., A. J. BOYCE, *editors*
   1972   *The structure of human populations.* Oxford: Clarendon.
LANGER, WILLIAM L.
   1963   Europe's initial population explosion. *American Historical Review*
          69:1–17.
MAC NEISH, RICHARD S.
   1967   Ancient Mesoamerican civilization. *Science* 143:531–537.
MAIR, LUCY
   1964   *Primitive government* (revised edition). Harmondsworth: Pelican
          Books.
MARSHALL, JOHN F., STEVEN POLGAR, *editors*
   i.p.   *Culture, natality and family planning.* Chapel Hill, North Carolina:
          Carolina Population Center Monographs.
MARUYAMA, MAGOROH
   1963   The second cybernetics: deviation-amplifying mutual causal processes.
          American Scientist 51:164–179.
NAG, MONI
   1962   *Factors affecting human fertility in nonindustrial societies: a cross-
          cultural study.* Yale University Publications in Anthropology No 66
          (Reprinted 1968 by Taplinger, New York).
NAG, MONI, *editor*
   i.p.   *Population and social organization.* World Anthropology. The Hague:
          Mouton.
NAROLL, RAOUL
   1956   A preliminary index of social development. *American Anthropologist*
          58:687–715.
ODUM, EUGENE P.
   1969   The strategy of ecosystem development. *Science* 164:262–269.
ORANS, MARTIN
   1966   Surplus. *Human Organization* 25:24–32.
PEARSON, HARRY W.
   1957   "The economy has no surplus: critique of a theory of development,"

in *Trade and market in the early empires*. Edited by K. Polanyi, C. M. Arensberg, and H. W. Pearson. New York: Free Press

POLANYI, KARL
1957 *The great transformation: the political and economic origins of our time.* Boston: Beacon Press.

POLGAR, STEVEN
1964 "Evolution and the ills of mankind," in *Horizons of anthropology* Edited by Sol Tax. Chicago: Aldine.
1972 Population history and population policies from an anthropological perspective. *Current Anthropology* 13:203–211.
1973 "Cultural development, population and the family," in *Symposium on population and the family*. United Nations, Economic and Social Council, E/conference 60, Symposium 2(3).
i.p. "Birth planning: between neglect and coercion," in *Topias and utopias in health*. Edited by S. R. Ingman and A. E. Thomas. Also in *Population and social organization*. Edited by Moni Nag. World Anthropology. The Hague: Mouton.

POLGAR, STEVEN, *editor*
1971 *Culture and population.* Carolina Population Center Monograph 9. Cambridge, Massachusetts: Schenkman.

SAHLINS, MARSHALL D.
1963 Poor man, rich man, big man, chief: political types in Melanesia and Polynesia. *Comparative Studies in Society and History* 5:285–303.
1968 "Notes on the original affluent society," in *Man the hunter*. Edited by I. DeVore and R. B. Lee, 86–89. Chicago: Aldine.

SANDERS, WILLIAM T.
1972 "Population, agricultural history, and societal evolution in Mesoamerica," in *Population growth: anthropological implications*. Edited by B. Spooner. Cambridge, Massachusetts: MIT Press.

SMITH, PHILIP E. L., T. CUYLER YOUNG
1972 "The evolution of early agriculture and culture in greater Mesopotamia: a trial formulation," in *Population growth: anthropological implications*. Edited by B. Spooner. Cambridge, Massachusetts: MIT Press.

SPOONER, BRIAN, *editor*
1972 *Population growth: anthropological implications.* Cambridge, Massachusetts: MIT Press.

STEVENSON, ROBERT F.
1968 *Population and political systems in Africa.* New York: Columbia University Press.

WORLD ARCHAEOLOGY
1973 *World Archaeology* 4(1) (entire issue).

WRIGHT, GARY A.
1971 Origins of food production in Southeastern Asia: a survey of ideas. *Current Anthropology* 12:447–478.

Determination of the Size, Density, and Growth Rate of Hunting-Gathering Populations

FEKRI A. HASSAN

INTRODUCTION

One of the most salient features accompanying the development of agriculture has been an unprecedented increase in the size of world population over a relatively very short time period. During the Late Paleolithic the world population is estimated at about three million (Deevey 1960). Within a span of four thousand years following the introduction of agriculture, the world population climbed to about ninety million (Deevey 1960). Today, the number of people born in a single year adds up to slightly less than the total world population during the Neolithic. This staggering explosion of the human population was accompanied by a tremendous increase in the size of local communities and, of course, population density.

The implications of these demographic changes cannot be ignored by the anthropologist. The relationship between population growth and cultural change already has been emphasized in a pioneer article by Dumond (1965), the relationship between the complexity of social organization and population size are discussed by Carneiro (1967), and the probable impact of population pressure on social evolution among agriculturists is treated by Harner (1970), to mention only a few of the anthropological studies which place population as a major force behind social dynamics. The relationship between population and disease, nutrition, and other aspects of human biology has been a matter of concern among physical anthropologists.

Fortunately, the interest among anthropologists in the direct or indirect role of population in cultural dynamics has grown considerably in the last few years. This must be regarded as a major development in anthropology. Indeed, one can observe the crystallization of what may be called a "demographic paradigm." The publication of a controversial work by the economist Boserup (1965) on the economics of agrarian change under population pressure has captured the attention of many anthropologists and has contributed thereby to the development of the demographic paradigm in anthropology. (For discussions of Boserup's thesis in the context of anthropology see Sheffer 1971; Spooner and Netting 1972; Polgar 1972; Smith 1972.) Binford's model (1968) on the probable role of population pressure in providing conditions favorable for the development of agriculture has also led to a widespread interest in the role of population dynamics in culture change.

Although one must regard with great satisfaction the recent upsurge of interest in the demographic dimension within the field of anthropology, one has to be cautious not to view population independently of its ecological and cultural matrix. The rate of population growth, for example, does not depend solely on man's biological potentials. Similarly, neither population size, nor population density are functions of population growth alone.

It is, therefore, our purpose to present a realistic picture of the biological, cultural, and ecological determinants of the size, density, and growth rate of hunting-gathering populations. In order to illustrate the significance of some of the concepts discussed, reference is made to the impact of an agricultural mode of life on population characteristics. It is hoped that this study may contribute to a more balanced view of the interrelationship between population dynamics and culture change.

For the sake of clarity in presentation, a separate treatment will be accorded to population density, size, and growth rate.

POPULATION DENSITY

The population density of hunter-gatherers is very low, varying in general from 0.01 to 2 persons per square mile (Figure 1). In some exceptional cases, however, e.g. the North American Northwest Coast, the population density is somewhat close to that of low-density agricultural groups.

The low population density of hunting-gathering population is a function of three major factors:
1. Resource potentials,
2. Food-extractive potentials, and
3. Consumption level.

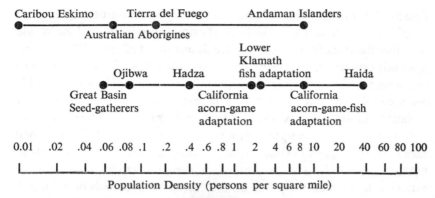

Figure 1. Population density of some hunting-gathering populations. Sources: Birdsell 1951; Baumhoff 1963; Kroeber 1953; Harrison et al. 1964.

The relationship between these three factors and population density can be expressed by the following formula:

$$PD = f(R, E)/L$$

where PD is the population density, R is the resource potential, E, the food-extractive potential, and L, the level of consumption. First let us examine each of these three factors.

Resource Potentials

The resource potentials of a region are much more than the biomass of food resources or the net amount of primary productivity. They are defined more appropriately in terms of (1) THE OPTIMUM YIELD TO MAN, i.e., the maximum sustained yield that can be removed without impairing the ability of the resources to replace the biomass harvested (Watt 1968: 125); (2) the TYPE AND NUTRITIONAL QUALITY of the resources; (3) the SPATIAL DISTRIBUTION PATTERN OF THE RESOURCES; and (4) the SEASONAL AND LONG-TERM FLUCTUATIONS IN THE ABUNDANCE OF THE RESOURCES.

Primary productivity, i.e. the productivity of autotrophic plants is indisputably the ultimate determinant of the biomass of primary consumers (e.g. herbivores), secondary consumers (e.g. carnivores), and other high-level consumers. The position of hunter-gatherers in the ecological network as consumers at varying trophic levels makes it impossible for them to override the limitations set by the amount of primary productivity. Primary productivity, however, is a poor index of human population density. For example, the maximum potential population density in a salt marsh biome, calculated on the basis of primary productivity alone, would be higher than that in a temperate deciduous forest (Casteel 1972). This is evidently erroneous, most probably because the proportion of edible foods available to man is not the same in the two biomes. The kind of edible resources also are not the same in different biomes, which leads to great variations in the amounts that can be extracted by man. The subsistence regime may also increase the resources within a territory through food exchange, trading, and extraction of resources such as migratory birds or fish (Casteel 1972). The percentage of net productivity which can be extracted by man also depends on the extractive potentials of man.

Utilization of the productivity of those resources that are actually under exploitation, as in the classic study by Baumhoff (1963) of the ecological determinants of California Indian populations, are very promising. In this study, Baumhoff was able to arrive at a successful mathematical approximation which expresses the relationship between the productivity of acorns, game, and fish with population density.

It should be noted here, however, that Birdsell (1957) has found that there is a logarithmic relationship between the population density of Australian aboriginal groups and the amount of rainfall in those areas where unearned water (e.g. riverine water) is not available. In this case, the amount of rainfall was taken by Birdsell as an index of the productivity of resources. Although there is certainly a close relationship between the amount of rainfall and primary productivity, there may be also a direct relationship between the amount of drinking water and population density.

A better index to the amount of food potentially available to man is the amount of "optimum yield to man." For example, deer can withstand a sustained annual catch of about 10 percent or more if the kill is appropriately distributed by age and sex (Watt 1968: 127), whereas the optimum catch of bison is only about 3.2 percent (ibid.: 122–123). The biomass of an animal herd in itself says very little about the proportion of the biomass which can be extracted by man without impairing the chances of that herd for survival. Differences between animal species in the amount available to man are governed by natural fertility, natural mortality, the size of the herd, predation by other animals, and disease. It also depends on age- or sex-specific hunting. The removal of females, for example, usually weakens the biotic potential of the animal population and reduces the optimum yield to man.

Overall similarities between two regions in either their primary productivity or optimum yield to man do not guarantee, however, that the food resources available from both regions are similar in kind or nutritional value. It is interesting to note in this regard that man's recognition of what constitutes profitable "food" is not cross-culturally uniform. The intensive exploitation of a wide spectrum of resources at the close of the Paleolithic in some areas of the Near East, e.g., Deh Luran (Flannery 1969) which were rarely exploited before, and the appearance of a coastal pattern of adaptation during the Mesolithic in Europe represent changes in prehistoric hunter-gatherers' recognition of usable food resources. The recognition of the potentials of cereal-type grasses as a major food resource by Paleolithic peoples in the Near East cannot be ignored in assessing the factors which led to the achievement of agriculture.

Changes in the kind of resources exploited usually imply nutritional changes. The nutritional value of human diet is extremely important in determining population density. The availability of animal protein or a combination of plant proteins provide adequate amounts of the essential amino acids seems to be particularly important. The common tendency to estimate population density on the basis of energy requirements should not obstruct our vision of the major role played by nutritional elements in determining population density. This point is of considerable significance with respect to the demographic transition during the Neolithic.

The dietary association of maize, beans, and chile peppers or squash in Latin America is apparently due to their complementary amino acid composition (Dornstreich 1972). Also, the close association between plant and animal domestication in the Near East during the Neolithic may have been necessitated to achieve a balanced protein diet. Similarly, garden vegetables and fruits were probably added to supplement the diet with minerals and vitamins. The influence of nutritional needs on the level of consumption among hunter-gatherers also has some effect on population density, and will be discussed below in dealing with consumption.

Another aspect of food resources which influences the density of hunting-gathering populations is the distribution pattern of the resources. This is reflected in the density, aggregation, and accessibility of the resources. In general, natural food resources are sparse and dispersed. Dense and concentrated food resources are encountered only under fortunate circumstances, along the routes of animal migrations, as those enjoyed by Siberian mammoth hunters during the Upper Paleolithic, or in the proximity of abundant fish and other complementary resources, as is the case along the North American Northwest Coast. Usually, coastal and riverine areas provide a greater and more concentrated supply of protein-rich foods, which partly explains the higher density of hunting-gathering populations in such favorable zones.

Probably one of the most important consequences of agriculture has been a sudden increase in the density of food resources. An increase in food supply without an accompanying localized increase in density probably would have failed to lead to many of the events which paved the way to the rise of complex civilizations.

Seasonal as well as long-term variations in the availability of foods, particularly those that are of key nutritional value, are also extremely influential in determining the maximum levels of population density. The relationship between seasonal fluctuations and population density are expressed in Liebig's "rule of the minimum" (Odum 1959: 88), which implies that maximum population density is regulated more by the amount of key resources during the time periods when these resources are most scarce rather than by the annual mean (see Bartholomew and Birdsell 1953; Thompson 1966; Smith 1972; Casteel 1972). The presence of greater amounts of food resources at the disposal of hunter-gatherers than what they would normally exploit (Lee and DeVore 1968; Lee 1969) therefore may be a long-term strategy to safeguard the population against seasonal or occasional shortage in food supply. In general, the exploitation of resources among hunter-gatherers seems to be restricted to about 30 to 40 percent, varying from about 20 to 60 percent of the carrying capacity, i.e., the maximum population size that can be supported from an ecological standpoint (Birdsell 1957; Lee and DeVore 1968: passim; Casteel 1972; Polgar 1972).

The tragic conditions of food shortage are all too familiar to us today from the sad experiences in India, Pakistan, and West Africa. Similar conditions probably produced long-lasting memories which were passed from one generation to another, leading not only to a conservation strategy but also to cultural controls on population growth. It may be noted in this regard that food-storage preservation of resources are successful methods to circumvent Liebig's rule (see Smith 1972). Although many food preservation techniques are known to hunter-gatherers, the practice of these methods among them is generally very small in scale. The maintenance of large storage facilities requires in most cases a settled mode of life, which a hunting-gathering subsistence pattern does not encourage. In those cases where a semisettled mode of life is possible, the practice of storage and preservation becomes prominent as on the North American Northwest Coast. Storage pits are also recorded from an Upper Paleolithic mammoth-hunters' village at Timonovka, Soviet Union (Mongait 1961: 91).

The development of multiannual cropping among agriculturists at the expense of somewhat poorer quality and quantity of each crop may have been probably favored more for its effect on ensuring a year-round food supply than for its contribution to a greater yield per annum.

In concluding this section on the impact of resource potentials on population density the following points should be emphasized. The amount of primary productivity or the biomass of food resources are not the sole determinants of population density. Only a certain amount of the total biomass can be extracted by man without endangering the biotic potential of the resources. In addition, the amount of food should not be considered in isolation of its kind and nutritional value, especially their amino acid composition. The spatial distribution pattern of the resources and their accessibility are other factors to contend with. Moreover, seasonal and occasional variations in the amount and kind of resources set strict limitations on the long-term well-being of the group and most hunting-gathering populations are bestowed with the wisdom of regulating their population density well below that during the times when essential resources are least abundant.

Food-Extractive Potentials

Throughout this discussion the term "hunting-gathering" is used to denote an extractive food-getting pattern. The term thus refers to a wide range of activities including sea-mammal hunting, fishing, fowling, shell-fish gathering, foraging, big-game hunting, small-game hunting, insect-collecting, etc. The relative dependency on any of these activities varies from one group to another. Hunter-gatherers differ also in their FOOD-EXTRACTING STRATEGY, and the METHODS AND TECHNIQUES involved in any of the above activities.

Generally, the major subsistence activities are conditioned by the most abundant food resources. In the tundra, for example, where plant food resources are scarce, emphasis is placed on hunting sea mammals and fishing in the coastal areas and caribou-hunting in the interior. In the tropical forest, at the other end of the spectrum, where the biomass of herbivores is low (Bourlière 1963), a great deal of emphasis is placed on gathering plant resources. The abundance of game in temperate and boreal areas seems to encourage intensive animal game hunting, as the evidence from prehistoric Europe suggests.

An abundant food resource, however, may be neglected in preference to another, and specialized subsistence regimes may coexist to avoid conflict or to ensure a more effective exploitation of the habitat.

There is also an element of selectivity in any subsistence regime. For example, of the 223 local species of animals known and named by the Bushmen, 54 are classified as edible, and of these, only 17 species were hunted on a regular basis. These animal species include in order of their importance, the warthog, kudu, duiker, steenbok, gemsbok, wildebeest, spring hare, porcupine, guinea fowl, francolin (two species), korhaan, tortoise, and python. Similarly, although 85 species of edible plants are known, only 23 species contribute 90 percent of the vegetable diet by weight (Lee 1968: 35).

Although the Hadza, as reported by Woodburn (1968), make no attempt at systematic cropping, impala, zebra, eland, and giraffe are the most frequently killed large animals. This "selectivity" may be a function both of "conscious" selectivity on the part of the hunters, and the ease by which a species can be caught. The degree of "catchability" is in turn a function of the behavior of the animal, technological skills, and the hunting strategy. Gregarious, placid animals can be easier to catch than alert, solitary, and agile ones. Cooperative hunting, on the other hand, enhances the chances for catching dangerous and large game. The procedure of hunting (stalking, trapping, or still-hunting) provides also another factor in determining the frequency of a specific catch. In the case of the Hadza, the biomass of the most frequently killed animals represent about 65 percent of the total biomass of ungulates, using Bourlière's estimates (1963) on ungulate biomass in Tanzanian thornbush savanna.

The impact of trade, as a part of the subsistence regime, on expanding the kind and amount of resources, must be also mentioned. Generally, however, the hunting-gathering system is a closed one, especially when considered by comparison to the agricultural system, in which trade is a very prominent component. Trade among agriculturists probably was not induced by the development of surplus but rather by the narrow range of subsistence activity, the development of storage facilities, and the settled mode of life, which not only limited the farmer's access to distant resources but also must have encouraged the establishment of fixed trade networks. Exchange of resources can be also a mechanism to offset seasonal scarcity (Smith 1972).

The food extractive potential can be measured in several ways. Harris (1971: 205) devised an index which he called "index of techno-environmental efficiency." The index is expressed by the formula:

$$e = O/I$$

where e is the value of the index; I, the caloric input invested in an average day of subsistence activity, and O, the average energy output in calories resulting from that investment. In essence, Harris' index measures the energy gain per unit of energy expenditure. For the !Kung Bushmen, Harris (1971) arrives at an estimate of 9.6, compared to 11.2 among the Genieri hoe agriculturists in Gambia, and 53.5 among the Chinese Luts'un irrigation rice farmers.

It must be remembered that the food-extractive potential has to be considered on an annual basis because many days per year are not usually devoted to nonsubsistence activities. Lee (1969: 68), for example, has found that 23 workdays are invested for a 100-day period of consumption. The food extractive potential of a group is also dependent upon the size of the labor force. Generally, producers constitute about 66 percent of the population (Wrigley 1969).

Among hunters the efficiency of hunting may be measured by the biomass of liveweight meat extracted per hunter per year, which may be considered as an index of "hunting success." According to Lee (1969), most hunters kill one large antelope or sometimes two antelopes per year. Woodburn (1968: 54) mentions that perhaps as many as 50 percent of the adult males fail to kill even one large animal a year and that there are some men who have killed scarcely one single large animal during their entire life! This means about nine to eighteen large animals a year are obtained by a group of thirty persons, which include nine adult males. The contribution of this seemingly low level of hunting success to the diet should not be underestimated. Given an average of 230 kilograms of liveweight per large animal and about 50 percent inedible material (White 1953), each person in the group would receive between 95 and 190 grams of edible meat per day from these large animals only. Usually, the meat of large animals is shared between contiguous groups which eliminates loss due to wastage (Lee 1969), guarantees an even distribution of meat among local groups, and cements, in the meantime, amicable social relations.

The extractive potentials, in sum, depend on the food-getting capabilities which are determined by the nature of the subsistence regime, the food-getting strategy (seasonal movements, food exchange, etc.), the food-getting methods, and the technological skills of the group. The food-extractive potentials may be measured thermodynamically by the level of extractive efficiency, which is a function of the caloric yield for each caloric unit invested per food-producer per workday, the percentage of workdays per year, and the size of the workforce.

Consumption

The level of consumption reflects primarily the basic biological requirements and secondarily, the additional social requirements. The lowest
level of consumption is usually referred to as the "subsistence" level. The
average subsistence caloric requirement according to the FAO standards
per capita per day is placed at 2,354 calories (Ehrlich and Ehrlich 1970:
69). In terms of protein, an intake of one gram per kilogram of body
weight from the time of maturity throughout adult life is considered near
the optimum (Dubos 1965). An average adult weighing about fifty kilograms would thus require about fifty grams per day. Children require a
higher intake of about 2.2 to 2.5 grams per kilogram of body weight
(Dubos 1965). The requirements also depend, in addition to age and body
weight, on sex, climate, and type of work. Data on the caloric intake of
hunter-gatherers indicate an average slightly below that recommended by
FAO. For example, !Kung Bushmen, have an average caloric intake of
about 2,140 kilocalories per day (Lee 1969: 71). Approximately similar
values are recorded for the Australian Aborigines (McCarthy and
McArthur 1960). The Eskimos show a higher value of 3,102. Agricultural
groups show values that vary between 2,000 and 2,700 with an average of
about 2,292 for African countries, 2,091 for Asian countries, and 2,126
for Latin American countries, with a world average of about 2,190 kilocalories per person (Clark and Haswell 1964: 21).

A subsistence caloric intake of about 2,200 kilocalories per person is
thus a likely estimate for hunter-gatherers in temperate areas. This is
equivalent to about 803,000 kilocalories per year per person or approximately about 8×10^5. In colder regions, an average of about 3,000 or
3,100 is more adequate because of the greater energy requirements. Generally, it can be assumed that "subsistence" levels of consumption would
be the norm during periods of high population pressure, a situation
characteristic of many contemporary agricultural societies (Clark and
Haswell 1964). During prosperous periods with low population pressure
higher consumption would be expected.

The amount of meat consumed, a major source of animal protein,
seems to vary considerably from one group to another. Lee (1969: 71)
found that the daily allotment per person among the Dobe Bushmen is
about 256 grams (34.5 grams protein per cooked portion) during a period
of twenty-eight days. Much higher estimates are given for the American
Indian buffalo hunters. Wheat (1972: 108–109), surveying historical
accounts, concludes that an average of about 1.36 kilograms (three
pounds) per person is a conservative estimate of the daily consumption.

It must be remembered, however, that the amount consumed of a specific nutrient is a function of the proportion contributed by the resource containing that nutrient to the diet. The Bushmen, for example, supplement their diet with mongongo nuts (33 percent) and other vegetable foods (30 percent). Meat constitutes only about 33 percent (Lee 1969: 69). The overall protein intake per person per day is thus about 93.1 grams. The Indian buffalo hunters, on the other hand, depended primarily on meat. In terms of protein intake, Wheat's estimates of 1.36 kilograms per person per day translate into about 293 grams of protein per person, a much higher value than the basic nutritional daily requirements. However, 1.36 kilograms of meat provide about 3,660 kilocalories, compared to a daily requirement of about 2,500 kilocalories. Thus, although the amount of meat seems excessive in terms of the amount of protein, it is within reasonable limits of the amount of calories required. The relative deficiency of meat in certain nutrients (vitamins or minerals) which would have been otherwise obtained from other vegetable resources may also account for the consumption of larger amounts of meat. Preference for certain parts of the animals, e.g. brain, tongue, liver, or other offals, also may be a function of the variations in the nutritional contents of these parts.

Reference must also be made to the percentage which is usually wasted through spoilage or negligence, as well as to the percentage of inedible constituents in the foodstuff. White (1953) estimates about 50 percent edible meat in large animals. Food-processing technology (grinding, soaking, etc.) and type of cooking lead usually to enrichment or impoverishment in certain nutritional components which would eventually influence the amount consumed of the processed food material.

Our discussion thus far has been focused on the relationships between resource potentials, food extractive potentials, and levels of consumption as they bear on the density of hunting-gathering populations. Throughout the discussion it is apparent that the supporting capacity of an environment is a function of both the ecological potential of that environment and the extractive capabilities of its inhabitants. Cultural factors unrelated to subsistence, however, may intervene at times to control population density.

Birdsell (1957) has shown that political organization has an effect on population density. Australian aboriginal groups with a more complex political organization than the average were found to have a higher population density than would be expected from the equation based on rainfall. Also, the fragmentation of a group as a result of differential intertribal adoption of circumcision and sub-incision was found to have a negative effect on population density. It thus may be inferred that the social coherence of a group would enhance population increase, probably through a better management of the resources and a more successful system of redistribution.

Population density may also be regulated by native concepts of "crowding." Such concepts could be of adaptive function. Social discomfort resulting from crowding would enhance fission or signal the need for population control by other means.

POPULATION SIZE

Generally speaking, hunter-gatherers do not live in large communities except temporarily and under exceptional conditions. Anthropologists seem to agree that bands, as local groups are referred to, vary between fifteen and fifty persons, with an average of about twenty-five persons. Regional groups, or band-aggregates, on the other hand, show a wider range of variations with an average of about 500 persons and a modal range from 200 to 800 persons (Birdsell 1957; Krzywicki 1934; Lee and DeVore 1968).

These numbers are quite intriguing because of their persistence regardless of the overall population density and the nature of the environmental conditions. It is proposed here that, given low population density, the 25-person-size mode is essentially a function of the optimal size for effective feeding strategy, interpersonal interaction, and defense, whereas the regional group size is most probably a function of the optimum size of an effective breeding unit.

Mathematically, population size is a function of the population density and area. The area which is regularly exploited by a group of hunter-gatherers may be called a "catchment territory," to use the meaningful term introduced by Vita-Vinzi and Higgs (1970). It generally has been observed that the catchment territory of hunter-gatherers usually lies within ten kilometers from the base camp (Lee 1968; Vita-Vinzi and Higgs 1970). The radius of the catchment territory, as Lee (1969) has observed is a function of the ratio of food yield to energy cost. The more distant the food resource, the greater the effort required. Consequently, as the distance to the resources increases, the ratio of yield to effort diminishes. Thus, beyond a certain distance the exploitation of resources ceases to be profitable. The effort expended in covering a given distance depends, of course, on the mode of transportation and the topography. The absence of effort-saving modes of transportation among most hunter-gatherers places physiological limitations on the distances traveled. Trade, food sharing between contiguous groups, and food exchange must be viewed partly as mechanisms to circumvent limitations imposed on subsistence effort. One must note, also, that the radius of a catchment territory does not measure the distance actually traveled. The actual distance is generally many times that of the radius because hunting-gathering activity usually is not carried out along a straight line. This is particularly important in determining the cost of the subsistence effort. In addition to effort relative to yield, the size of the catchment territory may be influenced by the relationship of the work schedule and the times of the day.

The area of the catchment territory increases logarithmically as its radius increases, assuming that the catchment area is circular. The area exploited thus may be expanded considerably by a slight increase in the radius of the catchment territory. However, due to physical barriers, the physical catchment territory may not be represented by a circle. It also may be defined by territorial boundaries which may not be compatible with specific hunting-gathering subsistence patterns. Territorial claims to specific resources also are known to exist, particularly when population pressure is high (Netting 1971: 8), but such claims, may be short-lived, lasting only for a few generations (Lee 1972: 129). If a given population size has to be maintained, areas with sparse, dispersed resources must require longer distances of travel than those with greater food potentials. The relationship between a group of twenty-five persons, population density, and catchment area are illustrated on Figure 2. When the food potentials dictate low population density, as in the case of Caribou Eskimos, for example, the area required for a band of twenty-five persons is about 2,500 square miles with a radius of 28 miles (about 6,450 square kilometers and 45 kilometers, respectively). In the case of the Hadza, on the other hand (Woodburn 1968) the area required for a band of twenty-five persons is about 63 square miles with a radius of about 4.5 miles (about 164 square kilometers and 7.2 kilometers, respectively). A population with greater density, e.g. the California Indians in the lower Klamath region with a fishing subsistence regime (Baumhoff 1963) needs an area of about 6 square miles with a radius of about 1.4 miles (about 16 square kilometers and 2.2 kilometers, respectively). If we assume, for the sake of argument, that an environment can support only as much as 0.001 person per square mile, a group of twenty-five persons would require 25,000 square miles, with a radius of about 90 miles (65,000 square kilometers and 144 kilometers, respectively). Without an energy-saving mode of transportation, such distance may induce the group to split, if the area is to be inhabited at all. It can be observed, however, that

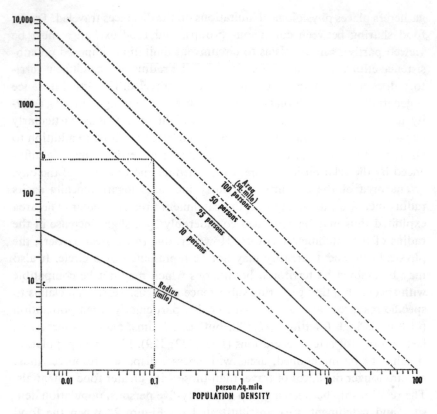

Figure 2. The relationship between population density, catchment territory, and group size. For example, the catchment territory required for a local group of twenty-five persons, at a population density of 0.1 persons per square mile (a) is 250 square miles (b). The radius of this area is about nine miles (c).

given the population densities of most hunting-gathering populations, which is probably between 0.1 and 1 person per square mile in most cases, group sizes up to one hundred persons or more can be easily accommodated within a reasonable limit of subsistence effort (Figure 2). It would seem, therefore, that a group size of about twenty-five persons is not primarily governed by the limitations imposed by subsistence effort given average resource and food extractive potentials. The size of a local group seems to be rather a function of the optimum size required for a stable organizational unit based on daily face-to-face relationship, which would be advantageous for cooperation in hunting, locating food, and defense.

A minimal group of one family, with two adults and two to three children does not seem to be a viable unit on a long-term basis because of its low chances of discovering or having access to widely dispersed resources, low hunting success, low defense capacity, and genetic viability. A very large group size, on the other hand, is not probably feasible without a strongly integrated social structure, which cannot be achieved under a mobile mode of life.

A great deal remains to be learned about the sociological significance of the small-size hunting-gathering local groups. The contributions of sociologists and psychologists to the field of small human groups provides a great wealth of information which should be tapped by anthropologists. Factors concerning cooperation, competition, suspicion, prestige, and conflict, among many others must be involved in regulating the hunting-gathering local group size from a sociological and psychological perspective. It may be added here that the observed fluidity of some hunting-gathering local groups is probably a mechanism to offset the impact of negative interpersonal relationships on the social stability of the group (Netting 1971: 7–8). It also may be a mechanism to regulate group size in response to seasonal variations in resource potentials. The sociological mechanism, however, may not be separable from the ecological, because social conflict may result from declining food yield and a corresponding decline in the standard of living (Netting 1971).

The size of a "regional group" or what we may call a "band-aggregate," on the other hand, seems to be controlled mainly by efficiency of communication and the optimum size of a viable breeding unit. At an average density of 0.25 persons per square mile, a regional group of 500 persons would cover a tract of land of about 2,000 square miles. At the low level of communication efficiency of hunter-gatherers, a large areal extent would lead to a dilution of the identity of the group at the margins, because there is a correlation between topographic distance and cultural distance (Howells 1966). The exchange of marriageable people, kinship, and ceremonial affiliations are probably some of the factors which foster the aggregation of bands into regional units. Seasonal abundance of certain resources may also encourage aggregation of bands, as shown, for example, by congregation of some Australian aboriginal groups during the season of high fish productivity (Birdsell 1957).

POPULATION GROWTH

It is clear from the slow increase in the human world population throughout the Paleolithic that exceedingly slow rates of population growth were involved. According to Polgar (1972: 204) the rate was probably below

0.003 percent. The present author (Hassan i.p.) estimated the rate at 0.001 to 0.002 percent on the basis of Paleolithic world population figures of Deevey (1960) and Keyfitz (1966). It also has been observed that only two to three children per adult female reach maturity (Carr-Saunders 1922; Krzywicki 1934) which would also reflect a very slow rate of population growth. However, a slow growth rate does not indicate that hunter-gatherers are less fecund than others. There is, in fact, no reason to believe that fecundity, the physiological capacity to reproduce, is lower among hunter-gatherers than among other groups. Population growth is not a direct function of fecundity but rather of fertility and mortality, assuming, of course, the absence of migration in or out of the group.

Several attempts were made to estimate the growth rate of the human population under hunting-gathering conditions on the basis of other estimates of both fertility and mortality. Polgar (1972), in an attempt of this nature, estimates a possible growth rate of at least 2 percent — 50 percent increase each generation with a generation span of twenty years. Sussman (1972), on the other hand, proposes that among hunter-gatherers, only two children would reach adulthood in view of a four-year child-spacing period necessitated by their high mobility. Elsewhere, the present author (Hassan i.p.) has presented a model by which the maximum potential annual growth rate among hunter-gatherers is estimated at about 1.8 to 2.7 percent with a natural child-spacing period, and about 0.4 to 1.3 percent with a spacing period of 3.5 years. This period is equivalent to a net spacing period of 3.3 years, considering infant mortality before one year of 20 percent as estimated from the data provided by Nag 1968. The figures were based on a reproductive span of eighteen years from the age at which the capacity for conception is attained — sixteen years according to Nag (1968) — to the end of adult life — about thirty-four on the basis of figures by Deevey, (1960). Application of the above model, using the data obtained by Angel (1972) on eastern Mediterranean Upper Paleolithic populations (adult female longevity estimated at about 28.7) leads to an estimate of about 0.7 to 1.7 percent maximum potential growth rate without birth control. Table 1 shows the estimates used to arrive at these figures. As may be seen in the table, allowance is made for child mortality as high as 40 to 50 percent, maternal mortality of 10 percent, sterility of 12 percent, and fetal mortality of 12 percent. These factors with their strong adverse effect on growth rate apparently are not sufficient to suppress fertility completely. The slow rate characteristic of hunter-gatherers does not seem, then, to be caused by any inherent incapacity; it seems to result, instead, from the application of birth control methods, notably abortion and infanticide, as Polgar

Table 1. Estimate of maximum potential population growth for Upper Paleolithic hunter-gatherers

Birth interval			
Amenorrhea	10	months	Wrigley (1969)
Interval before conception	3	months	Wrigley (1969)
Interval from conception to birth	9	months	Wrigley (1969)
Total	22	months	Wrigley (1969)
Live birth interval			
Birth interval	22	months	(see above)
Incidence of foetal death	12	percent	Nag (1968)
Sterility	12	percent	Nag (1968)
Live birth interval	27.3	months	Nag (1968)
		(or approximately 2½ years)[a]	
Age of initiation of conception capacity			
Age at menarche	15	years	Nag (1968)
Adolescent sterility	1	year	Nag (1968)
Age of initiation of conception capacity	16	years	
Reproductive span			
Adult female longevity	29	years	Angel (1972)
Age of initiation of reproductive capacity	16	years	(see above)
Reproductive span	13	years	
Number of live births per adult female			
Reproductive span	13	years	(see above)
Live birth interval	2¼	years	(see above)
Maternal mortality	10	percent	(Polgar 1972)
Number of live births per adult femals	4.7	children[b]	
Survivors per adult female			
Number of live births per adult female	4.7	children	(see above)
Infant mortality	50	percent	Deevey (1960)
Number of survivors per adult female	2.35	children	Polgar (1972)
Annual population growth rate[c]	0.73	percent	

[a] In a Monte Carlo simulation, Barrett (1972) arrived at an average of 28.4 ± 0.2 months and cites Perrin and Sheps as having reported an interval of 28.7 months.
[b] This is actually the same value estimated by Angel (1972) on the basis of skeletal evidence.
[c] A generation span of twenty-four years, as suggested by Angel (1969) is used.

(1972: 206) suggests. It is interesting to note here that Angel (1972) estimates the actual number of children who manage to survive until adulthood at 2.1, which would indicate a growth rate of about 0.2 percent. The difference between this figure and the maximum potential calculated above at 0.7 to 1.7 percent seems to indicate that cultural means were involved to reduce the growth rate. On the basis of the above estimates of maximum potential growth rate, about 23 to 35 percent of all potential offspring would need to be removed to achieve a zero-growth condition. The figure of about 32 percent infanticide, which represents the mean of the 15 to 50 percent suggested by Birdsell (1968), may be somewhat on the generous side, considering that abortion and other methods of birth control are employed.

In the light of these results, the demographic mechanism of temporary rapid population growth as those hypothesized for population expansion into Australia (Birdsell 1957) can be explained, therefore, in terms of the degree of birth control. On entering a pristine habitat, the population is far below the food potentials of the area, and a population buildup is possible. Under such conditions, some relaxation in the degree of birth control can lead to a considerable increase in the size of local populations, which may be followed by geographic population expansion. It is doubtful, however, that the population increase would proceed at the explosive rate of doubling each generation (about 3.5 percent), as suggested by Birdsell (1957), in view of the maximum potential rate of about 2.7 percent estimated above and in view of the restrictions placed on child-spacing by the young age of mothers, their work load, and their mobile mode of life (Polgar 1972; Hassan i.p.). It is unlikely also that birth control would come to a total halt considering its intricate social matrix. A rate in the proximity of 0.1 percent, which is the average growth rate during the Neolithic (Carneiro and Hilse 1966; Hassan i.p.), seems more plausible.[1] When the population reaches its optimum size, any further increase would mean a lower standard of living, a greater subsistence effort, and/or the adoption of social or technological innovations which can increase the level of extractive efficiency. If one of these things happens, the population would either have to repress fertility in excess of what is necessary to balance mortality or risk a progressive deterioration of the standard of living, as reflected in the level of consumption, which may lead to natural checks on the growth of population through disease, starvation, etc. If, on the other hand, the population takes the course of overexploiting its resources, it will risk its safety against seasonal or occasional fluctuations and in the long run would risk an irrevocable loss in the case of some resources and a reduction of the food potential of others.

Figure 3 presents a schematic chart which simplifies the relationship between population growth and optimum population size. Population pressure, which may be measured as the ratio between actual population size (P_1) and optimum population size (P_0), would indicate the degree of

---

[1] The figure cited represents an average. Rates probably as high as 0.5 to 1.0 per cent (Angel 1972:97; Hassan i.p.) apparently alternated with slower rates. De-population also may have occurred at times. This seems to have been the case at Nea Nikomedeia at circa 5800 B.C. Angel (1969) reports 1.9 surviving children only per adult female, mainly as a result of malaria.

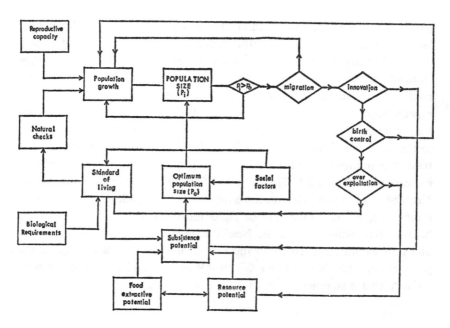

Figure 3. Population-regulating mechanisms

stress which controls population growth (a value approaching unity or greater would mean intensive population pressure). It must also be added that even if the population maintains an optimum population size, deterioration of climatic conditions may lead to decreasing the amount and/or quality of food resources and a new lower optimum population size would put tremendous stress on the actual population.

During the Neolithic period, there is no evidence of a significant increase in the longevity of adult females. According to Angel (1972) adult female longevity was about 29.8 years and 28.2 years in the Eastern Mediterranean during the early and late Neolithic, respectively, compared to the above-mentioned figure of 28.7 years during the Upper Paleolithic. Brothwell (1972) also reports 28.3 years as the average of adult female longevity during the British Neolithic. There is also no reason to believe that child mortality was lower during the Neolithic. On the contrary, it might have increased due to dietary changes and higher incidence of infectious diseases, malaria, dysentery, and hookworm, resulting from agricultural conditions (Cockburn 1971; Angel 1972). The new diet, with a high content of carbohydrates and, as the population grew in density, less meat, could have been particularly harmful to the children, who, with their high tissue-building activity, are least able to cope with long periods of inadequate amino acid intake, especially in the presence of intestinal parasites (Stini 1971: 1,021–1,022). It seems likely, therefore, that population increase during the Neolithic was achieved through partial release of such fertility-dampening controls as abortion, infanticide, and other cultural checks on population growth (Hassan i.p.). This seems to be confirmed by the demographic data available on the eastern Mediterranean populations. According to Angel (1972), the number of children born per female did not increase significantly from the Upper Paleolithic to the early Neolithic (4.7 to 4.9 from the former to the latter). In contrast, the number of surviving children per female shows a noticeable increase from 2.1 to 2.5. The number of survivors per female during the Neolithic would seem then to have increased as a result of a reduction in infanticide, if the above rate of child mortality remained constant or became even worse during the Neolithic. Reduction in the incidence of abortion would have led to an increase in the number of children born per female. The change from 4.7 to 4.9 (see above) does not seem to indicate that a significant reduction was involved.

SUMMARY AND CONCLUSIONS

The effect of population growth on food production is becoming a major theme in anthropological literature. The approach implied in this theme stands in sharp contrast with the Malthusian approach in which demographic conditions are viewed as dependent upon food production. The relationship between food production and population, however, is essentially reciprocal, although it is possible to consider either one as a short-term independent variable (Dumond 1965). Strong emphasis on the role of population growth as an independent causal force in long-term cultural changes thus may present a serious distortion of the intricate reciprocity between population and production, on the one hand, and between population and other cultural factors on the other. Moreover, the role of ecological and biological factors could be considerably obfuscated. The maximum reproductive potential of man cannot be given full expression without a rapidly expanding food production. The slow rate of human population growth in historic and prehistoric times, and the intensive efforts to control population growth even today indicate that suppressed rather than unrestricted population growth usually has been the norm.

Anthropological models which posit population increase as a causal force must therefore offer explanations for this increase. In this paper, the determinants of the density, size, and population growth of hunting-gathering population are discussed with the aim of shedding some light on the cultural, ecological, and biological matrix of these demographic elements.

Population density, population size, and population growth rate are mutually interdependent, yet each of these elements is influenced by a different set of variables (Figure 4).

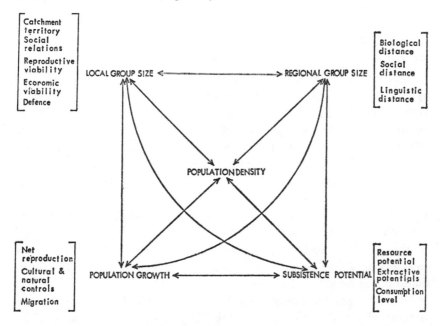

Figure 4. Ecological, cultural, and biological matrix of the density, size, and population growth among hunter-gatherers

The low population density among hunter-gatherers is essentially a reflection of their low food-extractive efficiency. The variations in population density from less than 0.01 to more than ten persons per square mile, however, are not necessarily determined solely by the level of extractive efficiency. Differences in resource potentials and consumption levels are usually involved. Seasonal fluctuations and annual variations in the kind and amount of resources are generally met by establishing a wide safety margin. Use of substitutes for the customary diet, food exchange, trade, intergroup food sharing, and food preservation dictated by residential mobility can be viewed as mechanisms to circumvent geographic and temporal fluctuations in resources.

The resource potentials usually influence and are influenced by the food extractive potentials. In addition to trade, food exchange, and other factors mentioned above, the potentials of an environment depend on the prevalent kind of subsistence activities and the methods and technology of food extraction. These factors, which contribute to the extractive potential, are in turn influenced by the dominant kinds of resources. Recognition of what constitutes an exploitable resource, however, can be governed by sociocultural considerations and demand.

By comparison with agricultural groups, the extractive efficiency of hunter-gatherers is low (Harris 1971), yet these peoples are believed to enjoy a great deal of leisure. The !Kung Bushmen, for example, invest only about eighty-four days in subsistence for a year of consumption. Considering the low level of resource potentials under food-extractive systems and the limitations demanded to secure long-term ecological equilibrium, intensification of labor would not lead to an increase in production, but to a degradation of the resource potentials. The leisure of the hunter-gatherers then may be regarded as the leisure of necessity rather than the leisure of affluence enjoyed by the lucky few under agricultural and industrial conditions. The hunters and gatherers, however, do not lead a life of starvation or hunger. On the contrary, they are well nourished according to recent nutritional studies (McCarthy and McArthur 1960; Lee 1969), but their level of consumption is barely influenced by the additional social requirements which are sometimes dramatically in excess of basic biological requirements among the "privileged" in agricultural and industrial societies.

The nutritional adequacy of the hunter-gatherer's diet reflects both the benefits of his diversified diet (Stini 1971) and the maintenance of an optimum balance between the number of people and the production. The small size of hunting-gathering bands can be viewed in this perspective, but it can be shown that if a large territory is exploited a large group size can be sustained without a greater investment of effort. That large groups are not generally common in areas with average food potentials seems to indicate that factors other than subsistence effort are involved. Such factors are probably related to the efficiency of cooperation under a mobile mode of life. A large group also would require a higher level of integration; this would limit the flexibility of the group in regard to economic and social advantages. A very small group, of two families or less, is not advantageous on a long-term basis. The extractive, reproductive, and defense potentials of such groups are too low to ensure survival. The size of an aggregate of bands or a regional group, on the other hand, is a function of biological, social, and linguistic distances. Group identity, which is defined in terms of these distances, cannot be maintained over long geographic distances given the low population density and the low levels of transportation and communication.

The limitations on the density and size of hunting-gathering populations, coupled with their low economic growth potentials, are not conducive to unrestricted population increase without jeopardizing the standard of living. Alternatively, the resources could be overexploited, but this would lead to serious reduction in their potential which would aggravate the situation. However, migration and/or innovation could alleviate the pressure, but migration cannot be continued indefinitely and the adoption of innovations, if they arise in the right time, may be obstructed by other factors. The low growth rate of population during the Paleolithic and the small number of children who survive to adulthood in ethnographic cases seems to suggest that cultural checks were exercised to curtail excessive population increases. The reproductive potentials of hunter-gatherers are indeed sufficiently great to permit rapid increase when favorable conditions exist. It is doubtful, however, that such increase over long time periods would have exceeded 0.1 percent per year in average.

REFERENCES

ANGEL, J. LAWRENCE
    1969   The bases of paleodemography. *American Journal of Physical Anthropology* 30:427–437.
    1972   Ecology and population in the eastern Mediterranean. *World Archaeology* 4:88–105.
BARRETT, J. C.
    1972   "A Monte Carlo simulation of reproduction," in *Biological aspects of demography*. Edited by W. Brass. London: Taylor and Francis.
BARTHOLOMEW, G. A., J. B. BIRDSELL
    1953   Ecology and the protohominids. *American Anthropologist* 55:481–498.
BAUMHOFF, M. A.
    1963   Ecological determinants of aboriginal California populations. *University of California Publications in American Archaeology and Ethnology* 49(2):155–236.
BINFORD, L. R.
    1968   "Post-Pleistocene adaptations," in *New perspectives in archaeology*. Edited by S. R. Binford and L. R. Binford 313–341. Chicago: Aldine.
BIRDSELL, JOSEPH B.
    1951   Some implications of the genetical concept of race. *Cold Spring Harbor Symposium on Quantitative Biology* 15:259–314.
    1957   Some population problems involving Pleistocene man. *Cold Spring Harbor Symposium on Quantitative Biology* 22:47–69.
    1968   "Some predictions for the Pleistocene based on equilibrium systems among recent hunter-gatherers," in *Man the hunter*. Edited by R. B. Lee and I. DeVore 229–240. Chicago: Aldine.

BOSERUP, ESTER
1965   *The conditions of agricultural growth.* Chicago: Aldine.
BOURLIÈRE FRANÇOIS
1963   "Obervations on the ecology of some large African mammals," in *African ecology and human evolution.* Edited by F. C. Howell and F. Bourlière 43–54. Chicago: Aldine.
BROTHWELL, DON
1972   Palaeodemography and earlier British populations. *World Archaeology* 4:75–87.
CARNEIRO, ROBERT L.
1967   On the relationship between size of population and complexity of social organization. *Southwestern Journal of Anthropology* 23:234–243.
CARNEIRO, ROBERT L., D. F. HILSE
1966   On determining the probable rate of population growth during the Neolithic. *American Anthropologist* 68:177–181.
CARR-SAUNDERS, A. M.
1922   *The population problem.* London: Oxford University Press.
CASTEEL, R. W.
1972   Two static maximum population-density models for hunter-gatherers: a first approximation. *World Archaeology* 4:19–40.
CLARK, COLIN, M. HASWELL
1964   *The economics of subsistence agriculture.* London: Macmillan.
COCKBURN, T. AIDAN
1971   Infectious disease in ancient populations. *Current Anthropology* 12: 45–62.
DEEVEY, EDWARD S., JR.
1960   The human population. *Scientific American* 203:195–204.
DORNSTREICH, MARK D.
1972   A comment on lowland Maya subsistence. *American Anthropologist* 74:776–779.
DUBOS, R.
1965   *Man adapting.* New Haven: Yale University Press.
DUMOND, D. E.
1965   Population growth and culture change. *Southwestern Journal of Anthropology* 17:301–316.
EHRLICH, P. R., A. H. EHRLICH
1970   *Population, resources, environment.* San Francisco: Freeman.
FLANNERY, K. V.
1969   "Origins and ecological effects of early domestication in Iran and the Near East," in *The domestication and exploitation of plants and animals.* Edited by J. J. Ucko and G. W. Dimbleby, 73–100. Chicago: Aldine.
HARNER, MICHAEL J.
1970   Population pressure and the social evolution of agriculturists. *Southwestern Journal of Anthropology* 26:67–86.
HARRIS, MARVIN
1971   *Culture, man, and nature.* New York: Crowell.
HARRISON, G. A., G. S. WEINER, G. M. TANNER, N. A. BARNICOT
1964   *Human biology.* Oxford: Oxford University Press.

HASSAN, FEKRI A.
 i.p.   On mechanisms of population growth during the Neolithic. *Current Anthropology.*
HOWELLS, W. W.
 1966   Population distances: Biological, linguistic, geographical and environmental. *Current Anthropology:* 7:531–535.
KEYFITZ, NATHAN
 1966   How many people have lived on the earth? *Demography* 3:581–582.
KROEBER, A. L.
 1953   *Cultural and natural areas of native North America.* Berkeley: University of California Press.
KRYZWICKI, L.
 1934   *Primitive society and its vital statistics.* London: Macmillan.
LEE, R. B.
 1968   "What hunters do for a living, or how to make out on scarce resources," in *Man the hunter.* Edited by R. B. Lee and I. DeVore, 30–48. Chicago: Aldine.
 1969   "!Kung Bushmen subsistence: an input-output analysis," in *Environment and cultural behavior.* Edited by A. P. Vayda, 47–79. New York: Natural History Press.
 1972   !Kung spatial organization: an ecological and historical perspective. *Human Ecology* 1:125–147.
LEE, R. B., I. DEVORE
 1968   "Problems in the study of hunters and gatherers," in *Man the hunter.* Edited by R. B. Lee and I. DeVore, 3–12. Chicago: Aldine.
MC CARTHY, F., M. MC ARTHUR
 1960   "The food quest and the time factor in aboriginal economic life," in *Records of the Australian-American Expedition to Arnhem Land.* Edited by C. P. Mountford. Melbourne: Melbourne University Press.
MONGAIT, A. L.
 1961   *Archaeology in U.S.S.R.* Baltimore: Penguin.
NAG, MONI
 1968   *Factors affecting fertility in nonindustrial societies: a cross-cultural study.* New Haven: Human Relations Area Files Press.
NETTING, ROBERT
 1971   *The ecological approach in cultural study.* Reading: Addison-Wesley.
ODUM, E. P.
 1959   *Fundamentals of ecology.* Philadelphia: Saunders.
POLGAR, STEVEN
 1972   Population history and population policies from an anthropological perspective. *Current Anthropology* 13:203–211, 260–262.
SHEFFER, CHARLES
 1971   Review of Boserup: the conditions of agricultural growth. *American Antiquity* 36:377–379.
SMITH, PHILIP S.
 1972   Changes in population pressure in archaeological explanation. *World Archaeology* 4:5–18.
SPOONER, BRIAN, ROBERT NETTING

1972 Boserup in the context of anthropology. *Peasant Studies Newsletter* 154–159.

STINI, WILLIAM A.
1971 Evolutionary implications of changing nutritional patterns in human population. *American Anthropologist* 73:1019–1030.

SUSSMAN, ROBERT W.
1972 Child transport, family size, and increase in human population during the Neolithic. *Current Anthropology* 13:258–259.

THOMPSON, H. P.
1966 A technique using anthropological and biological data. *Current Anthropology* 7:417–424.

VITA-VINZI, CLAUDIO, E. S. HIGGS
1970 Prehistoric economy in the Mount Carmel Area of Palestine – site catchment analysis. *Proceedings of the Prehistoric Society* 36:1–37.

WATT, KENNETH E. F.
1968 *Ecology and resource management: a quantitative approach.* New York: McGraw-Hill.

WHEAT, J. W.
1972 *The Olsen-Chubbuck site: a Paleo-Indian bison kill.* Memoirs of the American Society for American Archaeology 26.

WHITE, T. E.
1953 A method of calculating the dietary percentage of various food animals utilized by aboriginal peoples. *American Antiquity* 4:396–398.

WOODBURN, J.
1968 "An introduction of Hadza ecology," in *Man the hunter.* Edited by R. B. Lee and I. DeVore, 49–55. Chicago: Aldine.

WRIGLEY, E. A.
1969 *Population and history.* New York: McGraw-Hill.

The Earliest Farming:
Demography as Cause and Consequence

BENNET BRONSON

INTRODUCTION: DENSITY AND HUSBANDRY

I propose to discuss here the association between agriculture and population size in very early times in the millennia that separate the Palaeolithic from the first appearance of cities and states. That some such association exists, and that the association is in part causal, can hardly be doubted. But its precise nature remains elusive, the subject of many vexed and convoluted debates from Malthus' and Ricardo's time down to the present day.

Can the apparent explosion of population in the time of the early states be explained entirely by the Neolithic Revolution? Obviously not: the revolution precedes the explosion by several thousand years. Can the one partially explain the other, by saying that food production (i.e. agriculture) is a PRE-CONDITION though not a sufficient explanation for demographic expansion? Perhaps. Such explanations are a staple of elementary textbooks in anthropology (and nowadays even history) and may well be limitedly valid. But they suffer from a number of practical defects. They are no longer as productive of important new hypotheses, and stimulating research, as they were in the 1930's and 1940's. Moreover, they are not so subtle as to inspire anyone with respectful surprise. Such defects may contribute to the relative eclipse of agriculture-as-cause formulations among modern theorists.

On the other hand, the idea that the causality is reversed, with expansion in population supplying the motive force behind agricultural progress, is presently enjoying a modest vogue. One of the principal proponents of this position is the agricultural economist Ester Boserup (1965), who has elaborated a typology of agricultural stages arranged in order of increasing intensity (by which she means increased frequency of land use) which evolve from one to another under the influence of the exogenous variable, population density. An attractive feature of the Boserup formulation is that it does not simply assume that more intensive farming appears because increasingly dense populations need it but instead provides a mechanism to explain the changeover. This mechanism depends on the reasonable assumptions that (1) the technology for some kind of agricultural intensification is readily available to most peoples, and (2) that the average farmer is inhibited from employing this technology by the fact that the more intensive systems are also the most labor-demanding in terms of output per man-hour. Hence, all agricultural regimes, even if intrinsically quite intensifiable, will remain in the most extensive state possible until the farmers are forced to change through the pressure of population and an increasing scarcity of land.

This straightforward but novel view of agricultural evolution has been received by some (P. Smith and Young 1972; P. Smith 1972) with enthusiasm and has even been extended back into the prehistoric period (Cohen, this volume) on the grounds that hunting and gathering is still more economical of labor than the most extensive forms of true farming — thus, the very existence of agriculture is seen as a response to demographic factors. Others (Bronson 1972) have questioned the applicability of the Boserup model as originally presented, pointing out the lack of empirical evidence for the central proposition that extensiveness and labor efficiency are really correlated and suggesting that there are strong theoretical reasons for doubting that agriculture actually did evolve along a single track as Boserup proposes.

However, the details of this and similar models of agricultural change are not immediately germane. My concern here is to discuss the abstract issue of demographic explanations of subsistence systems, with reference not to recent alterations in farming methods but to the origins of farming itself. Can it be said that population pressure is a sufficient, or necessary, or even plausible precondition to the Neolithic Revolution? More importantly, is it an explanation? Do we gain anything in the way of theoretical rigor or predictive power by postulating a single demographic prime mover to explain all the manifold subsistence choices made by early man?

To answer these questions, I must redefine (or select among the definitions of) several concepts and reconstruct several models of subsistence economics and ancient demographics. Such concepts and models will be found to occupy the major portion of this paper.

DEFINITIONS AND RESTRICTIONS

Several terms in the following pages are likely to cause confusion unless the meanings assigned to them here are described. Among these are "efficiency," "intensiveness," and "permanence" as applied to subsistence regimes, and the more general terms, "agriculture," "cultivation," and "domestication."

"Efficiency" in this paper can be understood in two ways. When prefixed by the word, "labor," it refers to the success of a given subsistence method in minimizing the number of man-hours required for each unit of production. Prefixed by the word, "land," on the other hand, it refers to a related but sometimes opposed kind of success, the extent to which the subsistence method minimizes the quantity of land required for each unit of production. One could also evaluate efficiency according to other criteria (for instance, by social utility or effectiveness of capital utilization) but land- and labor-efficiency are what will mainly concern us here.

The concepts of "intensiveness" and "permanence" also have potential for causing misunderstanding. Both are applied to land use, but while the former is essentially a synonym of land-efficiency, the latter refers only to the relative frequency with which a plot of land is exploited. We know of subsistence regimes which are at once permanent and extensive (e.g. medieval plow farming — see Homans 1970 and Slicher van Bath 1963) and others which are intensive in spite of their impermanence (e.g. Ibo swiddening [Morgan 1955] which has a higher carrying capacity than many permanent regimes). The confusion between intensiveness and permanence is built into a good deal of the traditional terminology with which non-Western agriculture is described. Such terms as "shifting agriculture" have therefore been used sparingly here. They impute an excessive importance to simple permanence of field location, a datum which has only a limited relevance to demographic questions. We are far more interested in the land- and labor-efficiency of a regime than in whether its fields stay put from one year to the next.

"Agriculture" and "horticulture" are here treated as synonymous. Although some students of the subject have seen an evolutionary gap between *agris* and *hortus*, regarding one as an attribute of advanced societies and the other as intrinsically primitive, such an attitude is faintly ethnocentric. Many demographically successful modern peoples (e.g. the Javanese, Terra 1954) gain a major portion of their livelihoods from gardens, from plots of land too small and messy to be called, by our clean-cropping Western standards, "fields." Yet these plots may be centrally important from an economic point of view and, moreover, may be cultivated with a very high degree of skill, if not of hardware technology. My own feeling is that the owners of these plots are as much agriculturalists as any Ukrainian peasant or Nebraskan factory farmer. To treat horticulture as an essentially distinct system is misleading; it is equally misleading to talk as though horticulture is inferior from the standpoint of subsistence or necessarily early in an evolutionary sense. Some ancient farmers — wheat-growers in the Near East, for example — undoubtedly possessed plots a Westerner would call a field as soon as they began to cultivate a staple crop. But others — root-croppers in South America and Africa, mixed farmers in eastern Asia — began with small garden-like plots and have continued to depend on them down to the present day.

Agriculture is not, on the other hand, used synonymously with "cultivation," nor does either term necessarily mean "domestication." In the following pages, the term agriculture is reserved for contexts of substantial dependence on plants grown by humans, while cultivation denotes only that a useful species has been deliberately caused to reproduce by man. All agriculturalists are indeed cultivators, but a cultivator need not always be an agriculturalist; he may be just a gatherer (or a factory-worker) who occasionally puts a seed or cutting into the ground with the expectation of using the result. This distinction is unorthodox but useful. One consequence of it is that cultivation is seen to be more elementary and perhaps older than agriculture, a theme which will be expanded in a later section.

"Domestication" is used here in the strictly biological rather than partly cultural sense, referring not to taming, growing or other patterns of regular human utilization but instead to the genetic effects that sometimes accompany that utilization. The term is arbitrarily restricted to effects produced specifically by human use. Even though one can easily conceive that plants might become adapted to, and undergo genotypic changes because of, preferential utilization by cows, and even though one might plausibly call a plant adapted for growth in a field favored by cow manure a "bovine domesticate," our present interest is focused on the causal interactions between the natural environment and man.

Even within this limited sphere, under other circumstances it might be necessary to make a still narrower restriction in the meaning of domestication, confining it to meaning the effects produced specifically by cultivation and thus excluding the inherited phenotypic changes that frequently have attended the adaptation of weeds to human, but not necessarily subsistence-connected, habitats. Luckily, distinguishing between weeds and useful domesticates is not necessary to what follows. All that matters is to establish a conceptual separation between cultivating and domesticating and to observe that neither can be assumed invariably to accompany the other. Cultivation (and even agriculture) without domestication is perfectly conceivable; there is no necessary reason why even repeated cropping should always produce a phenotypically distinctive population. Likewise, a process much like domestication, and perhaps cytologically and morphologically indistinguishable from it, can be assumed to have occurred in numerous species of weed and perhaps in some selectively utilized wild species as well; hence, quasi-domestication without cultivation is also possible.

The conceptual distinction thus has a practical consequence. If we have no evidence but remains of plants, we cannot demonstrate conclusively that cultivation did or did not exist. The plant remains can of course indicate probabilities. I myself am inclined to feel that the abundant presence of domesticated characteristics yields a fairly strong presumption of cultivation and that their absence is indecisive, indicating no more than that the site in question MAY have been inhabited by pure gatherers. But in either case, plant remains by themselves are insufficient. Acceptable proof or disproof of cultivation requires the use of several additional lines of evidence.

A last comment should be made relative to cultivation and agriculture. Here, both terms are confined to plant-growing. Animal husbandry is indeed an integral part of many agricultural systems and the histories of the domestication of plants and animals in many areas are inextricably intertwined. Nonetheless, I have excluded animals from the following discussion. The reason is simple: I have not yet sorted out in my own mind how herding is related to population growth or whether, except insofar as traction power and manure are necessary to agriculture and scavengers to public health, it is related to population growth at all. Certainly, herding seems an inefficient way of getting protein and a most wasteful source of calories. In some environments it may be adaptive enough, but in others the idea of replacing the efficient wild fauna with domesticated animals seems demographic madness. If a causal relationship exists between population growth and herding, and if the adoption of herding is not due to quite different motives, that relationship is subtle and complex indeed.

With these distinctions and definitions in hand we can now return to the central subject, the association between population and agriculture. We must necessarily consider three sets of models before any conclusions are reached. The next three sections, accordingly, treat (1) the beginnings of cultivation, (2) the beginnings of staple agriculture, and (3) the history of population density.

BECOMING A CULTIVATOR

The proposition to be presented here is that the beginning of cultivation
— that is, of the habit of deliberately growing useful plants — was
neither a unique nor a revolutionary event. It probably happened
repeatedly in different places, starting at a very early date. Its causes may
have been comparatively trivial. And, for a period perhaps as long as ten
or more millenia, it may have had few discernible social or genetic effects.
The proposition is supported by the following arguments.

To begin with, cultivation is not in essence either a complex idea or one
difficult to develop. True farming — committing one's resources to the
establishment of an artificial ecosystem to yield a staple food supply —
may be filled with subtle risks and calculations, but small-scale non-
staple cultivating is elementary, so much so that it is not beyond the
inventive reach of almost any human being. We can be quite sure that
activities resembling cultivation go far back into the Palaeolithic. By the
time a modest degree of intelligence had appeared in the human stock —
certainly by the late Pleistocene if not before — extensive and in some
cases massive interference with the habitat of certain selected species
must have already begun. Even non-human predators (e.g. cows) are
often observed to feed with discrimination, singling out a small number
of species for special attention. But when the predators are intelligent and
use fire, the potential for sustained, focused, and drastic selective pressure
is clearly increased by several orders of magnitude. Through field fires
lit by humans and intelligent concentration on selected food sources,
numerous species must have been virtually exterminated long before the
famous extinctions of big game during the terminal Pleistocene. Numerous
others must have begun their adaptation to microhabitats influenced by
humans such as refuse piles and fireclearings, and thus started to become
quasi-domesticates. It should be remembered that domestication as
defined above is not necessarily a consequence of cultivation. Moreover
a few species must have been deliberately favored by man. Many recent
gatherers are reported to intervene extensively in the life cycles of wild
species, going so far as to replant them (wild yams among the Andaman
Islanders, wild rice among the Great Lakes Indians) or even to irrigate
them (among the Paiute). Ancient gatherers surely were also given to this
sort of intervention. One can easily imagine that a Neanderthaler had the
foresight to spare a fruit tree growing near a regular camping spot, or an
Upper Palaeolithic *sapiens sapiens* had the intelligence to remove weeds
from a bed of useful perennials.

It seems most realistic therefore to envision the process of human adaptation in the late Pleistocene as forming a continuum of selective exploitation, intervention, near-cultivation and quasi-domestication. Somewhere in this continuum the first act of deliberate cultivation must have occurred, without fanfare, or important consequences, or awareness that anything new had been done. The contemporaries of the pioneer among all cultivators were surely as aware as he or she that seeds sprout and planted cuttings become new plants. Accidental planting and subsequent utilization must already have occurred numberless times. The only new aspect of the situation was the element of deliberation, the decision to plant a seed or cutting with the intention of using the result.

We may assume that this first of cultigens had the following characteristics: (1) it was of a kind necessary or strongly desirable in the eyes of a group with a rather simple lifestyle; (2) it was in short supply within collecting range of this group's usual camping places; (3) it was not a major staple — if it had been, then planting a few individual plants would not have solved the problem of scarcity while planting a whole field full would probably have seemed to the group a dubious investment of their labor; they could for more easily have moved to an entirely new area; and (4) the plant may have been perishable, or rare everywhere in the region, or distributed in what the ecologists call a "fine-grained" fashion: that is, spread evenly over the landscape rather than in widely separated but easily harvested patches. This last set of characteristics would make resupply difficult even if the group should resort to the strategy of detaching a large part of its labor force to concentrate on long range foraging expeditions. If the plant is hard enough to procure even under those conditions then its labor-cost will be unacceptably high. The group will have no choice but to do without or to learn to cultivate.

Under the assumptions that this protocrop was highly desirable, quantitatively unimportant in the everyday diet, locally scarce, and difficult to keep in adequate supply even when areas outside the local zone were exploited, one might venture an *a priori* description of the plant. It should be native to a finegrained environment (like a tropical forest) or to an environment of low species and individual density (like a desert). It should have an annual habit and other traits that will make it likely to die off under careless exploitation (unlike a fruit tree or a grass). And it should contain some substance rarer than standard proteins, fats, sugars, and starches — perhaps an ester flavoring, an alkaloid stimulant, a glycoside poison, a fiber, or a dye. The theoretically ideal protocrop would be a non-staple plant with several important potential uses, such as flax, hemp, areca nut, turmeric, or the fruit banana. And empirically speaking, it is of interest that plants with these qualities are quite often found archaeologically in protoagricultural contexts — chile and agave in Mexico at Tamaulipas in the Infiernillo Phase (Manglesdorf, MacNeish, and Willey 1964: 430) and at Tehuacàn during the El Riego phase (C. E. Smith 1967: 232); nuts of *Piper* and areca in the lowest levels at Spirit Cave, Thailand (Gorman 1970: 100); and cotton and *Lagenaria* in early South America (Pickersgill and Heiser, 1975).

But detailed speculative models of this kind are a luxury at this eaɪly stage of prehistoric research. What matters more at present is to produce general models, and such a model can be abstracted from the preceding paragraphs. The probability of an early hunting-and-gathering group becoming cultivators is seemingly controlled by only four sets of factors:

1. Pre-existing technical knowledge — that is, familiarity with certain aspects of plant reproduction.

2. Sufficient rationality to be capable of acting for the sake of remotely rather than immediately anticipated gains.

3. A moderately strong locational constraint, which may be either positive or negative. It may be either (a) a focus of attraction, perhaps a natural resource that is difficult to transport and constantly used (e.g. a water source or a concentrated supply of a staple food) or a cultural resource with the same qualities (a defensible locale or, conceivably, a shrine); or (b) a circumscribing zone of negative attraction, rendered marginal by such factors as environmental poverty, climatic discomfort, military danger, or disease.

4. A botanical commodity which is both highly desirable and scarce, scarcity being defined in terms of the labor cost of collection when the collecting group is under a locational constraint.

Seen through the glass of such a model, the probability of early cultivation in any area might seem quite high. Certainly knowledge and rationality can be assumed to exist in some degree even in remote prehistoric times, and the coincidence of locational constraint with scarcity must be a well-nigh universal condition. We might therefore conclude without further ado that the inception of cultivation should itself be a near-universal. But first a few comments on the role of population density are in order.

The main effect of the model in this regard is to reduce the role of demographic pressure to that of one among several factors producing scarcity. Perhaps the commodity in question has become scarce simply because the increase of population has outrun the ability of the local habitat to maintain the commodity in steady supply. In such a case, demography is one of two producers of scarcity, the other being the always-necessary factor of locational constraint — if no constraint exists, and the group is free to wander anywhere in search of what it needs then "scarcity" can hardly exist. But the commodity may be unobtainable for reasons other than straightforward population growth. Perhaps a small and non-increasing population has eaten all the commodity up over the years it has remained in a certain locality. Here, demographics remains a factor but in a rather less decisive way. Conceivably the commodity may never have existed in adequate quantities within foraging range of the place where the population is constrained to live. The population might have migrated to that place and brought their knowledge of the scarce plant with them, or might have acquired a taste for a previously unknown plant through chance discovery or trade. A case in point is the interest in and subsequent cultivation of tobacco among the Northwest Coast Indians during the eighteenth and nineteenth centuries. Tobacco can be said to have become scarce among the Kwakiutl as soon as they discovered its existence, but in "scarcity" of this kind demographics plays no role at all.

A last point to be considered is that resource scarcity (and for that matter, population pressure) is a highly subjective matter as far as causation in human societies is concerned. Whether a commodity has really become scarce and whether it really is necessary to survival are not entirely relevant when we seek to explain actual human decisions and actions. As modern specialists on agricultural development have begun to emphasize (e.g. Found 1971) what counts most in subsistence decisions is PERCEPTION. If a technique is perceived to be laborious then it will be resisted even if, from the standpoint of an outside observer, it is convenient and economical. And if a commodity is perceived to be scarce, even though it may in actuality be abundant enough, then appropriate action will be taken. Possibly the original cultivator decided to plant his crop because he wrongly evaluated the difficulty of finding the plant growing wild.

But if we ignore this problem of perception for the moment, we can arrive at four interim conclusions. First, cultivation of an elementary kind should be extremely old; there is no reason why it should not have come into being quite far back in the Pleistocene. Second, this rudimentary cultivation need not have had any decisive genetic effects on the plants involved. If only a few individuals were grown at once and especially if the parts of the plant utilized were not the flowers or the seeds, a protocultigen might be indistinguishable from its wild congeners. Third, early cultivation need not have had much effect on human populations. Perhaps it enabled a few groups to lead more comfortable lives and encouraged some to slow their wanderings, but it may not have contributed directly to any kind of archaeologically discernible population. And fourth, increase in density of population need not have played a decisive causal role. Although a plant may have occasionally come into cultivation as a response to demographically-induced scarcity, there are many alternative routes to that result.

All these conclusions are of course predicated on the notion that cultivation and agriculture, a substantial dependence on cultivated plants, are quite distinct institutions. As will be seen in the following sections, the interconnections between staple agriculture and demography are of a rather different kind.

BECOMING A FARMER

At this point we should inquire why the appearance of staple crop farming was delayed so long. Even if we reject the almost unprovable possibility of a Pleistocene origin for casual plant tending, we must still account for the fact that full-scale dependence on agriculture lags a surprising distance behind the known beginnings of cultivation. In Mexico, Peru and Southeast Asia, although perhaps not in the Near East, this time-lag seems to amount to at least several thousand years. What is the reason for such a long delay?

Several explanations can be invented. One of the most attractive is a hypothesis based on Boserup's model (see above) of agricultural development — that just as "extensive" agriculture is less labor-demanding and therefore preferable to "intensive" agriculture, so gathering is still more economical of labor than agriculture itself. There is even some empirical evidence for such a hypothesis. Sahlins (1972: 1–39) has pointed out that many hunters and gatherers, contrary to what once was generally believed, are comparatively affluent. Both the Hadza (Woodburn 1968, 1972) and the !Kung Bushmen (Lee 1972a, 1972b) are said by their ethnographers to lead an easy life, devoting no more than a few hours a day to subsistence activities even (in the case of the !Kung) in distinctly marginal environments. Thus one can argue that the apparent reluctance of early gatherers and casual cultivators to convert to true farming may have been due to a simple lack of incentive. Before the appearance of the incentives of the later prehistoric period — denser populations, markets, perhaps government persuasion — remaining a gatherer may have been the economically rational course.

However, the labor-saving explanation is difficult to accept as a universally applicable rule. As I have argued elsewhere (Bronson 1972), a great many other factors enter into decisions concerning subsistence besides labor-efficiency: considerations of security, of prestige, of comfort, of health. For instance, nomadic gathering usually seems to exact a rather high price in natural and induced mortality among the very young and very old. It also limits substantially the possibilities of owning weatherproof dwellings, of developing non-subsistence technologies, and of storing food against times of scarcity. One is not convinced that the desire to do as little work as possible will invariably offset such considerations as these. It is far from certain, in fact, that gathering is always less work than some kinds of farming. Numerous food-production regimes, both shifting and permanent, require no more than a few hours' work each day in order to keep a family in food; most known hunter-gatherers (including the Hadza and !Kung) work at least this much, particularly when the labor cost of trekking from camp to camp is counted in. The labor-efficiency of gathering is indeed a factor to be considered, but it is not adequate as a full explanation for the apparent fact that substantial dependence on cultivation appeared so tardily.

An alternative explanation is that time was required for productive and trustworthy staple crops to evolve, and that the delay in the appearance of farming was thus due to a built-in lag in genetic possibility. But this explanation seems weak. Except for a few especially intractable species (perhaps maize), few staple crops can have needed more than a century or two of human attention to reach an adequate level of productivity.

A third explanation, which might be called the "naive-demographic" model, depends heavily on the idea that the development of farming was a straightforward adaptive response to the development of large, dense populations. Thus, it could be argued, true agriculture did not appear earlier simply because it was not needed until the time it did appear. But there are a number of serious objections to such a baldly eufunctional proposition, among them the fact that demographic development on a local scale is inherently too fast-moving to explain a series of events that extends over several millennia. As will be pointed out in a succeeding section, if demographic necessity were the only cause, agriculture would have appeared much more quickly than it did.

The fourth explanation that suggests itself has to do with the minimization of risk. When the casually cultivating hunter-gatherer turned to farming, he may not necessarily have had to work harder, and he may have obtained a number of benefits from the settled life that then was possible. But it is undeniable that he took a considerable gamble. He committed a substantial amount of labor to a course of action from which he could receive no immediate return. Indeed, in those days of pristine farming when no one had successful agriculturalist neighbors to observe, he could have reasonably doubted that he would receive any return at all. Even nowadays crops frequently fail, and still more frequently return no profit on the labor and capital expended, in spite of some nine or ten millenia of agronomic experience. Back in the days when farming began, the risk must have seemed and been very great indeed. While other factors may have contributed, simple caution is an almost adequate explanation for the reluctance of early cultivators to engage in full-scale farming.

The problem that remains is to find a model to explain why agriculture came to exist at all, why men everywhere, perhaps through judicious use of infanticide, war, and other fertility-controlling measures, did not remain casually cultivating hunter-gatherers down to the present day. The model that seems most useful is described below.

In its most generalized form, this model has a good deal of similarity to the one presented in the preceding section for the probability of becoming a cultivator. Again one must postulate a locational constraint and a scarcity of an important commodity. But here the commodity must be essential rather than simply desirable — that is, a staple food. And the question becomes more acute of why the proto-farmers stayed put when faced with this scarcity rather than just moving on. The risk they took by staying and attempting to grow the commodity was, as has already been pointed out, considerable. We must therefore assume that the locational constraint was very strong.

A number of more detailed submodels can be generated by considering the possible nature of this constraint.

The first submodel is a classically simple one — an island or otherwise circumscribed environment from which, for reasons of military danger, epidemiology, or sheer physical impossibility, the inhabitants cannot migrate. Within such an area it is plausible that population densities will increase quite quickly beyond the point where a hunting and gathering way of life can be sustained. In later times, such densely populated enclaves have been observed often to produce strikingly land-intensive agricultural systems, even in the midst of regions where most subsistence is of a very extensive kind. Numerous examples of what Clark and Haswell (1967: 50) call "societies under siege" occur in East and West Africa, Central and Southeast Asia, the Pacific, and the New World (see also Bronson 1972: 216). Since these isolated enclaves are often rather idiosyncratic in terms of the intensive farming technologies they use (e.g. the Haya — Allan 1965), one concludes that many of these technologies have evolved *in situ* in response to the fact that no one could migrate out when land grew scarce. But if constraints on out-migration can thus render inefficient farming systems efficient, then why could they not at an earlier date make a casual cultivator become a full-scale agriculturalist? Many of the same constraining forces were as operative in the early Neolithic as in recent times. It seems plausible that they could have had similar effects.

A rather more complex submodel is generated when the constraining forces are considered to be centripetal and positive: when, for instance, a population is drawn to a given place by the abundant presence of a second staple commodity different in kind from the one which is becoming scarce. A fishing lagoon on an otherwise unproductive coast would meet these requirements, as would a water source in a generally waterless region. The attractions of an abundant supply of protein or water might easily counterbalance the disadvantages of a shortage of a starchy staple in the eyes of a hunting-and-gathering group, causing them to attempt to raise that staple rather than move on to another place.

It will be observed that this two-staple model is a generalized version of two well known theories of the origin of food production. The idea that the first agriculturalists may have been fishermen was originally suggested by Sauer (1952: 23) and has been subsequently taken up by several more recent authorities (e.g. Adams 1966: 40–1). The latter sources emphasize the importance of sedentarization as a factor in the decision to plant a staple crop; here, the conflict between two separate locationally-fixed staples is assigned the central role. Sedentarization undoubtedly predisposes to agriculture but is not a necessary precondition in this model's terms. A conflict between the need for fish and the need for grain could result in the adoption of agriculture even in the absence of a settled life. The fishermen could use the vicinity of the lagoon only seasonally, planting a (necessarily pest-resistant) crop and then continuing on a gathering circuit for the remainder of the year.

The water-source-centered version of the model rather resembles the somewhat discredited "oasis theory" of agricultural origins, whereby the first domestication was assumed to have occurred within oases isolated by increasing regional dessication. The main difference between this model and the oasis theory in its more highly elaborated form (e.g. Peake 1928) lies in the way the future farmers are assumed to get into the oasis in the first place. While Peake and Pumpelly postulated that the farmers had to be trapped there by a vast climatic change, here no catastrophe is necessary. Many nomadic pre-farming groups must have stayed within oases for long enough to consume most of the food supply inside the watered area and within the exploitable zone surrounding the oasis. That the group would always attempt to farm rather than move on to another oasis is of course unlikely. But, given a sufficient scarcity of water elsewhere and perhaps a reluctance to split the group into smaller units, it is entirely plausible that agriculture would sometimes have been the result.

A last submodel worth considering is the most diffuse and indeterminate of all. Let us assume that most of the conditions laid down previously do not always hold — that under some circumstances agriculture is less risky and easier than collecting, that no locational constraint exists, and that the desired staple commodity, although in short supply, is not necessary to survival. A wandering band of gatherers in an almost deserted rainforest will serve as an example. What is to keep them from cutting down a few trees and planting a moderately large crop of, say, manioc? The labor investment need not have been excessive. If they girdled the trees they would have had to do little cutting and if the forest was deserted, and hence primary, the undergrowth would have been minimal. A quarter hectare of cleared area might have needed no more than two weeks' work and could have produced, in the case of manioc, enough calories to live on for a year. Moreover, since manioc has few natural enemies, the members of the band would not have been obliged to wait around until harvest time; they could have gone off and gathered wild foods elsewhere in the forest while the crop took care of itself. The band thus took no risk, made little commitment, and enjoyed a greatly increased level of security — if the supply of other staples failed, it could always have fallen back on the manioc, which can be expected to remain in edible condition in the ground for several years. Whether such farming as this is theoretically significant—whether it would ordinarily lead to any kind of sociocultural or demographic progress — may seem questionable. But that it is farming cannot be denied. Agriculture in some instances can have evolved for reasons which are both unrecoverable and trivial.

In summary, one can produce a number of quite disparate models of agricultural origins, varied according to the constraints and commodities assumed to be necessary. I myself see little to choose between them. Any could have happened. If we assume that agriculture was independently "invented" often enough, then all of these causal sequences should have unrolled at least once somewhere in the world.

As for the role of growth of population, this clearly varies from case to case. In the model of the population under siege, it is always present but not, as will be pointed out shortly, as a truly independent variable. In the two-staple model, increasing density may or may not be present, and demographic causation is entirely absent from the model of the part-time forest-farmers. But before demographic issues can be dealt with properly two observations on that subject must first be made.

THE NATURE OF POPULATION PRESSURE AND INCREASE

The two observations in question have to do with (1) the *a priori* probability of being able to project demographic growth curves into the past and so to make assumptions about the size of ancient populations, and (2) what does and does not constitute demographic pressure.

Increase Curves and Frame-Dependence

It is usual, when discussing the influence of demography on societal and economic development, to consider that long-term population-growth is represented by the familiar exponential curve (Figure 1).

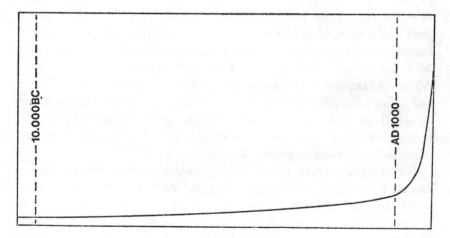

Figure 1.   Model of population increase on a worldwide scale

A curve much like Figure 1 would, with somewhat varying parameters, be accepted by most specialists as a fair model of worldwide demographic trends between the Palaeolithic and the present. It would be accepted validly; that international population growth has actually followed such a curve is not open to doubt. But its usefulness is quite another matter. There are reasons for questioning whether the exponential-curve model has any explanatory relevance to early socioeconomic evolution.

The main reason is that socioeconomic events do not (or did not until recently) happen on a worldwide scale. They take place instead within restricted blocks of area measuring at most a few hundred miles on a side, and have their roots in causes which operate within a similarly reduced frame. If we are interested in demographic causation then densities of continental populations are of no interest to us; such data are meaningless abstractions. And if we come to consider the probable history of populations within restricted regions and localities, the exponential-curve model becomes unsatisfactory as a predictor of demographic density.

Empirically speaking, it is difficult to find a single example of a regional or local population before the era of modern medicine known to have followed a steady pattern of exponential increase for longer than a few centuries. Virtually every population of this kind for which we have long-term documentary records can be shown to have undergone substantial fluctuations. If we consider only the period before A.D. 1800, taking the diffusion of the Jenner vaccine as the cut-off point for the beginning of demographically effective medicine, we find that the late eighteenth century rarely marks the known apogee of any regional population. Northern Europe may be an exception, but in most regions the premedical peak was reached long before 1800 and was followed by a considerable decline afterwards. Aztec Mexico, Byzantine Anatolia and Egypt, pre-Mongol Persia, and perhaps Sung China and Roman Italy and northern Africa are examples of such early peaks. And in areas smaller than regions and nations, the short-term fluctuations must completely overwhelm any secular trend toward gradual increase. Seen within a frame of this size, the exponential curve cannot be expected to resemble the actual histories of populations except in a small fraction of cases.

The theoretical explanation for the "frame-dependence" of demographic models is obvious and need not occupy much of our time. Human populations are capable of intrinsically high rates of increase — even under premedical conditions — of a doubling rate of less than fifty years. The inhabitants of a given locality should therefore be able to fill it solidly with human bodies within the space of one or two millennia. The probability that a population will actually sustain such an increase rate over a large area is of course vanishingly small, but as the spatial frame shrinks the probabilities change. If the frame is a region of 10,000 square kilometers, possibly this regional population has at some time in its history remained free from excessive mortality for long enough to produce a substantial population boom. And if the frame is a locality measuring only 500 square kilometers in size, the probability approaches certainty. Given a moderate reduction in mortality, the likelihood of in-migration, and the absence of controls over fertility that is almost universal among modern peoples, we may assume that almost all 500 square-kilometer local populations have undergone a number of extreme fluctuations during the last ten millennia. The actual population curve for a locality of such a size would probably resemble Figure 2 more closely than Figure 1.

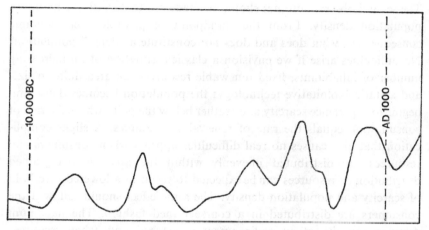

Figure 2.   Model of population increase on a local scale

One interest of this indeterminate population model is that it frees us of the need to find mechanisms by which low densities of continental populations can be assumed to exert significant pressures on resources of land and labor. There is no need, for instance, to postulate that pre-Neolithic gatherers were driven to adopt a major subsistence change because of crowding at high relative densities of several persons per hundred square kilometers. If high absolute local densities are needed for a hypothesis, then they can be assumed to have existed almost anywhere and at any date.

But this conclusion has a corollary, and the corollary is of equal interest and importance: high densities of population do not invariably lead to the adoption of agriculture. Density-induced resource scarcity must have occurred in numerous localities during the late Pleistocene; even though these densities must sometimes have been considerable, not once are they known to have resulted in the large-scale cultivation of staple crops. In the early Holocene, such densities must have occurred at numerous times and places again; yet in only five or ten small regions can they be shown to have led to farming. Demographic pressure is thus a most inefficient cause. When response follows the presumed stimulus only once in each ten thousand trials, one is justified in doubting the adequacy of that stimulus as an explanation.

Density versus Pseudo-Density

The second observation that should be made has to do with the nature of population density. From the standpoint of possible socioeconomic consequences, what does and does not constitute a "dense" population? No difficulties arise if we envision a classical situation of an increasing number of inhabitants, fixed renewable resources, an area finite in size, and a static exploitative technology; the population becomes dense and begins to experience scarcity at or rather below the point where the rate of consumption equals the rate of renewal of resources. A slight complication that also causes no real difficulties appears when consumers and resources are distributed unevenly within the area. A fine-grained distribution of resources can be expected to result in a lowered threshold of scarcity and population density. The same effect should follow if the consumers are distributed in a coarsegrained fashion. The maximum carrying capacity of an environment is reached only when resources are clustered into easily exploitable nodes, and when the exploiters are spread out as evenly as possible.

On the other hand, there are some sorts of complications which cause real difficulties for the concepts of density and scarcity. One is the probability that any resource which is not necessary for survival can be exhausted eventually by a bare handful of consumers, just as long as these consumers are sufficiently omnivorous, determined, and improvident. Into this category fall almost all individual species of plants and animals. The consumers can exterminate any one of these by falling back on others when the preferred species grows scarce. The category also includes all non-staple species as a class; a few consumers can exterminate these without suffering any consequences except perhaps for a certain regret at the disappearance of a favored condiment. Hence, we cannot always glibly say that some sorts of scarcity are due to population pressures; they may be due to simple overconsumption. Population pressure is not a meaningful concept except when referred to a critical class of resources, so critical that increasing scarcity can be presumed to bring Malthusian demographic checks into operation.

Another serious complication arises when we consider more carefully the subject of population distribution within the local area. Let us imagine, for instance, an underpopulated valley inhabited by a number of house-holds which are relatively dispersed but focused around a single non-subsistence feature in the center, such as a shrine or defensible hilltop. The resulting settlement-pattern might resemble Figure 3. The issue here involves the problems of supply faced by households located at differing distances from the focal feature. The household marked B on Figure 3 is out at the edge of the settled area; its inhabitants may be far from the population focus but are otherwise in an advantageous position, closer to their fields, to wild resources, and to most other things necessary to the household economy. As a consequence, B's resupply costs, measured in time and effort of transportation are relatively low. Household A, on the

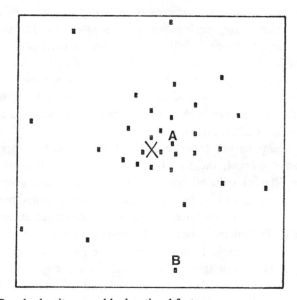

Figure 3.   Pseudo-density caused by locational factors

other hand, is in a high-cost location. It may gain some advantages from its proximity to the center, but few of these advantages are economic. It is further from most resources and must regularly expend more time and labor in obtaining them, in spite of the fact that the valley contains adequate land and that no resource is scarce in an absolute sense.

The model being constructed here is only a restatement of the familiar "Isolated City" model of Von Thünen (Chisolm 1967; Chayanov 1966), whereby locational considerations — factors of distance and ease of transportation — are said to be decisive in optimizing the choice of crops and farming techniques in a marketized regional economy. However, this particular version of the Von Thünen model is being used to point up a somewhat different conclusion: that even in an unmarketized pure subsistence economy, locational variations will still produce cost differentials and hence exert the same kind of economic pressure as does genuine scarcity. From an operational point of view, cost (in this case, labor cost) is the only meaningful measure of scarcity. That a given resource is actually common somewhere within the valley makes no difference to the inhabitants of Household A. For them, the resource is hard to get, and they are therefore under economic pressure, a kind of pressure which is most difficult to distinguish from the pressure caused by over-population.

Analogous forms of "pseudo-populational" pressure can be presumed to exist at some level in all societies for whom the choice of a place to live is not dictated by the location of a single food resource. If the location of the settlement, whether temporary or permanent, is chosen partly on the basis of defensibility, sociability, or the presence of a second critical resource, then some members of the society will be under appreciable pseudo-pressure. Depending on the keenness with which this pressure is felt, those members will be more or less receptive to the idea of new subsistence alternatives.

The last complication for the concept of population pressure has already been discussed, the fact that increased density must first pass through the filter of cultural perception before it is likely to have any socioeconomic effect. In human as distinguished from animal populations, pressure, scarcity, and stress are to a considerable extent states of mind. A group which feels itself in need of *Lebensraum* may take steps to solve the problem even though, by a more objective measure, the shortage of living space is largely imaginary. Likewise, the scarcity of a resource is not measured in actual labor cost but instead in terms of PERCEIVED labor, and this will clearly depend on a whole host of variables besides caloric expenditure and man-hours worked. In all probability such perceptual factors will usually tend to lower thresholds of pressure and scarcity rather than raise them. But how much these thresholds will be lowered in any particular case is impossible to predict. Thus it follows that an appreciable percentage of ancient subsistence changes will not be explainable by objective economic and demographic factors. Repugnant though it is to our nomothetic instincts, we must consider the possibility that some changes, including some instances of the inception of agriculture and cultivation, may have been caused by a perceptual mistake.

THE LIMITS OF DEMOGRAPHIC EXPLANATION

None of the foregoing is meant to deny the validity of some demographic explanations. Unquestionably population pressure has been significant and sometimes decisive in documented cases of recent alterations of subsistence patterns. The twentieth century intensification of farming by the Ibo (Netting 1969) is quite clearly a more or less direct effect of the recent population boom in Eastern Nigeria, and a whole series of historic shifts in English agriculture have been convincingly tied by Slicher van Bath (1963) to price fluctuations and, through this intermediary market mechanism, to long-term national demographic changes. But there are also numerous countervailing examples. Many of the pre-modern agricultural innovations in Tokugawa Japan (T. Smith 1968) seem to have been accomplished through administrative fiat, because of a concern for increased productivity on the part of landlords and tax collectors. Similar incentives to agronomic change are also known to have been present in eighteenth-century England and in Rome at the time of Virgil. Many modern changes of subsistence in Africa are better interpreted as responses to market development than to increase in population — witness the appearance of land-extensive commercial agriculture among the Gishu (Allan 1965) and Kofyar (Netting 1968). A twentieth-century farmer in New Jersey or Kent selects techniques and crops with regard only to input costs and output prices; he (and, one imagines, his counterparts on the outskirts of any ancient city) farms in a singularly labor- and land-intensive fashion because land is dear, transport to urban markets cheap, and prices for perishable produce high. Whether the total population within the city's hinterland is dense or sparse makes no difference to his choice of farm technology. If he is close to the city, even though that city may be in the midst of a fertile and uninhabited wasteland, he will be an intensive farmer.

Numerous other examples could be cited but there is no need. It is absurd to maintain that, in the modern and recent world, simple demographic density is invariably the prime mover of subsistence change. It may be important in many cases and decisive in some, but too many other factors affecting subsistence exist — market forces, administrative controls, limitations on information, differences in perception — for one to conclude that population pressure alone is an adequate explanation for the majority of ethnographically and historically known instances of the intensification of subsistence methods.

Perhaps it may seem that the early days of farming represent a more pristine and simpler pattern, when the primacy of population pressure should emerge more clearly. However, as the preceding pages have tried to show, this commonsense expectation encounters a number of theoretical difficulties.

The inception of cultivation (as distinguished from full-fledged farming) would seem to have a most tenuous *a priori* connection with increase in population. This follows directly from the postulate that the first cultivated plants need not have been staple crops. If they were not staples, or were not treated as staples, then they can hardly have begun to be grown because the growers were faced with imminent starvation. One of the archetypal instances of pre-agricultural cultivation is the El Riego phase at Tehuacán, where the ordinary diet, on the evidence of coprolites, is said by MacNeish (1972: 71) to have contained between 0 and 6 percent of cultivated plants. Now, this quantity of food may have made a considerable difference to the comfort and even nutrition of the ancient Tehuacanos. But it did not save anyone from starving to death. One cannot believe that the Tehuacanos began cultivating in order to obtain 6 percent more of a staple, or because they sensed that a decline of 6 percent in gathering output meant future disaster. Whyever they began, there was no perceptible wolf at their door.

The beginnings of agriculture, on the other hand, may have had a firmer relationship with demographic factors. If the knowledge of cultivation was already widespread, it is entirely plausible that a population crisis could have turned a group of hunter-gatherers into farmers almost overnight. But one can think of other equally plausible reasons for taking that drastic step — locationally-generated pseudo-pressure, conflicts between positionally-fixed resources, the social benefits of sedentism, perhaps even at times the increased ease and diminished risk of farming as against gathering. It is true that these other reasons may have had a demographic component, but then demographic causes themselves must always have been much diluted by other factors. The model of straight population pressure is inadequate as an explanation even of situations where a marked demographic increase can be shown to precede staple agriculture, for of necessity the increased population must be a purely local phenomenon which cannot exist without factors — called here, "locational constraints" — that keep the excess people from wandering off into the surrounding emptiness. And so which is the independent variable, the population increase or the constraint?

To my mind, such questions are both unanswerable and unnecessary. What we are dealing with is a complex, multifaceted adaptive system, and in human adaptive systems (as in real natural and human systems of any kind), single all-efficient "causes" cannot exist. True, it may be advantageous occasionally to construct models of such systems in which a single factor is given paramount status. But in the case of this particular system, the heuristic value of a simplex model is most doubtful, perhaps especially when the paramount factor is to be demography. Population pressure is not the only possible explanation of farming. Nor does it invariably lead to farming. As pointed out earlier, high local densities must have occurred very early in man's history and with great frequency; only in a small percentage of post-Pleistocene cases can these have led to the adoption of large-scale food production. Thus, increase in population is neither necessary nor sufficient as an explanation. It is also among the most difficult of all data to recover archaeologically, depending as it does on excavations on a tremendous scale and on datings of an improbable accuracy. Even if it were true that in a given case a rapid increase in population had immediately preceded and thus presumably caused the appearance of true farming, that fact would be most difficult to demonstrate through any conceivable excavation. And, as I say, the farming may have many other explanations. The population-centered model of subsistence-evolution may be pedagogically useful but it is of doubtful value as a research guide.

Much more satisfactory is the rather subliminal model that seems actually to guide much of the research on post-Pleistocene adaptations, whatever the explicit theoretical orientation of the individual researcher may be. The leading characteristics of this model are complexity, factor feedback, and instability. A great many agencies — sedentariness, epidemiology, genetics, environmental structure, technologies of subsistence and non-subsistence, political evolution, economic development, warfare, the density and distribution in space of populations — are recognized as potential influences, without seriously contending that any have necessary priority. The relationship between each pair of these is visualized as one of feedback; the chicken-and-egg quality of interactions between adaptational factors has long been recognized by most specialists. And the rather Augustinian notion that all recent (i.e. post-Pleistocene) adaptive patterns are intrinsically unstable is gaining ground again after a brief setback during the heyday of functionalism. Change, driven by the sheer impossibility of keeping so many interacting factors out of disequilibrium, is a normal condition. What requires explaining is stability, not change.

Under the influence of this implicit model, a considerable quantity of significant work has been done. Indeed, in spite of the regrettable lack of detailed and overt consensus, the model has probably generated as much useful research as has the average paradigm of we of the Kuhnian "normal" sciences. It is too good a model to be replaced casually.

However, beyond question it will be replaced. The appearance of numerous proposals for new explicit models of socioeconomic evolution, together with a growing feeling that the field is on the edge (or over the edge) of a breakthrough, signals the old model's approaching demise. As yet the few comprehensive models that have been attempted have not been unqualified successes. But a number of partial models, focused on disentangling only a few strands of the web of factor relationships, have done quite well in terms of generating research hypotheses that are at once testable, non-trival, and interesting. It would seem that studies of ancient demography could be aimed best at producing partial models like these, at clarifying the connections among a small number of precisely defined and quantified variables of which one is size of population. Such an aim may seem dishearteningly modest when compared with the dimensions of the overall problem of why the long Pleistocene stasis did slip over into a disequilibrating mode and produce the world as we now know it. But a sharply limited approach is the only one that is likely to be productive. Testable explanations for grand patterns are not necessary for research, nor are they practicable in the present state of the art.

REFERENCES

ADAMS, R. M.
   1966   *The evolution of urban society.* Chicago: Aldine.
ALLAN, W.
   1965   *The African husbandman.* Edinburgh: Oliver and Boyd.
BOSERUP, E.
   1965   *The conditions of agricultural growth.* Chicago: Aldine.
BRONSON, B.
   1972   "Farm labor and the evolution of food production," in *Population growth: anthropological implications.* Edited by Brian Spooner, 190–218. Cambridge, Massachusetts: M.I.T. Press.
CHAYANOV, A. V.
   1966   *The theory of peasant economy.* Homewood, Illinois: American Economic Association.
CHISOLM, N.
   1967   *Rural settlement and land use.* New York: John Wiley.
CLARK, C., M. HASWELL
   1967   *The economics of subsistence agriculture* (third edition). New York: St. Martin's Press.
FOUND, W. C.
   1971   *A theoretical approach to rural land-use patterns.* New York: St. Martin's Press.

GORMAN, C. F.

1970 Excavations at Spirit Cave, Thailand, *Asian Perspectives* 13:79–108.

HOMANS, G. C.

1970 *English villagers of the thirteenth century*. New York: Harper and Row.

LEE, R. B.

1972a "Population growth and the beginnings of sedentary life among the !Kung Bushmen," in *Population growth: anthropological implications*. Edited by Brian Spooner, 329–342. Cambridge, Massachusetts: M.I.T. Press.

1972b "Work effort, group structure, and land-use in contemporary hunter-gatherers," in *Man, settlement and urbanism*. Edited by P. J. Ucko, R. Tringham, and G. W. Dimbleby, 177–186. Cambridge, Massachusetts: Schenkman.

MACARTHUR, R. H., E. O. WILSON

1967 *The theory of island biogeography*. Monographs in Population Biology 1. Princeton, New Jersey: Princeton University Press.

MACNEISH, R. S.

1972 "The evolution of community patterns in the Tehuacan valley of Mexico and speculations about the cultural processes," in *Man, settlement and urbanism*. Edited by P. J. Ucko, R. Tringham, and G. W. Dimbleby, 67–93. Cambridge, Massachusetts: Schenkman.

MANGLESDORF, P. C., R. S. MACNEISH, G. R. WILLEY

1964 "Origins of agriculture in Mesoamerica," in *Handbook of Middle American Indians*, volume one. Edited by R. C. West, 427–445. Austin: University of Texas Press.

MORGAN, W. B.

1955 The change from shifting agriculture to fixed settlement in southern Nigeria. *Department of Geography Research Notes* 7. Ibadan, Nigeria: University College of Ibadan.

NETTING, R. M.

1968 *Hill farmers of Nigeria*. Seattle: University of Washington Press.

1969 Ecosystems in process: a comparative study of change in two West African societies. *National Museum of Canada Bulletin* 230:102–112.

PEAKE, H.

1928 *The origins of agriculture*. London: E. Benn.

PICKERSGILL, BARBARA, CHARLES B. HEISER, JR.

1975 "Origin and distribution of plants domesticated in the New World tropics," in *Origins of agriculture*. Edited by Charles A. Reed. World Anthropology. The Hague: Mouton.

SAHLINS, M.

1972 *Stone age economics*. Chicago: Aldine.

SAUER, C. O.

1952 *Agricultural origins and dispersals*. New York: The American Geographical Society.

SMITH, C. E.

1967 "Plant remains," in *The prehistory of the Tehuacan Valley*, volume one. Edited by Douglas S. Byers, 220–255. Austin: University of Texas Press.

SMITH, P. E. L.
   1972 "Land use, settlements patterns, and subsistence agriculture: a
         demographic perspective," in *Man, settlement and urbanism*. Edited
         by P. J. Ucko, R. Tringham, and G. W. Dimbleby, 409–426. Cam-
         bridge, Massachusetts: Schenkman.
SMITH, P. E. L., T. C. YOUNG
   1972 "The evolution of early agriculture and culture in Greater Mesopota-
         mia: A trial model," in *Population growth: anthropological implications*.
         Edited by Brian Spooner, 1–59. Cambridge, Massachusetts: M.I.T.
         Press.
SMITH, T. C.
   1968 *The agrarian origins of modern Japan*. Stanford: Stanford University
         Press.
SLICHER VAN BATH, B. H.
   1963 *The agrarian history of western Europe A.D. 500–1950*. London:
         Edward Arnold.
TERRA, G. J. A.
   1954 Mixed garden horticulture in Java. *Journal of Tropical Geography* 3:
         34–43.
WOODBURN, J. C.
   1968 "An introduction to Hadza ecology," in *Man the hunter*. Edited by
         R. B. Lee and I. DeVore, 49–55. Chicago: Aldine.
   1972 "Ecology, nomadic movement, and composition of the local group
         among hunters and gatherers," in *Man, settlement and urbanism*.
         Edited by P. J. Ucko, R. Tringham, and G. W. Dimbleby, 193–206.
         Cambridge, Massachusetts: Schenkman.

Population Pressure and the Origins of Agriculture: An Archaeological Example From the Coast of Peru

MARK N. COHEN

Since the time of Morgan's comprehensive statement (1877) on the nature of cultural evolution in which he embodied themes of considerable antiquity, two main ideas contained in his work have dominated our ideas about the development of cultural systems: first, that the process of cultural change is primarily an accumulation of technological capabilities and that the level of technological development is the primary determinant of the culture system as a whole; and second, that cultural evolution consists of a succession of well-defined and relatively static stages separated by abrupt revolutionary transitions. The combination of these two themes has led anthropology toward a one-sided view of the relationship between technology and population growth. Technology is considered an independent variable; technological changes modify the carrying capacity of the environment; population simply adjusts to the new limits in a Malthusian sense and is not seen as having any significant effect on technological change; as a result, the history of population growth is assumed to have a stepped pattern in which periods of stable equilibrium alternate with periods of rapid population growth.

Perhaps the most explicit modern expression of these two themes and the resulting model of population growth is in the work of Childe (1951) who discussed the development of European civilization in terms of a series of technological revolutions (for example the "Neolithic" or food-producing revolution) involving relatively short term massive reorganizations of technology which resulted in periods of rapid population growth and reorganization of social institutions.

Recently, however, the assumptions about the revolutionary nature of technological changes and culture growth have been questioned. For example, Adams (1966) has questioned the applicability of the revolution concept in explaining the development of urban society in Mesopotamia or Mexico which he describes as a gradual (although not necessarily continuous or homogeneous) process. As another example, local sequences worked out for the Tamaulipas, Tehuacán and Oaxaca regions of Mexico (MacNeish 1958, 1967; Flannery 1968) have all demonstrated quite convincingly that the transition from hunting and gathering to agriculture was extremely gradual rather than revolutionary.

The assumption of technological determinism and the related assumption of the dependent, responsive nature of population growth, has had a much more pervasive influence, however, and still persists as a major, if tacit, assumption in much work on cultural development. The assumption is so pervasive for example that it has survived even the introduction of systems-models in the analysis of cultural change. The systems approach (not necessarily to be confused with the more recent explicit use of systems-theory terminology) has the advantage of viewing cultural change (for example, the evolution of domestication) not simply as a sequence of isolated historical events, but rather as a series of shifts in the balance between a number of interrelated variables. This approach allows us to consider multiple dimensions of feedback between variables instead of making simple cause-effect or independent–dependent variable statements. As a result, the potential for accurate analysis of the processes of cultural evolution is greatly enhanced. However, the full potential of this method is lost since we are tending to retain our traditional assumptions about causal relationships and tending simply to translate our old assumption into the new language. Flannery (1968), for example, described the evolution of agriculture in Oaxaca, not as a series of discoveries, but as a series of quantitative shifts in the balance between alternative strategies of getting food. However, pressed for an explanation of these shifts, Flannery has argued that the original nexus of change in the system is a mutation of the maize-plant which increases its productivity and therefore increases the efficiency of one part of the human economic cycle, and that on this basis there was a shift in human economic strategy toward domestication. Here Flannery has made two assumptions which reflect old biases of traditional anthropology and which produce a logically impossible result. First, he has presumed that human population simply remains in (or actively seeks) one equilibrium level until that equilibrium is upset by an outside event. And second, he has assumed something which is implicit in technological determinism — that the critical event which triggers the adjustment must be an increase in the AVAILABILITY of food-resources (increased productive CAPACITY).

He has assumed that new productive potential is the key to change and that the other elements in his system simply respond to this altered productivity in maize. Here he betrayed his intellectual ancestry, but he was also forced into a logical error. Mutations are recurrent aspects of the environment which occur with statistical regularity. The mutations which increased the productivity of maize would have been regularly available to primitive hunter-gatherers dealing with wild populations of maize, and they cannot logically therefore account for a shift in their exploitative system. We must instead look for the reason behind the altered human response to this aspect of the environment. Why did the hunter-gatherers choose to make use of a mutation which they had previously ignored? The way out of this problem lies in a slightly more complex model in which we view human population not simply as an equilibrium-seeking system responding to altered productive potential but rather as a system with inherent growth, actively redetermining the nature of its relationship with the environment. Such a model can be constructed if we consider population growth (or population pressure defined in terms of the degradation of existing resources whether or not accompanied by actual increase of population) as an inherent feature of the human adaptive system and not simply as a response to environmental or technological changes. Such an approach would solve Flannery's dilemma. We could simply assume that his population began to make use of the potential of the mutated maize-plant when the population was too large to manage easily with its traditional strategies.

There is, of course, a certain basic logic in considering population growth as a contributing factor in culture change. We know that human populations have enormous growth potential (Polgar 1972: 205; Birdsell 1957: 193) and we know that population growth is one of the most noticeable trends of human history. Moreover, a model emphasizing population growth would correspond well with the newly discovered gradual nature of the major features of cultural evolution.

A number of recent studies have attempted to demonstrate the importance of growth and pressure of populations in contributing to the process of cultural growth rather than simply resulting from technological change (e.g. Dumond 1965; Boserup 1965; Harner 1970; Spooner 1972). The basic discussion of the role of population growth as a determinant of technological change is that provided by Boserup (1965) who argued that agricultural technology is largely a function of population density and that the various known technologies represent a continuous series of more or less elastic responses to growing population. Despite these studies, and despite what I consider to be the cogency of Boserup's logic (if not always of her supporting data) this approach is not widely recognized. It is explicitly dismissed in a number of recent studies (Polgar 1972; Sheffer 1971) and it is ignored (see e.g. Flannery 1968) where it might provide useful insights.

I believe that such dismissal is unfortunate. I intend to argue that population growth and population pressure are in fact contributing factors in the origins and growth of an agricultural economy and, incidentally, I intend to suggest that the model of human cultural systems as equilibrium seeking and maintaining systems must be replaced with a model stressing their inherent growth through expanding population. I do not intend simply to replace technological determinism with a new population determinism or assume that population grows independent of other factors. I do intend to argue that population growth is an inherent factor in the adaptive histories of many, if not most, human populations and that such growth can be used to explain aspects of the development of agriculture which are otherwise inexplicable.

THE THEORY OF POPULATION GROWTH AND AGRICULTURAL ORIGINS

In order to get around the legacy of technological determinism and look at population growth as a factor in the origins of agriculture, we must deal with a number of myths concerning agriculture and its origin. The first myth is that agriculture is a difficult concept, whose discovery was a major obstacle in human progress. There are a number of lines of eivdence which refute this assumption and suggest in fact that the concept of agriculture was probably readily available to evolving human populations. First, it is becoming increasingly apparent that agriculture was in fact discovered independently a number of times. A recent review of agricultural origins by Harlan (1971) indicated that the origins of our major domesticates must be traced over an extremely broad area of the New and Old Worlds and that defined centers of domestication are recognizable only in certain cases. He pointed out in addition that there are a large number of genera of plants in which two or more species were domesticated at different times and in different places. The evidence of interregional contacts of great antiquity is sufficient to suggest that many of these regions learned the idea from others. However, to account for all of these several origins by assuming that the concept of agriculture spread from one or a few hearths is not supportable in terms of known patterns of diffusion: the indigenous crops occur earlier than the imports in too many regions. Hence, we can assume that there were at least several independent discoveries of agriculture. Moreover, our knowledge of the ecology of hunter-gatherer groups suggests that the independent discovery of the concept of domestication by several of these groups is not only possible, it is highly probable, and I maintain that lack of insight into the process of domestication would rarely have offered an obstacle to the progress of any group. The techniques of agriculture are self-evident to any hunter-gatherer group. We know, for example, that even nonhuman primates regularly accumulate around their home-ranges gardens of their favorite produce grown from seeds or vegetative parts dropped in the course of eating or in feces (Jolly 1972: 59). We know that human hunter-gatherers also tend to collect gardens of their favorite foods near their houses quite independent of any attempts at domestication (Schwanitz 1966: 12). And we know that these people often unintentionally propagate their food plants by accidentally re-sowing parts of their crops in the process of harvesting (Schwanitz 1966: 12). We know that pre-agricultural man created new open habitats for plants in the form of dumps, pathways, and recently burned areas (Anderson 1969: 144) and that many of man's cultivated plants originated as species which enjoyed these disturbed habitats (Anderson 1969: 144; Sauer 1952: 71). We know that most hunting and gathering groups have a very thorough knowledge of the characteristics and ecological needs of the species of their preferred food and that they even know how to assist them in their survival (Stewart 1956: 120). We know that hunters and gatherers are aware, for example, of the value of a fire in promoting the growth of preferred species. (Stewart 1956: 120; Sauer 1952: 11; Isaac 1970: 18–19). We know also that desirable morphological changes such as gigantism of edible parts, and early maturity, have occurred in plants growing in the vicinity of human settlement although without direct human participation (Isaac 1970: 18).

All this suggests that the break between gathering and agriculture is not very sharp and therefore, that the conceptual break was not very difficult. In fact, I maintain no such break occurred. There is rather a continuum in degrees of assistance offered to the plants on which one depends. This sort of continuum is reflected in Anderson's (1969: 131ff) description of primitive gardens with their haphazard organization of crop plants and the graded distinction from weeds which are discouraged, through tolerated weeds, through unplanned but cultivated plants to purposefully planted domesticates. With these considerations in mind, the view that the bulk of humanity was seriously blocked from the discovery of agriculture for any period of time is untenable. Local inequities in the type of plants available might have hindered individual populations, but given the range of plants which have been cultivated at various times and places, this cannot have been a widespread limitation. In addition, I must stress that even people of those regions which learned about agriculture from others or imported their cultigens from other areas probably would not have been delayed for lack of access to agricultural techniques. We are finding increasingly that cultural contacts between regions are of great antiquity (see for example Lanning 1967a and MacNeish 1969, 1970 concerning the distribution of early artifact styles in Peru). The suggestion, therefore, is that even those regions lacking suitable cultigens had access to agricultural knowledge and to suitable cultigens long before they were needed or utilized as is true in the case to be discussed. What this suggests is that we must look for some reason other than ignorance why some people have remained hunters, and conversely, some reason other than discovery why some became farmers.

The second myth concerns the benefits which result from the transition to an agricultural economy. Recent studies of the diet of hunters and gatherers by Lee (1968, 1969) by Woodburn (1968) and by Neel (1970) indicate that modern hunters and gatherers are commonly well nourished and healthy. Their diets are found to be sufficient in total caloric intake, and also in protein and necessary elements. This is true despite the fact that modern hunters and gatherers (for example Lee's Bushmen in the Kalahari desert) have been pushed by political pressure into marginal environments which are presumably less productive than the environments of their prehistoric counterparts. It is questionable, therefore, whether agriculture would have brought any significant dietary improvement to hunting and gathering peoples. There is even indication that the quality of the diet will decline with agriculture since agriculture presumes concentration on a relatively small number of food-sources. By reducing the dietary variety inherent in a gathering economy, agriculture may actually reduce the balance of the diet. (As Lee points out, hunter-gatherers may be better nourished than their agricultural neighbors.) Agriculture may also reduce rather than increase the reliability of the food sources. The natural plant-community is buffered against ecological disaster by its very complexity. The number of species represented in the wild community means that some edible parts will be available at most seasons and, more important, assures that some foods will survive droughts, fires and other natural disasters, especially since the plants represented have already undergone a long process of selection for tolerance to these particular conditions. The replacement of the natural community by an artificial plant community of fewer members means that the food-supply will be more seasonal (geared to the cycles of the few crop plants) and much more susceptible to ecological breakdown. Lee also suggested (1969: 73) that the Bushmen suffered less from a drought experienced prior to his visit than had their agricultural or pastoral neighbors.

The work of Lee and Woodburn also destroys one other misconception about the benefits of agriculture, the assumption that agriculture makes food-getting easier (i.e. less costly in terms of labor). Lee's statistics and Woodburn's description indicate that hunters and gatherers, again in marginal, difficult environments, put in very little time in the food quest. Lee indicated, for example, that the bulk of the food for the Bushmen is gathered by a fraction of those we would consider able-bodied adults working only a very few hours per week. This is not surprising when we realize that their labor is generally equivalent only to the harvesting portion of an agricultural cycle. Sufficient figures are not available to demonstrate conclusively the greater ease of hunting and gathering, especially since it is difficult to compare labor figures cross-culturally. However, Lee's figures are sufficiently striking to suggest that leisure time does not appear for the first time with agriculture and that labor-saving is hardly likely to have been an incentive for technological change. Once these myths are destroyed, we arrive at a new problem about the origins of agriculture. If agriculture provides neither better diet, nor greater dietary reliability, nor greater ease, but conversely appears to provide a poorer diet, less reliably, with greater labor costs, why does anyone become a farmer? (Lee's Bushmen who know all about planting seeds argue that this would be silly since it is much easier to harvest wild foods.) What does agriculture actually accomplish? It provides only one economic benefit: the ability to grow and harvest more food from a unit of space in a unit of time. In other words, agriculture permits denser food-growth supporting, denser population and hence larger social units, but at the cost of lower dietary quality, less reliability, and more work per unit of food. If I am correct then that agriculture is not a difficult concept, but something readily available to hunting and gathering groups, and if I am correct then that its only advantage is in the greater density of food available, then it follows that agriculture will occur primarily in response to a situation of need resulting either from population growth or from resource degradation. The hunter-gatherers in Oaxaca (Flannery 1968) shifted their ecological response to favor maize-agriculture when the need arose, not because the mutation became available. I will argue further that while resource degradation (or even political incentive to greater production) may have played a part under certain circumstances, the predominant historical motivation for agriculture has been growth of population.

To understand the latter position, a third major misconception that underlies prevailing assumptions about the technology/population inter-action must be considered: the uncritical use of models of carrying capacity in the study of human society based on the assumption that human population historically has simply responded to fixed population ceilings established by available resources. Many, but by no means all, populations of non-human animals tend to reach stable levels balanced at, or near, the optimum level which the environment can support without resource degradation. Working with modern hunter-gatherers, anthropologists like Birdsell (1957) have demonstrated that human populations also achieve relatively stable optimum levels balanced with their resources. The failure here is the failure to realize that these studies of modern hunter-gatherers are studies on populations which are anomalous precisely because their populations have remained small. I would argue that the concept of carrying capacity as a fixed ceiling to which population responds, although applicable to specific populations under particular conditions, has little general validity for human history. Human populations, aware of agricultural potential, know that they can expand their resources by intensifying their labor-inputs if it should become necessary. Such a population has a choice whether to stabilize at a given level of population and a given productivity or to expand its population and work harder. We do not need to consider a stable population growing to a new stable ceiling whenever technology permits, although such may, of course, happen in some historical events. We can rather visualize a population growing and pushing its technology with it. Human populations have grown historically. The remaining populations of hunters and gatherers are anomalous groups which either by cultural choice or by reason of unidentified biological factors have remained small and survived. Let us consider for a moment the model of a hunting and gathering population and consider its alternatives. If the Kalahari Bushmen are in any way typical, we can assume that such a population obtained an adequate and nutritious diet with a minimum of work by exploiting the wild resources within a loosely defined radius of its camp. Typically, such exploitative systems appear to support less than one person per square mile, (Lee and DeVore 1968: 11) so that the size of the group is limited by the distance people are willing to walk to obtain food. Among modern hunter-gatherers an exploitative radius of a few miles seems typical. A radius of 6 miles brings 100 square miles within the area of exploitation so that it is again typical of such groups that the population of a single camp is rarely more than 100 people and typically closer to one-half or one-quarter of that figure (Lee and DeVore 1968: 11). Depending on local conditions, the group may be required to move once or more during the year to exploit new areas.

The high quality of diet and the low labor costs involved can be maintained as long as population is constant, but this nice balance is threatened if population tends to grow beyond these limited figures, and my contention is that for many, if not most, human populations, this tendency had constantly to be dealt with. Increased population threatened the group with a decline in the quality and quantity of food available, an increased work load, or both, and I think we must assume that the people involved were capable of realizing as a practical matter, if not theoretically, that the more mouths there were to feed, the harder the gathering process would be. The group then had several alternative solutions to its dilemma. First, it could limit population either by infanticide, which is obviously available to all human populations, or by techniques of abortion or contraception which are also almost universal (Birdsell 1968; Devereux 1967: 98). This is the solution most in keeping with retaining both the quality of diet and low labor costs, but it is not the only solution. The alternatives are to increase the radius exploited (which implies increased labor-costs in travel); to search harder for the less readily available food sources within the area exploited (again implying increased labor-costs); to move from camp to camp more often (increased labor-costs); or to settle for less desired and less nutritious foods. We can be sure that some combination of these alternatives entered into the response of any particular population. But, these responses are limited in their adjustive capacity. An increase in the radius of exploitation leads eventually to the budding off of new village units by persons who feel that they are forced to walk too far from new resource-areas to old villages, or who realize that they can get food for less work by starting a new smaller social group. This is, I suspect, the process by which hunter-gatherers populated the world. But, eventually this sort of territorial expansion abuts against natural barriers to migration or against the ranges of competing groups. Similarly, working harder on finding wild foods within the same area or settling for lesser foods are only temporary solutions to growing populations. Again, the decision may be made belatedly to limit population and stabilize labor-costs at the new higher level. For those who do not take this option, and continue to allow population to grow, the only other alternative is to begin artificially to increase the density of desirable crops within their gathering radius by the use of one of a number of techniques which must have been known to them: removing the competing plants (weeding); protecting from other animals; improving the physical environment (hoeing etc.); placing the plants in areas where they did not formerly grow (planting); selecting and selectively aiding the most productive plants. These techniques add up to agriculture, but it is important to stress that the techniques probably accumulate *de facto* and piecemeal as responses to the need for more food, long before the concept of agriculture was developed. Also important to note is that these changes which we call agriculture only occurred when the people decided that the labor involved in these practices was the least of evils. Each technique represented higher labor-costs and would only have been added when the costs were outweighed by the costs of retaining old methods.

All of this, of course, allowed for a wide range of latitude in group decision. Were there good rational reasons for wanting or needing a larger population despite the costs? Were there cultural norms favoring the prestige of large families or preventing the use of techniques of population control? Did the joys of parenthood outweigh the additional labor-cost? Was it considered harder to walk farther to collect food, to move the village more often, or to weed the plants close to home? Are there biological reasons why some populations grow and some don't?

Clearly, given these alternatives, populations have an enormous number of possible strategies. Some in fact chose to limit population at the hunter-gatherer level. Some just as clearly did not. These variables however are ultimately regulated by the one overwhelming factor of competition. If we assume that various groups of hunter-gatherers made different decisions in these situations and some limited population while some did not, how do we explain the scarcity of hunter-gatherers? The simple answer is that those who for one reason or another chose to allow populations to grow and responded to the need by putting extra labor into agriculture were able to compete successfully for space with those groups that chose to remain small (or who for biological reasons did not grow). Thus, even if only a relatively few populations allowed population growth and compensated with agriculture, they would over a period of time replace hunter-gatherers in all but the most marginal environments. (Moreover, the awareness of such competition may very well have been one factor involved in the original choices). (Also to be noted: it is not population growth *per se* which is the critical variable, but demand for production outstripping the wild resources of a given region for whatever reasons. A similar result will occur with a stable population if it stabilized above the carrying capacity of the land for a given technology and therefore progressively degraded resources. Such results would also occur if climatic change eliminated resources or if social factors required new production standards.)

In sum, I am suggesting a model in which expanding population (along with environmental changes or altered sociopolitical conditions) may cause a more or less continuous modification of adaptive strategy. The population has a choice of several adaptive strategies at any point in time, but only one choice, the intensification of resources by application of agricultural techniques, is viable for most populations in the long run. The other choices either provide only temporary solutions which delay but do not eliminate the beginnings of agriculture, or they lead to evolutionary dead ends since such populations cannot ultimately compete with those utilizing agriculture. (One other alternative, that of exploiting other agriculturalists, is, of course, available but only to a few populations.) The point is that although the intent at all times is to retain a balance between population and resources, the system is not simply designed to maintain stable equilibrium. The continual tendency for population to grow, and the ready availability of techniques for intensifying resources (agriculture) mean that new equilibria are constantly being redefined. This does not, however, imply that population growth is an independent variable in any simple sense. Clearly rates of population growth are subject to cultural choice. Moreover, nothing in this model precludes feedback from technological or social changes to the rate of population growth. The achievement of a certain level of agricultural competence (for example, the development of sedentary life) may subsequently alter either biological factors or cultural values concerning population growth.

This model helps to account for the apparently gradual nature of much major technological change, since it implies that technological change does not occur solely by its own momentum but in large part occurs only as necessitated by the demand for new resources. The model also implies that population growth historically may be smoother and more gradual than is commonly assumed, and that it may approximate a ramplike model or a stepped ramp, rather than the simple stepped model which is commonly applied in anthropology (e.g. Deevey 1960:198; Polgar 1972: 204). (There is, of course, no need to assume that population growth is totally gradual since I do not assume that it is an independent variable.)

This in turn requires us to explore one more myth in anthropological thinking concerning the reconstruction of prehistoric population curves. The archaeological record is commonly read in such a way as to support the assumption that population is constant before agriculture and that rapid revolutionary population growth follows the discovery of agriculture suggesting a Malthusian model. (See, for example, Braidwood and Reed 1957.) Such a conclusion may, however, represent a misreading of the evidence. In the first place, archaeological techniques for reconstruction of populations invariably rely on counting the number of units of some parameter representing population which are in use at the same time, for example the number of archaeological sites of a given period, the number of houses, the number of square meters of floor space, the number of grindstones. While this method has inaccuracies in dealing with population of sedentary peoples, it is totally inadequate to deal with mobile populations. Moreover, the nature of temporary campsites suggests that they will be underrepresented in the archaeological record. They are harder to find and identify and more easily obliterated than permanent villages. Since the inception of agriculture is roughly associated with the beginnings of sedentary villages it is hardly surprising that the archaeological record shows a marked increase in the number of settlement units at this time. The apparent enormous expansion of population after the beginning of agriculture may simply reflect the inaccuracy of archaeological samples and the growth curve of the historical population may have been somewhat smoother than a direct reading of the evidence suggests.

Ultimately, of course, the issue of the role of population-growth in culture change needs to be settled empirically by the study of culture systems in transition. Ethnographic examples of the transition to agriculture are hard to come by. Reconstruction from archaeological evidence is difficult because all of the important variables (population, resources, agricultural techniques etc.) can be reconstructed only from indirect evidence which is prone to sampling errors of many kinds. For these reasons, I do not think that it is possible to prove my case archaeologically. However, I do believe that it is possible to present archaeological sequences which are best interpreted according to the model I have suggested.

The Peru Coast, where I have done my field work, provides what is in many ways an ideal area for testing. The dry climate results in excellent preservation of organic remains so that the status of agriculture can be readily assessed. The desert conditions also mean that archaeological sites are readily amenable to surface description and survey (although there are important limitations which weaken the argument). In addition, the long history of sophisticated, anthropologically oriented archaeological work in Peru, particularly the emphasis on settlement pattern analysis, means that there is a well defined prehistoric context in which to work.

Finally, the nature of the coast provides well bounded ecological units of study.

My example from the Ancón-Chillón Region of the Peru Coast is not a perfect model of agricultural origins since the evidence suggests that the people of this region imported their first cultigens from other regions rather than developing indigenous food resources domesticates. The value of the evidence from this region is fourfold. First, the data indicate that the hunting and gathering population of the region was growing (if slowly); that it was degrading its resources; and that it was being forced to modify its collecting strategy prior to the beginnings of agriculture in the region. Second, the data indicate that the people of the region had access to agricultural techniques and resources at least several hundred years before they were used as evidenced by established diffusion-contacts with agricultural regions. (In particular I will show that the Ancón-Chillón region lags at least several hundred years behind the Ayacucho region of the Peruvian highlands in the development of agriculture and the domestication of major crops despite the fact that more direct diffusion-contacts between the two regions can be demonstrated.) Third, the data suggest that agricultural technology, when it does appear in the region, does so in a period of ecological crisis following the progressive exhaustion of the wild resources of the region. Fourth, the data suggest that even after the beginning of agriculture in the region, new domestic crops and animals and new technologies appear slowly and gradually in response to need rather than in correspondence to known diffusion patterns.

THE ANCÓN-CHILLÓN REGION OF THE PERU COAST

Between 1961 and 1971, Edward P. Lanning of Columbia University, Thomas C. Patterson, now of Temple University, M. E. Moseley of Harvard and their students engaged in a systematic study of the archaeology of the lower portion of the Chillón Valley and the adjoining Ancón region of the Central Coast of Peru. (See Figure 1.) As a result of their studies, a complete archaeological sequence for the last 12,000 years has been worked out. The distribution of archaeological sites and environmental zones can be determined or inferred for each prehistorical period; and organic collections from site excavations are available for each of the main time periods (Lanning 1967a,b; Patterson 1966a,b, 1971; Patterson and Moseley 1968; Moseley 1968, 1972). In 1969–1971, working under the guidance of Dr. Margaret Towle of Harvard University, I undertook a study of the botanical remains from the region. My intention

A   Ancón-Chillón region
B   Ayacucho
C   Callejón de Huaylas (Ancash)
D   Huarmey

Figure 1. Peru (showing the location of the Ancón-Chillón region and regions referred to)

was to describe economic changes through time and to relate these changes to population growth and settlement patterns.

The region studied includes the delta of the Chillón River and an area of the coastal desert to the north covering a total of approximately 360 square kilometers (see Figure 2). The area measures 29 kilometers north to south with an east to west distance which varies between 9 kilometers and 16 kilometers because of the irregularity of the coastline. The zone is located just to the northwest of Lima (11° 58′ to 11° 40′ South latitude by 77° 13′ to 77° 03′ West longitude). The area is predominantly an extremely dry desert due to the cold offshore ocean currents, and over much of the land no natural biological communities exist. Within the area there are, however, three major communities utilized as resource-zones by pre-

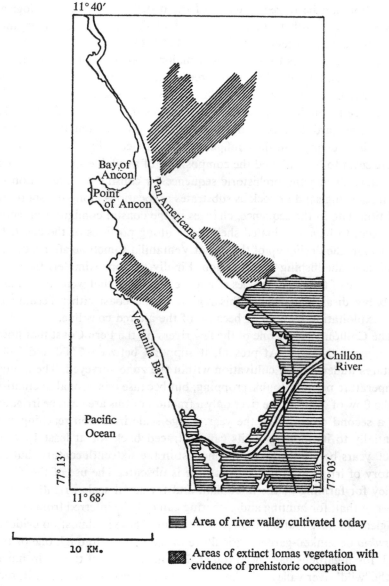

11° 40'

Bay of
Ancon

Point
of Ancon

Pan Americana

Bay of
Ancon

Ventanilla Bay

Chillón
River

Pacific
Ocean

Lima

77° 13'

77° 03'

11° 68'

10 KM.

▤ Area of river valley cultivated today

▨ Areas of extinct lomas vegetation with
evidence of prehistoric occupation

Figure 2. The Ancón-Chillón region

historic populations: the ocean itself with its rich marine fauna; the
river's valley with its riverine fauna and its naturally irrigated forest later
replaced by cultivated fields and extended by artificial irrigation; and
patches of *lomas* vegetation or vegetation supported by the moisture of
fogs on the upper slopes of hills facing the sea. The history of human

occupation can be traced in terms of the distribution of archaeological sites associated with these three zones and the appearance of organic refuse pertaining to each zone found in the sites.

The ocean appears to have been a major food source throughout the sequence. Fishing sites have been recorded all along the coast of the survey zone. Marine fish and shellfish, as well as shore-birds, appear in abundance throughout the sequence. Changes in the productivity of the oceans are hard to assess, but certain changes are well documented. First, slight changes in the configuration of the coastline have occurred. These seem to have altered the composition of available shellfish at various times during the prehistoric sequence by causing an alternation of molluscs using sand or rock as substrates at locations along the shore. In addition, late in the sequence, changes in the coastal configuration actually seem to have eliminated shellfishing along portions of the coast. In particular, the drying up of the bay at Ventanilla sometime after A.D. 600 eliminated shellfishing in this region. Finally, at approximately the same date, some of the major species of marine mammals that were hunted had probably disappeared from this region of the coast either because of over-exploitation by man or because of the altered coastline.

The Chillón River is one of the few rivers on the Peru Coast that flows throughout the year. At present, it supports between 6,000 and 7,000 hectares under annual cultivation within the zone surveyed. The annual temperature permits double cropping, but because of seasonal fluctuation in the flow of water in the river only a fraction of this area can be irrigated for a second crop during the year. Large scale irrigation reaching substantially to its modern limits can be traced back for at least 1,000 to 1,500 years before the Spanish conquest in the sixteenth century, but the history of irrigation prior to that time is obscure. The use of the river's valley for farming of the floodplain and for small scale irrigation, and, prior to that, for hunting and gathering can only be inferred from archaeological site-distribution and refuse-content. There is almost no evidence of *pukio* or sunken-garden agriculture in the region although one or two such fossil gardens have been found. Reconstruction of the environment of the 'wild' river valley prior to human interference is a problem. Ramón Ferreyra of the *Museo de Historia Natural*, Lima (personal communication), has cited evidence in the form of modern remnants of primary forest and fossilized seeds which suggests that the river may once have supported a forest in a band several kilometers in width. In this case, the primary forest would have been substantially equal in area to that of the modern cultivated zone, and as such the valley would have been a rich source of varied fauna and flora for early man.

The vegetation of the *lomas* is the most problematic of the three zones. The vegetation is dependent on moisture from fogs and as such only occurs today in locations (hillsides near the sea above 300 meters) and at seasons (mid-winter) when the fog is densest. During this period, a highly visible green patch occurs on isolated hillsides in the region. The vegetation of the *lomas* is a loosely knit community of herbaceous annual plants plus a number of tuber-, bulb- and rhizome-bearing plants, some species of which could have provided food for early inhabitants in the region, as well as supporting grazing fauna which could be exploited (Weberbauer 1932: 16ff.). At present these regions are used for grazing domestic herds but there is no evidence in this region at least that the areas of *lomas* have ever been farmed or contributed any species which have become domesticated.

In 1970, during my visit, the vegetation of the *lomas* consisted only of tiny patches in one or two restricted locations in the survey zone. These patches contained tubers of the edible species *Solanum tuberiferum* in great abundance. I estimated ten such tubers (not to be confused with true potatoes) per square meter (or a total of about 150,000 tubers in one patch) which along with other edible species of plants and small fauna even today would have provided rich resources for exploitation by a small human population. These resources would be available not only in the winter season when the *lomas* blooms, but throughout the year since the tubers would remain available for harvest long after the superficial parts of the plants which provide the *lomas* with its temporary bright green color had disappeared.

The extent of this vegetation at various times in the past, however, is in dispute. There is abundant historical evidence that the distribution of the vegetation of the *lomas* responds markedly to the alternation of wet and dry years (Goodspeed and Stork 1955) and there is extensive evidence of fossil plants and snails covering a much larger area of the survey-zone of the *lomas* than that which supported active vegetation in 1970 (Figure 2). Lanning (1967a, b) has argued that the expanse of fossil vegetation represents a period of generally wetter conditions in the areas of the *lomas*, corresponding to a period of warmer climate between 6000 and 2500 B.C., and he has argued that the vegetation of the *lomas* was extensively utilized by man only during this period. He has been criticized by Parsons (1970), who has claimed that the fossil *lomas* vegetation is nothing more than the remains of occasional wet years which do not correspond to any particular time-period. The carbon 14 dates and the artifactual content of Lanning's sites, however, are so consistent (Cohen 1971) that there is no question that these sites in the *lomas* represent

individual industries and exploitation of particular portions of the vegetation corresponding to particular time-periods. Lanning's climatic
hypothesis, however, is questionable. Judging by the position and content
of the various sites in the *lomas* apparently there was a trend in the use
of the vegetation (see below) that suggests that the pattern of its use and
subsequent abandonment owe more to human population pressure than
to climate. In short, clearly the vegetation of the *lomas* was exploited
primarily during one prehistoric era (just prior to the advent of agriculture. It is not clear that this use pattern necessarily reflects climate
change, and for reasons which will be discussed below I prefer a model
that emphasizes population pressure as a cause of their decline. In either
case, I intend to show that the origins of agriculture in the region are
bound up with the declining productivity of the vegetation of the *lomas*.

Lanning and Patterson (Lanning 1967a; Patterson 1966a; Patterson
and Moseley 1968) have divided the prehistory of the region into six
preceramic and six ceramic periods (Table 1), following the standard
Peruvian chronology. They recognized approximately forty separate
phases with finer discriminations still being worked out. Threehundred
archaeological sites have been mapped from the area so that settlement
patterns for all periods are known (Figures 3 and 4). Occupation of the
region appears to have been continuous from about 14,000 B.P. to the
Spanish conquest in the 16th century with only one possible break. The
gradual nature of the changes which occur in the artifact content, site-
distribution and refuse suggest that we are dealing with a continuous
process of cultural development *in loco*. Outside influences are felt but
there is no evidence of wholesale replacement of population or culture
with the possible exception of the one gap in the sequence. Approximately
50,000 floral specimens have been analyzed by the author from 105
excavation units at ten sites representing the entire sequence with only
one or two gaps. The plant material represents a total of thirty-nine taxa.
The taxa identified are listed in Table 2, and are broken down into three
groups: Those definitely or very probably wild species indigenous to the
area; those of unresolved origins; and those which are clearly domestic
imports into the region. The latter category, it will be noted, includes
almost all of the significant food plants. Some of the wild plants and
plants of unknown origin are now grown under conditions of domestication, but in these cases there are insufficient data available to distinguish
domestic and wild types from the archaeological record. I also undertook
a crude sorting of the faunal material, sorting out the domestic groups,
llamas and guinea pigs, marine mammals, nondomestic terrestrial mammals such as deer, fish and various types of shellfish. These data are

Table 1. Chronological table of prehistoric periods for Peru and approximate chronology of archaeological assemblages in the Ancón-Chillón Region

Prehistoric period		*Ancón-Chillón*	
Late Horizon	A.D. 1534 A.D. 1476	(Late Horizon)	
Late Intermediate Period	1000 B.P.	(Late Intermediate)	
Middle Horizon	1400 B.P.	(Middle Horizon)	
Early Intermediate Period	2200 B.P.	Lima (8 phases) Miramar (4 phases)	
Early Horizon		8–10 unnamed phases	
Initial Period	2900 B.P. 3800 B.P. 3500 B.P.	Colinas Thick Brown Ware Thin Brown Ware	3350–2900 B.P. 3650–3350 B.P. 3750–3650 B.P.
Preceramic 6	4500 B.P.	Gaviota Conchas Playa Hermosa Pampa	3900–3750 B.P. 4100–3900 B.P. 4300–4100 B.P. 4500–4300 B.P.
Preceramic 5	6200 B.P.	Encanto Corbina	5600–4500 B.P. 6200–5600 B.P.
Preceramic 4	8000 B.P.	Canario Luz Arenal	7000–6200 B.P. 7500–7000 B.P. 8000–7500 B.P.
Preceramic 3	10,000 B.P.	(Hiatus in occupation?)	
Preceramic 2	10,500 B.P.	Chivateros II Chivateros I	10,500–10,000 B.P. 11,500–10,500 B.P.
Preceramic 1		Oquendo Red Zone	12,500–11,500 B.P. 14,000–12,500 B.P.

supplemented by descriptions of organic remains of sites in the region provided by Lanning (1967a, b; Patterson and Moseley 1968; Moseley 1968).

A summary of the major changes in settlement-patterns and organic refuse follows.

Table 2. Botanical remains identified from archaeological samples in the Ancón-Chillón Region

Taxa considered to be definitely or probably wild species indigenous to the region	
Inga feuillei	*Asclepias* sp. (Milkweed)
Sapindus saponaria	*Typha* sp. (Cattails)
Caesalpinia sp.	*Cyperaceae* spp. (Sedges)
Prosopis	*Equisetum* spp. (Horsetails)
Schinus molle	*Tillandsia latifolia*
Galactia striata	*Gramineae* sp. (Grasses)
Jusseia peruviana	*Hymenocallis amencaes*

Taxa of undefined origin	
Psidium guajava (Guavas)	*Cucurbita ecuadorensis* (Squash)
Lagenaria siceraria (Gourds)	

Domestic plants imported into the region	
Zea mays (Maize)	*Solanum* spp. (Potatoes)
Cucurbita ficifolia (Squash)	*Oxalis tuberosa* (Oca)
C. moschata (Squash)	*Polymnia* sp.
C. maxima (Squash)	*Bunchosia armeniaca*
Phaseolus lunatus (Lima beans)	*Campomanesia lineatifolia*
P. vulgaris (Common beans)	*Lucuma bifera* (Lucumas)
Canavalia sp. (Jack beans)	*Persea americana* (Avocados)
Arachis hypogaea (Peanuts)	*Capsicum baccatum* (Peppers)
Erythrina sp.	*Erythroxylon* sp. (Coca)
Ipomoea batatas (Sweet potatoes)	*Gossypium barbadense* (Cotton)
Manihot esculenta (Manioc)	
Canna sp. (Achira)	

THE ARCHAEOLOGICAL SEQUENCE TO 4500 B.P.

The sites of the first five periods (Preceramic Periods 1–5, 14,000 to 4500 B.P.) represent a period of nomadic or transhumant hunting and gathering prior to the introduction of domestic crops or animals. They are without exception thin superficial surface sites with no permanent structures or other indication that habitation was other than temporary, and their organic refuse, with one exception late in the sequence, consists entirely of remains of wild plants and animals. However, although a hunting and gathering economy is retained throughout this portion of the sequence, the content and distribution of the sites demonstrate economic trends leading to, and helping to account for, the origins of agriculture and settled life.

The sites of the earliest assemblages are all quarry-sites located on the top of a hilly massif within the valley near the mouth of the Chillón River. The actual camp-sites, presumably on the valley floor, are unknown since sites on the valley floor have regularly been covered or destroyed by

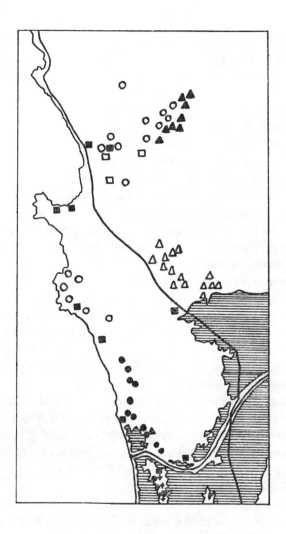

▽ Red Zone Complex   O Canaric Complex
+ Oquendo Complex   ▢ Corbina Complex
● Chivateros Complex   ▲ Encanto Complex
△ Arenal and Luz Complexes   ◼ Preceramic Period 6

Figure 3. Preceramic sites in the Ancón-Chillón region

4,000 years or more of subsequent cultivation. But since there is a dearth of usable stone throughout the survey area and no evidence of contemporary sites outside this limited area, clearly the quarries indicate the approximate position of the camp-sites. The quarry sites are almost totally lacking in organic preservation, possibly because food was rarely consumed at those locations. Nevertheless, certain inferences about exploitative patterns can be made on the basis of site distribution and content.

The Red Zone assemblage (Figure 3) dated 14,000 to 12,500 B.P. is represented only by a single site, a quarry at the mouth of the Chillón River (Patterson 1966b). The industry consists entirely of chipped stone. It is characterized by small tabular pieces of quartzite and flakes with steep edge retouch. The tools identified include spokeshaves, perforators, and scrapers and burins, but the assemblages lack projectile points. Little of a positive nature can be said about the economy of the site based on its artifacts. However, the site-location within the river valley and close to the coast indicates, despite the lack of refuse, that it was situated to permit simultaneous exploitation of the wild resources of these two zones. This interpretation is supported by Lanning's suggestion (1967b: 11) that the assemblage was adapted for woodworking.

The Oquendo complex (12,500 to 11,500 B.P.) is represented by seven small superficial sites, all quarries, again on the top of the hills at the mouth of the river. Again they lack refuse, but again they are situated so as to be able to exploit coast and valley simultaneously. The industry resembles that of the Red Zone, retaining burins, scrapers, perforators and spokeshaves as well as the technique of edge retouch, but it displays minor differences both in technique and in tool-kit which mark it as a separate assemblage. Again projectile points are lacking, suggesting that the hunting of large animals is still not a significant part of the economy. The industry is again characterized by Lanning (1967: 12) as being a woodworking assemblage.

The sites of the Chivateros complex (11,500 to 10,000 B.P.) are again quarries without refuse except some shells of marine molluscs. The sites again focus at the mouth of the river, but now they expand out of the river's valley along the coast (Figure 3). Six sites occur on the hilly region at the foot of the Chillón River; nine sites occur just outside the valley on the coast and nine more occur slightly to the north of the valley on the south shore of Ventanilla Bay. Site distribution again indicates exploitation of a combination of coast and valley, but for the first time there is evidence that the area of exploitation has expanded beyond the valley's margins, presumably because a larger area was needed to feed a growing population or because the population had begun to exhaust the food available at the mouth of the river. The industry, as described by Lanning (1967b: 13), consists of bifaces, long thin spear points, denticulates, spokeshaves, flakes and scrapers. Again Lanning considered this a woodworking assemblage, but he noted the existence of spear points as the first evidence of specialized tools for hunting of big game.

Period 3 represents the one apparent hiatus in the occupation of the area. The area possibly was unoccupied at this time. However, if quarrying activities on the hilltops were abandoned as is true of subsequent periods, but no other shift in economy and site-distribution had occurred (i.e. if the economy of this period, as might be expected, was at an intermediate stage of development between that of the preceding and following periods), we would expect to find no evidence of sites of this period because of destruction of sites even if the valley was occupied. Such a pattern is, I think, the best explanation of the hiatus, but whether the apparent hiatus in the occupation sequence is real or is merely a result of destruction of sites does not affect the major logic of the analysis although it would affect the time sequences involved.

The sites of Periods 4 and 5 are almost all located outside the river's valley in areas of extinct *lomas* (Figure 3). Only an occasional site related to these complexes is found in the valley, but the presence of such occasional sites, the existence of culturally related sites in other river-valleys along the Central Coast, and the content of the sites in the *lomas* (which include the refuse of plants from the valley) indicate strongly that we are dealing with people who are exploiting and probably camping both in the valley and on the *lomas*. The abandonment of quarrying activities of the type described above and the history of subsequent cultivation on the floor of the valley account for the scarcity of preserved valley-sites. Since the vegetation of the *lomas* blooms in winter, the season of reduced flow of water in the river, possibly we may be dealing with seasonal transhumance between valley and *lomas*. On the other hand, since much of the produce of the *lomas* is available year-round, there is no reason to assume that this pattern represents strictly seasonal movement.

The earliest of the known *lomas* complexes are the Arenal and Luz complexes dated between 8000 and 7000 B.P. These sites are small superficial patches of refuse or huge coalescences of such patches in areas of extinct *lomas* vegetation. The twenty-three sites occur in a single cluster nine kilometers from the river but averaging only three kilometers from the modern valley margin, and they are about six kilometers from the coast. The refuse of the sites regularly consists of twenty to thirty centimeters of sand and ash with fragments of wood and wood charcoal in addition to culms of grass (*Gramineae* spp.), fragments of *Tillandsia* (*T. latifolia*), a desert dwelling plant usable only for fuel (and often charred), and fragments of gourd-rinds (*Lagenaria siceraria*). In addition the shells of marine molluscs occur along with the bones of fish, large birds, and land-mammals. These sites, relatively, have a high content of mammalian bone and a small content of shell. Although the sites, by their location, are primarily for exploitation of the *lomas*, the presence of gourd (a plant of requiring much water and thus clearly unsuited to growth in the *lomas*) and of marine molluscs indicates that the river's valley and the coast were part of the exploitative pattern. The tool-kit demonstrates two new techniques, pressure flaking and pecking. Scrapers, core tools and cobble flakes (which Lanning (1967b: 19) considered to have been used as sickles) were found in addition to projectile points. Most important, rare grinding tools including milling stones and manos occur. The Arenal and Luz assemblages are related by typological similarities in the manufacture of projectile point to the Jaywa complex of the Ayacucho region of the Peruvian highlands (MacNeish 1970: 37), indicating some degree of cultural contact between the two regions even at this date, before agriculture is known in either region.

The twenty-two sites of the following Canario complex (7000–6200 B.P.) occur in two clusters, one in the hills north of the town of Ancón, the second just north of the Bay of Ventanilla, both clusters substantially farther from the river than those of the preceding complexes. Again the sites consist of shell and ash and again they appear to represent non-permanent seasonal or temporary camps of people utilizing resources of valley and coast as well as those of the *lomas*. The refuse of the sites on the *lomas* (Lanning 1967: 19) differed from that of earlier complexes in having a higher content of seeds but less wood, more shell and fewer remains of vertebrates. Compared to the previous assemblages, the stone-industry characterizing the Canario sites displays an increase in the frequency of cobble flakes (sickles?) and grinding equipment (milling stones, manos, mortars and pestles) suggesting an increased reliance on the harvesting and grinding of seeds. However, there is no evidence of domestication (Lanning 1967b: 19). In this light the tool assemblage, culturally related to the Piki complex in Ayacucho in the Peruvian highlands where agriculture with squash is well attested (MacNeish 1970: 38; 1969: 38), is of extreme interest. Agriculture may be found in the Canario complex on the coast when river valley sites as opposed to sites on the *lomas* are found and excavated. I consider this highly unlikely, however, for two reasons. First, the *lomas* sites consistently contain produce from the valley so we would expect cultigens to be represented if they were being utilized in the valley. Second, a site of the Canario complex has been excavated by Patterson in the Lurín Valley immediately to the south of the survey area. I have had a chance to study the refuse from the site and it too is devoid of cultigens. All this strongly suggests that the absence of cultivated plants in the Canario complex is historically significant and not just a function of lack of preservation.

After the Canario complex, two further complexes associated with the *lomas* are identified: the poorly defined Corbina complex (6200 to 5600 B.P.) and the Encanto complex (5600 to 4500 B.P.). Corbina is identified at only three sites at the northern end of the Canario cluster. No collections of refuse have been made and little need be said. The fifteen Encanto sites occur in a single cluster at the northern end of the surveyed area over 20 km. from the river and appear to represent seasonal or temporary camps forming part of an exploitative pattern of people utilizing resources of coast and valley as well as those of the *lomas*. One site, a quarry, was actually preserved from this period in the river's valley. The industry consists primarily of milling stones, manos and small projectile points. Lanning (1967b), Patterson and Moseley (1968), and Moseley (1968) have all done test-excavations of Encanto sites. The refuse has produced shellfish (in great abundance), crayfish, fishbone, and mammalian bone (deer in very small quantities) in addition to *Tillandsia*, sedge (*Cyperaceae* spp.) gourd, fragments of bulbs (*Hymenocallis amencaes*?), fragments of pods of unidentified wild legumes, fragments of the river valley fruit *Jusseia peruviana*, and a variety of the vegetative portions of unidentified wild plants. In addition, two items of particular importance have been found. Lanning found seeds of grass (*Gramineae* spp.) in enormous concentrations, clearly representing a pattern of harvest and (temporary?) storage, which along with the incidence of milling stones indicates the importance of seed-grinding in the economy. In addition, squash seeds were found in both Moseley's and Patterson's excavations. The seeds, twenty-six in all, are clearly domestic on the basis of the size criteria published by Cutler and Whitaker (1961: 478) and are tentatively identified as *Cucurbita ficifolia*.

In summary, the sites of these earliest assemblages all represent quarries or temporary camps of nomadic hunter-gatherers who utilized wild resources from the coast, river's valley and, somewhat later, of the vegetation of the *lomas*. For most of the period the only possible domestic crop is the gourd whose status in this regard cannot be assessed. At the end of this period, squash appeared, the size of the seeds indicating that it was imported fully domesticated. The squash was at first utilized as part of the old economy, occurring in *lomas*-camps of a type essentially similar to those of earlier periods.

Analysis of the sites of these hunting and gathering periods provides a number of clues about the circumstances surrounding the inception of agriculture in the region. The earliest quarry sites occur only at the foot of the river suggesting (since there was no limit to potential quarry areas *per se*) that the pattern of exploitation of the group was limited to resources of the coast and valley and to the small area at the mouth of the river where these resources occur together. Subsequently the sites occur at the mouth of the river as well as extending along the coast outside the valley, suggesting an expanded radius of exploitation. The exploited area continued to expand in subsequent periods. Sites of the following periods occur primarily in the areas of *lomas*, but their content (gourd, squash, *Jusseia peruviana*, and sedge, as well as crayfish, bones of fish, and shells of molluscs) along with occasional preserved river-valley sites indicates that these sites on the *lomas* are a preserved remnant of an exploitative pattern utilizing coast, valley and *lomas* together. As such it is of great interest that the sites on the *lomas* get progressively further from the valley with time, again indicating an enlarging area of exploitation.

I suggest that the picture presented is that of a hunting and gathering population needing to travel progressively farther afield to obtain food, because its population was expanding and because resources closer to home were being exhausted. This interpretation is supported by three other types of evidence. First, the refuse of the sites on the *lomas* shows a progressive decline in the hunting of land-mammals and increased reliance on shellfish as a source of protein, suggesting increased pressure of population on land-resources (Harner 1970: 71) and suggesting also, perhaps, the degradation of the environment of the *lomas*. Second there is a progressive decrease of wood in the sites on the *lomas* and an increase in remains of herbaceous plants, again suggesting a degrading of resources. Third, there is a progressive increase in the importance of grinding tools in the assemblages which, along with the large quantities of grass-seed in the Encanto sites, suggests progressive emergence of more and more intensive patterns of utilization of wild resources. The implication of the distribution and content of the sites is, therefore, that population pressure on resources was increasing. The population was being required to move farther to obtain food and was utilizing resources requiring more intensive preparation. The appearance of domestic squash in sites of the Encanto group appears to have been a response to the increased difficulty of a hunting and gathering economy and as such, the use of agriculture seems at first to have been intended as a minor dietary supplement in order to preserve the old way of life.

There are, then, two lines of evidence from this sequence contributing to the assumption that agriculture responds to need rather than to the availability of new technology. The first is the evidence outlined above which suggests that, prior to the beginnings of agriculture, hunting and gathering was becoming increasingly difficult and probably was resulting (in combination with climatic change?) in degradation of the wild resources of the area. The second is the date of arrival of agriculture itself. Agriculture is first attested in this region sometime after 5600 B.P., at least 700 years and possibly as much as 2,000 years after its appearance in the highland region of Ayacucho. This time-gap is significant only because there is evidence of repeated culture contact between the two regions well before this date and evidence that styles in the manufacture of projectile points were shared by diffusion between the regions much more rapidly. The beginnings of agriculture in the Ancón-Chillón region thus do not seem to correspond to known diffusion horizons as might be expected if agricultural technology were inherently desirable.

I believe that, clearly, imbalance between population and resources results in the beginning of agriculture, but the separation of the roles played by population growth *per se* from the decline of the vegetation on the *lomas* by reason of changing climate is not easy. The evidence for climatic change, as it affects the vegetation of the *lomas*, is largely speculative and cannot be considered here except to point out that degradation of resources by climate alone would not be expected to produce the steady pattern of movement of *lomas* vegetation and archaeological sites away from the river. It would instead result in remnant patches of vegetation in climatically favored locations with the result that the archaeological sites of the various periods would be mixed. The consistent outward movement of the exploitation of the sites on the *lomas* argues for the role of human populations in the degradation of the environment. However, we are still faced with the difficulty of assessing the actual growth of population. Analyzing such growth in the pre-agricultural period is difficult since, as indicated above, good parameters for estimating population are lacking. There is evidence that part of the occupation of each period is not preserved. Quarry sites give no indication of population and the superficial *lomas* sites are mostly large, poorly defined scatters, often of great extent, with no definition of individual camping areas. Determining how many sites are strictly contemporaneous is impossible. Lanning (1967a: 50) found a cluster of seventeen milling stones at one Encanto site which he takes to represent a population of fifty to seventy-five people. But there is no way of determining what fraction of the total population this represents. We can, however, get a crude estimate by working back from the population of the first agricultural settlement. I have estimated on the basis of the extent of preserved village space that there were at least 200 to 300 persons living in the survey zone in the first permanent villages just after the beginning of agriculture (Cohen 1971: 193).[1]

If we take these figures as the ceiling for the preagricultural population, then we can visualize the expansion of population in the survey zone from a minimum of perhaps twenty-five to fifty individuals (roughly standard size among hunter-gatherer groups) at about 12,000 B.P. to a maximum of 200 to 300 by 4500 B.P. This represents an increase of population of at least 400 percent and possibly as much as 1200 percent. Stated in terms of populational growth rates, however, this averages out to only about .01 percent per year or less, indicative of very slow average growth. (There is, however, no way to determine the extent to which population growth was balanced by out-migration, and a possible interpretation is that a growing population at once shunted off excess population by migration and gradually expanded its exploitation of wild resources, finally turning to agriculture when neither recourse remained possible.)

GROWTH OF POPULATION AND AGRICULTURAL DEVELOPMENT AFTER 4500 B.P.

In the period following the inception of agriculture, Preceramic Period 6, there is a marked change in economy and settlement patterns, resulting from the progessive exhaustion of the resources of the *lomas* and of land mammals as sources of food, plus the availability of the new agricultural produce. Permanent villages were then located on the coast and in the river's valley. Most of the known sites (Figure 4) in fact are found on the coast outside the valley and outside the areas of potential cultivation, but the rich agricultural refuse of these coastal sites leaves no doubt that they were part of a cooperative economic pattern involving agricultural sites in the valley which have been destroyed by subsequent cultivation. The areas of vegetation on the *lomas* were at the time almost entirely abandoned. Cotton (*Gossypium barbadense*) is found in refuse of sites of this period, and with the exception of the earliest of the coastal sites, the sites of this period are characterized by twined cotton textiles and cotton fish nets and lines along with other fishing equipment. Pottery is not yet encountered and chipped stone tools and grinding tools of the previous periods gradually disappear (Moseley 1968).

---

[1] Patterson (1971b) has more conservatively estimated only a hundred persons for the same period of time, but his estimate fails to account for the population in the valley's bottom, for which no sites are preserved but which is attested by the quantity of agricultural produce in preserved coastal sites which are outside the agricultural areas.

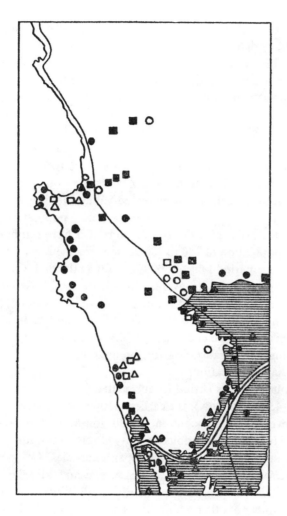

□ Initial Period   ▲ Middle Horizon
△ Early Horizon   ▨ Late Intermediate Period
● Early Intermediate Period   ○ Late Horizon

Figure 4. Ceramic sites in the Ancón-Chillón region

Two major trends are observable in the sites of this period, both presumably related to agriculture and sedentary living. First, there is evidence
suggesting a very high rate of growth of population. The existence of
permanently bounded habitation sites whose extent can be measured and
whose duration of occupation is known allows us to assess the total area
of sites occupied (i.e. the total area of village space) at various points in
time. By assuming that the density of population of villages is at least

roughly constant we can determine the relative size of population at various times, by determining the relative site-areas occupied. The method is crude, first because the population density of villages, of course, is not strictly constant and second, because only a portion of the sites of each period are preserved. But the method does provide at least a crude estimate of change in population. At the beginning of Preceramic Period 6 there was only a single small coastal village, and allowing for at least an equivalent population of the valley, of which the evidence has been destroyed, we can estimate that total occupied villages covered no more than perhaps two to four hectares. By the end of this period, the total site-space occupied, including a preserved valley site, was at least on the order of fifty to sixty hectares, suggesting that population may have increased on the order of 2000 to 3000 percent. I have estimated (Cohen 1971: 193) a population of 200 to 300 persons for the survey region at the beginning of this period and of 3000 to 6000 at the end. Over a span of 750 years this represents an average growth-rate of between .4 and .7 percent per year, so obviously the rate of growth has responded markedly to the combination of sedentary living and agriculture. In addition, by the end of this period we encounter the first evidence of centralized political and economic organization for the area and possibly the first evidence of social stratification.

The first phase of this period is represented at a single coastal site, the Pampa site (4500–4300 B.P.), the earliest permanent village in the region. The lower levels of the site contain, in addition to quantities of shell and other marine refuse, an enormous quantity of remains of squash including seeds, rinds and peduncles of three separate species, two domesticates, *Cucurbita ficifolia* and *C. moschata* (Patterson and Moseley 1968: 117) and a wild form, *C. ecuadorensis* (Cutler and Whitaker 1969). I have identified a number of other minor plants occurring for the first time in the area in the refuse of this site including *pacae* (*Inga feuillei,*) Achira (*Canna* sp.), guavas (*Psidium guajava*), milkweed (*Asclepias* sp.) and a small-seeded legume (*Galactia striata*). In addition, Patterson and Moseley (1968: 116) reported jack beans (*Canavalia* sp.) from a portion of the refuse I have not had an opportunity to study. These are accompanied by gourd, a number of unidentified tubers and rhizomes, plus the usual assortment of *Tillandsia*, cattails, sedges, grasses and twigs. The fauna includes abundant remains of shellfish, shorebirds and sea-mammals, particularly sea lion. Bones of land-mammals are extremely scarce, and from this time on, until the introduction of domestic mammals sometime after 2200 B.P., land-mammals played only a very minimal part in the economy of the region.

In the subsequent Playa Hermosa and Conchas phases of Preceramic Period 6, the overall pattern does not change significantly. Again, we appear to have had small permanent coastal villages gradually increasing in size and number on the coast outside the river's valley, but these coastal sites are filled with vegetable produce indicating that additional sites in the valley existed but have been destroyed. The subsistence pattern remained largely unchanged except that squash declined as a major staple.

During the Playa Hermosa phase (4300–4100 B.P.) only one new cultigen, peppers (*Capsicum baccatum*), occurred. In the refuse of the Conchas phase (4100–3900 B.P.) lima beans (*Phaseolus lunatus*), lucumas (*Lucuma bifera*), and sapindus seeds (*Sapindus saponaria*) all occur for the first time. Bones of land-mammals are again very rare and protein was provided primarily by fish, shellfish, shorebirds and sea-mammals. The persistence of large numbers of unidentified tubers and rhizomes along with milkweed, cattails, sedge, grasses, and twigs indicate that a proportion of the diet was still obtained from wild vegetables.

In the Gaviota phase of Preceramic Period 6 (3900–3750 B.P.) in addition to the coastal villages, we actually encounter three sites preserved in the river's valley, the most important of which is Chuquitanta, a large site with stone ruins located at the foot of the Chillón River on the same hilly massif as the quarry sites of earlier periods. The site itself is located near a wide expanse of river, and Patterson and Moseley (1968: 125) suggested that the site represents floodplain farming. For this reason it is important that Patterson (1971a: 197) has recorded the existence of populations farther up in the valley, outside the survey zone, at this time, which because of their location far from a cultivable flood plain must have been using small-scale irrigation. The Chuquitanta site is a large town or small city, whose population I have estimated at 3,000 to 4,000 people (Cohen 1971: 179). Moreover, the symmetry of its stone construction involved a large well-organized labor force and suggests political centralization and possibly social stratification, and it is interesting that this large population and highly evolved society occurred in the apparent absence of either irrigation or maize, which are often considered the *sina qua non* of New World civilization. Engel (1967), who excavated the site, reported cotton, gourds, *archira*, lima beans, guavas, *lucumas*, *pacae* and *jicama* (*Pachyrrhizus tuberosus*), the latter being the only new cultigen mentioned. In addition, my own studies of the refuse from the Gaviota phase from coastal sites added peanuts (*Archis hypogea*), and possibly sweet potatoes (*Ipomoea batatas*), to the list of cultigens.

Beginning with the Initial Period (3750 to 2900 B.C.) and extending through the Early Intermediate Period (2200 to 1400 B.P.) we witness a gradual expansion of the valley's population accompanied by a progressive increase in the number of occupied sites. The growth of population during this span, however, was markedly less than that of Preceramic Period 6. Judging by the number and size of sites occupied, the peak population in the prehistoric valley was reached by about the third quarter of the Early Intermediate Period (1800 to 1600 B.P.).

The peak population of the area is estimated at 25,000 to 50,000, roughly ten times that of the end of Preceramic Period 6, representing an average annual rate of population-growth between 3750 B.P. and 1600 B.P. of only about .1 percent, a much slower growth rate than during Preceramic Period 6 (Cohen 1971: 196). This expansion of population was accompanied by a gradual change in location of sites outward from the banks of the river to the modern margins of the river valley; growth of a valley-wide system of irrigation and the gradual accumulation of new and significant crop plants are suggested.

In the Initial Period (defined by the arrival of pottery in the area) there is no direct evidence of irrigation in the survey region. Moseley (1972: 41) suggested that the abandonment of Chuquitanta implies a shift from floodplain farming to irrigation agriculture, but the few sites known in the valley are still near its bottom, suggesting that floodplain agriculture still predominated (Figure 4). The refuse from the early part of the Initial Period is very similar to that of the preceding periods. The only new cultigen in the early part of the period is coca (*Erythroxylon* sp.), identified from chewed quids complete with well-defined tooth rows. Late in the Initial Period, however, three significant new cultigens were added: potatoes (*Solanum tuberosum*), polymnia tubers (*Polymnia* sp.) and maize (*Zea mays*). The appearance of maize can be dated by careful pottery seriation to a very late phase of the Initial Period, about 3200 B.P., long after maize is known elsewhere in Peru (see below). The cobs are large; the broken fragments are fifty to sixty millimeters long and the diameters range from thirteen to eighteen millimeters which, on size alone, makes these cobs comparable to all subsequent prehistoric maize from the region. There is clearly no evidence of wild, or even of primitive maize in the region.

During the Early Horizon (1750–1050 B.P.) nine sites occur in the river's valley (in addition to those along the coast) and most still cluster close to the river, indicating again a predominance of floodplain agriculture (Figure 4). However, two sites occur on the margins of modern cultivation where the valley is narrow, and appear to suggest small-scale irrigation. The only additions to the organic refuse during this period are avocados (*Persea americana*), ciruelas (*Bunchosia armeniaca*), campo-manesia (*C. lineatifolia*), manioc (*Manihot esculenta*), and the common bean (*P. vulgaris*). The latter occurs first in levels dated to about 2900 B.P., again long after its first appearance in other regions of Peru. Middens of this period also mark the last time when large sea-mammals are encountered in this region, suggesting that from this point on this source of protein was either no longer available or no longer utilized.

During the Early Intermediate Period (2200 to 1400 B.P.) we witness the sudden blossoming of archaeological sites along the modern margins of the river valley. The size and quantity of these sites occupied at any one time during this period appear to indicate that the maximum prehistoric population of the area had now been achieved, and from this time on, with the exception of a decline in the Middle Horizon, the population, as measured from the size and number of habitation-sites, appears to have remained approximately constant until the Spanish conquest. The location of these sites at the edge of the valley indicates that by this period the valley's irrigation system had been developed to its fullest prehistoric extent, which is equivalent, as far as can be determined, with the present-day extent of the valley's irrigation. During this period the whole of the coast appears to have been utilized very intensively, judging by the number of sites found here, and a few sites even occur in areas of *lomas*-vegetation, indicating continued but small-scale use of the products of the *lomas*. No new cultigens appear in the middens of this period, although the fauna of the period show some significant changes. Bones of sea-mammals are notably absent from the refuse for the first time, and as indicated, these animals are never again encountered along this region of the coast. At the same time, bones, pelts and coprolites of llamas and guinea pigs provide the first evidence of domestic animals in the region (at a remarkably late date).

After the end of the Early Intermediate Period there were only minor economic changes. One species of squash (*Cucurbita maxima*) and a number of inedible or minor legumes (*Casealpinia* sp., *Erythrina* sp. and *Prosopis* sp.) are found for the first time in the Late Intermediate Period (A.D. 1000 to 1476) and oca (*Oxalis tuberosa*) is tentatively identified in my samples from the Late Horizon (A.D. 1476–1534). In addition, Towle (1961) lists a number of taxa identified by various workers from mummy-bundles at the Ancón Necropolis in the Late Intermediate or Late Horizon, of which only quinoa (*Chenopodium quinoa*) and cherimoyas (*Annona cherimolia*) are of particular significance.

The distribution of the main archaeological sites remains basically the same after the end of the Early Intermediate Period, although two new related patterns become evident. First, certain areas of the coast utilized for fishing in the Early Intermediate Period were abandoned. Since the sites of the Early Intermediate Period are now stranded well behind the modern coastline, apparently abandonment of the region was due to modification of the coastline which eliminated the region as a source of fish and shellfish. Possibly by way of compensation, in the Late Intermediate Period and Late Horizon, a number of superficial archaeological sites occur in the regions of *lomas*-vegetation, often including rectangular stone corrals which appear to suggest the use of this vegetation for grazing domestic flocks. In short, while no major shifts in the vegetable portion of the diet occurred after the Early Intermediate Period, apparently declining coastal resources were gradually replaced by domestic flocks as sources of protein.

Analysis of the Ancón-Chillón Sequence and Conclusions

The general patterns of changes in the subsistence-economy of the region may be summarized as follows:

In the sites of Preceramic Periods 1 to 4, the diet appears to have been composed entirely of wild foods. Wild plants, game, fish and shellfish are all represented in the refuse. During this period, however, four important trends are apparent. First, the sites show a progressive increase in the relative importance of shellfish over land-mammals as sources of protein; second, they demonstrate an increasingly intensive use of harvested wild grass seeds as a vegetable stable; third, they demonstrate a gradual replacement of woody by herbaceous plants; and fourth, the area exploited grows increasingly larger. As indicated above, all of the trends suggest increased pressure of population on wild resources, and I have suggested that population growth during this span of time is on the order of 400 to 1200 percent.

In the sites of the Encanto complex (Preceramic Period 5) these trends continued, so that shellfish dominated the protein sources in the almost total absence of evidence of land-based hunting, and remains of grass grain occur in great abundance. At this time, the first domesticated plant food (squash) occurred, but appears to have been only a minor portion of the diet. Agriculture appears to have occurred out of the need to supplement the old economy, and at first it appear to have had little influence on that economy.

In Preceramic Period 6, however, there was a shift in the location of known sites from the areas of vegetation on the *lomas* to the seacoast, prompted by the exhaustion of that vegetation and of land-animals to be hunted, plus the availability of agricultural produce. The economy shifted to a mixture of agriculture and coastal gathering. At the beginning of the period, squash was the major item in the diet, but this was gradually replaced by a series of other cultigens. The settlements of the period were permanent villages which increased in size and number throughout the period, suggesting a period of rapid growth of population. By the end of the period there is some evidence of the emergence of a complex society involving centralized political authority and possibly social stratification. What evidence there is, however, suggests that agriculture was still of a relatively simple floodplain type although irrigation is attested in nearby regions. Evidence for the crops which later become the staples of Peruvian agriculture, maize and common beans, has not yet been found, although lima beans, peanuts, jack beans, sweet potatoes, *achira*, *lucumas*, peppers, guavas and the squashes do occur.

From the Initial Period through the Early Intermediate Period there is evidence of a slower expansion of population, accompanied by a gradual extension of irrigation in the valley and a gradual accumulation of new cultivated plants. Maize, potatoes and *polymnia* occur late in the Initial Period; common beans, manioc and avocados occur in the Early Horizon. By the early Intermediate Period the maximum prehistoric population of the area occurred; irrigation reached its modern limits, and the main domestic animals (llamas and guinea pigs) were present for the first time, correlated apparently with the decline in sea-mammals in the area.

After the Early Intermediate Period, except for a decline and resurgence during the Middle Horizon and the Late Intermediate Period, population growth ceases. Since the leveling off of such growth is coincident with the expansion of irrigation to its modern limits, we may have had for the first time in the region a truly Malthusian situation in which population was limited by the capacity of the technology to expand agricultural production. During the next 800 years, until the Spanish conquest, the main agricultural patterns appear to have remained unchanged, although a new pattern of grazing domestic herds did appear in the later periods.

If we analyze the patterns of the archaeological sequence, a number of points emerge. First, the Ancón-Chillón region clearly received all of its major cultigens from other regions, since none of these are traceable to local origins. Moreover, there is no evidence of any independent experimentation with the domestication of lesser local crops, since the first plausible cultigen (squash) was clearly an import. The most striking pattern, however, is the absence of correlation between the arrivals of new cultivated plants (and animals) in this region and the dates at which they appeared in nearby, culturally related areas. Table 3 summarizes the arrival of new crops by period, and Table 4 lists the first arrivals of the major cultigens in the area in comparison with their known occurrences elsewhere in Peru. The time-gap in the two dates is often striking, especially since cultural contact of a much more direct nature can often be attested between the two regions in question. For example, domestic squash, which in the Ancón-Chillón region represented the beginning of agriculture, did not occur here until the Encanto Complex (5700–4500 B.P.), whereas it is definitely known in the Piki Complex in the Ayacucho region of the Peruvian highlands between 7500 and 6300 B.P. (MacNeish 1969: 38). Significantly, the Piki complex shows definite cultural affiliations in artifact forms with the earlier Canario complex of the Ancón-Chillón region (MacNeish 1970: 38). Similarly, maize did not appear in the Ancón-Chillón region until the Initial Period (about 3200 B.P.), whereas it is known in Ayacucho in the Chihua complex, 6300–4800 B.P. (MacNeish 1970: 38), a complex which again had earlier and more direct cultural ties with the Encanto phase of the Ancón-Chillón region (MacNeish 1969: 42). Moreover, maize is known from another region of the Peruvian Coast (Huarmey), which again shows cultural affiliations by about 3800 B.P. (Kelley and Bonavia 1963). Similar delays can be observed in the case of other cultigens including many of the important ones. Common beans (*P. vulgaris*) occurred in the region during the Early Horizon between 2900 and 2600 B.P. although they are known in Ayacucho in the Chihua or Cachi complexes between 6300 and 3700 B.P. (MacNeish 1969, 1970) and have been found in the Callejón de Huaylas, Ancash, Peru between 10,500 and 7500 B.P. (Kaplan et al. 1973). Lima beans (*Phaseolus lunatus*), occurred at Ancón as early as the Conchas complex, 4100 to 3900 B.P. but are also known in the Callejón de Huaylas by 10,500 to 7500 B.P. (Kaplan et al. 1973). Moreover, the technique of irrigation is not evident here at least until the Initial Period and probably not until the Early Horizon although it is in evidence elsewhere in adjoining areas as early as Preceramic Period 6.

Although the dates of first occurrence of cultigens in the region do not correspond well with those of other regions, they do show correlations with growth of population and ecological crises in the survey-zone. In the case of squash in particular, a case has been made to the effect that this cultigen and the whole concept of agriculture appeared in the region at a time of critically diminished wild resources. Agriculture, in other words, appears to have been adopted not when first exposure might have occurred, but rather at the point when the absence of wild resources necessitated cultivation. Domestic crops first appeared in a hunting and gathering context where they supplemented and supported the old economy in a time of increasing shortage. Only later did any revolutionary effects emerge in the form of stable settlement and accelerated growth of population. A similar, though more speculative case, can be made for maize and common beans and for irrigation. Perhaps these three late arrivals were related, and maize and beans were only utilized here in conjunction with irrigation. What is more important is that all three occurred in the area AFTER the period of rapid growth of population was completed, and during a period of more gradual growth. I suggest that the rapid expansion of population in Preceramic Period 6 represented the relatively easy expansion of pre-maize floodplain agriculture, which reached its limits by 3750 B.P. or shortly thereafter. Maize, beans and irrigation arrived when the potential of this relatively easy agriculture in the valley's bottom had been exhausted, and when continued growth of population began to necessitate the more tedious expansion of farmland by artificial irrigation and experimentation with more productive crops.

The evidence for domestic animals shows similar patterns. Llamas and guinea pigs appeared here, at least in quantity, only in the Early Intermediate Period (2200 to 1400 B.P.) although the former was found elsewhere on the Coast in the Initial Period (3750 B.C. to 2900 B.P.) (Lanning 1967a: 82) and the latter occurred on the coast by the end of Preceramic Period 6 (2500 to 3750 B.P.) (Lanning 1967a: 63), while both have been reported in Ayacucho in the Piki Complex between 7500 and 6300 B.P. (MacNeish 1969: 38). Here again they appeared in the survey zone when sources of wild protein appear to have been diminishing, as evidenced by the disappearance of sea-mammals from the middens, and later, by the decline of coastal sites as related to eustatic or tectonic modification of the coastline.

In general, the history of technology and of growth of population in the region is totally in keeping with the assumption that the technology of domestication developed in response to the pressure of population. Technological change is slow — belated relative to nearby regions — and closely associated with population pressure on resources. This evidence suggests that attempts to deal with technological change as an independent variable must be questioned. For example, attempts to trace the spread of cultigens as a pattern of simple diffusion does not work. We cannot hope to isolate simple patterns of symmetrical diffusion of crops or technology from hearths of domestication. Instead we are forced to consider the ecological requirements of various localities in understanding the appearance of economic changes. In particular, apparently economic conservatism is the rule, to be broken in a region only when pressure on existing resources necessitates change.

Table 3.   First occurrence of the main economic plants in the Ancón-Chillón region by period or complex

Late Horizon:	*Oxalis tuberosa* (?), (*Chenopodium quinoa*)
Late Intermediate Period:	*Cucurbita maxima, Caesalpinia* sp., *Erythrina* sp., *Prosopis* sp.
Middle Horizon:	No sample
Early Intermediate Period:	(domestic camelids and guinea pig)
Early Horizon:	
Late	No sample
Early	*Phaseolus vulgaris, Bunchosia armeniaca, Manihot esculenta, Campomanesia lineatifolia, Persea americana*
Initial Period:	
Late	*Zea mays, Solanum* spp. (?), *Polymnia* sp. (?)
Middle	None
Early	*Erythroxylon* sp.
Preceramic Period 6:	
Gaviota	*Archis hypogaea, Lucuma bifera, Ipomoea batatas* (?), *Pachyrrhizus tuberosus*
Conchas	*Phaseolus lunatus, Lucuma bifera,* ? *Sapindus saponaria*
Playa Hermosa	*Capsicum baccatum*
Pampa	*Cucurbita moschata, Cucurbita ecuadorensis, Inga feuillei, Galactia striata, Canna* sp., *Psidium guajava, Asclepias* sp., *Gossypium barbadense, Canavalia* sp.
Preceramic Period 5:	
Encanto	*Cucurbita ficifolia*
Corbina	No Sample
Preceramic Period 4:	
Canario	None
Arenal-Luz	*Lagenaria siceraria*

Table 4.   First occurrence of the main economic plants in the Ancón-Chillón region by cultigen

Cultigen	Date of appearance Ancón-Chillón region	First appearance in Peru
Zea mays	Late Initial Period 3200 B.P.	Huarmey 3800 B.P.[a] Chihua Complex, Ayacucho[b] 6300–4800 B.P.
Cucurbita cicifolia	Encanto Complex 3600–4500 B.P.	(Cucurbita sp. Piki Complex, Ayacucho 7500–6300 B.P.)[b]
C. maxima	Late Intermediate Period A.D. 1000–1476	Ica Valley, 1400 B.P.[c]

Cultigen	Date of appearance Ancón-Chillón region	First appearance in Peru
C. moschata	Pampa Complex 4500–4300 B.P.	(Cucurbita sp. Piki Complex, Ayacucho 7500–6300 B.P.)[b]
Phaseolus lunatus	Conchas Complex 4100–3900 B.P.	Chilca Valley 5800 B.P. (?)[d] Ancash 7500–10,500 B.P.[f]
P. vulgaris	Early Horizon 2900–2600 B.P.	Chihua or Cachi Complexes[b] Ayacucho, 6300–3700 B.P. Ancash 7500–10,500 B.P.[f]
Canavalia sp.	Pampa Complex 4500–4300 B.P.	Cachi Complex, Ayacucho[b] 4800–3700 B.P.
Archis hypogaea	Gaviota Complex 3900–3750 B.P.	
Erythrina sp.	Late Intermediate Period A.D. 1000–1476	
Ipomoea batatas	Gaviota Complex (?) 3900–3750 B.P.	
Manihot esculenta	Early Horizon 2900–2600 B.P.	
Solanum tuberosum	Late Initial Period 3200 B.P.	
Polymnia sp.	Late Initial Period 3200 B.P.	
Bunchosia armeniaca	Early Horizon 2900–2600 B.P.	Huaca Prieta (Chicama)[e] (3900 B.P.)
Campomanesia lineatifolia	Early Horizon 2900–2600 B.P.	Huaca Prieta (Chicama)[e] (3900 B.P.)
Lucuma bifera	Conchas Complex 4100–3100 B.P.	Chihua Complex, Ayacucho[b] 6300–4800 B.P.
Persea americana	Early Horizon 2900–2600 B.P.	Early Horizon on coast
Capsicum baccatum	Playa Hermosa Complex 4300–4100 B.P.	
Erythroxylon sp.	Early Initial Period 3700–3600 B.P.	
Gossypium barbadense	Pampa Complex 4500–4300 B.P.	Chihua Complex, Ayacucho[b] 6300–4800 B.P.
Inga feuillei	Pampa Complex 4500–4300 B.P.	
Canna sp.	Pampa Complex 4500–4300 B.P.	
Psidium guajava	Pampa Complex 4500–4300 B.P.	
Lagenaria siceraria	Arenal and Luz Complexes 8000–7000 B.P.	Jaywa Complex, Ayacucho[b] 8600–7500 B.P.

[a]   Kelley and Bonavia (1963)
[b]   MacNeish (1969, 1970)
[c]   Cutler and Whitaker (1961)
[d]   Engel (1964)
[e]   Towle (1961)
[f]   Kaplan et al. (1973)

Conversely, population growth in the region clearly was not constant but responded markedly to technological changes. Population growth was slow in the pre-agricultural period, rapid immediately after the beginning of agriculture when the floodplain was being farmed, slower when the cultivated area was being expanded by irrigation, and finally limited in a Malthusian sense when irrigation reached its practical limits. This in turn suggests that we cannot consider population growth an independent variable and should not expect smooth, regular population curves.

Much of this analysis is, of course, tenuous. Interpreting sequences of cause and effect or the interaction of various factors of change from archaeological evidence requires indirect interpretations of such evidence. Moreover, the existing archaeological evidence, in this region, as in other well studied areas, is still no more than a (fairly minor) sample of the potential evidence. The interpretation, therefore, is subject to modification as further evidence accumulates. This discussion is not offered as a final statement on the nature of population and technological growth in the region, or as proof of a population-oriented hypothesis about culture growth. The population-growth hypothesis is, I believe, worthy of further consideration on logical grounds alone. The result of the study of the archaeological sequence from the Peruvian coast is an attempt, first, to suggest that this hypothesis can and should be considered in the evaluation of sequences of cultural growth; second, to suggest that archaeological evidence can be used, albeit crudely, in the analysis of patterns of change and, therefore, should be applied to the consideration of large theoretical issues in anthropology; and third, to suggest avenues of approach to theory in anthropology necessitating refinement of archaeological techniques and necessitating new approaches to the interpretations of archaeological sequences.

REFERENCES

ADAMS, R. M.
  1966   *The evolution of urban society.* Chicago: Aldine.
ANDERSON, EDGAR
  1969   *Plants, man, and life.* Berkeley: University of California Press.
BIRDSELL, JOSEPH
  1957   On population structure in generalized hunting and collecting populations. *Evolution* 12:189–205.
  1968   "Some predictions for the Pleistocene based on equilibrium systems among recent hunter-gatherers," in *Man the hunter.* Edited by R. B. Lee and Irven DeVore, 229–240. Chicago: Aldine.

BOSERUP, ESTER
1965   *The conditions of agricultural growth.* Chicago: Aldine.

BRAIDWOOD, R. J., C. A. REED
1957   The achievement and early consequences of food production: a consideration of the archaeological and natural-historical evidence. *Cold Spring Harbor Symposia in Quantitative Biology* 22:19–31.

CHILDE, V. G.
1951   *Man makes himself.* New York: New American Library.

COHEN, M. N.
1971   "Population growth, subsistence and settlement in the Ancon-Chillon region of the central coast of Peru." Unpublished doctoral dissertation, Columbia University, New York.

CRAIG, A., N. P. PSUTY
1968   *The Paracas papers: studies in marine and desert ecology 1, reconaissance report.* Occasional Publications of the Department of Geography, Florida Atlantic University 1.

CUTLER, H. C., T. W. WHITAKER
1961   History and distribution of the cultivated cucurbits in the Americas. *American Antiquity* 26:469–485.
1969   A new species of *Cucurbita* from Equador. *Annals of the Missouri Botanical Garden* 55:392–396.

DEEVEY, EDWARD
1960   The human population. *Scientific American* 203(3):194–204.

DEVEREUX, G.
1967   "A typological study of abortion in 350 primitive, ancient and pre-industrial societies," in *Abortion in America.* Edited by H. Rosen, 97–152. Boston: Beacon Press.

DUMOND, D. E.
1965   Population growth and cultural change. *Southwestern Journal of Anthropology* 21:302–325.

ENGEL, F.
1964   El preceramico sin algodon en la costa del Peru. *Actas y Memorias del XXXV Congreso Internacional de Americanistas.* Mexico. 3:141–152.
1967   Le complexe précéramique d'el Paraiso (Pérou). *Journal de la Société des Americanistes,* n.s., LV–1:43–95.

FLANNERY, K. V.
1968   "Archaeological systems theory and early Mesoamerica," in *Anthropological archaeology in the Americas.* Edited by Betty Meggers, 67–87. Washington: Anthropological Society of Washington.

GOODSPEED, T. H., H. E. STORK
1955   The University of California Botanical Garden Expedition to the Andes, 1935–1952. *University of California Publications in Botany* 28(8):97–142.

HARLAN, JACK
1971   Agricultural origins: centers and non-centers. *Science* 174:468–474.

HARNER, MICHAEL
1970   Population pressure and the social evolution of agriculturalists. *Southwestern Journal of Anthropology* 26:67–86.

ISAAC, ERICH
  1970   *Geography of domestication.* Englewood Cliffs: Prentice-Hall.
JOLLY, A. J.
  1972   *The evolution of primate behavior.* New York: Macmillan.
KAPLAN, LAWRENCE, T. F. LYNCH, K. A. R. KENNEDY
  1973   Early cultivated beans *(Phaeolus vulgaris)* from an intermontane
         Peruvian valley. *Science* 179:76–77.
KELLEY, DAVID, DUCCIO BONAVIA
  1963   New evidence for pre-ceramic maize on the coast of Peru. *Nawpa
         Pacha* 1:39–41.
LANNING, EDWARD
  1967a *Peru before the Incas.* Englewood Cliffs: Prentice-Hall.
  1967b "Preceramic archaeology of the Ancon-Chillon region, central coast
         of Peru." Report to NSF on research carried out under grant GS869,
         1965–1966.
LEE, RICHARD
  1968   "What hunters do for a living or how to make out on scarce re-
         sources," in *Man the Hunter.* Edited by Richard Lee and Irven De-
         Vore, 30–43. Chicago: Aldine.
  1969   "!Kung Bushman subsistence: an input-output analysis," in *Eco-
         logical studies in cultural anthropology.* Edited by A. P. Vayda, 47–79.
         New York: Natural History Press.
LEE, RICHARD, IRVEN DEVORE
  1968   "Problems in the study of hunters and gatherers," in *Man the hunter.*
         Edited by R. Lee and I. DeVore, 3–20. Chicago: Aldine.
MACNEISH, RICHARD S.
  1958   Preliminary archaeological investigations in the Sierra de Tamaulipas,
         Mexico. *Transactions of the American Philosophical Society* 48(6):1–
         210.
  1967   "A summary of subsistence," in *The prehistory of the Tehuacan Valley.*
         Edited by D. S. Byers, 209–309. Austin: University of Texas Press.
  1969   *First annual report of the Ayacucho Archaeological-Botanical Project.*
         Andover, Massachusetts: Robert S. Peabody Foundation on Archaeo-
         logy.
  1970   *Second annual report of the Ayacucho Archaeological-Botanical Project.*
         Andover, Massachusetts: Robert S. Peabody Foundation on Archaeo-
         logy.
MORGAN. LEWIS HENRY
  1877   *Ancient society.* New York: Henry Holt.
MOSELEY, M. E.
  1968   *Changing subsistence patterns: late preceramic archaeology of the
         central Peruvian coast.* Unpublished doctoral dissertation, Harvard
         University.
  1972   Subsistence and demography: an example of interaction from pre-
         historic Peru. *Southwestern Journal of Anthropology* 28:25–49.
NEEL, J. V.
  1970   Lessons from a primitive people. *Science* 170:815-822.
PARSONS, M. H.

1970 Preceramic subsistence on the Peruvian coast. *American Antiquity* 35:292–304.

PATTERSON, THOMAS

1966a Pattern and process in the Early Intermediate Period pottery of the central coast of Peru. *University of California Publication in Anthropology* 3:I–IX, 1–180.

1966b Early cultural remains on the central coast of Peru. *Nawpa Pacha* 4:145–153.

1971a "The emergence of food production in central Peru," in *Prehistoric agriculture*. Edited by S. Streuver, 181–208. Garden City: Natural History Press.

1971b Population and economy in central Peru. *Archaeology* 24:316–321.

PATTERSON, THOMAS, M. E. MOSELEY

1968 Late preceramic and early ceramic culture of the central coast of Peru. *Nawpa Pacha* 6:115–133.

POLGAR, STEVEN

1972 Population history and population policies from an anthropological perspective. *Current Anthropology* 13:203–209.

SAUER, CARL

1952 *Agricultural origins and dispersals*. New York: American Geographical Society.

SCHWANITZ, FRANZ

1966 *The origin of cultivated plants*. Cambridge: Harvard University Press.

SHEFFER, CHARLES

1971 Review of Boserup: *The conditions of agricultural growth. American Antiquity* 36:377–389.

SPOONER, BRIAN

1972 *Population growth: anthropological implications*. Cambridge: MIT Press.

STEWART, OMER C.

1956 "Fire as the first great force employed by man," in *Man's role in changing the face of the earth*. Edited by William L. Thomas, 115–133. Chicago: University of Chicago Press.

TOWLE, MARGARET

1961 *Ethnobotany of precolumbian Peru*. Chicago: Aldine.

WEBERBAUER, A.

1932 "Phytogeography of the Peruvian Andes," in *Flora of Peru* (volume one). Edited by J. F. Mac Bride, 18–31. Chicago: Field Museum of Natural History.

Scarcity, the Factors of Production, and Social Evolution

MICHAEL J. HARNER

An immense growth in human population has been one of the fundamental facts of man's existence since the beginnings of agriculture in Neolithic times. From the archaeological record we can read of the unmistakable multiplication of human populations in most areas of the Old and New Worlds. Although of course there admittedly have been fluctuations, the overall trend of this growth has been extremely obvious. By the usual standards of measuring adaptation in biology, that is, in terms of the ability of a species to increase its numbers, man has been most "successful." However, this growth in numbers upon the necessarily finite natural resources of our planet has meant an increase in population pressure, and more specifically, changes in the ratio of land to labor. Changes in the relative scarcity of these two factors of production have implications for social evolution, and I am particularly interested in these implications with respect to precapitalistic societies.

As I indicated in an earlier paper (Harner 1970: 68–69), the first consequences of the adoption of agriculture tend to be a temporary decrease, rather than increase, in the scarcity of land or natural resources:

...the innovation of agriculture ... provides a new subsistence base or means of production, which heretofore has been unexploited for this purpose and thus is relatively open-ended in its productive potentialities. Furthermore, since time is required for population growth to catch up with the new potential carrying capacity of the land, overall competition for food-producing resources is temporarily less than in the preceding period of the final pre-agricultural

This paper was presented, in a slightly different form, at the Columbia University Seminar in Ecological Systems and Cultural Evolution on February 9, 1970, under the title "Scarcity and Society."

phase and relatively slight compared to the eventual time when the population will increase sufficiently to effect a significant scarcity of productive agricultural and herding land. This temporary "free" land situation accompanying the agricultural innovation tends to undermine any pre-existing unilineal kinship units, ranking, or class stratification by undercutting the social power conferred through control of scarce wild subsistence resource territories and by relieving the need to organize to defend or acquire scarce natural resources. Thus, in this early phase of agricultural dependence, because of the relative abundance of agricultural and livestock-raising land, kinship will tend to be cognatic or bilateral, i.e., without unilineal kin groups, and there also will tend to be no class stratification. Eventually, however, the innovation of agriculture results in population growth; and as population density increases, subsistence resource land will become scarcer and hence more valuable, leading to competition for its control. Competition for scarce subsistence resources will, in turn, lead to ever larger local and inter-local cooperative social units to ensure success in holding and acquiring scarce resources.

Thus, within the category of societies having some degree of dependence on domesticated food production, we can find a remarkable range of difference in terms of the degree of scarcity of land. Often this is due not to the recent adoption of agriculture but to the immensity of the exploitable area, such as the Amazon basin, which agriculturalists occupy but have not yet had time to fill through multiplication of their numbers since their immigration into the area (see Carneiro 1961). In any case, in the ethnographic laboratory we can find the variations we seek and can use them to develop and test our theoretical approaches.

But first, let us consider the scarcity concept to be employed as a major focus of this essay. It means simply that with reference to someone, the demand for something exceeds the supply. This essentially elementary concept does not, in itself, require external value judgments as to what is necessary to the survival or the standard of living of a population. Another main focus is on the means of production, in terms of the three chief factors of production: land, labor, and capital. Although looking at the social universe in connection with a factor of production, especially capital, is not dissimilar from the approach of traditional Marxists, focusing on scarcity is something the Marxists have often failed to do, particularly with regard to societies viewed as precapitalistic. At the same time, while we share with market economists the assumption of the fundamental importance of the imbalance of supply and demand known as scarcity, we part ways with most of them by attempting to relate it to social structure. Therefore, in a sense, it is a new field, but one that may come very naturally to anthropologists. Of all scholars, they alone have a great archive of some hundreds of diverse cultures in which to test hypotheses, specifically, hypotheses that involve such logical factors as the nature and scarcity of subsistence resources and such questions as the relationship between certain kinds of economies and certain kinds of social structures throughout the known diachronic and synchronic spread of the human universe.

One very simple, fundamental, and useful concept that will be proposed here is that scarcity is essential to any social situation. That is, two or more persons will not interact unless there is a demand beyond the supply of something. Now this position, that scarcity is basic to action and, more specifically, to social life, runs counter to the view of one major school of economic anthropology, the substantivists, who have maintained, following Polanyi in particular, that scarcity is not necessarily present in all societies. While we do not want to push the substantivists to the wall on this point or to say that they all have adhered to this view completely, this position has typified many of them and has impeded progress in developing serious theories for the application of economic and ecological principles in anthropological analysis.

On the positive side, the substantivists have emphasized the importance of the material aspects of life, particularly of subsistence, and there is little question that subsistence, together with the scarcity factor, is the basis for economic life. Certainly, other factors, especially clothing and shelter, can be essential for survival in certain ecological situations, but basic subsistence requirements are not easily modified.

In the other camp in economic anthropology, that of the formalists, the emphasis is on the study of the allocation of scarce resources amongst alternative ends; the problem of making choices with regard to these scarce resources is a focal point. A great many journal pages have been used in recent years in disputes between these two schools, and I shall not attempt to pursue or perpetuate the debate here. Rather, I wish to point out that there is another area, which is very close to ecology, that belongs to neither school. Here we do not deal with the question of the allocation of scarce resources, which presupposes that they are controlled by someone, but rather with the more fundamental issue, to my mind, of what conditions determine which resources are scarce in given situations and what actions populations undertake to acquire and hold them. And finally, what are the social consequences of the acquisition and control of these scarce resources?

What do we mean by resources? Here I include all the chief factors of production: land, labor, and capital. Of course, in any specific empirical situation, these can be more closely defined, but for broad cross-cultural comparisons, the encompassing scope of these three terms permits degrees of understanding not normally possible within the framework of historical particularism.

I use the term land in the very broad sense, the way economists classically have used the term, i.e. as natural resources, including air, water, and natural flora and fauna. Labor here refers to the enculturated aspect of a person as a producer or an energy source. According to one definition, the individual whose services are represented by the term "labor" can be viewed just in terms of his energy potential and output. From another point of view, however, he can be viewed as having certain skills and other conditioning, often called by economists human capital. For purposes of the present analysis, I find it useful to think of labor as conditioned manpower.

This paper deals with societies having a relatively low degree of capital accumulation, in other words, those that are not characterized by a predominately capitalistic mode of production. The primary focus of such societies in terms of the three main factors of production is labor versus land.

First, let us briefly review the ecological basis for such a focus. The technological level is relatively low compared to mercantile or industrial societies; in fact, many of our subject societies have not passed beyond the use of a stone technology or have done so only recently. The environmental and demographic factors of the ecological situation are, in contrast, quite variable. In other words, population pressure can be minimal or extreme. In those cases where population pressure is low, by definition land is abundant. In those cases where population pressure is high, by definition land is scarce, i.e. demand exceeds supply. Conversely, because in these relatively low technology societies the abundance of land is defined essentially in terms of the resident population or labor supply, the abundant land situation represents a condition of labor scarcity, in the sense that the limiting condition on production is the availability of labor, not land. Similarly, in the high population pressure areas, where land resources are scarce, the limiting condition on production is natural resources rather than labor.

The limiting factor exerts its influence not only on production for direct subsistence but also on production for prestige. Years ago, Thorstein Veblen (as well as others before him) pointed out that human wants are insatiable simply because men vie with one another in all social situations in some way or another. Veblen focused primarily on prestige, and in his theory of conspicuous consumption he proposed that there was no upper limit to man's desire for goods that might be expended in the competition for status or "invidious distinction" (Veblen 1953:

35). From an anthropological perspective, this indeed does seem to be a mechanism widely used by human populations. It suggests that because in any ecological, economic, or social situation one of the chief factors of production will tend to be less abundant than the others, that factor will be the limiting one in achieving "invidious distinction." As the scarcest essential factor of production, it will be the focus for competition and the keystone for social prestige and power.

The kind of behavior Veblen was talking about is cross-culturally widespread and quite possibly universal, provided we include the conspicuous expenditure of services as well as of material goods. We must again note that our concept of scarcity is simply that of demand exceeding supply, and nothing more. It does not include value judgments on our part as to whether the excess of demand over supply in any particular case is justified.

For "precapitalistic" societies with low population pressure, the postulated limiting factor on production is labor, whether for subsistence or prestige production. In such a society, labor, not land, should be the basis for competition and social inequality. One such case is represented by the Jívaro Indians of the Upper Amazon, whom I have studied first-hand (see Harner 1972). Their food supply comes from a mixture of hunting, fishing, gathering, and agriculture. Fertile, productive land is abundant, and when weeds become too thick in the garden, the Jívaro simply clear another plot somewhere else in the forest and move on. Famine is utterly unknown. The population density is approximately one person per square mile, and there is virtually no territoriality or ownership of land, even of a communal nature. Competition for land in any form is completely unheard-of. Obviously, power and prestige in this economy cannot be attained by acquiring and controlling land. There is no significant capital to accumulate and monopolize as a factor of production in order to obtain power and prestige, because everyone can make his own weapons, utensils, houses, and so on. Therefore, all that remains to acquire and accumulate as the path to power and prestige is labor, and this means agricultural labor, i.e. women. Women are wanted because they are the scarce means of production, that is, the only limitation on the production of food in a household is the number of wives a man has, not the amount of land at his disposal. A man wishes to have plural wives in order to produce large quantities of food and beer so that he may give feasts in order to gain prestige. This kind of food gift-giving is found in many primitive societies where land is not yet scarce and thus only the accumulation of labor, not land, is the way to obtain prestige.

Because of the demand for women, one of the ways to get social power among the Jívaro is for a father to give his daughters in marriage on the condition that their husbands take up residence at or near his household and shift their allegiances to him. This form of prestige acquisition through the control of labor but not land is commonly known in the ethnological literature, particularly in that of New Guinea, as the "big man" phenomenon. But it is a very weak way to gain power; because the "big man" does not control land, there is no stable basis for hereditary chieftainship or class distinctions to develop.

The Jívaro are important from several theoretical and evolutionary points of view, but especially because of how closely their basic ecological and economic circumstances resemble those that Engels, in *The origin of the family, private property, and the state*, postulated for his ideal or model society for Lower Barbarism. In this stage he hypothesizes the equality of men and women, in contrast to the subsequent stage when herding gives rise to sexual inequality because males have a monopoly on wealth represented by livestock.

The population is extremely sparse; it is dense only at the tribe's place of settlement, around which lie in a wide circle first the hunting grounds and then the protective belt of neutral forest, which separates the tribe from others. The division of labor is purely primitive, between the sexes only. The man fights in the wars, goes hunting and fishing, procures the raw materials of food and the tools necessary for doing so. The woman looks after the house and the preparation of food and clothing, cooks, weaves, sews. They are each master in their own sphere: the man in the forest, the woman in the house. Each is owner of the instruments which he or she makes and uses: the man of the weapons, the hunting and fishing implements, the woman of the household gear. The housekeeping is communal among several and often many families. What is made and used in common is common property — the house, the garden, the long-boat. Here therefore, and here alone, there still exists in actual fact that "property created by the owner's labor" which in civilized society is an ideal fiction of the jurists and economists, the last lying legal pretense by which modern capitalist property still bolsters itself up (Engels 1942:144–145).

The Jívaro and the closely related Jivaroan Achuara of eastern Ecuador, with whom I have also worked, fit this description almost perfectly, except that males and females are not equal in these societies; in fact, women are both formally and informally subordinate to men. There are no herds yet, nothing to fit Engels's qualifications for the subordination of women to men. What, then, has gone wrong? I would argue that Engels was insensitive to the importance of labor scarcity in affecting the social structure; he assumed that simply because capital was not unequally controlled between the sexes, the sexes would be socially equal.

Let us review Engels's own data to seek the solution. He has told us "the population is extremely sparse"; thus we know, even if he does not, that land is abundant and labor is scarce. Because there is labor scarcity, we can predict with relative confidence that there will be competition between men to accumulate the labor of women through polygyny. Perhaps more basically, by telling us that "the man fights in the wars," Engels has also told us that male adult mortality tends to be higher than female adult mortality, as among the Jívaro. This means that there is an imbalance in the sex ratio between adult males and females, in the absence of special factors. A polygynous society will result, so that in the typical household, adult male labor will be scarcer than adult female labor. While, as Engels says, the males and females are each masters in their own economic spheres, the males, by having the scarcer labor vis à vis the females, will exert the greater influence and control in the household. In fact, the individual male head of the polygynous family will have a monopoly in supplying meat from the hunt, while no woman will exercise such a monopoly on her means of production, because it is identical to that controlled by each of the other wives.

Here then, is an example of the inadequacy of a focus on capital in order to understand societies in which competition, dominance, and subordination are understood primarily in terms of scarce labor or land.

Understandably, because of the poor state of ethnological knowledge at the time, Marx was among those who paid very little attention to the societies with relatively low population densities, where land was not scarce compared to labor, and where, if there were a means to social power, it had to derive from control of labor. Instead, he tended to derive his comparative data from medieval Europe, classical Greece and Rome, and the Orient, all of them being cases where land was already scarce. Thus, land undoubtedly appeared to Marx as something that always had value and thus was always a basis for power.

It might be thought that because of the need for services, societies with the greatest scarcity of labor would have the most elaborate formalized descent and alliance structures for assuring the supply of that labor. Actually, however, such structures only evolve when there is increasing scarcity of land to support them. The formalized structures, which are hereditary, cannot exist and persist without a stable and valued material base to support them. Thus, we find that the Jívaro, without land scarcity, have no formal kin or descent units, despite their often desperate need for labor for defense and household production. The need for labor is not enough in itself for the development of elaborate kinship systems in precapitalistic societies; such systems occur when the supply of land is not adequate to the demand, and kinship structures must be seen first and foremost as units for holding natural resources. (Herding societies may seem an exception unless one keeps in mind that they are not precapitalistic, because of their heavy dependence on large livestock which constitute important productive capital.) The reason that kinship systems are emphasized in societies with relatively low population pressures is not that land is not scarce, but that it is still not scarce enough to have given rise to super-skin systems of class and state organization that would supplant kin-based landholding units. In addition, non-land-holding sibs or clans may be present to provide alliances over a large area between members of the more localized natural resource-holding units. This cooperation may be for competition in the form of war against outsiders or for reciprocal access to each other's territory in times of differential water or food scarcity between local regions. In either case, the non-residential sibs or clans can be seen as a response to natural resource scarcity, whether occurring evenly throughout an area or unevenly in terms of differential famine. To facilitate the alliance aspect of these sibs or clans, they are normally exogamous under such circumstances, to permit the welding together of as many persons as possible.

The chiefdom is a generally recognized phase of sociopolitical evolution, but discussions of the basis for its formation have largely overlooked the issue of relative scarcity in the factors of production. In terms of our model, however, the chiefdom is the logical consequence of growing land scarcity, and it derives directly from the increasing formalization of unilineal descent structures which themselves derive from increasing natural resource scarcity.

The development of unilineality, by permitting the growth of exogamous sibs or clans, can thereby create alliances throughout an entire dialect group or, as among the Iroquois, even among a number of dialectally distinct tribes. Because the chiefs tend to come from the ranks of lineage leaders, the development of unilineal kinship organization goes hand in hand with the evolution of political organization. Unilineal descent is thus seen as an important condition for the development of permanent chieftainships.

For the earlier stages of rising land scarcity, before the pressure is sufficient to necessitate the political innovation of permanent chieftainship, I hypothesized the gradual evolution of principles of kin descent from the nonterritorial cognatic type to unilineal forms associated with particular territories (Harner 1970: 69). Specifically, these are lineages which may, on occasion, compete for land through mild mechanisms not yet involving warfare. The principle of unilineal descent also provides for peacemaking by the highest-ranking elders within the descent unit. This principle of governance by the elders of the lineage becomes centralized into chieftainship as population grows, land becomes more scarce, and war for it increases; the ranking lineage member or chief has the responsibility to coordinate the defense of the territory of his lineage against other groups bent on conquest, as well as to arbitrate potentially disruptive internal disputes within the descent group. In the interest of successful defense of their territory, lineages join together, placing themselves under the general authority of one such chief, often the leader of the largest and strongest local lineage. In this way, the transition is made from a petty to a paramount chiefdom.

Because the lineage is the landholding unit, the development of lineage chieftainship is accompanied by the assumption of managerial responsibility by the chief for the allocation of rights of access to the scarce natural resources belonging to his lineage. The scarce land under his jurisdiction becomes his power base, and he is now able to expect tribute in terms of goods and services in exchange for the rights to exploit what eventually becomes essentially "his" territory and is typically passed on to his descendants as their inheritance of the chieftainship.

Here we have laid then, the foundations for the transition to a dual class stratified society. However, the chiefdom phase does not reach that transition point as long as the chiefs primarily classify themselves as members of the descent groups whose land they administer. Gradually, as competition for the available land becomes increasingly intense, class stratification can come about through three main mechanisms. The first and often-hypothesized one is through the seizure of new territory, with the victors becoming the upper class. The second process is the in-migration of outsiders seeking access to land who find themselves having to accept a subordinate status in return for the privilege of using the land. The third, and generally overlooked process, is simply internal evolution, in which the chiefs, for purposes of strengthening their military alliances, marry their offspring primarily to those of neighboring chiefs. In a matter of a relatively few generations, the chiefs and their immediate families may comprise an in-breeding aristocracy, easily distinguishable from the commoners in terms of marriage patterns and inheritance of land.

The unequal inheritance of scarce natural resources has been recognized, of course, by a number of writers as the basis for precapitalistic class stratification. And it is only a short step from the territorially based paramount chiefdom to the early state, with its emphases on the defense and conquest of land and on the maintenance of internal order. In such a precapitalistic state, the high degree of land scarcity provides the basis for both class stratification and military-political organization.

By the time this high degree of population pressure is reached, however, social and political structures are developing which shortly start to undermine the material basis of kin organization as far as land ownership or control is concerned. The evolution of class stratification and of the state, by moving the area of competition for, and control of, natural resources to new loci in the society, reduces the role of descent groups and leads to their gradual return to the cognatic or bilateral form (Harner 1970: 82–84). Although more detailed elaborations of the evolution of kinship need to be worked out, we have here within the framework of the relative scarcity of the factors of land and labor in premercantile and preindustrial societies a basic model of a process that can be tested in terms of cross-cultural research.

Now let us turn to the impact of the relative scarcity of labor and land on fighting and warfare. As we have seen in the case of the land-abundant Jívaro, competition and fighting for territory are completely unknown. At the other end of the spectrum from the Jívaro, we have the land-scarce societies, which are more familiar to us and whose focus is upon the seizing and defending of territory. There are many examples in the ethnographic literature of societies where the concept of territorial possession exists and territorial boundaries are delineated. In elementary cases, there is pure conquest of land alone, not of the land with its occupants, who are expelled or exterminated. It seems that only later, with the development of chiefdoms or states, do we have the refinement of tribute or taxation as a means of siphoning off surpluses from the interaction of both alien labor and alien land. But even this development only occurs where there is a substantial land scarcity, as indicated by the fact that the labor is left resident on its own land, rather than brought back to exploit the victor's own territory; under conditions of high population pressure the latter arrangement would not yield as great a marginal return as does the vanquished labor pool exploiting its own region.

In terms of this model, then, the objectives and nature of warfare change according to the labor/land ratio. In societies without land scarcity, war takes the form of "raiding," that is, expeditions that seize captives, especially women and children, to augment the raiders' own households and that typically take trophies, such as scalps or human heads, to enhance the status of those wishing to be recognized as "big men" on their return home. The "raiding" form of warfare is characterized by hit-and-run expeditions whose purpose is not to hold territory and which involve ambush tactics and an ephemeral military organization. "Conquest" warfare, on the other hand, derives from a scarcity of land, and here are found strong tendencies toward a stable military organization with authority concentrated in permanent chiefs responsible for the defense of clearly recognized territories. Tactics tend to emphasize mass formations in open combat, with emphasis on "no retreat" principles. The need for centralized war-chief leadership to defend territory against mass "conquest-type" attacks within a general region of scarce land reinforces internal political tendencies toward permanent centralization and authority.

The assumption should not be made that higher population pressure leads simply to increased warfare. It appears, rather, that the most unremitting warfare is more often found among such land-abundant groups as the Jívaro, which lack any unilineal descent groups and chiefs to preserve domestic tranquility or to act in unison against outside aggressors. Rather, it is suggested that the land-scarce groups, through their more evolved permanent mechanisms for maintaining local peace and through their relative disinterest in labor-seizing raiding activity, may tend to experience actual outbreaks of warfare less frequently. Such societies, however, tend to have campaigns and outbreaks of violence on a much larger scale when they do occur.

Part and parcel of the labor-scarce versus the land-scarce kind of warfare is the question of the occurrence of slavery, which is defined here in broad anthropological terms as the utilization of the involuntary labor of persons brought in from other societies, usually as war captives. There is a variety of subtypes of slavery, including the hereditary/non-hereditary distinctions, which need not be discussed for our present broad comparative purposes. What is essential to our argument is the recognition that such labor, when imported on a mass scale, obviously is brought in because the demand for it exceeds the supply. Therefore, it is not surprising that in our cross-cultural research we find that the highest incidence of mass slavery in precapitalistic societies is not among those with class stratification or state organization (in other words, high population pressure societies) but rather in the non-class-stratified societies (in other words, those with an abundance of land). This correlation between frequency of slavery and abundance of land has long been recognized (see Nieboer 1900).

Conversely, we should expect slavery to be essentially absent as a productive force in the societies with the greatest land scarcity. Thus it is no surprise to find that the most densely populated islands of the Pacific, which had class stratification, lacked slavery; examples of these are Ponape, Samoa, Tikopia, Tonga, the Marquesas, and Tahiti (Murdock 1967). These societies were so land-starved that often substantial portions of their populations chose emigration despite high degrees of uncertainty with regard to their survival and success in finding new island homes. Under conditions of such high population pressure it would have been absurd to seek slaves, to bring in additional mouths to feed, when such a large labor pool was already locally available. Obviously, there is a point of diminishing marginal productivity where the recruitment of labor from other societies is not matched by the rewards of obtaining it.

The relative scarcity of land and labor also affects the nature of the technology emphasized. As some economists have pointed out, a distinction can be made between labor-saving and land-saving devices. The latter can be seen as primarily a response to conditions of high population pressure and consist essentially of technology designed to increase the production of a given unit of area, not of a given member of the labor force. The transition from hunting and gathering to agriculture was probably a development of this nature, domestication serving to increase the carrying capacity of the land in response to population pressure. Similarly, agricultural intensification in precapitalistic societies apparently has been primarily due to the same forces (cf. Boserup 1965). For a land-scarce society, land-saving activity is an alternative choice to expansion through conquest warfare, that is, land acquisition, although over any period of time both techniques tend to be used to increase food production.

In such land-scarce and therefore labor-abundant societies, we would not expect a great emphasis on labor-saving technology. Because labor is cheap, any labor-saving invention would presumably not be adopted as readily as it would be in a society where labor is scarce and valuable. Everything else being equal, therefore, labor-saving technology should be more emphasized and more commonly adopted in societies of low population pressure. In this connection, we note that the greatest elaboration of labor-saving technology among the aboriginal inhabitants of the New World was among the sparsely settled Eskimo. Their inventions for moving heavy weights are unparalleled in anthropological museum collections. In contrast, the greatest development of land-saving technology in the New World was among the most densely settled peoples. The Incas of Peru, for example, depended heavily upon irrigation, terracing, and fertilization to increase land productivity; the Aztecs of Mexico depended in addition upon the *chinampa*, basically a technique for obtaining earth from lake and swamp bottoms to create fields for cultivation.

While it is not my intention to deal with mercantile or industrial societies, I would like to note that this type of model is not inconsistent with the leadership of Western Europe, not densely populated China, in exploiting labor-saving technology, even though the latter society had long had many of these inventions "on the books." And even Europe did not have as low a labor/land ratio as did the early United States, so that it is not inconsistent that innovations in labor-saving technology (i.e. "Yankee ingenuity") should have eventually become even more a hallmark of the American economy, for the same basic reasons of labor scarcity and land abundance that seem to be ultimately responsible for both the American "frontier democracy" in the North and West (à la Turner and Webb) and slavery in the South.

A problem that remains to be solved in employing the concepts embodied in this paper is the development of methods for measuring the relative scarcity of land and labor. Because one is seen primarily as a function of the other in precapitalistic societies, it may be sufficient to simply develop scales for measuring the degree of land scarcity; thus, by implication, we would have an inverse scale for labor scarcity. In any case, such scales or indices need to be devised.

One possibility might be to develop a scale based upon the "price," in human life, that populations are willing to pay to seize and defend land. The lowest rating, of course, would be the complete absence of any practice of competition for land. Slightly higher on the scale would be nonviolent competition, such as tugs-of-war at boundaries; next might be violent competition that is decided by inflicting a nonfatal wound, as known for some central California tribes; next, competition that is decided by inflicting a single fatality on one side or another; and finally, all-out mortal combat for land, perhaps with the measurement of differing degrees of escalation. It might be argued, however, that such a scale may embody a significant cultural component that does not necessarily directly represent the relative scarcity of land at a particular historical moment.

Another possible scale might be sheer population density, but this suffers from a serious liability in that the relative scarcity of land is also influenced by whether or not there is domesticated food production, by the general level of technology, and by variations in the nature of specific environments.

Boserup (1965) offers a progressive scale of degrees of agricultural intensification with the frequency of cropping as the indicator of growing land scarcity, but her schema has a number of flaws. It is designed for forest environments, and two of its five categories ("annual cropping" and "multi-cropping") are susceptible to the influence of climate, while a third ("short fallow") is primarily a function of the use of the plow, as Boserup herself notes. Among other problems it is by no means clear how applicable her sequence is, even in forest environments, to cultures lacking steel tools for forest clearing.

In an earlier paper I presented one possible scale for measuring natural resource scarcity in agricultural societies, which is based on the following reasoning (Harner 1970: 71):

In societies dependent upon both domesticated and wild foods obtained from the land, the growth in population density deriving from the expandability of domesticated food production will contribute to an increasing degradation of the non-domesticated food resources of the land through over-hunting and over-gathering, and through the conversion of areas of wild subsistence resource land to agriculture and livestock-raising. Aside from degradation of wild food land resources, simple growth in population density by itself will heighten the pressure on non-domesticated resources, with the effect that, taking the pattern of subsistence dependence of the population as a whole, the proportion of the diet deriving from wild food land resources will decline. This buildup of pressure on the land subsistence resources should be reflected in a diminishing dependence on hunting and gathering. Using this model, it is therefore proposed that an inverse correlation exists between the degree of dependence on hunting and gathering and the degree of population pressure in societies having any agriculture, and that the total degree of dependence on hunting and gathering in such societies provides a scale for measuring population pressure.... This is a gross scale, proposed as a tool to ascertain broad statistical tendencies rather than to accurately represent the population pressure on subsistence resources in every specific case.

That it may, to some degree, help us to predict the social consequences of land scarcity may be seen by examination of tables in that paper, which involved samples of up to 838 societies. In every table where the scale was used against known social evolutionary levels the chi-square computations resulted in a "p" of less than .000001.

As has been observed, the basic approach taken here runs counter to some of the avowed positions of substantivists in economic anthropology. For example, in contrast to Polanyi, I consider scarcity to be a universal fact of social life. On the other hand, Polanyi (1957: 255–256), among the substantivists, has particularly tried to relate the integration of the chief factors of production to social evolutionary stages, and in that respect, my position shares more with his than it does with that of the formalists in economic anthropology, who have almost entirely neglected the question of the evolutionary relationship between economic and social structures. It is, however, only the formalists who have consistently argued for the importance of the scarcity postulate in economic anthropology. Thus, the approach used here belongs to neither camp, but reflects certain aspects of both positions. The formalist-substantivist opposition may possibly be on the way to a partial synthesis within a causality-oriented evolutionary framework.

In addition, the present approach shares much of the Marxist tradition of respect for the social impact of the forces of production, but emphasizes that in precapitalistic societies the relative scarcity of land versus labor must be considered in order to understand and predict loci of power. Marx's *Pre-capitalist economic formations* (1965: 82–83) suggests that he had some nascent glimmerings of the importance of population growth in preindustrial society, but on the whole his insights are disappointing, and he seems unaware of the possibility or importance of "free land" primitive societies as opposed to his frequently mentioned "communally owned" land cases. Within our framework the latter evolve only after land is sufficiently scarce to be claimed or owned at all, a development that fits our phases of unilineal descent and chieftainship. But then, it would be surprising if, more than a century after Marx wrote *Pre-capitalist economic formations*, anthropology were not able to gradually move forward in its understanding of the economic and social structures of premercantile and preindustrial societies. While Marx and Engels emphasized the evolutionary role of the social relations of production and of vertical competition for the means of production, the present approach emphasizes in addition the evolutionary role of horizontal competition for the means of production. Furthermore, it should be observed that our theoretical framework is not at all unrelated to the thrust of Darwinian organic evolution, with its emphasis upon competition deriving from scarcity of natural resources under the impact of growing population.

I wish to conclude by suggesting that a scarcity of any factor of production can underlie economic exploitation and social inequality. This has been obscured because capital is always scarce — that is, it is created and maintained by people through effort only because the supply, from their viewpoint, does not, or is not expected to, meet the demand. Thus, the hidden, but inherently present, scarcity aspect of capital, together with the scarcity of land in our own relatively high population pressure state societies, has obscured the fact that scarcity in any of the chief factors of production, even labor, can provide the basis for competition, exploitation, and social inequality and has done so in the course of human social evolution.

REFERENCES

BOSERUP, ESTER
  1965   *The conditions of agricultural growth: the economics of agrarian change under population pressure.* Chicago: Aldine.
CARNEIRO, ROBERT
  1961   "Slash-and-burn cultivation among the Kuikuru and its implications for cultural development in the Amazon basin," in *The evolution of horticultural systems in native South America, causes and consequences.* Edited by Johannes Wilbert, 47–67. Anthropológica Supplement Publication 2. Caracas: Sociedad de Ciencias Naturales La Salle.
ENGELS, FREDERICK
  1942   *The origin of the family, private property, and the state.* New York: International Publishers. (Originally published 1884.)
HARNER, MICHAEL J.
  1970   Population pressure and the social evolution of agriculturalists. *Southwestern Journal of Anthropology* 26:67–86.
  1972   *The Jívaro: people of the sacred waterfalls.* Garden City, New York: Doubleday and Natural History Press.
MARX, KARL
  1965   *Pre-capitalist economic formations.* New York: International Publishers.
MURDOCK, GEORGE P.
  1967   Ethnographic atlas: a summary. *Ethnology* 6(2).
NIEBOER, H. J.
  1900   *Slavery as an industrial system: ethnological researches.* The Hague: Martinus Nijhoff.
POLANYI, KARL
  1957   "The economy as instituted process," in *Trade and market in early empires: economies in history and theory.* Edited by Karl Polanyi, Conrad M. Arensberg, and Harry W. Pearson, 243–270. New York: Free Press.
VEBLEN, THORSTEIN
  1953   *The theory of the leisure class: an economic study of institutions* New York: Mentor. (Originally published 1899.)

Population and Social Variation in Early Bronze Age Denmark: A Systemic Approach

KLAVS RANDSBORG

> I always think within myself
> That there is no place
> Where people do not die.
>
> PROVERB OF NORTHWEST COAST
> TLINGIT INDIANS

1. INTRODUCTION

A characteristic of human populations is their ability to evolve differences in their access to material goods. Often these differences are linked up with sets of symbolic behavior, as in political systems. In the following, population density is related to status differences or social stratification in a group of prehistoric societies that occupied a relatively homogeneous habitat. These societies seemed to be in posession of the same technology. It is not implied, however, that the structure of the economy was the same, a fact that unfortunately is obscured by poor data on the subsistence. The quantification of the archaeological information on the mentioned variables permits a study of their systemic — or functional — variability. The regulating nature of the operations of the societies is thus exemplified. Some major changes in population density and social stratification illustrate variation at the limits of the general system.

The focus of the investigation is Denmark in the so-called Early Bronze Age (approximately 1800 to 1000 B.C.). The southern Scandinavian societies of this age were practicing a plow agriculture with some cattle and sheep breeding, but evidence of settlements was found almost lacking

I am grateful for the help given to me by various institutions and individuals including my assistants since 1970, the starting year of this study. I am further indebted to the State Research Council for the Humanities for grants at important steps of the investigation.

from the materials and, with them, further information on economic dimensions. From other sources it is clear that the technological level was fairly high concerning work in both wood and metal: for instance, pictographs reflect the existence of light chariots and long boats (huge canoes). As copper, tin, and gold are not found naturally in the soil, some trading over longer distances must have existed. No monumental buildings were undertaken, apart from the numerous burial mounds. From the settlements come only a few traces of post houses.

2.   THE DATA

The graves, which number many hundreds, constitute the traditional data for investigations into the Early Bronze Age. As burial goods they contain bronzes and gold objects of mostly the same types as found in the smaller number of "hoards and offerings." From an aesthetic point of view the metal artifacts are traditionally considered fairly satisfying, and they have long since been appreciated by archaeologists for their typological and chronological potential as well. In 1885 the data served to make a classical model in archaeology: Montelius' division of the entire "Nordic" Bronze Age into six periods, of which the Early Bronze Age occupies numbers I to III, each for a length of 200 to 300 years.

Nearly all the graves were found in burial mounds that frequently contained several interments. Only a few graves were not covered by a barrow. The mounds, which often seem to follow the ancient dirt track systems, were constructed of turf, obtained from about 1.0 to 1.5 hectares of grassland, giving the circular mound a height of three meters, and a diameter of approximately twenty meters. The interments themselves were almost always single graves, comprising a wood coffin of a man's height, usually a cleft and hollowed oak trunk, supported and often covered by stones. In many cases, especially in the northwest of Jutland, the dead were laid in stone coffins. The normal burial state of the body is inhumation, which in Period III became rivalled by cremation, but skeletons were rarely preserved. Anyway, it is possible to determine the sex of most of the deceased by means of the combinations of the accompanying artifact types, though some small ornaments are common to both sexes. Judging by the length of the inhumation coffins, children very rarely seem to have been buried in the mounds. Another direct observation concerns the women, who numbered only half as many as the men. Consequently, the graves do not represent a random sample of the population.

In the graves were found what looks like personal equipment of the deceased — for the men swords, daggers, and axes, and a little jewelry; for the women jewelry (often of impressive sort) and not seldom a dagger. To be mentioned also are amber and glass beads, and pottery. Tools were very rarely found, apart from some male firestroke flints, razors and tweezers plus minor knives. Only a few arm rings—and no other objects— occurred in a child's size, which confirms the aforementioned observation as to the lack of children in the barrows. In a smaller number of graves — the famous "oak coffins" (Boye 1896) — full woolen dresses for men and women, blankets, and wooden objects, e.g. bowls and folding chairs, were found along with the oxskins that wrapped up the dead (Plates 1 and 2). A few of the graves from the mounds containing no metal objects are dated to the Early Bronze Age by means of stratigraphy. They are not included in this material.

The "hoards and offerings" will play a smaller role in the investigation and shall not be commented upon here. The prime data consist of the grave finds. As the major part of the Bronze Age material from Denmark is housed in the collections of the National Museum — and this sample is a reliable one for the country as a whole — the data are thus restricted, The number of reliable grave finds from Period I is only twenty-one, while Periods II and III, in spite of the more or less equal length of the three periods and identical circumstances of find, yielded, respectively, 426 and 552 graves. Graves equipped with artifacts of metal were very rare in the beginning of the Bronze Age.

The choice of Denmark as focus for the investigation is of a purely practical nature, as southernmost Sweden (Scania) and Schleswig-Holstein might have been included as well, environmentally speaking.

3. GEOGRAPHICAL DISTRIBUTION OF THE GRAVES

From distribution maps of the graves of Periods II and III, which contained a very large number of finds, it is seen that the scattering is not random. Some areas are left open while others are densely populated. (The few Period I graves were found in the settled areas of the two later periods.) In Figures 1 and 2 are depicted the distributions, respectively, for Periods II and III in the northwestern parts of Jutland. We do not here concern ourselves with the minor fluctuations from period to period but only with the general picture, where, for instance, the southern parts of the Danish Islands and the southern part of eastern Jutland are practically devoid of finds. The northern part of Zealand and northwestern Jutland are both rich in graves and contain soil of almost the same high quality as the above mentioned areas. It has therefore been proposed that

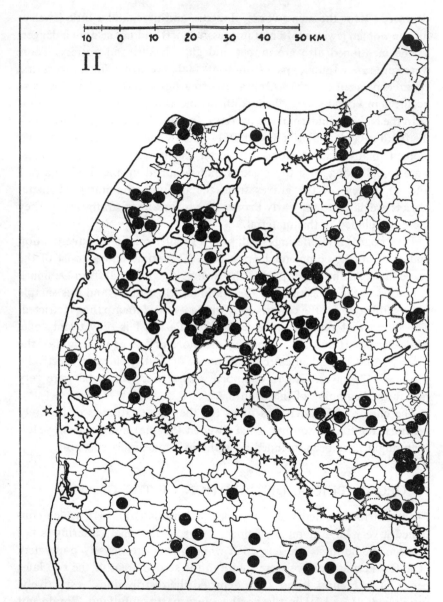

Figure 1. Distribution of graves in the northwestern parts of Jutland in Period II. The starred borders run between zones (see Figure 3). The small units are parishes.

the distribution of the graves is partly disturbed by later farming, even on a regional scale (Müller 1897: 296; Brøndsted 1958: 41). To test this proposition the following strategy is applied.

The Early Bronze Age finds contain not only more costly artifacts of

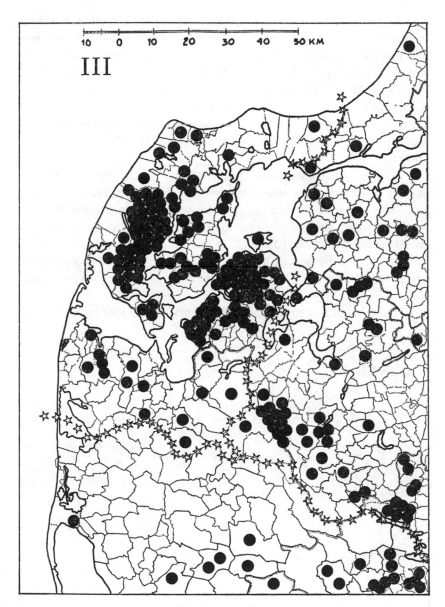

Figure 2.   Distribution of graves in the northwestern parts of Jutland in Period III.
The starred borders run between zones (see Figure 3). The small units are parishes.

metal but also some made from stone (such as flint daggers) and especially
firestroke flints. These latter items were probably of no importance to
later farmers, especially not to those of the second millennium A.D. period
of intensive agriculture. If the above "empty" areas were in fact settled in

the Early Bronze Age, the destroyed barrows of the occupation, if not the settlement sites themselves, would have left a considerable number of such stone artifacts. This, however, is not the case, neither concerning the flint daggers of Type VI, dated to Periods I and II (Lomborg 1973: 60, Figures 38–39), nor the firestroke flints. For the flints especially the types of Periods II and III were selected and the one-of-a kind specimens have not only the same distribution as the graves of Periods II and III, but occur in the same relative number as the graves from zone to zone (see below).

It is therefore assumed that the distribution of the graves, when the number of finds is reasonably high, reflects the regional settlement pattern. This proposition is in accordance with the observation that the graves strikingly seem to avoid the old areas of dense deciduous forest on the Islands and in eastern Jutland, as well as the poorest heather soil in western Jutland. No test can be made of the commonsense acceptance of a relatively close geographical relation between settlement site and graveyard.

To facilitate further investigation Denmark was divided into five zones

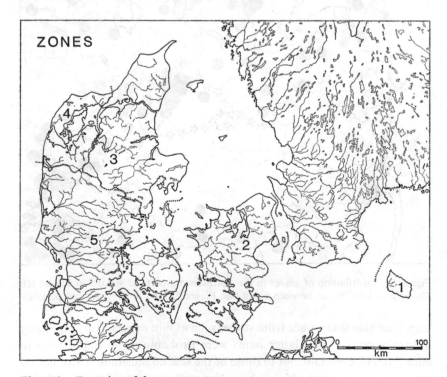

Figure 3. Extension of the zones

according to the number of graves, their distribution and certain environmental criteria. The zone of good soil in northwest Jutland (Zone 4) is thus isolated from the surrounding poorer soils, while Zones 3 and 5 are separated by areas of practically no finds (see also Figures 1 and 2). The five zones are (Figure 3):

1. The island of Bornholm (in the Baltic)
2. The Danish Islands
3. Northeastern Jutland
4. Northwestern Jutland
5. Mid- and southern Jutland

Another observation from Figure 4 concerns the movement of settlement onto better soils from Period II to Period III with the ensuing possibility of a higher production. This result is valid for all zones apart from Zone 1 (Bornholm), where the average values of the settled areas are almost the same for the two periods, a fact that might be explained in terms of population pressure on available land on the relatively small island (see next section). The general improvement of arable land is especially observed in Zone 3, where the rich soil of the peninsula of Djursland (on the east coast of Jutland) was densely settled in Period III.

The aforementioned fluctuations must indicate a general change in the subsistence strategy, but due to the lack of relevant information it is not possible to elaborate on this point.

4. AGRICULTURAL VALUE OF THE SETTLED AREAS

Accepting the distribution of the graves as reflecting the regional settlement pattern, we now attempt to describe — in quantitative terms — the agricultural value of the settled areas. For the description two variables are employed, hectare (ha.) and the so-called "hartkorn" (hard corn, e.g. barley), which is a Danish unit of land valuation measurable in "tønder" [barrels] and abbreviated "td.H.". Thus, on poor soil the number of hectares needed per barrel of hard corn is higher than on good soil.

Two calculations are made thereupon: the first one refers to the average number of hectares per barrel of hard corn of all five zones, the second one to the average number of hectares per barrel of hard corn in the settled areas as measured parish by parish. It is thus possible to observe not only the selective strategy for land but also the fluctuations from period to period. In Figure 4 are shown the results for Periods II and III, while the small number of observations from Period I is the reason for omitting this period.

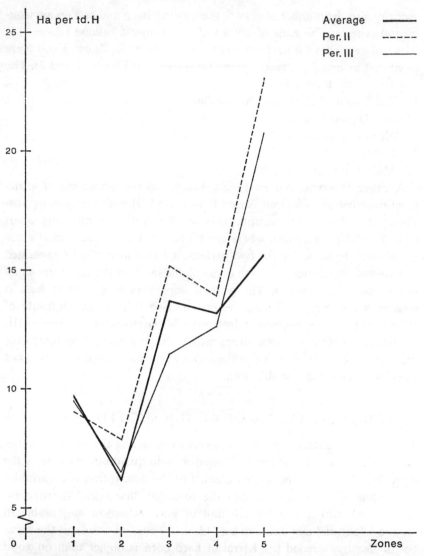

Figure 4. Average number of hectares (ha.) per barrel of hard corn (td.H.) of the entire zones and of the settled areas within the zones for Periods II and III. These measurements indicate the quality of land.

Heretofore, the archaeological literature has been in odd agreement that the Bronze Age people preferred poorer soils to the good ones, yet avoiding the poorest areas of western Jutland (e.g. Broholm 1944: 226 ff.; Brøndsted 1958: 25, 40 ff., 109). This proposition is only partly in accord with the representation in Figure 4, where it is seen that the average settlement within a zone is situated on average land. To choose the very best soil only may have required too much cutting (see foregoing Section 3). Only in Zone 5, mid- and southern Jutland, whose good eastern soils remain an unsettled question, a clear difference from the average is seen with the choice of poor land. It is tempting to propose a heavier stress on animal breeding in this zone, where the Early Bronze Age landscape is known to have been fairly open pasture.

5.   POPULATION SIZE AND QUALITY OF THE LAND

It is seen from the distribution maps of the graves that the settled parishes generally contain only a few graves each, and that they occur more or less scattered within the zones. A typical picture is shown in Figure 1, which reflects the scattering within the northwestern part of Jutland in Period II. The tendency to form clusters of more densely populated parishes is not pronounced. In Figure 2 a somewhat different picture is seen with two distinct clusters of rich parishes. Again, the geographical area is northwestern Jutland, but the time is Period III. The "centers" are situated, respectively, in the southern part of the peninsula of Thy (on the North Sea) and in the western part of the peninsula of Salling. The clusters cannot be due to differences in the circumstances of the finds, and their occurrence raises the question as to the extent to which the numbers of graves reflect the intensity of settlement, or rather, the population density.

In preindustrial Denmark the size of the rural population was in direct proportion to the quality of land, as measured in barrels of hard corn (td.H.). The organizational and technological level being held equal, the td.H. variable is the most important one in determining the so-called carrying capacity of fields and pastures. Now, it is postulated that the td.H.-population size connection is valid for the agricultural societies of the Early Bronze Age as well. To test the proposition a simple scatter diagram was made (Figure 5), from which is obtained a very good correlation between the total number of graves in the zones of Period II and III, and the corresponding barrels of hard corn values of the settled areas within the zones. It is noted that it is possible to depict the two periods together. Only one observation (Zone 4, Period III) falls outside the regression curve. The "centers" of this zone and period result in a density of population that breaks the system of the rest of the zones/periods. It should be added that both the correlation between barrels of hard corn and the male graves alone and the corresponding one with female graves alone produce poorer results than the one depicted in Figure 5. Consequently, the total number of graves is accepted as the best

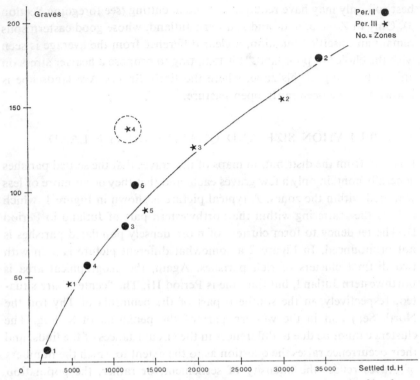

Figure 5. Relationship between the number of graves and settled barrels of hard corn (td.H.) in the zones for Periods II and III

measurement of the relative population size. Between the corresponding amounts of settled hectares and the numbers of graves a very poor correlation is noted, reflecting the considerable differences of land quality within Denmark. Also, between the total numbers of barrels of hard corn in the zones and the numbers of graves practically no correlation is seen. This latter observation confirms the use of the settled parishes as foci for the determination of the Early Bronze Age settlement pattern.

The correlation depicted in Figure 5 has some bearing also on the use of land in the Early Bronze Age, which must have been as flexible as in later, historic times. The same number of people was supported by one barrel of hard corn on poor soil as by one on rich soil. The strange case of Zone 4, Period III indicates, however, an increase in population — and consequently also in production — out of proportion to prior estimates of the economic potential. As no change in the technology is seen, only two major sets of explanation seem to apply to the situation, both involving an alteration of the organizational structure of the society. The first one indicates the existence of a subsistence base beside the traditional farming system, for instance, a sudden abundance in the marine resources. Zone 4, with its long coastline, would provide a good opportunity to exploit these. The second explanation implies an increase in work hours used in the agricultural system, where the number of animals may have been augmented and the fallow periods shortened, a factor Boserup (1965) recently has stressed with some impact even on archaeological studies.

Other possible explanations of the Zone 4 observation may take the form of acquisition through trade or warfare. However, as there were no parallel changes in the adjoining zones a considerable increase in the trade of food is hardly believable. There seem to have been no surplus of manpower in the Zones 3 and 5 of Period III, and, if the production was in fact augmented in these zones, it would have happened — as we shall note from the following — without apparent changes in the social dimension of the societies. The last observation may also reject warfare as the sole explanation of the case. It should be added that the phenomenon in question has a duration of a couple of hundred years, in which a certain degree of stability must have been acquired. Consequently, we are inclined to believe that major changes would have made themselves observable in the cultural system even when, as in the present investigation, only a limited number of variables was studied.

6.   THE GRAVES AS REFLECTORS OF SOCIAL
STRATIFICATION: PRIOR VIEWS

In the last section it was shown that the total number of graves seem to reflect the population size in the different zones/periods. But it was not proposed that the graves were a random sample of the entire population. Such a statement would also be in disagreement with the finding that children are almost entirely lacking from the data, and that the female graves comprise only one-third of the adult interments. Looking at the male graves alone two views heretofore have been given as to their social placement (see Moberg 1956):

1.   The graves represent the "upper stratum" of a two-class society (Müller 1897: 401 ff.; Brøndsted 1958: 10, 90 ff.).
2.   The graves represent a sample of the entire society (Broholm 1944: 257 ff.).

The first proposition, which is the common one, is obviously colored by comparisons with societies of state character (generally ignoring the rest of the cultural factors of these societies). Brøndsted, for instance, supports his view with the idea that the so-called "corded-ware people" in the Middle Neolithic Period subjugated the "funnel-beaker people" and established themselves as an "upper class," ruling through the Late Neolithic Period and the Bronze Age. In a way, the second of the aforementioned propositions is a sounder basis for speculations, though it may exaggerate the egalitarian character of primitive societies. Thus, the small number of male graves in Period I (20) compared to Periods II and III (258 and 293 respectively), must reflect differences in the mortuary ritual as to the equipment of the graves with artifacts of the costly metal.

But even though no "lower-stratum" interments are registered, this observation cannot be used as an argument for the second proposition, as also half of the women — at least — are lacking burials known to the archaeologist. The problem, which is not irrelevant to the understanding of the population dynamics we have just mentioned, must be solved by other means.

7.   MORTUARY WEALTH AND SOCIAL STATUS

The buried artifacts made by the exotic raw materials of bronze and gold must be ascribed a special value because the rest of the grave goods were made of local wood, clay, wool, etc. In the following the metal is used as a reflector of wealth differences in the burials and a quantitative method applied for the sake of comparison (see Randsborg 1973).

The content of golden and bronze objects was weighed for each grave with the assumption that the amount of imported and costly metal used is equivalent to the "price" of the artifacts. (This proposition is tested below.) The ratio between bronze and gold is not known, but it is rendered probable through a series of "best fit" experiments that it comes close to 100:1. (Contemporary historical sources from the Near East report on a fluctuation of 500–1,000:1 for COPPER and gold [Heichelheim 1958: 197 ff.]. These values fall far away from the European one, and the discrepancy may even erode the earlier notions of metal trade between "barbarian" Europe and the eastern Mediterranean civilizations.) Another problem is the deterioration of the bronzes (physical and to some extent also chemical), which can be shown to have operated with the same relative strength in the different zones/periods.

Chi-square tests were used to try whether significant differences exist between zones in the distribution of wealth. (Period I is omitted owing to a low number of observations.) For the women of Periods II and III no zonal difference has been noted. In Period II the same also applies to the men, while in Period III homogeneity exists between Zone 1 and 3 only.

Plate 1. Rich male grave from Muldbjerg, western Jutland (Zone 5, Period II). After Boye 1896. See Plate 2.

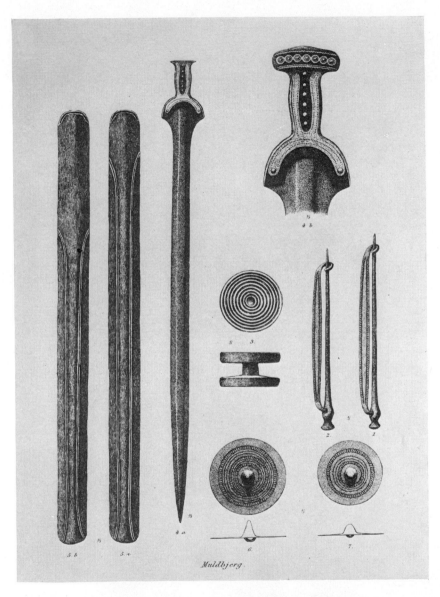

Plate 2.   Artifacts from the Muldbjerg grave. After Boye 1896. See Plate 1.

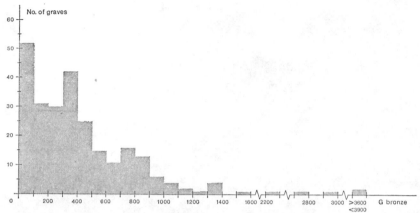

Figure 6. Histogram for the distribution of the sum of male graves from Period II
(1 G gold = 100 G bronze).

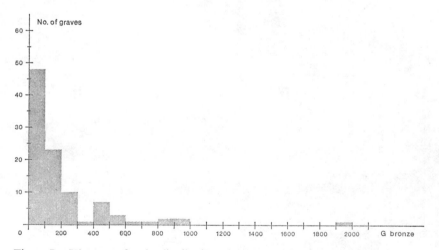

Figure 7. Histogram for the distribution of the sum of female graves from Period II
(1 G gold = 100 G bronze).

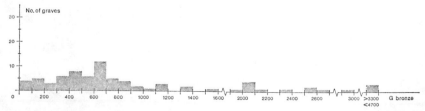

Figure 8. Histogram for the distribution of male graves from Zone 4, Period III
(1 G gold = 100 G bronze).

In this period especially Zone 4 differs from the rest of the distributions in having considerably more rich graves than poor ones at the 400 G bronze level of distinction. This division breaks the general triangular pattern of wealth distribution, though a faint tendency in the same direction is observable for the men of Zone 4, Period II, too. As the triangular model — with more poor than rich graves — seems to be a general one for social division of wealth, the notions from Zone 4 must indicate that A CONSIDERABLE GROUP OF MEN IS NOT REPRESENTED IN THE FIND MATERIAL. To these men we rank a concomitant number of women and children plus the rest of the women, and the children, of the men in the barrows. Consequently, it is more than plausible that the male graves in the data do not represent a random sample of the entire male population. On the other hand, the number of high-status graves (from the mounds) must be proportional — within certain limits — to the burials that are not archaeologically registered. This proposition raises some questions as to the interchangeability between male and female (burial) status, which we shall comment upon in the next section.

With respect to the homogeneity tests, it should be mentioned that also artifact styles show a difference in the zonal variability from Period II to Period III. In Period II the five zones are fairly homogeneous, while in Period III Zones 1 and 2 — and, to some extent also Zone 3 — display a strong continuity in style of artifacts as opposed to Zones 4 and 5. In these western areas the Period III "style" arose (Randsborg 1968). This observation may indicate the existence of correlation between social variability and those cultural features that traditionally are well treated in archaeology, such as art and artifact styles, types of graves, etc. Archaeological "Lokaltypen und -gruppen" may fruitfully be studied in terms of social variation. In the present case we suggest that communication, as reflected by the spread of artifact types, is facilitated if the social units involved are identical.

In the homogeneity tests 200 G classes were generally used, but histograms with smaller classes give a more detailed picture of the distribution of wealth. In Figure 6 a 100 G histogram for the male graves of all zones of Period II is shown and in Figure 7, the corresponding one for the female graves. For both groups certain peaks occur in the distribution. The male graves expose peaks around 0 G, 300–500 G, and around 700–900 G bronze. These "anomalies" seem to be an essential property of the division because they are similar from zone to zone. It might be suggested that the peaks were due to variations in the kinds of artifacts found in the graves; this, however, is not the case because the weight distribution of the single type of artifact is bimodal. Consequently, the peaks must reflect levels in the allotment of grave goods, or, in other words, signify the existence of different status strata within the general population of high-ranking men and women. It has not been possible by the way of independent information — like differences in the mortuary ritual — to separate these status strata in a clear way. But it is noticeable that graves with gold make up a major part of the richest graves. In these graves also considerably more bronze was found than in the graves without gold. THIS IMPORTANT OBSERVATION IS A TEST OF THE APPLICATION OF BRONZE AS AN INDICATOR OF WEALTH and at the same time a hint as to the social reality of the differences of wealth reflected in the graves. Comparing the sexes, it is noted that the fewer female graves with metal are also poorer than the male ones.

Besides the artifacts of gold a few made of generally less than 100 G bronze are also found in the rich graves only, though, according to their weight, we would expect them to be randomly distributed. These objects further develop the social reality of the wealth differences. In the rich male graves of Period II sometimes occur fittings and nails for wooden folding stools, that in one case has been even totally preserved. Next to be mentioned are some ornamental plates, which have been worn on the mantle. Also bowls and — perhaps more surprising — socketed chisels belong to this group. The "chisels" are probably not tools, at least not in a burial context, but rather, like other socketed implements, shoes for staves.

It is natural to stress the symbolic value of these artifacts, in the social dimension of the Early Bronze Age community. Though wealth normally bolsters social status (e.g. Kuper 1947: 180ff. for burials), the occurrence of the mentioned objects in the rich male graves clearly confirms this proposition. To find the heavy swords in the wealthiest graves is, of course, not surprising, but adds to the picture of the highest-ranking men. In Period III only gold objects and heavy weapons are found in the rich graves, indicating that the high-status positions may have lost some of their personal content, and consequently certain symbols of authority — like stools, badges and staves — were not buried with their holders. Golden arm rings, on the other hand, are much more plentiful in Period III.

The rich female graves do not contain objects parallel to the "cheap" ones from the male graves of Period II. The highest status is demonstrated only by the occurrence of impressive ornaments and daggers with elaborate handles, which are of the same type as on the heaviest swords in the male graves. But the difference between wealthy and poor graves should not be overestimated when describing the present social structure. Half of the female relatives, and most of the children, of the men in the barrows were never given such a burial. And, wherever they were disposed of, their graves were never equipped with metal artifacts.

As shown by the distribution of the objects of authority, burial wealth and consequently also the burial type as such, reflect differences in status. The fixed nature of the status positions is revealed by those same objects and further supported by the fact that there seem to be no age distinctions between rich and poor graves. Finally also, the peaks in the histograms for the distribution of wealth are clearly due to the existence of certain status levels. We are observing a series of societies in which some social relations have taken a stratified form. However, perhaps, apart from the men — and only the men — of Zone 4, Period III, no clear-cut contrasts are observed; this must be due to the existence of a certain degree of mobility.

Though the relation of social stratification to population factors is our main theme, it should not be forgotten that a number of social positions refer to nonstratified dimensions of the society. In the present case we can point to differences in mortuary practices (e.g. the occurrence of a cist of stone, cremation, etc.) or to a number of artifacts in the grave equipment, such as firestroke flints, which come from the male graves only, and razors. All these traits are randomly distributed according to wealth.

8. POPULATION DENSITY AND SOCIAL STRATIFICATION: THE PROBLEM OF THE FEMALES

In using the amount of metal in the burials as an index of social stratification two major problems immediately appear. The first one refers to the sexes. Should males and females be considered together, or would it be more appropriate to concentrate on the men in measuring degrees of social stratification? The second problem at first seems to be a more "technical" one having to do with possible regional differences in the inclination, or the ability, to dispose costly artifacts with the dead. But actually, this question involves population variables in an attempt to estimate the capability of the zones to invest metal in the rituals. We shall now provisionally leave the first problem and instead concentrate on the group of "hoards and offerings" (mentioned in Section 2) in an attempt to solve the second difficulty.

The "hoards and offerings" occur almost exclusively in the eastern zones (1 to 3); and they generally contain the same types of object as the graves do, though, for instance, the coarse "work axes" are more plentiful in the hoards. The locations of the finds are often peatbogs or streams, but a number of hoards come from "dry land," and these latter finds are often thought of in terms of "trading depots" or depositories from times of unrest. Both interpretations, however, can be rejected as general explanations by referring to the geographical distribution, which remains constant over a period of 800 years (Periods I to III). The hoards from the peatbogs are commonly interpreted as "religious offerings," an interpretation supported, for example, by the find of the famous model of a "sun-chariot" in the bog at Trundholm on Zealand (Zone 2). Though this is the most plausible holistic explanation, it would be somewhat dangerous to extend it to cover all finds. What we can do, is to note that the eastern zones knew of a series of ritual actions, which took the form of the disposal of valuables. These actions have a strong economic overtone as they require a lot of metal to be carried out. Under this point of view it is very important to observe that there is a strong correlation (for the zones of Periods II to III) between population number and the total amount of bronze from both graves and "hoards and offerings." (1 G of gold is here given the previously mentioned value of 100 G bronze; see Section 7).

In the different zones the societies have made different choices as to the type and character of the rituals, but the amount of metal invested is always proportionally related to the size of the population and thus also to the general level of production. The greater the production, the more metal has been imported. The geographical position of the zones consequently has only little or no significance for the ability to invest metal in the graves, and the splendor of the burial of high-ranking persons is weakened exclusively by rival offerings in moors, ceremonies involving the destruction of property. The quantity of metal in the single hoard is normally considerable, and it would be natural to imagine that the rituals connected with the hoards were controlled by the high-ranking persons. It is noteworthy, too, that gold, which is practically never found in the hoards, is much more abundant, especially in Period III, in the western zones (4 and 5), where there are only graves. The import of the two metals is thus weighted as to the ritual investment.

We conclude that, due to the distribution of the hoards, the eastern graves are generally poorer than the western ones. This fact must influence the pattern or the degree of social stratification if measured by the division of wealth in the graves, and we should proceed with our investigation along these lines very carefully. The problem now to be handled is the relationship between the sexes in connection with the high status positions.

In section 7 we noted that it is the entire number of high-status burials, not the male graves alone, which seem to be proportional to the group of burials of lower status not recognizable in the archaeological data (see Section 5 and Figure 5). This observation is important because it hints at an otherwise unexpected interchangeability between male and female high-status positions. It should be remembered that it is not a question of male and female status in general; if that were the case, we would have expected to find twice as many female graves as we do. Incidentally, the prior view on the position of the woman is that she is more or less "equal" to the man, given the same sort of burial (Müller 1897: 400, 1909: 55). As in the case of the "social structure" it is hardly possible to comment upon the traditional notions; the premises are too different from the present ones.

There is no significant difference between zones in the ratio of male and female graves from Periods II and III as measured by chi-square tests. But in Period III the variation is greater than in Period II. In the later period the female graves of Zone 5 comprise only 30 percent of the male ones, while in Zone 3 they amount to 70 percent. On the peninsula of Djursland (on the eastern coast of Jutland, and within Zone 3) the female interments even outnumber the male ones twelve to ten. Generally, the female graves in Period II amount to 40 percent of the male ones, in Period III to 50 percent.

In Figure 9 the density of population, expressed in number of graves per 1,000 hectares, is plotted against the female-male index. This index is calculated by dividing the number of female burials by the corresponding number of male ones. On the diagram in Figure 10 the relationship is depicted between the population density and the index of invested metal in the female and male graves, the indication of respective status. This latter index is calculated by dividing the sum of bronze and gold from the female graves — giving I G gold the value of 100 G bronze — by the corresponding sum from the male graves. For both figures Zone 1, Period II is omitted for small number of observations, while the rest of the zones of Periods II and III, as previously, are grouped together. As expected, the two charts show the same picture stemming from a general correlation between number of graves and amount of metal. In both cases FEMALE STATUS VARIES SYSTEMATICALLY WITH POPULATION DENSITY, BEING HIGHEST IN THE DENSE AREAS. This result also accounts for the periodic rise in the percentage of females. The best correlation is seen in Figure 10, which, among other observations, confirms the value used for gold.

We might imagine that the status of the females was dependent exclusively on that of their male relatives. But illustrative enough, the promo-

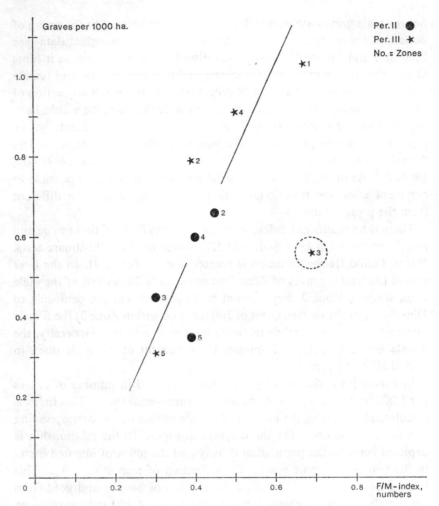

Figure 9. Relationship between population density and the female-male (F/M) index of the zones for Periods II and III. The population density is expressed in number of graves per 1,000 hectares; the F/M-index is calculated by dividing the number of female graves by the number of male graves. Zone 1, Period II is omitted for low number of observations. (See Figure 10.)

tion of the men of Zone 4, Period III did not result in a parallel rise of the women; the distribution of wealth in the female graves is identical for all zones. Incidentally, the same result is already hinted at by the notion of the interchangeability between male and female high status. Instead, the role of the high-status women in the functioning of the society is closely linked to the population density variable, which, moreover, is highly dependent on the quality of the farmed land. And it is just in the agri-

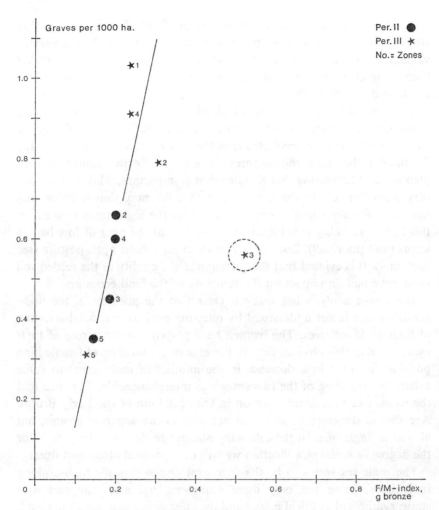

Figure 10.   Relationship between population density and the female-male (F/M) index of the zones for Periods II and III. The population density is expressed in number of graves per 1,000 hectares; the F/M-index is calculated by dividing the amount of bronze in the female graves — giving 1 G gold the value of 100 G bronze — by the amount of bronze in the male graves. Zone 1, Period II is omitted for low number of observations. (See Figure 9.)

cultural system that we may find an explanation of the variations in female status. The extra-systemic increase in population size in Zone 4 did not proportionally improve the status of the women. In Zone 3, Period III, however, female status reached a level far higher than predictable from the rest of the observations (Figures 9 and 10). This is especially due to the many women on the peninsula of Djursland, whose fertile soil was settled with the advent of Period III. Because of the Djursland settlement

Zone 3 shows the most marked improvement of soil of all zones in Period III (Figure 4). It is thus tempting to relate the role of the high-status women to activities carried out in connection with agriculture, rather than to intergroup regulations in general. A few speculations can be mentioned in further discussion of this proposition.

The nonsettled parts of eastern Jutland probably were once covered by woodland. An extension of the settled area would have caused a lot of cutting, and it is more probable that this work was done to enlarge the farmland rather than the pastures. It is especially in connection with planting and harvesting that female labor is important, while the women play a smaller role in the rearing of cattle. We may thus imagine that nontrivial female activities were regulated by the high-status women. In this line of thinking it is important to note that the area of low female status (and poor soil), Zone 5, is known to have been open pasture (see Section 4). It is evident that the variation in the quality of the settled soil must have had an impact on the structure of the land economy.

The above analysis has made it clear that the position of the high-status women is not understood by referring only to the social standing of their male relatives. The women have played a distinct role of their own. But it is also obvious that an increase in the number of female high positions resulted in a decrease in the number of male ones; to some extent, the standing of the two sexes was interchangeable. The men and the women of prominent position in the social life of the Early Bronze Age should therefore be analyzed not only as two separate groups, but also as a single one. In the following attempt to describe the pattern or the degree of social stratification we will thus proceed along two lines.

The male sex seems to be the dominant one among the high-ranking individuals, being not only more numerous, but also equipped with status symbols of political power and the most costly equipment in metal. To determine the degree of inequality among these men, the following rough measurement of the social stratification was applied. The number of graves with more than 400 G bronze was divided by the number of graves with less than 400 G bronze. This calculation was made for all zones of the Periods II and III, omitting Zone 1, Period II because of the small number of observations. In Figure 11 this degree of social stratification (among the high-ranking men) is plotted against the population density expressed in numbers of graves per 1,000 hectares within each zone/period. It is immediately noted that Zone 4, Period III falls apart from the rest of the observations, having a very high degree of stratification, as already indicated by the histogram in Figure 8. The other eight observations seem to divide into two groups, both showing — in spite of

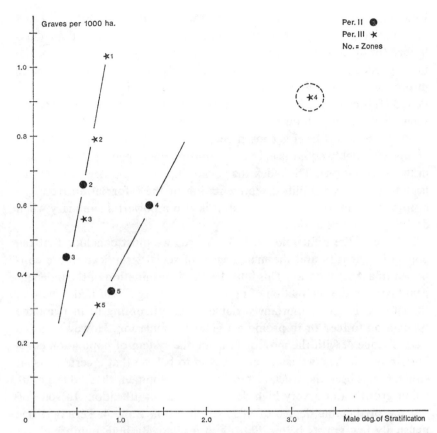

Figure 11. Relationship between population density and the male degree of social stratification of the zones for Periods II and III. The population density is expressed in number of graves per 1,000 hectares; the male degree of social stratification is calculated by dividing the number of graves with more than 400 G bronze — giving 1 G gold the value of 100 G bronze — by the number of graves below that level. Zone 1, Period II is omitted owing to a low number of observations. (See Figure 12.)

the very low number of observations — a very strong correlation between population density and male degree of social stratification, THE INEQUAL-ITY BEING HIGHER THE DENSER THE SETTLEMENTS.

It is perhaps hardly surprising that Zone 4, Period III does not conform with the general picture, being already divergent in having an unusually high population for the amount of barrels of hard corn. The rest of the zones/periods, however, show an almost identical type of variation, and yet they are distinct. The eastern zones (1 to 3) of the two periods have a relatively low degree of male social stratification, while the western zones (4 and 5) form a second group having a high one. Now, it is exactly the eastern zones in which the amount of metal was divided between the graves and the hoards, and we should in fact be astonished that relatively fewer graves in the east are equipped with more than 400 G bronze (or an equivalent amount of gold). The only condition is that the metal yielded in the hoards is "taken" from the different groups of males in proportion to their wealth. This prerequisite is fulfilled at least for Period II, because the homogeneity test mentioned in the previous section shows no significant difference between zones in the distribution of wealth. The 400 G level is chosen because it divides the graves into two groups of roughly equal size, thus minimizing the impact from anomalies in the distributions. The index that makes up the male degree of stratification is a very simplified representation of the information from the histograms; but, on the other hand, it is also a powerful summary when dealing with correlations.

In spite of the difficulties with the hoards we must conclude that the population density and the male degree of social stratification are connected in a systemic way. This impedes the determination of the independent factor in the interaction of population and organizational structure, the latter being an important variable when attempting to increase the production to feed or to promote a greater population. However, in the case of Zone 4, with the movement from one system of population equilibrium to another, we have some reason to believe that a certain social structure has been the crucial factor in the development that led to population growth and a very high degree of male stratification. In spite of just the predictable degree of male stratification Zone 4, Period II has unusually few graves below 200 G and a relatively high number above 600 G bronze. The more detailed pattern of distribution can — to some extent — be described as something in between the normal Period II pattern and the division of Zone 4, Period III. What we note is a greater distance between the high-ranking men and the men of low rank, whose burials are unknown to us — in other words, a more authoritarian relationship between men of high and low rank. Such a structure may strengthen the commands and demands of the top of the society and perhaps increase the production with a concomitant result of a greater population. It is worthwhile now to recall the establishment of population clusters, or "centers," in the Zone 4 of Period III; these have widened also the geographical distance between high and low.

This representation may have some dialectic value at a time when many archaeologists have become increasingly attached to the Boserup concept of population increase and decrease as the independent variable in economic and in social development (e.g. Smith 1972).

In measuring the degree of social stratification we will now include in the analysis the female high positions. A female degree of stratification is calculated for each zone/period except Zone 1, Period II, that has no female tombs. It is done by dividing the number of graves with more than 200 G bronze by the number of graves below that level; 1 G gold is also here given the same value as 100 G bronze. It is noted that the degree of female social stratification generally goes up with the population density expressed in number of graves per 1,000 hectares. However, the correlation is considerably poorer than the ones we have just treated in connection with the male degree of social stratification. And what is important too, the variation in degree of social stratification is relatively limited.

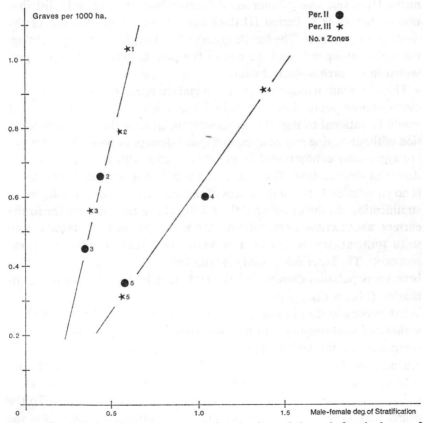

Figure 12. Relationship between population density and the male-female degree of social stratification of the zones for Periods II and III. The population density is expressed in number of graves per 1,000 hectares; the male-female degree of social stratification is calculated by dividing the number of graves with more than 400 G bronze — giving 1 G gold the value of 100 G bronze — by the number of graves below that level. (Zone 1, Period II is omitted owing to a low number of observations. See Figure 11.)

A more significant picture emerges when data on the two sexes are joined together, and the degree of social stratification is calculated as above, with 400 G bronze as the level of distinction. A plot of this degree of stratification against the population density, expressed in number of graves per 1,000 hectares, gives the same general pattern as Figure 11 (see also Figure 12). The eastern zones (1 to 3) — with Zone 1, Period II omitted due to paucity of observations — show, like the western zones (4 and 5), a strong correlation between degree of social stratification and population density, only at a lower level than the western zones. This, again, is due to the greater investment in the burial rituals in the west, where there are no hoards, as in the east, to compete for the "surplus" metal. However, a very important difference from the Figure 11 distribution is that Zone 4, Period III does not fall aside from the rest of the western observations. The female graves fill in the gap, so to say, between the high-ranking men and the rest of the population, which is unrepresented in the archaeological data.

This observation indicates that the social change in connection with the extrasystemic population growth in Zone 4 is relatively simple, and it would be rational to regard it as an attempt to raise the level of production without having any new technological devices at hand. The changes are apparently concentrated in the male sector with its unusually high degree of stratification. The female sector is in one way unaltered: there is no correlation between the status of the woman and the male degree of stratification. In the other way, the results above have demonstrated the current REGULATION BETWEEN NOT ONLY THE NUMBER OF FEMALE AND MALE HIGH STATUS POSITIONS, BUT ALSO THE RELATIVE RANK OF THESE POSITIONS. The latter relationship is reflected by the very good correlation between population density and the male-female degree of social stratification (Figure 12).

Extrasystemic rises in population size seem to be regulated by a more authoritarian arrangement of the male status, probably to strengthen the commands of the high-ranking men. This development is hardly surprising in dealing with societies which have a graded access to status and wealth. Observing, too, the distribution of weapons, we must note a clear concentration of these in the hands of the men of highest status. To the degree that physical force is important for the fulfilment of the ends of the society, this monopoly also is controlled by the social apex. But it should be remarked that the high-ranking men themselves execute this power, as no warriors are found who do not belong to the group of men of highest social standing. Also in this respect the Early Bronze Age society is of graded rather than of "class-ridden" nature.

In connection with the Zone 3, Period III notion of an unusually high status for women, we suggested that this was due to a marked improvement of the quality of the farmed land (due to an expansion), because no other remarkable differences were observable in the zone. We know, too, that the status of the women is correlated with the population density variable, which in turn is also dependent on the quality of land. We speculated that the status of the high-ranking women might have a connection with the stress on female labor in the subsistence sector. Parallel to this representation, we can now add that traditional male activities like cattle breeding and, to some extent, also fishing, are exactly those types of work into which Zone 4, Period III might have expanded to feed a larger population. A greater importance of these activities may in turn have promoted the high-ranking men in control of the work. However, this hypothesis can hardly be tested on the present data.

The discussion of the events in Zone 4, Period III has served to illustrate the fund of adaptive mechanisms with which the Early Bronze Age society controlled and regulated variations in its cultural systems. The high male stratification and the sharp and extrasystemic population growth in the aforementioned zone and period might be termed components of the "evolutionary potential" of the society. But even these deviations are coped with by the systems, and integrity is thereby retained. It is exactly systemic variability and continuity that we have demonstrated in this section.

9. CONCLUSION

The investigation terminates with the advent of the Late Bronze Age (Period IV), where materials found take on a somewhat different character, thus demanding further elaboration of the methods used. For instance, the more politically oriented display at the entombment gives way almost completely to the material investment in the rituals connected with the hoards. In the Early Bronze Age we have been restricted by the absence of information on the economic variables. But, in spite of the exclusive use of earlier data it has been possible to enlarge the knowledge of the population and social dimensions by applying a few simple quantitative methods. In doing so, we have noted especially the systemic variability in the cultural systems.

We have dealt with a series of societies with unequal distribution of status and wealth, two concepts which are shown to relate to each other. The population is divided into the high-status men and women who are buried in the barrows, and a larger group of "commoners" who are not. At least a part of the latter group is directly akin to the persons of high rank. This observation makes the division less sharp than it otherwise would be interpreted. Among the people of high status, great, but graded, distinctions in wealth are noted. A number of rich men are, besides their exquisite weaponry, in possession of staves, stools and badges, which are interpreted as symbols of fixed-status positions. The status of the high-ranking women is generally only half that of the corresponding men; yet, the number and the wealth of the women is inversely proportional to that of the men of a given zone and period. In this way the degree of social stratification for men AND women is kept rising with the population density in spite of a systematically declining number of males. The size of the populations is very well correlated with the agricultural quality of the different areas. However, in one area (Zone 4, Period III) the size of the population is far too great for the agricultural potential, and with the technology unaltered, food must have been acquired through an intensification of the subsistence base. In the social sector, the men of this zone/period show a very high degree of stratification, which has made the society a more authoritarian one. In Zone 4, Period III we also note a different settlement pattern. Two centers are created with a very high population density. The mutual position of the centers, which as the crow flies are less than forty kilometers away from each other, gives us, finally, some information about the maximum size of the social units in the Early Bronze Age.

The deviations in Zone 4, Period III reflect some of the factors, like population growth, which might have brought the Early Bronze Age society up the evolutionary ladder. But concerning, for instance, the population growth, we have some information that hints at a change in the social sector prior to the population deviation. Biological and environmental factors do not seem to have destroyed the cultural systems, and what the archaeologists call "change," i.e. changes in the styles of artifact, are not really systemic changes. And yet, also traditional archaeological units, like periods and cultural groups, may be fruitfully studied in terms of population and social variation.

It is tempting to fit the Early Bronze Age society into Service's "chiefdom" level of social integration (1971: 133ff.), but this identification does not really take us very far: we are dealing with a fairly homogeneous environment and a limited span of time for the societies in question. It would be of much greater importance to obtain quantitative data from anthropological studies of burials, offerings, etc., seen as reflectors of social and ecological structures of populations with a simple technology.

Though at present there are few such studies the investigation of "dead" societies would benefit very much from them.

REFERENCES

BOSERUP, E.
1965 *The conditions of agricultural growth: the economics of agrarian change under population pressure.* London.

BOYE, W.
1896 *Fund af Egekister fra Bronzealderen i Danmark.* Copenhagen. (French edition: *Trouvailles de cercueils en chêne de l'age du bronze en Danemark.* Published in Copenhagen.)

BROHOLM, H. C.
1944 *Danmarks Bronzealder II.* Copenhagen.

BRØNDSTED, J.
1958 *Danmarks oldtid II. Bronzealderen* (second edition). Copenhagen. (German edition: *Nordische Vorzeit 2. Bronzezeit in Dänemark.* Published in Neumünster, 1962).

HEICHELHEIM, F. M.
1958 *An ancient economic history I* (second edition). Leiden.

KUPER, H.
1947 *An African aristocracy: rank among the Swazi.* London.

LOMBORG, E.
1973 *Die Flintdolche Dänemarks, Studien über Chronologie und Kulturbeziehungen des südskandinavischen Spätneolithikums.* Nordiske Fortidsminder, Serie B-in quarto 1. Copenhagen.

MOBERG, C.-A.
1956 Till frågan om samhällsstrukturen i Norden under bronsåldern. *Fornvännen* 51:65–79.

MÜLLER, S.
1897 *Vor Oldtid.* Copenhagen. (German edition: *Nordische Altertumskunde nach Funden und Denkmäler aus Dänemark und Schleswig.* Published in Strassburg, 1897–1898.)
1909 *Bronzealderens Begyndelse og aeldre Udvikling i Danmark, efter de nyeste Fund.* Aarbøger for Nordisk Oldkyndighed og Historie. (French translation: *Début et première évolution de la civilisation du bronze en Danemark, d'après les découvertes les plus récentes.* Mémoires de la Société Royale des Antiquaires du Nord, Nouvelle Série 1908–1913).

RANDSBORG, K.
1968 Von Periode II zu III, Chronologische Studien über die ältere Bronzezeit Südskandinaviens und Norddeutschlands. *Acta Archaeologica* 39: 1–142.
1973 "Wealth and social structure as reflected in bronze age burials — a quantitative approach," in *The explanation of culture change: models in prehistory.* Edited by C. Renfrew, 565–570. London.

SERVICE, E. R.
   1971   *Primitive social organization: an evolutionary perspective* (second edition). New York.
SMITH, P. E. L.
   1972   Changes in population pressure in archaeological explanation. *World Archaeology* 4(1):5–18.

Paleoecology, Paleodemography and Health

J. LAWRENCE ANGEL

Population increase for the past several generations has become the ultimate threat against mankind, the threat behind war, urban blight, nuclear and other destructive horrors, wasting of the environment and fuel resources, and empty autocracies. Yet population increase is the usual measure of evolutionary success: for other life forms the upper limit of density of population is the inevitable negative feedback from lack of food, increase of (enemy) competitors, change in climate or soils, and lack of actual space in a particular ecologic niche. Plant populations show a sequence of successful species. Animals show fluctuating densities, especially in a predator-prey feedback balance, and even a drive for self-destructive migration (lemmings, bats) when crowding produces unbearable emotional stress. And as Malthus saw clearly, the same logistic limit is ultimately true for man too (Wrigley 1969). Man's cultural skill in creating his own living conditions has insulated him, but at the same time

I studied the skeletons discussed in this paper on eight field trips from 1937 to 1972 with support from Harvard traveling fellowships, J. S. Guggenheim and Wenner-Gren Foundations, National Institutes of Health (A-224), American Philosophical Society, and the Smithsonian Institution (Aleš Hrdlička Fund); with permission and encouragement of the Archaeological Services in Greece, Cyprus, and Turkey, of the Jefferson Medical College and University Museum in Philadelphia, of the American School of Classical Studies in Athens, of the British Archaeological Institute in Ankara, and of many archeologists, anthropologists, and administrators; and with active help also from several assistants and from my wife. I thank the following people for help in recent years: T. Blackburn, E. Bostanci, J. L. Caskey, S. Dietz, D. Ferembach, D. H. and L. W. French, M. Gough, H. Gurçay, R. and Y. Harper, K. Holland, T. W. Jacobsen, D. Johnson, J. S. Lea, M. Matthews, J. R. McCredie, M. J. Mellink, J. Mintzes, M. Önder, S. Payne, E. Protonotariou-Deïlakis, H. S. Robinson, R. J. and J. M. Rodden, R. Sando, T. L. Shear, Jr., L. Sternberg, T. D. Stewart, W. Taylor, R. Temizer, H. Thompson, C. K. Williams and J. Wiseman.

it erodes his broadening ecological niche and produces paradoxically this impasse: that health and long survival of mothers and children now produce an urban population avalanche (Dubos 1965) which can bury all of us, but which may also return our survivors to a prehistoric level of living. Submission to cultural and ecological destruction might seem the "natural" mode of limiting our too great evolutionary success. But in spite of excesses, our civilization's themes, capitalist and communist alike, include a flexible ingenuity in response to challenge. We do not intend to let our problems bury us. To learn from past experience we must ask if anything like the present population avalanche has happened before. It has happened at least twice. First, at the very end of the Upper Paleolithic period, the grassland game herds of bison, horse, cattle, mammoth, and reindeer allowed a great efflorescence, then suddenly began to decline under the combined pressures of human overkill and rapid environmental fluctuations ending with spread of Boreal forests at the Pleistocene-Recent transition from about 12,000 to 7500 B.C. (Butzer 1971). Second, a population avalanche preceded the urban population loss (after soil destruction and epidemics) in the collapse of the ancient Mediterranean (imperial Roman) culture during the first millennium A.D. There have been many other sharp local rises and drops in population density — for example, in the late second millennium B.C. in Greece (Angel 1972a) and in late Han empire times (second century A.D.) in China (Goodrich 1963: 44–114) — and fluctuation is frequent. In each case the ultimate reaction is a strong revival, with a resynthesis of culture based on new discoveries and inventions, often made during the times of disturbance.

The ecological variables involved are geographic barriers; climate; sea levels and hydrography; soils, food plants, and trace minerals; and animals for meat protein. The major demographic and health variables are female longevity, reproductive capacity (parity or fecundity and also fertility), survival of children to adulthood, disease-carrying capacity, and available physical and psychological energy. Fetal loss and infant deaths are not very important in terms of health, though they limit reproductive capacity chronologically and tax energy. Actual disease varies greatly as a limiting factor unless it directly restricts fecundity (cf. the malarias, syphilis) or causes early death (cf. tuberculosis, plague): a truly healthy population can carry a big load of minor and chronic disease. Yet child disease and malnutrition can limit growth and warp the pelvis, so that stature and pelvic inlet index are good indicators (Nicholson 1945) of child growth conditions; pelvic flattening can also limit average parity by causing death of newborn and mother. In addition, for psychological reasons overpopulation limits fecundity. All of these are secondary negative feedback forces.

The samples for data on these biological variables for fourteen successive culture periods from Upper Paleolithic to modern times mainly in the Eastern Mediterranean are 2,200 skeletons or skulls from sites mostly in the circum-Isthmian area of Greece. I include other regions for certain periods: all of Eurafrica for Upper Paleolithic and Mesolithic; Macedonia for Early and Late Neolithic and Classic; Kephallenia for Early Iron Age; Leukas and Acarnania for Late Neolithic; Messenia for Late Bronze; Laconia for Middle and Late Bronze and Roman; Kea for Late Neolithic; Lycia for Early Bronze, and the Konya Plain for Early Neolithic. In general, conditions of preservation are poor to medium: obviously poor in terra rossa soils and better in more sandy and well-drained soils (for example at Lerna [Angel 1971a]), but even there very much poorer than in Midwest or Southwest United States Indian cemeteries. Burial customs greatly influence the completeness of skeletons preserved, the age brackets sampled, and of course the amount of decay. Mesolithic and Neolithic burials in actual living areas in Franchthi Cave (Jacobsen 1969), Nea Nikomedeia (Rodden 1965), Lerna (Caskey 1956, 1957), and Çatal Hüyük (Mellaart 1967) include complete and careful interments, scattered human bones apparently resulting from disturbance (sometimes mixed with animal bones and rarely burnt or partly changed by heat), and occasional secondary burials. Early Bronze Age burials in Greece (Mylonas 1959) and Late Neolithic burials at Kephala on Kea (Caskey 1966) are multiple secondary burials in stone cists and obviously much disturbed, in some contrast to Early Bronze Age family burials in pithoi under stone circle markers at Karatas in Lycia (Mellink 1964–1970, especially 1969), where individuals are usually distinct and a little better preserved; in all these groups infants seem relatively too uncommon, and I suspect that unnamed (newborn or fetal) individuals were usually not buried. This contrasts with the Greek Middle Bronze cemeteries, where families including infants are found around or under their houses (Angel 1971a; Caskey 1954–1959), and the sample for demography and health is unbiased. This is not true in Late Bronze Age chamber tombs, where each new burial tends to disturb earlier ones. The stone cists and tile graves of Early Iron Age and Classic to Hellenistic times give good sampling of all but infants except where (as at Olynthus [Robinson 1942]) infants are in amphorae and demographic counts are possible still. Roman period columbaria and other secondary burials do not give good preservation of bones, and Byzantine family and mass graves are more frustrating. Finally, the church crypt bone piles of Baroque to modern times select against juveniles. Under most of these circumstances selection by the excavator is almost unavoidable because in general stronger and more massive bones tend to resist decay longer than others.

ECOLOGY

The Eastern Mediterranean setting for the change from hunting to farming to civilization owes to continental drift and vulcanism (Dewey 1972) its many islands, long and varied coastlines, protected harbors around the unifying sea, and mountain barriers around small demesnes of rich but stony soil (Angel 1971a and 1946 quoting many sources including Stéphanos 1884; Maull 1922; Jardé 1925; Butzer 1965, 1971). The sinking, overriding, and tilting of old crystalline blocks (parts of Hellenic, Turkish, and Arabian plates) under curving festoons of new limestone mountains pushed up mostly in Oligocene and later times between the Alps, Caucasus, and Pamirs produced the irregular variety of the Balkans, Greece, the Aegean area, Anatolia, and the Levant, accompanied by the volcanic activity and earthquakes associated with subduction and compression stress zones of continental drift (Dewey 1972). The climate is Mediterranean with winter rains and no distinct autumn. Soils range from rocky mountain slopes with podsolic soils under conifers, via the widespread Pleistocene fossil terra rossa soils in karst basins or washed down into sea plains, some arid steppe soils in Anatolia, some rendzina soils, flysch, and marls to the volcanic soils rich for grapevines and olives, and finally to the broader lower valleys and sea plains filled with stony and calcareous silt (only occasionally acid terra rossa) usable for cereals — wheat, barley — or grassland for cattle and horses. The formation of silt in the lower valleys and deltas at the shoreline obviously has depended on a postglacial rise in sea level, as well as on precipitation, the rising mountain frost line, vegetation, and the water table. There have been two major phases of eustatic rise in sea level from worldwide melting of glacial ice, with reversals, fluctuations, and of course local sinking or uplift of land produced by vulcanism (as in the general tilt of the island of Crete, where nine meters of western uplift and two meters of eastern submergence hinge on the Rethymno region [Flemming 1972]) which sometimes blur the overall eustatic changes. Both sequences of rising and high sea levels involved silting, with soil renewal in valleys extremely important in relation to farming, soil minerals, and diet (Raikes 1967; Vita-Finzi 1969), and formation of coastal and other marshes critical for anopheline mosquitos, malarias, and other diseases.

The first and greater rise in sea level was during the Boreal climatic period (mid-eighth millennium to about 6000 B.C.) when the 3°C. post-glacial warming saw sea level completing its 100-meter rise above the Würm II glacial low point to a level about two meters higher than today's. This level continued into the warm but moister Atlantic phase, favoring the Neolithic population overflow in the Eastern Mediterranean and through Europe. Then came the drier Sub-Boreal phase (3000–400 B.C.) of lowering sea levels responding to slight glacial readvance, with reduction of marshes and river cutting during Bronze Age to Classical times. There followed the generally wetter Sub-Atlantic climate phase, with its later Byzantine drier warming and one or more episodes of silting as sea levels rose and marshes spread (Vita-Finzi 1969) up to the time of the Little Ice Age of the seventeenth to nineteenth centuries A.D. (Denton and Porter 1970) from which we are emerging. As a result, most Mycenaean and Classical coastal sites and harbors are a meter or more below modern sea level; we must, however, always remember the added effect of local volcanic forces. I think that the hydrographic and coastline changes since Mesolithic times (ninth and eighth millennia B.C.) have been more important than climatic fluctuations in temperature or even in rainfall because the extent of salt or fresh marshes and of lakes and running streams provides one control over the mosquitos *Anopheles sacharovi* and *Anopheles superpictus*, which are vectors for malarial plasmodia (the other control, of course is the density of human populations [cf. Cockburn 1967]), and because trade, cultural exchange, and unity and movements of people depend much more on sea than land routes in this ecological setting.

East Mediterranean climate has a long and rainless summer when evergreens, bulbs, and other plants estivate or wither and people use cisterns and springs for water. Then comes a rainy season from October to March, when 75 to 95 percent of the rain and snow falls, and temperature is like a New England autumn with occasional cold spells (9–12°C.) except in the snowy and more continental (0°C.) Balkan and Anatolian uplands (Butzer 1965: Figure 3). After the late winter gorgeous bloom of wildflowers, the spring growing season lasts through May, with a temperature rise to 20° and finally 25° C. Raising crops depends critically on rainfall, not just on temperature. With west winds, rain varies sharply from 80 to 130 centimeters annually in the western mountains of Greece down to 35 to 50 centimeters in the Aegean (Maull 1922) and inland Anatolia; it goes below 30 centimeters only in the desert zone to the south, where rivers supply the moisture. The limited cultivable area (only 20 to 25 percent of the area, even with terracing), mainly the 100-kilometer deep coastal strip, also restricts crops. The contrast between the long rainless summer and the wet winter and growing season allows inadequate replacement of minerals lost to crops, especially phosphoric acid, nitrogen, and potassium. Fallowing, manuring, plowing-in of legumes, and burning-over have to be fairly frequent, therefore, and with the stony, lime-rich soil even cultivation with the ard or scratch-plow allows eventual loss of minerals, especially potassium (Angel 1971a, quoting Dorigny 1908; Jardé 1925; Michell 1940). Hence cash crops like olives, grapes, or other fruit tend to become more important than barley or wheat, and in times of full population density grain must be imported, typically from the Ukraine and North Africa.

In the Upper Paleolithic period of relatively intense cold, hunting populations occupied caves (and unexcavated open campsites) in valleys and along coasts (Petralona, Louros valley, Copaic basin, Kaki Skala, Franchthi, Kara In, Beldibi, Ksar Akil, Mount Carmel, Zarzi, Karim Shahir, Hotu) in cold temperate woodland, avoiding the partly glaciated high mountains and plateaus. The great ungulate herds of the steppe and tundra country were not available, but these hunters could eat deer (fallow, red, and roe), wild cattle and pig, and wild ass *(Equus hydruntinus)*; in western Asia there were wild sheep and goat, brown bear, wolf, fox, hyena, leopard, lion, various smaller animals (Jacobsen 1969; Butzer 1965), and such vital vegetable foods as pistachio, hazel, and other nuts, fruits and various wild grains. The warm Alleröd phase at the end of the Upper Paleolithic in the tenth millennium B.C. and especially the immediately postglacial pre-Boreal Mesolithic warming that started before the eighth millennium helped to produce a great growth and spread of woodland with a slight change in fauna making red deer, pig, and cattle predominant. This was the basic drought-resistant evergreen and coniferous woodland that lasted through the Bronze Age until men destroyed it. The Pleistocene coniferous mountain forest moved higher and warm-temperate juniper, black pine, evergreen oak, and other hard-woods displaced it in the mountains. At altitudes below 900 meters ever-green oaks predominated, with umbrella and maritime pines and wild olives, and occasional meadows, marshes, and rocky areas covered with evergreen scrub or maquis. This included heather, myrtle, rhododendron, pistachio, bulk plants like asphodel and amaryllis, poppies, anemones, and wild grasses (Maull 1922: 32–42; Butzer 1965: 9, 1971: 472–540). Mesolithic hunters were handicapped by this forest and by the postglacial spread of malarias (cf. Angel 1966, 1971b: 77–79; Bruce-Chwatt 1965), certainly including the new and relatively fatal falciparum form. Local isolation of sites (e.g. Franchthi, Beldibi, Wadi-en-Natuf, Jericho), overhunting, and cultural differences may temporarily have been as great as in Europe and North Africa, but the decline in population may have been less (cf. Butzer 1971: 536–537) because the original Upper Paleolithic population, unsupported by steppe game herds, was probably less dense. Then, during the eighth millennium B.C., the people developed boats for coastal sea trade (Weinberg 1965) as well as for fishing (Jacobsen 1969), apparently in part because of demand for obsidian rather than flint for blades for the new composite tools using microliths. Obsidian came from Armenia, the Hasan mountains east of Çatal Hüyük on the Konya plain, and the Aegean island of Melos.

Jacobs (1969) makes an imaginative case for regular trade, based on easily fortifiable camp-towns with secure food supply, as the key motive for the very rapid spread in postglacial climate of newly invented farming in the East Mediterranean from the late eighth through the seventh millennium B.C., from Tell Mureybat and Jericho west to Çatal Hüyük, Hacilar, Argissa, Nea Nikomedeia, Franchthi, Lerna, and south to Egypt. The actual experimenting and invention of agriculture had begun a little further east among separate groups of latest Paleolithic hunters on the edge of and in the highlands. Reed (1960) suggests that some of them had started domestication of sheep and goats by winter feeding and its selective effects. The ancestral grain crop plants are of highland origin: Helbaek (1960) and Harlan and Zohary (1966) show wild barley stretching east as far as Turkestan and wild wheats in the same area, with ancestral einkorn *(Triticum aegilopoides)* northwest into Thrace. Trees from the edge of the highlands such as pistachio, apple, almond, and flame oak also were domesticated early. The twin processes of domestication of animals and of plants were complex, although in some ways culturally predetermined (Flannery 1965) as an outgrowth of a tradition of maximizing all environmental resources during a time (9000 to 7000 B.C.) when better climate allowed hunters to camp in highland country in a more permanent fashion that was good for trade in both foodstuffs (as between Suberde and the Konya plain circa 6500 B.C. [Perkins and Daly 1968]) and raw materials. Trial plantings certainly had begun earlier, whenever the relatively poor (compared to steppe-area hunters) and quite diverse groups of hunters in the Near East were pressed for meat supply; in the few millennia before 7000 B.C., grain raising was normal in some places, as indicated by silica polish on Mesolithic or proto-Neolithic sickle blades, and had produced six-row barley, emmer, and einkorn. In other areas, trees, and in yet others sheep, goat, pig, and then cattle, were domesticated.

One important ecological point is that the extra Boreal and Atlantic period warmth of perhaps 1°C. over today allowed the spread of grain and other crops to river basin and other environments. Second, by facilitating the spread of woodland this same climate forced proto-Neolithic people to plant and to settle where soft soil free of trees was available — near rivers or on the edges of lakes and marshes within range of anopheline mosquitos. Third, the cultural diversity in different specialties of domestication and hunting promoted trade, and with the population overflow as farming advanced also promoted hybridization of man and of his animals (Angel 1971a, 1972a), as in the diversity of origins of sheep selected for wool production. Fourth, a new feedback was starting: by Early and Later Neolithic times the digging stick, then hoe farming and inexpert irrigation saw the beginning of cultural destruction of land added to the drain on game animals.

During the whole rise of civilization from 6000 to 600 B.C., population pressures rose steadily and the overuse of soils, of grassland, and then (after the invention of stone and later bronze axes, adzes, and other tools) of forests increased; farming practice improved only slowly, and such endemic diseases of crowded settlement as the malarias, hookworm, amoebiasis, and other dysenteries could spread. On the other hand, the early beginning of fallowing (Clark 1952), the development by the third millennium B.C. of the ox-drawn scratch-plow and of new crops such as grapes and olives (Hopf 1962), and the development by the Late Bronze Age of totally improved farming methods (with manuring, alkaline ash from burning-over, irrigation, and proper drainage [cf. Seymour 1908]) checked the ecological deterioration in part and laid down the dietary and land base for city-state urbanism. Mycenaean Greeks successfully drained such marshy areas as the Copaic basin and still had available trees of ship-mast size, as seen in the timber supports of the siege-fountain staircase descending 30 meters down through the rock of the Athenian ancropolis (Broneer 1939). But Plato describes Attica as skeletally bare, perhaps as treeless as after World War II. Local timber went not only for trading ships and the navy but also for balks and wagons for the new silver mines at Laureion — the military and economic force that kept Europe free in 490 and 480 B.C. — not to mention industrial and domestic charcoal use. Importation of grain helped to conserve soil temporarily, as did new dietary protein such as hen's and duck's eggs and more fish (Michell 1940), so that human diet stayed good well into Hellenistic times. But Gejvall (1969) observes that cattle and domestic animals were diminishing in size from Early Bronze to Roman times.

By imperial Roman times the population was tending to concentrate in mob cities and hence overall density was clearly diminishing (though probably still above the modern level of more than thirty per square kilometer for the whole area). Neither grain imports nor slave farms (latifundia) could provide enough food, and Roman trade balance was declining. Increasing use of wood and overgrazing by the sheep and goats that were now tending to replace cattle contributed to increasing erosion, with massive silting in valleys, later accelerated by the rise in sea level (Vita-Finzi 1969). Marsh control became more difficult, therefore, and increasing malaria weakened the fecundity of the already diminished rural population and helped to reduce its ability to recover from three massive epidemics in the second to fourth centuries A.D., culminating in true plague from A.D. 531 (under Justinian) until 590, with loss of as much as half the population and as great social change and demoralization as during the later Black Death (Ackerknecht 1965: 7–22). Slaves were especially affected and people deserted villages and areas of countryside. The culture lacked vitality: people could not rebuild temples, cities, or sometimes even aqueducts that earthquakes had thrown down (as at Olympia or Antioch). Science was no help after the burning of the library and then the museum at Alexandria. Warfare also continued to strain the people and environment, and the total background — ecological, political, and military — for the rise of Christianity and then of Islam was bleak.

The vitality of the new Christian Byzantine culture is amazing: it could build domed churches through most of the towns which had Hellenistic theaters and Roman baths (including the miraculous domed basilica of Santa Sophia in Constantinople) and hold an empire in spite of a chaos of wars and invasions: Goths, Huns, Avars, Slavs, Viking Russians, Albanians, Muslim Arabs, then Seljuk Turks, and Aragonese and Venetian Crusaders. Cities and monasteries had to become small and defensible (except Constantinople). It was the survival of the Bronze Age type of village farming that saved the culture and allowed the ninth to eleventh century Byzantine cultural revival during the drier climatic interval mentioned above (Denton and Porter 1970), because the rich Byzantine families tied down the small farmer with heavy taxes plus laws prohibiting his travel. But although silting valleys were beginning to restore soil minerals, there was no recovery in land use.

During and after the great plague pandemic in the fourteenth century A.D., the Osmanli Turks conquered Anatolia and the Balkans, took Constantinople in 1453 (delayed slightly by Mongol conquests under Timur reaching Ankara in 1402), and by 1517 had conquered Greece and the Crusader-Arab-held Levant and North Africa. During the sixteenth-century golden age of the Ottoman Empire, farmers freed from the hated

Byzantine taxes grew more rice (first introduced in Roman times) to supplement bread, eggs, and herbs; more fishing was possible to supplement rare goat meat and mutton, while the new sugar cane from Southeast Asia added calories, and coffee and tea eventually replaced wine as a stimulant. But except for tobacco, the Ottomans failed to adopt the New World crops, failed to innovate in land use or in preventing a new slavery, partly of Africans, and failed to compete economically with a Western Europe stimulated by new currencies of New World silver and gold. The climate became cooler and somewhat wetter; marshes remained undrained, and malaria increased and remained endemic until DDT in the 1940's wiped out anophelines. Plague was also endemic until 1845 (Ackerknecht 1965: 7–22). Farming also remained on a Bronze Age level through the Romantic revival and up to modern times.

This is the ecological background with its feedback keys with which I shall try to relate the changes in demography and health shown in a total sample of 2,200 skeletons from the East Mediterranean and 310 from Upper Paleolithic and Mesolithic sites in the Old World.

DEMOGRAPHY AND HEALTH

As mentioned earlier and shown in Table 1 between pages (182 and 183), the criteria available for demography are in Acsádi and Nemeskéri (1970) and Angel (1969a, 1971a, 1972a):

1.   Adult longevity of each sex, but especially of females, from age fifteen upward, as determined by the usual criteria of age and sex (Todd 1920, 1921; McKern and Stewart 1957; Krogman 1962; Stewart 1968; Gilbert and McKern 1973);

2.   Number of births per female pelvis as guessed from the degree of pit formation, grooving, and distortion on the posterior or visceral surface of the pubic symphysis resulting from stretching and reattachment of ligaments and from tears or bruises [hematomas] (cf. Putschar 1931; Angel 1969a, 1971b; Stewart 1970; Gilbert and McKern 1973);

3.   Number of juvenile deaths, i.e. infants plus children in the cemetery sample, per female;

4.   Survivors per female each generation as determined by subtracting juvenile deaths from births; death ratio or proportion of infant and of child deaths to adult deaths taken as ten, done in order to minimize the distorting effect of sampling errors of infant deaths (from cultural burial practice as well as from archaeological selection);

5.   Population density per square kilometer as determined (Angel 1972a)

from a number of archaeological sites (McDonald and Simpson 1969; Weinberg 1965), assuming average town populations of 1,000 in Early Neolithic, 1,500 in Late Neolithic, 2,000 in Early Bronze, 2,500 in Middle Bronze, 3,000 in Late Bronze, 2,500 in Early Iron, and 4,000 in Classical times, from census and historical data (Gomme 1933; Sargent 1924; Stéphanos 1884) and city areas (Westfall 1968);

6.   Population composition mean variability as determined from Howells' sigma ratio (1941) based on relatively uncorrelated characters (horizontal circumference, auricular-vertex height, chin height, minimum jaw ramus breadth, face profile angle, cranial breadth-length index, fronto-parietal index, upper facial index, and nasal index).

Man is no exception to the rule that all animals carry a large variety of parasites, from viruses, bacteria, various protozoans, and metazoan internal worms and fungi, to such actual ectoparasites as lice, leeches, ticks, and many other arthropods. Some of these, for example in the bacterial flora of the intestine, are so commensally adjusted to man that they are necessary for his normal survival. Others cause active destructive disease and sometimes death when they invade man's tissues in too great numbers. Most are relatively neutral hangers-on. We also need adequate amounts of proteins, fat, leafy vegetables, starchy carbohydrates, and vitamins or their precursors as well as proper cellular regulation and handling of these foods in order to grow and have enough energy for mature life. Disease occurs when for some reason there is a breakdown either of these anabolic and regulatory processes or of defensive reaction (for example, the excess formation of proper antibodies). Health, therefore, is the state of relative balance between constructive and destructive forces. It is never a lack of disease parasites, because such a state in biological terms is virtually impossible. Some diseases, like cancer, tuberculosis, gout, or rickets, leave marks on the skeleton; others do not. But all disease affects bone to some degree when it interferes with growth, shortens life, or prevents implantation or growth of an embryo or fetus. Hence the prime indicators of health are: first, adult longevity for both sexes; second, parity or fecundity at the birth rather than the conception level; and third, the healthy survival of children. These are necessarily part of the demographic picture already sketched.

I take age fifteen as the biosocial divider between childhood and adulthood (with "adolescence" on each side of this divider) because, with menarche very soon after the thirteenth birthday, as seems likely for prehistoric as well as ancient times (Amundsen and Diers 1969), fifteen is the earliest likely time for conception, allowing for adolescent sterility. The period between the ages of fifteen and twenty is the prime time for marriage and first childbearing. Male maturation is at least two years slower. Health in this five-year period is critical for both sexes and this is the time when female deaths first exceed male deaths (Angel 1969a, b, 1971a). The length of a generation is the average age at female marriage plus one half of the childbearing period. Whether average age at death for adult females is thirty to thirty-two, as in the Bronze Age (Table 1), or thirty-six to thirty-seven, as in the historical period (with marriage at seventeen to eighteen, the generation length is either slightly under or slightly over twenty-five years. More children are born in the first half than in the second half of the childbearing period, so that it is the age span from fifteen to twenty-five that which is critical for female health and fecundity.

Quite direct indices of nutritional health are stature, as derived from long bone lengths by the Trotter (1958) formulas, and depth index (Anteroposterior/Tranverse diameter) of the true pelvis inlet or brim. The former clearly reflects childhood nutrition as well as genetic background and the latter is extremely responsive to overall nutrition and child health (as seen in the effect of World War I in lowering this index by about four units in those who were young children in England between 1915 and 1918 [Nicholson 1945] and in the American upper to lower "class" difference [Greulich and Thoms 1938]). The ancient to modern difference is at least ten units, and the Industrial Revolution to modern change is apparently greater still. Because the pelvis transmits body weight to the femur heads by a curved arch (sacrum and ilia) whose tendency to spread apart under pressure is resisted only by the anteroinferior arch of the pubic bone, pelvic depth is the diameter reduced if pelvic bone growth is hindered by poor nutrition in childhood. This in turn can decrease the effective size of the birth canal: extra large fetuses will be more likely to die from birth trauma and also to endanger their mothers if this A-P diameter drops below ten centimeters. Hypoplastic or growth-arrest lines in tooth enamel can occur from any stress or insult to the enamel organ as it forms the crown of a growing tooth. This can be local, but if similar lines ring the crowns of all teeth at a given time of formation, the inference of a specific illness, stress, or starvation is fairly sound (Clement 1963), although there is individual difference in response. Harris lines of growth arrest in diaphysial bone are similar indicators, except that remodeling can remove them.

The occurrence of actual dental lesions in adulthood is a less direct indicator of stress when the teeth were forming, though a diet inadequate in protein may predispose to inadequate enamel and dentine (Sognnaes 1956), and traces of dietary selenium and fluoride apparently have opposite effects — weakening versus hardening — on tooth enamel in relation to cariogenic mouth conditions and bacteria (Keyes 1969). Loss of teeth can be caused either by periodontal disease and the resulting tissue inflammation and alveolar bone atrophy or by periapical abscess resulting from bacteria reaching the tip of a tooth root through caries and infected dental pulp. I include both types of dental disease in the lesions listed in Table 1, and I show these as the actual number of teeth or dental spaces affected per mouth.

For the Eastern Mediterranean the most interesting and probably also the most handicapping, though not the most lethal, disease spectrum has been the malarias and especially falciparum malaria (Jones 1907; Acker-knecht 1965) endemic in lowland and marshy areas until use of DDT wiped out anophelines at the end of World War II. Falciparum malaria in particular allowed selective survival of those children heterozygous for one of several abnormal hemoglobins — thalassemia, sicklemia, and favism or G6PD deficiency — which through increased red cell cytoplasm viscosity (cf. Moulder 1962) or a similar mechanism prevented amoeboid entrance of *Plasmodium falciparum* sporozoites and thus protected young children until their reticulo-endothelial systems had time to develop antibodies (cf. Allison 1964). Because in a sufficiently malarious environ-ment the homozygous normal children will very often die of falciparum malaria and those homozygous for an abnormal hemoglobin will die of the resulting hemolytic anemia, the situation produces the best known of the balanced polymorphisms and may have a considerable micro-evolutionary effect. In children thalassemia and sicklemia cause enlarge-ment of marrow space of long bones (really striking only in homozygous thalassemia) and hyperostosis of the skull diploë almost always combined with porosity and then thinning of the outer table of the vault and roofs of the orbits (Moseley 1965; Caffey 1937). This porotic hyperostosis occurs in slight to pronounced degree in adults and children from Mesolithic times onward (Angel 1966, 1971a) and tends to confirm the inference of malariologists that the falciparum species of plasmodium is a recent mutant form, perhaps appearing first in Paleolithic times (cf. Bruce-Chwatt 1965), whether first in the Near East or Mediterranean being uncertain.

Table 1 suggests a real depression of health as well as a decrease in population density following the relatively high point of the Upper Paleolithic. The decreases in stature and in longevity are especially striking. Although there may have been some temporary dietary cutback in the Eastern Mediterranean with the forest spread and change in fauna until fishing began, I suspect that malaria and other diseases were more important factors, resulting from lessened mobility and the start of the tendency to overuse a given campsite. In Early Neolithic times, with real settlement in fixed villages and trading towns supported by a cereal diet, there was some recovery, even though the meat ration per person was probably one-fifth or one-tenth what it had been in the Upper Paleolithic (Angel 1971b), because of the twentyfold increase in population made possible by the added year of female life span (five years over the Mesolithic level) and a considerable increase in fertility. Male longevity shows virtually no increase over the Upper Paleolithic level until after 2,000 B.C., perhaps because the adaptation to endemic malaria (produced by larger, fixed populations living near rivers or marshes in areas available to anopheline mosquitos) put stress on adults as well as children, especially at the beginning when the frequency of anemia from abnormal hemoglobins was rising. The key cultural change which affected the two sexes differently was the shift to permanent houses: the males still had to go out hunting and trading (cf. Mellaart 1967) and probably did more of the new farm work than the women, especially if women now became as socially dominant as seems indicated by shrines and figurines at Çatal Hüyük; the women had the opportunity for less mobile lives and in particular were no longer forced to trek between camps while pregnant. Stature recovers about four centimeters, as expected, but pelvic depth apparently decreases and dental lesions increase, perhaps because of the increased ratio of carbohydrate to protein.

During the three millennia of the rest of the Neolithic and Early Bronze Age, stature and fertility both decline somewhat and longevity does not increase, presumably because population density tends to put pressure on the food supply; the relative amount of meat decreased as the supply of wild game dropped (Gejvall 1969), probably from overhunting. Improvements in farming as well as the slow beginning of a drop in sea level tended to reduce marshes and breeding places for anopheline mosquitos by the third millennium, and there was probably a decrease in malaria and thalassemia, though less clear-cut than appears in Table 1 because the Neolithic sample includes a majority from Kephala (a Latest Neolithic site on a rocky headland of the island of Kea near Attica where anophelines are virtually impossible) and the Early Bronze Age sample, in addition to the Greek coastal sites (Corinth and Aghios Kosmas), includes a majority from Karatas in the Elmali plain of Lycia, over fifteen kilometers from a possible marsh or lake. At this time population increase may have slowed temporarily because of the first encounters with overpopulation: there are signs of hostilities in repeated walling of towns and strongholds (as at Troy, Chalandriani, and Lerna) and in parry fractures and a skull split open by a battle-ax (Angel 1968a), and the second half of the third millennium B.C. is the time of movements of Indo-European-speaking intruders from the steppe country, perhaps Kazakhstan, westward into Anatolia, Greece, the Balkans, and then Europe.

After 2000 B.C., in the Middle Bronze Age, there is a definite improvement in health, though porotic hyperostosis continues and analysis of the cemetery at Lerna indicates that the usual microevolutionary effect of relative fertility includes slight selection favoring porotic hyperostosis and facial linearity. Certainly the incredible heterogeneity occurring as a direct result of migration and trade favors microevolutionary change. Stature in Greece probably increased slightly, for the Early Bronze Karatas, stature dominant in Table 1 is one or two centimeters above that indicated by the small Greek sample. But dental health now deteriorates quite sharply. Why? Can it be from more fruit, such as grapes, and more cereals? In striking contrast the aristocrats or rulers in the Middle Bronze Age are six centimeters taller than ordinary people and have very much better teeth, although their life span is no greater and they have the same amazing diversity of genetic trends. Apparently they consumed much more meat, as indicated by Homeric tradition in the next millennium (Seymour 1908) and by gallstones in at least one of them (this might also suggest more wine drunk). Perhaps they more often died from violence, though only one has a trephined head wound (Angel 1971a), and this should not apply to the women (queens?), where there is a hint of greater longevity and possibly greater fertility (however, we need a larger sample to determine this). Fertility in general has risen, apparently because a year added to the female life span means on the average one more birth per woman. The increasing population shown by the archaeological and demographic evidence in inland as well as coastal sites (McDonald and Simpson 1969; Angel 1971a, 1972a) now became large enough to support epidemic diseases (cf. Cockburn 1967), especially those of childhood, which the sudden increase in incidence of hypoplastic growth-arrest lines in tooth enamel indicates. The rise in number of infant deaths and failure of child deaths to decrease probably also reflects infections added to endemic malaria.

There are three really striking interactions of ecology, demography, and health extending through the Late Bronze Age or Mycenaean period. First, the lower sea level plus increasing success in drainage of marshes apparently steadily reduced anophelines and malaria, as indicated by a straight-line drop in porotic hyperostosis actually down to Classical times (i.e. a drop in frequency of abnormal hemoglobins). This in turn allowed longer lives for women and slightly greater parity and fertility, which in turn allowed the (perhaps expected) logarithmically straight-line population density increase (Angel 1972a), leading to eventual inevitable overpopulation at the literate "urban" level and then to overseas expansion. Second, with adjustment to childhood diseases the child death ratio decreased, a trend continuing from the Middle Bronze high of five children to ten adults to the Classical period low of three children to ten adults; this is the key cause of increasing fertility. Third, the increasing populations promoted continuing hybridization and cultural mixture among pre-Hellenes; various groups of Hellenes, Minoans, Lydians, Balkan peoples (Illyrians?), Levantines, and Cypriotes; and Aegean islanders. As a result, the Mycenaean norm is a panmixia with much lower, in fact normal, variability and heterogeneity. This mixture is the source of the healthy and vigorous reactions of the Mycenaean Greek peoples. But health is not complete by any means. There is no improvement in stature, pelvic depth (possibly shallower), or dental health, and very likely not in diet. Probably reaction to crowding is starting, limiting health and finding cultural expression in the first waves of overseas war and colonization, e.g. of Crete, the Anatolian coast, Cyprus, and Palestine, together with the Trojan and other wars for control of the new metal, iron.

With the southward movements of Dorians, West Greeks, and others, and the equally massive overseas colonizing across the Aegean, the Early Iron Age begins with enough cultural confusion so that epic poetry replaces writing temporarily; there is considerable political and social as well as economic change and apparently a major temporary reduction in population. Longevity and fertility drop, expectably. Variability rises and will readjust to normal in the next period as invaders mix. Stature puzzlingly tends to rise at first, perhaps because of the invaders, then drops two centimeters in Geometric times, probably for nutritional reasons (not shown in Table 1). Then, as the creative leap of Classical times develops and population virtually doubles (Angel 1972a, based on Gomme 1933 and McDonald and Simpson 1969) despite the major colonizing effort, there is a corresponding jump ahead in health status: longevity advances five to six years and juvenile deaths drop, with a corresponding spurt in fertility; the pelvis deepens and stature rises three to four centimeters, in step with the addition of eggs to the diet, as well as more meat and fish and imports of wheat; added protein is the plausible cause for much better dental health. Malaria has virtually disappeared with careful farming plus the lower sea levels. Positive feedbacks between ecology, demography, health, and society are at maximum effectiveness.

The brilliant but militarily unstable Hellenistic period saw the start of a millennium of decline, almost straight-line decline, in all the indices of demography and health except stature. Population growth leveled off and then started its decline in the first century B.C., coincident with a major movement into cities and an increasing dependence on slaves (hence the philosophical opposition to slavery), so that the psychological, social, economic, and disease pressures of overcrowding began to operate. Both contraception and female infanticide tended to produce families with a single male child among the rich (Tarn 1930), and an apparent decrease in fecundity (despite no shortening of female life span) and increase in infant deaths resulted. The same results came also from wars and epidemics (e.g. the first century B.C. well in the Athenian Agora contains more than 380 newborn infants plus more than 100 dogs put in more or less simultaneously) and from malaria, which now began to increase (Stéphanos 1884; Jones 1907), as Table 1 also suggests. Malaria can have a direct effect on fecundity as well as on general energy and survival of young children. Malaria must have had a considerable selective microevolutionary effect, as it did in the Bronze Age (Angel 1969b, 1971a). The decrease in enamel growth arrests may mean fewer survivors of childhood diseases. At the same time diet continued at a reasonably good level for the middle and upper classes, though perhaps with less protein, and stature may even rise while dental health declines. If we had any sample of the slaves, the entire health picture would be very much more depressed; this is even more true of the imperial Roman period.

The Roman system of slave farms began to break down concurrently with erosion and exhaustion of soil and the slight rise in sea level and increased marshiness of the Sub-Atlantic's first brief warm spell (Denton and Porter 1970) from about A.D. 100 to 400. Endemic malaria could increase, therefore, and the climate probably also facilitated the spread of three major epidemics in the third and fourth centuries A.D. before the true plague in the fifth. Longevity decreased a little, with perhaps little change in fertility; certainly there was no vitality to overcome the epidemic and endemic disease pressures for which slave and city populations became reservoirs. MacDonnell (1913) shows the demographic and health situation of urban Romans to be far worse than in North Africa and other provinces, as seen in tombstone data which I have used in Table 1: with female longevity at 30.5 and marriage at 17.8 years, their fertility was so low that virtually the entire population had to be replaced each generation by immigration from the countryside. Lead poisoning as well as malaria and overcrowding may have been a causal factor. This demographic catastrophe was even worse than the ecological one. Rural areas were better off, but the Byzantine period began with populations fleeing the plague and with continued decline at about the Middle Bronze Age level, probably with some recovery after the major invasions and during the remarkable cultural revival of the tenth and eleventh centuries, coincident with the warm spell. Malaria may have lessened, but in the mid-fourteenth century plague again halved the population and there was no recovery.

As cities shrank and monasteries and villages became the effective units, local isolation led to variability, which continued to increase into the Muslim Baroque period. At this time the cooler winter climate and continuing silting of valleys helped grain crops, though possibly restricted the new major crops of rice and sugar; in any case, stature stayed relatively tall despite relative lack of meat protein. Porotic hyperostosis approached the Neolithic level, and despite the lack of urban concentration both malaria and plague remained endemic. Longevity (below prehistoric level), fertility (below replacement), and population density (at Early Bronze level) reached their low points, actually considerably later than the apparent ecological and economic causes.

After sinking to a claimed low of 5.4 per square kilometer in 1692 (Stéphanos 1884), population density rises steadily to 20 per square kilometer in 1820, so that both demographic and health recovery begin in the eighteenth century; between 1700 (9.3 per square kilometer) and 1900 population doubles twice — even faster than the Archaic into Classical increase from 650 to 450 B.C. Recovery is in part reaction to the new soils brought into most valleys and in part from stimulation from Baroque and Romantic Europe, which ends in religious, military, and political revolution during the 1820's as the Romantic period begins. The largely carbohydrate diet improves only in volume, accommodating the rise in population, so that dental health begins its sharp decline to a level as terrible as in modern America, while stature changes little. Female longevity shoots up to the Classical level, and by 1928–1929 (Michalopoulos 1932) reaches 54.3 — with males then at 56.1 — and fertility skyrockets despite continuing malaria, which actually does restrict average parity apparently. In 1928 parity is 3.9 (birth rate 29 per 1,000) and survivors are 2.5 female; I have interpolated the Romantic period data in Table 1 from this, assuming one birth every five years, as only one female pelvis is available for parity data. For this Romantic and modern improvement in longevity and health, improved winter housing, water supply, drainage, and sewage disposal seem more important than diet, and medical care plays a role only very recently. In 1929 child deaths (3.9

child deaths: 10 adult deaths) were still above the Early Iron to Roman period levels, though infant deaths (at 3 to 4: 10) were lower.

In a challenging ecological setting like the Eastern Mediterranean, change in population size depends closely on fertility, which is in turn dependent on health based on living conditions, diet, and ecology. Because women on the average died well before menopause during the whole time span from the Paleolithic through the nineteenth century A.D., adult female longevity is the major operative factor relating health to fertility, with survival of infants and children secondary though important. Female longevity is equally important for relative fertility as a force in microevolution, perhaps more than in modern times. Positive interactions between population density, female longevity, health, and fertility (as estimated) are clearly much stronger than those between population and cultural and ecological factors. In this area the feedback relations are indirect and subtle, and there is usually a considerable time lag before a change — a new food or farm method, the plow, endemic malaria or plague, or deforestation — has full effect on population growth or decline. The cycle set off by gradual human destruction of natural resources, soils, and forests of the Eastern Mediterranean began in the Late Bronze Age, but produced its full effect more than a millennium later. How long do we wait for the full demographic effect of modern environmental destruction?

REFERENCES

ACKERKNECHT, ERWIN H.
  1965 *History and geography of the most important diseases.* New York and London: Hafner.
ACSÁDI, GY., JANOS NEMESKÉRI
  1970 *History of human life span and mortality.* Translated by K. Balás. Budapest: Akadémiai Kiadó.
ALLISON, A. C.
  1964 Polymorphism and natural selection in human populations. *Cold Spring Harbor Symposia on Quantitative Biology* 29:137–149.
AMUNDSEN, DARREL W., CAROL J. DIERS
  1969 The age of menarche in Classical Greece and Rome. *Human Biology* 41:125–132.
ANGEL, J. LAWRENCE
  1946 Social biology of Greek culture growth. *American Anthropologist* 48: 493–533.
  1966 Porotic hyperostosis, anemias, malarias, and marshes in the prehistoric Eastern Mediterranean. *Science* 153:760–763.

1968a "Ecological aspects of paleodemography," in *The skeletal biology of earlier human populations*. Edited by Don Brothwell, 263–270. Oxford: Pergamon.

1968b Human remains at Karatas. *American Journal of Archaeology* 72: 260–263.

1969a The bases of paleodemography. *American Journal of Physical Anthropology* 30:427–437.

1969b Paleodemography and evolution. *American Journal of Physical Anthropology* 31:343–353.

1971a *The people of Lerna: analysis of a prehistoric Aegean population*. Princeton and Washington: American School of Classical Studies at Athens and Smithsonian Institution Press.

1971b Early Neolithic skeletons from Çatal Hüyük: demography and pathology. *Anatolian Studies* 21:77–98.

1972a Ecology and population in the Eastern Mediterranean. *World Archaeology* 4:88–105.

1972b Biological relations of Egyptian and Eastern Mediterranean populations during Pre-dynastic and Dynastic times. *Journal of Human Evolution* 1:307–313.

BRONEER, OSCAR
1939   A Mycenaean fountain in the Athenian acropolis. *Hesperia* 8:317–430.

BRUCE-CHWATT, L. J.
1965   Paleogenesis and paleo-epidemiology of primate malaria. *Bulletin of the World Health Organization* 32:363–387.

BUTZER, KARL W.
1965   "Physical conditions in Eastern Europe, Western Asia and Egypt before the period of agricultural and urban settlement," in *Cambridge ancient history*, fascicle 33, chapter 2. Cambridge: Cambridge University Press.

1971   *Environment and archeology: an ecological approach to prehistory* (second edition). Chicago and New York: Aldine-Atherton.

CAFFEY, JOHN
1937   The skeletal changes in the chronic hemolytic anemias. *American Journal of Roentgenology and Radium Therapy* 37:293–324.

CASKEY, JOHN L.
1954   Excavations at Lerna, 1952–1953. *Hesperia* 23:3–30.
1955   Excavations at Lerna, 1954. *Hesperia* 24:25–49.
1956   Excavations at Lerna, 1955. *Hesperia* 25:147–173.
1957   Excavations at Lerna, 1956. *Hesperia* 26:142–162.
1958   Excavations at Lerna, 1957. *Hesperia* 27:125–144.
1959   Excavations at Lerna, 1958. *Hesperia* 28:202–207.
1966   Excavations in Keos, 1964–1965. *Hesperia* 35:323–376.

CLARK, J. G. D.
1952   *Prehistoric Europe: the economic basis*. New York: Philosophical Library.

CLEMENT, A. J.
1963   "Variations in the microstructure and biochemistry of human teeth," in *Dental anthropology*. Edited by Don R. Brothwell, 245–269. New York: Pergamon.

COCKBURN, T. AIDAN
  1967 *Infectious diseases: their evolution and eradication.* Springfield, Illinois: C. C. Thomas.
DENTON, GEORGE, H., STEPHEN C. PORTER
  1970 Neoglaciation. *Scientific American* 222(6):100–110.
DEWEY, JOHN F.
  1972 Plate tectonics. *Scientific American* 226:56–68.
DUBOS, RENÉ
  1965 *Man adapting.* New Haven: Yale University Press.
FLANNERY, KENT V.
  1965 The ecology of early food-production in Mesopotamia. *Science* 147: 1247–1256.
FLEMMING, NICHOLAS C.
  1972 "Analysis and interpretation of vertical earth movements, Crete." Paper presented at the meeting of the Archaeological Institute of America, December 28, 1972.
GEJVALL, NILS-GUSTAF
  1969 *Lerna: a preclassical site in the Argolid,* volume one: *The fauna.* Princeton: American School of Classical Studies at Athens.
GILBERT, B. MILES, THOMAS W. MCKERN
  1973 A method for aging the female *os pubis. American Journal of Physical Anthropology* 38:31–38.
GOMME, A. W.
  1933 *The population of Athens in the fifth and fourth centuries B.C.* Oxford: Blackwell.
GOODRICH, L. CARRINGTON
  1963 *A short history of the Chinese people* (third edition). New York: Harper and Row.
GREULICH, WILLIAM W., H. THOMS
  1938 The dimensions of the pelvic inlet of 789 white females. *Anatomical Record* 72:45–51.
HADJIMARKOS, D. M., C. W. BONHORST
  1962 Fluoride- and selenium-levels in contemporary and ancient Greek teeth in relation to dental caries. *Nature* 193:177–178.
HARLAN, JACK R., DANIEL ZOHARY
  1966 Distribution of wild wheats and barley. *Science* 153:1074–1080.
HELBAEK, HANS
  1960 "The paleoethnobotany of the Near East and Europe," in *Prehistoric investigations in Iraqi Kurdistan.* Edited by R. J. Braidwood and Bruce Howe, 99–118. Chicago: Oriental Institute and University of Chicago Press.
HOPF, MARIA
  1962 Nutzpflanzen vom Lernäischen Golf. *Jahrbuch des Römisch-Germanischen Zentralmuseums, Mainz* 9:1–19.
HOWELLS, WILLIAM W.
  1941 The Early Christian Irish: the skeletons at Gallen Priory. *Proceedings of the Royal Irish Academy,* Section C, 46:103–219.
JACOBS, JANE
  1969 *The economy of cities.* New York: Random House.

JACOBSEN, THOMAS W.
   1969   Excavations at Porto Cheli and vicinity, preliminary report II: the Franchthi Cave 1967–1968. *Hesperia* 38:343–381.

JARDÉ, AUGUSTE
   1925   *Les céréales dans l'antiquité grecque: la production.* Paris.

JONES, W. H. S.
   1907   *Malaria, a neglected factor in the history of Greece and Rome.* Cambridge: Macmillan and Bowes.

KEYES, PAUL H.
   1969   Present and future measures for dental caries control. *Journal of the American Dental Association* 79:1395–1404.

KROGMAN, WILTON M.
   1962   *The human skeleton in forensic medicine.* Springfield: C. C. Thomas.

MacDONNELL, W. R.
   1913   On the expectation of life in ancient Rome, and in the provinces of Hispania and Lusitania. *Biometrika* 9:366–380.

MAULL, OTTO
   1922   *Griechisches Mittelmeergebiet.* Breslau: Ferdinand Hirt.

MCDONALD, WILLIAM A., RICHARD H. SIMPSON
   1969   Further explorations in southwestern Peloponnese, 1964–1968. *American Journal of Archaeology* 73:123–177.

MCKERN, THOMAS W., T. DALE STEWART
   1957   *Skeletal age changes in young American males.* Technical Report EP-45. Natick: Quartermaster Research and Development Command.

MELLAART, JAMES
   1967   *Çatal Hüyük: a Neolithic town in Anatolia.* New York: McGraw-Hill.

MELLINK, MACHTELD J.
   1964   Excavations at Karatas-Semayük in Lycia, 1963. *American Journal of Archaeology* 68:269–278.
   1965   Excavations at Karatas-Semayük in Lycia, 1964. *American Journal of Archaeology* 69:241–251.
   1966   Excavations at Karatas-Semayük in Lycia, 1965. *American Journal of Archaeology* 70:245–257.
   1967   Excavations at Karatas-Semayük in Lycia, 1966. *American Journal of Archaeology* 71:251–267.
   1968   Excavations at Karatas-Semayük in Lycia, 1967. *American Journal of Archaeology* 72:243–263.
   1969   Excavations at Karatas-Semayük in Lycia and Elmali. *American Journal of Archaeology* 74:245–259.

MICHALOPOULOS, J. G.
   1932   *Statistical yearbook of Greece, 1931.* Athens: National.

MICHELL, H.
   1940   *The economics of ancient Greece.* Cambridge: Cambridge University Press.

MOSELEY, JOHN E.
   1965   The paleopathologic riddle of "symmetrical osteoporosis." *American Journal of Roentgenology, Radium Therapy and Nuclear Medicine* 95:135–142.

MOULDER, JAMES W.
1962   *The biochemistry of intracellular parasitism.* Chicago: University of Chicago Press.

MYLONAS, GEORGE E.
1959   *Aghios Kosmas: an Early Bronze Age settlement and cemetery in Attica.* Princeton: Princeton University Press.

NICHOLSON, G.
1945   The two main diameters at the brim of the female pelvis. *Journal of Anatomy* 79:131–135.

PERKINS, DEXTER, JR., PATRICIA DALY
1968   A hunters' village in Neolithic Turkey. *Scientific American* 219:96–106.

PUTSCHAR, WALTER
1931   *Entwicklung, Wachstum and Pathologie der Beckenverbindungen des Menschen, mit besonderer Berucksichtigung von Schwangerschaft, Geburt, und ihren Folgen.* Jena: Gustav Fischer.

RAIKES, ROBERT
1967   *Water, weather and prehistory.* New York: Humanities Press.

REED, CHARLES A.
1960   "Animal domestication in the prehistoric Near East," in *Prehistoric investigation in Iraqi Kurdistan.* Edited by R. J. Braidwood and Bruce Howe, 119–145. Oriental Institute of the University of Chicago, Studies in Ancient Oriental Civilization 21. Chicago: University of Chicago Press.
1970   "The pattern of animal domestication in the prehistoric Near East," in *The domestication and exploitation of plants and animals.* Edited by Peter J. Ucko and G. W. Dimbleby, 361–380. London: Gerald Duckworth.

ROBINSON, DAVID M.
1942   *Excavations at Olynthus*, part eleven: *Necrolynthia, a study in Greek burial customs and anthropology, with the assistance of Frank P. Albright and with an appendix on skeletons excavated at Olynthus by John Lawrence Angel.* Baltimore: Johns Hopkins Press.

RODDEN, ROBERT J.
1965   An early Neolithic village in Greece. *Scientific American* 212:82–90.

SARGENT, R. L.
1924   *The size of the slave population at Athens during the fifth and fourth centuries before Christ.* University of Illinois Studies in the Social Sciences 12(3). Urbana, Illinois: University of Illinois Press.

SEYMOUR, THOMAS D.
1908   *Life in the Homeric Age.* New York: Macmillan.

SOGNNAES, REIDAR F.
1956   Histologic evidence of developmental lesions in teeth originating from paleolithic, prehistoric and ancient man. *American Journal of Pathology* 32:547–577.

STÉPHANOS, CLON
1884   "Grèce. Géographie médicale (orographie, hydrographie, géologie, flore, faune, ethnologie, anthropologie, démographie, hygiène,

pathologie)," in *Dictionnaire encyclopédique des sciences médicales, Série IV, 10.* Edited by A. Déchambre, 363–581. Paris.

STEWART, T. DALE

1968   "Identification by the skeletal structures," in *Gradwohl's legal medicine,* 2nd edition. Edited by Francis E. Camps, 123–154. Bristol: John Wright and Sons.

1970   "Identification of the scars of parturition in the skeletal remains of females," in *Identification in mass disasters.* Edited by T. Dale Stewart, 127–135. Washington: National Museum of Natural History, Smithsonian Institution.

TARN, W. W.

1930   *Hellenistic civilisation* (second edition). London: Arnold.

TODD, T. WINGATE

1920   Age changes in the pubic bone, I: The male White pubis. *American Journal of Physical Anthropology* 3:285–334.

1921   Age changes in the pubic bone, II: The pubis of the male Negro-White hybrid. III: The pubis of the White female. IV: The pubis of the female Negro-White hybrid. *American Journal of Physical Anthropology* 4: 1–70.

TROTTER, MILDRED, GOLDINE C. GLASER

1958   A re-evaluation of estimation of stature based on measurement of stature taken during life and of long bones after death. *American Journal of Physical Anthropology,* n.s. 16:79–124.

VITA-FINZI, CLAUDIO

1969   *The Mediterranean valleys: geological changes in historical times.* Cambridge: Cambridge University Press.

WEINBERG, SAUL S.

1965   "The stone age in the Aegean," in *Cambridge ancient history,* volume I, fascicle 36, chapter 10. Cambridge: Cambridge University Press.

WESTFALL, JOHN

1968   "Estimation of ancient population." Unpublished doctoral dissertation, George Washington University.

WRIGLEY, E. A.

1969   *Population and history.* London: World University Library.

Population Pressure, Land Tenure, and Agricultural Development in Southeastern Ghana

G. K. NUKUNYA

The Anlo are the most numerous and perhaps the best-known of the Ewe-speaking peoples who now live in southeastern Ghana and southern Togo. Oral tradition, identifiable locations, and historical records suggest that the Ewe had lived in or around Ketu near the present Dahomey-Nigeria border in Yoruba country before migrating in separate groups to their present country. It is not known for certain for how long they had been living in Ketu nor whether they had moved there from another country. The details of their migratory movements from Ketu and the socioeconomic conditions of the period also are not clear, apart from their settlement in the ancient walled city of Notsio (*nuatja*) in central Togo under the tyrannical rule of King Agokoli. How and why they came to live under Agokoli also remain a mystery. Nor are we certain about the sequence or time of their settlement in Eweland.

What is known is that by the middle of the seventeenth century the Anlo had established themselves in their present country surrounding the Keta Lagoon, east of the Volta estuary. Today the Ewe speak one language with slight local variations, and they share the consciousness of being one people although they never lived under a single political authority. But while forming a broad cultural group, differences exist in their social and political institutions, making generalizations very misleading. Thus, what is said here about the Anlo does not necessarily refer to the other Ewe groups unless it is so stated.

The present study is also very much restricted in area, though this by no means limits the scope or importance of the subject matter it proposes to discuss. It is concerned with the southern half of Anlo country, where the inhabitants have managed over the last fifty years to develop a system of farming around their traditional capital of Anloga, which changed the harsh environment into an oasis of progress and prosperity. Faced with problems of land shortage, unbelievably poor sandy soil, sea erosion, drought as well as the constant threat of flooding from the unreliable rains, and the periodic rising waters of the Volta and the lagoons, they introduced a system of cultivation based on irrigation, heavy fertilization, rotation of crops, and intensive cultivation.

The main crop grown under this system is shallot [*Aillium ascolonicum*], locally known as *sabala*, introduced into the area towards the end of the last century, but corn, pepper, okra, tomatoes, and other vegetables are also grown. The elaborate, often meticulous, preparations for cultivation and the type of organization that goes with them, form the subject matter of this study. But the study also has significance for students of tropical agriculture who have too often criticized farmers of the region for failure to adapt themselves to modern innovations. In south Anlo all the intricate techniques associated with the industry have been developed by the farmers themselves, who are predominantly illiterate. Indeed, the problem with the industry is not the inability of the farmers to adapt themselves to more scientific methods of cultivation. It is rather the failure so far of the more scientific methods of the Ministry of Agriculture to provide the farmers with less expensive and more effective tools of production to improve the farmers' own methods.

It is important to emphasize from the outset the intensive nature of shallot cultivation, for it is only with this knowledge that the problems associated with the industry can be clearly understood. Intensive agriculture may be described as a "system by which soil fertility is continuously maintained or restored, allowing successive food crops to be produced with little or no intervening fallow period. This may take place naturally as a result of the periodic deposit of nutrient elements by water or wind, or through human intervention" (Netting 1968: 55). In south Anlo, as we shall see, the soil is naturally very poor, and continuous cultivation is made possible only because of the regular fertilizing, which has become part and parcel of shallot farming. The amount of labor expended is also considerable and often additional labor has to be hired from outside the family or household. But before going into the details of cultivation certain general points about Anlo will be given.

PHYSICAL FEATURES AND TRADITIONAL ECONOMY

Anlo country, which is also known in government circles as the Keta district after its largest town, lies halfway across the dry coastal plains which extend from Ghana into Dahomey. It covers an area of nearly 900 square miles of which about a quarter is occupied by lagoons, but only two-thirds of the total area is good for cultivation and human habitation due to the marshy nature of the areas surrounding the lagoons. Besides, even some of the drier and more sheltered patches also get flooded in years of heavy rainfall. Thus, if allowance is made for these lagoons and their surrounding areas, the population figure of nearly 250,000 returned in 1970 (Ghana 1970) should give a density much higher than the area would lead us to believe.

The Anlo are surrounded on all sides by other Ewe subtribes except in the south, where their land is bounded by the Atlantic ocean. In the west live the Tongu, in the north the Ave, and in the east the Bε and Noefe, both in Togo. The forty-mile stretch of sand bars, which borders on the ocean, runs roughly northeasterly and until recently was fringed with coconut trees. Sandwiched between the sea in the south and the numerous large lagoons in the north, it is a narrow strip of land barely exceeding two miles at its widest portions and only one hundred yards wide in some places. Yet it contains many thickly peopled settlements of different sizes, lying in a continuous stream, like beads along a string. In fact, the twenty-five-mile-long portion of the coast between Aflao and Anloga, where the population density exceeds 500 per square mile looks like a long rural conurbation. Of these towns Keta with its 14,446 inhabitants, lying roughly halfway along the belt is easily the largest. Besides being until recently a port of call for cargo ships, it is the commercial and administrative center of the Anlo district and has large European stores, several government offices, and two secondary schools. As the first town of missionary activity in what is now the Volta Region,[1] it has a large Christian community. The Keta market, which like all others in the area falls on every fourth day, attracts traders and customers from all over Ghana, Togo, Dahomey, and Nigeria. But its importance is now declining on many fronts due to the increasing menace of sea erosion from which it has been suffering for a long time.

Twelve miles to the west lies Anloga (population 14,032), the traditional capital and ritual center of Anlo which is rapidly developing at the expense of Keta. It has a large, flourishing market now comparable in importance to that at Keta, a teacher training college and two secondary schools. It is here that the shallot-growing industry was started several

---

[1] The Volta Region, the home of the Ghanaian Ewe is one of the eight regions of Ghana, with Anlo (Keta) as the most populous of its five administrative districts. The others are Sogakofe (Tongu), Ho, Kpandu and Buem-Krachi (Jasikan).

decades ago. It is also hoped that in the very near future Anloga will become an industrial center because of the reportedly rich deposit of oil discovered there recently. But, unlike Keta, it embraced Christianity very late and the first school was not opened there until 1907. Accordingly, its population is predominantly illiterate and the Christians are less than 20 percent of the population.

Halfway between these two settlements is a cape named St. Paul on which in 1900 the then Gold Coast Government built a lighthouse, about one mile north of which lies the small township of Woe (population 4,060) another center of the shallot-growing industry. It is an important historical town whose chief in the past commanded the "Right" (Dusi) division of the Anlo army. It also accepted Christianity as early as 1887, and has a fairly large Christian population. Other important settlements on the littoral are Aflao (population 11,397), Denu (2,675), Tegbi (6,628) and Dzelukofe (5,153).

Behind the sandbars stretch the lagoons, fed by numerous creeks and streams, and also by the Volta River. The main lagoon, named after Keta, which covers an area of nearly 200 square miles, is brackish water, the coasts and shallow portions of which dry up during years of scanty rainfall, leaving large incrustations of salt, which provide an important article of trade. In extremely dry years almost the whole lagoon is dried up, but in years of heavy rainfall, which comes mainly in May and June, the waters of the lagoon rise to flood the surrounding lands for several months. The lagoon is navigable for boats and large canoes as far as Blekusu and for small canoes as far as Amutinu. During the rains canoes reach Adafienu, where the lagoon terminates in a swamp which extends to Aflao, Togo. Of the remaining lagoons, Angaw and Avu are by far the largest and most important.

The northern fringes of the Keta lagoon are marked by heavy clayey soils and a belt of mangrove swamps and reeds, the higher grounds of which contain such large towns and villages as Anyake, Afiadenyigba and Atiavi. Inland from here and stretching northwards to the northern boundary lies a different soil, red laterite alternating with sand, whose almost flat surface is covered with grass and shrubs interspersed with only borassus palms and baobab trees. The population is not as dense as along the littoral, the only large town being Abor. Towards the northeast, however, the higher rainfall supports a more luxuriant vegetation of palm groves and taller bushes, especially around the large town of Dzodze.

An essential feature of the area between the sea and the lagoons is the presence of two or three narrow depressions across the belt which runs

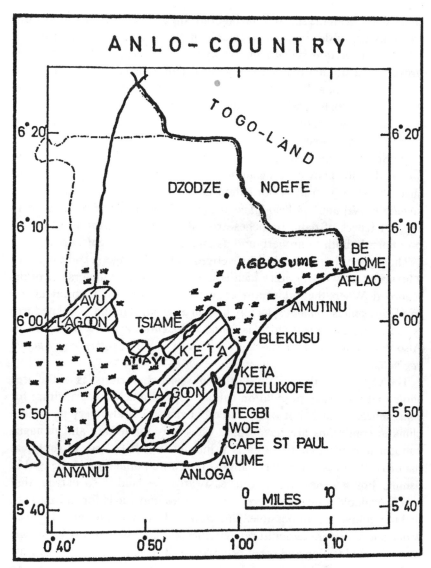

Map 1

almost parallel to the coastline. They also get flooded after the main rainy season, to support a luxuriant species of thatch locally known as *ava* [*typha antralis*]. In the west some of these depressions are covered by small lagoons and ponds (see Map 1).

The land immediately bordering on the seashore is very sandy and its vegetation is greatly limited. Where the land is a little coarse and is underlain by a thicker layer, thorny creepers with large burrs are found. But midway between the sea and the lagoons, the soil is darker and richer due to admixture of decomposed vegetable matter, and here we find a species of thatch [*imperatus cylindrica*], locally known as *be*. Also found here are groves of "a stunted tree with very hard stem, tangled branches and stiff leaves" (Chapman 1943: 56) called *fetigba* [*chrysobalamus orbicularis*]. Mangoes and palm trees are also found in fairly large numbers, but the coconut trees which once flourished throughout the belt are now restricted to Anloga and areas to the west, the others having been killed by the Cape St. Paul wilt.[2] Another common tree is a species of the fig [*ficus polita*], locally known as *agbafloti*, which is planted solely to provide shade because its fruit is not eaten. Other common trees are *avia* [*newbouldia locuis*] and *kpokplo* [*ficus umbellata*], both of which are used to support fences of palm branches around homes. The *avia* also features prominently both as an herb and as an essential ingredient in rituals.

The lagoon shores, marked by wetter and heavier lagoon soils, produce a luxuriant growth of grass which is softer and shorter than grasses of the seaboard. Where the soil is more compact and less moist, a typical lagoon tree [*avicennia germinanus*] locally known as *amuti* is found. A related tree is the mangrove, *atra* which is found in localities near the Volta River. Also common here is a short grass known locally as *gbekle* [*paspalum vaginatum*].

The vegetation, the soil, and other physical characteristics of the area show that the heavy population cannot depend much on agriculture for subsistence. Land is not only scarce but the soil is also very poor, and climatic conditions are hazardous. Thus it is for fishing and nonagricultural pursuits that the area is primarily suited. Indeed, in the great majority of towns and villages almost the entire population is engaged in fishing. For instance, from Keta eastwards the land is so narrow that every available space is covered with houses and sheds for drying nets, making cultivation impossible. But west of Keta the land area is much wider and therefore agricultural activities in many settlements have long supplemented fishing and other occupations. It is here that the flourishing shallot-growing industry has developed over the past few decades to transform both the landscape and the living conditions of the people. In Anloga, the center of the industry, almost the entire population depends on the industry. But the character of the industry can only be clearly understood if the physical limitations of the area are fully appreciated.

[2]   This disease is named after the place of its first attack. Its root cause is not officially known, but it is generally believed to be an insect pest whose stings cause the death of the trees. It has wiped out all the trees in the Cape St. Paul area as well as a considerable part eastward of this spot as far as the Togo border.

It will have been seen that water dominates the Anlo landscape and presents it with most of its problems — and opportunities, like fishing. The sandbar we are considering is almost completely surrounded by water, and its only land link with the outside world is the precarious Anloga-Denu road. Like other parts of southern Anlo it is made further vulnerable by its low relief which barely rises above sea level. Periodically, especially around September, the surf becomes wild and erodes substantial portions of the coast, only — fortunately — to redeposit the silt later. However, the erosive effects seem to get the upper hand year after year, with the result that every year the sandbar becomes narrower. September is also the month in which the waters of the Volta rise and spill over into the lagoons to raise the water level above the surrounding lands. When the lagoon flooding and sea erosion are preceded by heavy rainfall in May and June, the main rainy months, the effect is disastrous because they often render thousands of people homeless and threaten the road, as was the case first in 1963 and again in 1968, when it became necessary to close the road for over one year.

The effects of flooding are no less hazardous for agriculture in the west. By an unfortunate coincidence it is only the low-lying areas around the Keta and Angaw lagoons and the elongated depressions which can support the shallot crop. Thus, when the flooding havoc comes, these are the places which bear the brunt of it. The farmers have no technique for solving this problem. Flooded farms simply are left uncultivated until the situation improves on its own.

Anlo is a land of contradictions and contrasting features, for, alternating with the flooding, are periods of drought due mainly to the nature of the local rains which are not only scanty but also irregular and extremely variable. And to offset this other menace, irrigation from wells has become another important aspect of the Anlo farmer's life. But the plight of the inhabitants would not have assumed such serious proportions if the population were less dense.

Because of the population density every available part of the land, "including cemeteries is therefore put under cultivation" (Benneh 1971: 74). Yet not every piece of available land is suitable for cultivation. Even cassava (manioc), considered among the most hardy of local food crops, cannot grow in some places, especially along the immediate sea coast. The shallots also grow only in the areas already referred to, namely, along the Keta and Angaw lagoons, where the soil is much wetter and heavier, and also in the narrow depressions. It is also worth noting that about half of the shallots are grown on a narrow four-mile stretch of land on the shores of the lagoon between Anloga and Woe. The estimated total acreage under cultivation is just over 3,000.[3] Individual holdings are therefore small, barely exceeding half an acre, making intensive cultivation inevitable. The scarcity also affects building plots, whose prices compare with those in Accra, that is, about 500 pounds an acre. In short, land is so scarce that, although shallot farms provide the great majority of the population with their living, not every family or even clan has direct access to them. We therefore have many systems of land alienation by which plots are made available to those who cannot obtain them through inheritance.

The final physical problem is the poverty of the soil which is such that even those places considered suitable for shallot cultivation cannot meet the requirements of the crop without heavy fertilizing. The coarse sandpit which covers the immediate seashore and extends to about half a mile in some places supports nothing apart from coconut. It is only where the Cape St. Paul wilt has killed the trees that decomposed roots have fertilized the ground to make possible the cultivation of cassava. The shores of the Keta and Angaw Lagoons are made of finer, heavier soil but they are also too salty to support most crops without intensive fertilizing. In the west, where agriculture is possible, it is therefore only a narrow belt lying between these extremes that is capable of supporting any cultivation. Unfortunately, these are also the only areas suitable for human habitation. Consequently it is the less unsuitable depressions and the lagoon shores which have become the saviors of the Anlo cultivator. By heavy fertilizing and sanding he has been able to neutralize the effect of extreme salinity of the lagoon shores and has brought the land under cultivation. And by the same process he has rendered the depressions less vulnerable to flooding.

Before the development of shallots on commercial scale, however, cultivation was not an important occupation, and coconut was the only cash crop. Fishing and poultry keeping were the major economic activities. As we have already seen, the coastal strip is very well placed for an important fishing industry as it lies between the sea and the lagoons. In the sea, seines, each operated by a gang of about thirty men are used, but in the lagoons and streams smaller nets are employed together with weir baskets, traps, hook-and-line, and dams. In the past few decades, however, as a result of population pressure and increased dependence on the sea, it has become necessary for large numbers of fishermen to migrate to other parts of West Africa in search of richer waters.

The coastal Anlo are also well noted for their poultry. As early as 1850

---

[3]   This figure represents the total acreage available, but because of floods only about half of it is actually cultivated each year.

Governor Winniet, the British governor of the Gold Coast, who took over the Danish fort at Keta, reported the importance of the industry in his journal thus:

Bounteous nature supplies the natives with an ample share of the necessities of life; turkeys, ducks, fowls, bullocks, sheep, goats, etc., abound along this part of the coast .... Indeed, it was from this part of the country that nearly all the live-stock consumed by the European and respectable natives throughout the Gold Coast were supplied.

Forty years later in 1891, Keta was still "the poultry market of the Gold Coast," according to the Government's population census report of the year. Today, although Keta does not occupy such a prominent position in this regard, poultry is still important in the area's economy. Almost every Anlo settlement has a poultry farm, where fowl, together with goats, sheep and pigs, are reared, but the cattle population is now quite small. It is interesting to note that despite the abundance of poultry, their meat does not feature significantly in Anlo diet, which is made up almost entirely of fish and vegetables. Perhaps the equally abundant fish and the high prices the fowl and beasts can fetch are responsible for this.

The coconut plantations were also a major source of income for those who had them. While a large proportion of the crop was sent to Accra for export in the form of copra, the bulk was processed into coconut oil and sold in Keta to be sent to other parts of the country. Cloth, mats, mattresses and baskets are also made here but this and pot making are more important along the northern shores of the Keta Lagoon and settlements to the north, where maize, cassava and oil palm are also cultivated.

The various economic activities and forms of local specialization described have resulted in an exchange system among the various localities. This has made trading an important additional occupation, especially among women. It also makes meaningful the four-day market cycle by which the major towns hold their markets on different days (Nukunya 1969). Cassava and corn, as well as the woven articles and pottery produced in the north, are brought to the coast in exchange for fish and shallots. In fact, trading among women is so common that a foreign observer could not help remarking that "there is hardly anyone who does not trade" (Westermann 1949: 48). But it is now for shallots, not poultry or trade, that the area is noted.

SOME ASPECTS OF THE SOCIAL SYSTEM

The Anlo formed a distinct subgroup within the larger Ewe entity, which migrated from the east to occupy the present country. Thus, while they share many cultural traits with the other Ewe groups, differences are also discernible in a number of institutions. For instance, while their political structure and religious organization follow the same general pattern described for other Ewe, details of their clan and lineage organization show marked differences from the Ewe groups on which there is material. Anlo social organization itself has been described in great detail elsewhere (Nukunya 1969). In this present account emphasis will be placed on the organization of descent groups at the various levels because of the close bearing they have on questions of land tenure and inheritance.

The key to an understanding of Anlo social organization is patrilineal descent based on clans and lineages. There are at least fifteen clans around which the social fabric of the society is woven. As in some other clan-based societies, the number of Anlo clans is sometimes subject to argument. In certain parts of northern and eastern Anlo there are some lineage groups which are not generally accorded independent clan status though they sometimes claim to be independent of the main clans. However, because they are not officially recognized at Anloga and differ both in structure and organization from the recognized clans, we shall omit them from our list. According to Anlo tradition, the fifteen clans are listed in order of their settlement in Anlo as Lafe, Amlade, Adzovia, Bate, Like, Bames, Klevi, Tovi, Tsiame, Agave, Ame, Dzevi, Vifeme, Xetsefe, and Blu.

The Anlo *hlɔ*, translated here as "clan," may be described as a group of people who are believed to have descended patrilineally from a common putative ancestor and who share the same totemic and other observances. Membership is normally obtained by birth, but strangers and slaves were sometimes incorporated into the clans of their hosts or masters, and were accorded full membership status. Strangers not specifically attached to any particular Anlo clan were grouped into one special clan created for strangers only. Descendants of this special clan are known today as the Blu clan. The composition of the Blu clan is unique in clan organization; although recruiting members has been and still is based on patrifiliation, those who originally composed it did not have any common patrilineal ties. The only thing they had in common was in fact their foreign origin irrespective of tribe.[4] As such, the definition of the clan as

---

[4] Most Blu lineages are of Ada, Adangbe, and Krobo origins, but the name Blu (the Anlo name for the Akans) suggests that the Akans probably formed a substantial portion of the early membership.

a group of agnates, tracing patrilineal descent from a common ancestor does not apply to them.

All fifteen clans are dispersed throughout the entire tribe in such a way that every large settlement has a branch of most of them living in it. Although they are dispersed, they have many characteristics of corporateness. They own land and palm groves and have appointed leaders known as chiefs in whom are vested legal and ritual powers. They also meet regularly to discuss matters of common interest, and have their ancestral shrines at Anloga, except the Xetsofe who have theirs at Tsiame, where every year clansmen from all over Anlo make pilgrimages. In the past these pilgrimages were made for specific ritual and ceremonial purposes. Apart from the usual offerings and prayers, children were brought to the shrine to be washed in the clan's ritual water and inducted into the clan cult. Today, though prayers are offered during those visits, they are more of sightseeing ventures than religious pilgrimages.

In the past vengeance was also a clan function: an offender would have a fellow clansmen taken or killed if he ran away or somehow evaded the punishment applicable to the offense committed. Likewise, an offended party was entitled to help from his fellow clansmen. Within the centralized political system of the Anlo these interclan relations — the retaliatory measures and compensations — were channeled through the king's court and those of the smaller chiefs.

There are no aristocratic clans in Anlo on the lines described for some traditional kingdoms like the Nyoro (Beattie 1960) or the Bemba (Richards 1940: 83–120). All are equal in status but perform different functions in the localities and the kingdom. The paramount stool belongs to the Adzovia and Bate clans, who alternately provide the king; the Lafe are the kingmakers at the national level; the Lafe and the Amlade are the hereditary ritual specialists in each settlement and at the tribal level,[5] while the Dzevi provide the chief priest for the war god, Nyigbla. But, in each settlement, selection of the chiefship, now hereditary within certain lineages, was determined by a number of factors including dominance in terms of numbers, first settlement in the town, bravery in war, and wealth. Almost all clans have chiefships in one locality or the other.

Membership in a clan carries many distinctive attributes. Some of these are names, food taboos, avoidances and injunctions. For instance, every clan has a pair of names, one applying to men, the other to women. Each

[5] These joint functions by the Lafe and Amlade clans are usually performed at village, town, and national meetings by the senior lineage heads at each level. As the acknowledged first settlers in Anlo, it is their duty at these meetings to ask permission from their respective apical ancestors to allow gatherings to pass off smoothly.

has its own totems which are related to stories about the clan and its origin, especially some exploit of the founding ancestor. Every clan also has its own funeral customs. Again, membership in a particular clan is believed to imply certain personal qualities. Members of a clan may be spoken of as being addicted to certain practices or as being notably wicked, even-tempered, violent, or fertile. The Anlo clan is not exogamous. On the contrary, in the past and today in some remote villages, marriages are encouraged between clan folk between whom close relationships could not be traced; endogamy is never enforced, however.

All large settlements have segments of most clans living in them. Members of these local segments who trace common descent from a known ancestor form what we have called the lineage. Thus defined, there are in some settlements two or more lineages of the same clan. This is particularly the case at Anloga, where each of the fifteen clans is represented by several lineages.

The lineage may be defined as that branch of a clan found in a settlement which comprises all persons, male and female, who are able to trace relationships by a series of genealogical steps through the male line to a known ancestor and theoretically to each other. It is an exogamous group of nearly ten generations which is named after its founding ancestor and has as symbols of interest and unity, a stool, an ancestral shrine, a lineage head, and common property. Within this group, members are entitled to a number of rights and privileges, including a plot of land to cultivate, a creek to fish in, a place to live, and a group to care for them in time of need. The lineage head was usually its oldest male member of the oldest living generation, and the older he was the greater his authority and ritual powers. Today, however, the office is elective and therefore younger members with qualities of leadership may be preferred to older men. Whatever his age, the head administers the lineage land and other property, and no transaction concerning this or other lineage interests may take place without his knowledge and approval. He judges disputes involving members of the group and he is their representative on the town's governing council. As the chief ritual specialist of the lineage, he is believed to be the link between the living and the dead and the only one who can officiate with sufficient authority to the understanding of the ancestors.

Marriage among the Anlo is usually virilocal; therefore, a lineage is almost always confined to a section of the town although, as usually happens, some members will be living with their maternal relatives elsewhere in the town. Today an important development in Anlo residential pattern is the overcrowding in the old settlement areas leading to the movement of many members to the outskirts to occupy what was originally regarded as farm land.

These, in brief, are the main features of Anlo descent groups. It will be seen that it is primarily as members of these groups that individual Anlo get access to land. Thus, the amount of land a person possesses would be related to the size of his descent group and available land. This is very important because not only are some lineages and clans richer in land than the others, but the richer descent groups are not necessarily the larger ones. Yet, although this is an important determining factor in the size of individual plots, the patrilineal principles described are counterbalanced by many bilateral institutions, especially those concerned with inheritance. It is therefore possible for individuals to inherit land and other property from outside their descent groups.

LAND TENURE: GENERAL PRINCIPLES

It will be helpful to begin our description of Anlo land tenure with a brief discussion of the traditional political organization because the former greatly depends on the latter.

Anlo political system may be described as centralized because it provides for a constituted executive authority, an administrative machinery and judicial institutions (Fortes and Evans-Pritchard 1940:5). At the head is the *awoamefia*, the king, who lives in a sacred place made holy by the presence of the gods. Though highly respected, his powers are greatly circumscribed. Below him are the three senior chiefs, who in the past commanded the three divisions in the traditional military formation (Amenumey 1964: 51–60; Nukunya 1969: 9–15). Next in the hierarchy come town and village chiefs, followed by the ward and lineage heads respectively.

Although the system is centralized, descent groups are very powerful and often enjoy a good deal of autonomy. The chief advisers of the *awoamefia*, for instance, are the heads of the fifteen dispersed patriclans around which the social fabric of the society is woven. But nowhere is the power of the clans displayed more clearly than in the system of land tenure, for the ultimate title in land is vested in them and not in the *awoamefia*. The king as protector of his subjects and their property has to defend the land against outsiders, but within the kingdom, the clans are not answerable to him for any questions concerning land. It is true that land cases between clans are often referred to him for settlement, and his authority is recognized in such matters, but he owes this position to the status of his court as the highest adjudicating body and not as a land overlord. He is responsible only for land standing in the name of his clan or lineage, which as head of the clan, he administers like any other clan head.

Although land may stand in the name of a clan it is usually vested in a localized segment or lineage, which holds it to the total exclusion of all others except where no such segment has yet worked or laid claim to it. Such unclaimed lands no longer exist in Anlo.

Within the lineage itself formal demarcations are made, roughly once in a generation, which determine the portion of lineage property an individual may cultivate without let or hindrance from any other member of the group. Before this formal demarcation all descendants of the previous user as well as his close relatives such as brother and sister may have access to his land.

The result of this continuous demarcation is that in every generation the land is divided, according to the number of eligible heirs, into smaller units. This means that after every generation a lineage member receives much less than, in fact only a fraction of, what members of the preceding generation cultivated. For some lineages, the time of reckoning has already come, with lineage patrimony clearly inadequate for subsistence. For others, and this now appears to be the trend, the effects of formal education have greatly helped to reduce the number of the younger generation willing or able to subsist on agriculture.

As a rule, school leavers migrate to the cities and employment centers to work as artisans and clerks, so that any farmer who sends his children to school reduces the burden on the land for future generations. Another factor which tends to offset the effects of continuous division of land is no doubt the fact that sea and lagoon fishing is an important occupation in settlements surrounding Anloga, and therefore those who are affected by land shortage readily can turn to fishing. Even in Anloga town itself many farmers are also part-time fishermen, while others follow the two occupations side by side. Thus, although individial plots are becoming smaller and therefore insufficient for subsistence, a number of factors are working to alleviate the situation.

Whatever the internal divisions of the lineage land, its overall administration remains in the hands of the lineage head who, with the stool itself, is the most important symbol of unity of the lineage group. At the same time, the divisions and demarcations just mentioned have shown one important element in African land tenure which hardly needs emphasizing now: while land is generally regarded as belonging to a corporate entity, it is worked individually by families within the corporate descent groups.

It often happens that a piece of land is associated with one person rather than a whole clan or lineage. Such land is usually one of the numerous patches of land which were not claimed by any of the clans during the time of their early settlement in the area because the sites were considered unproductive or useless at the time. Therefore, they remained something like no man's lands until much later, when they were claimed by such individuals. The interesting thing about some of these plots is that they originally were claimed by women, from whom they were handed via the male line to their present descendants. Much of the shallot-growing area bordering on the Keta Lagoon between Tegbi and Anloga falls within this category. Because of its marshy nature its importance as a farming area was not realized until the introduction of sugar cane and shallots in the nineteenth century. Before then, women basket weavers claimed them for growing reeds and wickers. The plots passed down in the female line until men found use for them, when they changed into the hands of male offspring. Land traced to a woman in this way is referred to as *mamanyigba* [grandmother's land].

In view of this, Benneh's statement that there is a male "at the head of each genealogical table" (1971: 78) can be misleading. On the one hand, while the statement is essentially correct with regard to descent groups, it is not correct when applied to genealogies relating to land which he was in fact considering. On the other hand, one can even go further to say that kinship itself, as opposed to descent, is always bilateral and therefore for purely genealogical purposes the two apical ancestors, male and female, are equally important. As such the opposite of what he said is indeed the fact. There are both male and female at the head of each genealogical table.

But while Anlo social structure works within a patrilineal ideology, the system is flexible enough to enable adjustments to be made to cater to maternal ties (Nukunya 1969). Whether this flexibility results from the kinship system itself or the physical environment is difficult to say, but it is worthy of note that the importance of "both sides" of the family in inheritance is always emphasized throughout Ewe country, even in areas with different physical features. In addition to having access to land by inheritance there have developed over the last few decades several forms of alienation including pledges, mortgages, tenancies and direct purchase.

MAIN ASPECT OF SHALLOT CULTIVATION

As a result of land shortage and the difficult terrain, individual farms are quite small, as we have already seen. Only the low-lying areas surrounding the Keta Lagoon and the elongated depressions may be used because the beds upon which the crop is grown are made on very low ground, barely a few feet above sea level. Even then, no area neatly fits the required level without much attention and detailed manipulation. In short, where the land is too high the surface layers need to be removed and where it is too low sand has to be added to bring it to the required level.

The specialized nature of the plots shows that only those whose lineages and other relations have land in the correct locations have access to it through direct inheritance. In this respect the system of divergent transmission has the effect of making land available to people who would not get it through their lineages. But as we have just seen, within the context of general land shortage in the area it has the additional effect of further fragmentation, leading to smaller portions per capita. Individual holdings are therefore very small averaging something like half an acre. But in almost every year nearly half of the total area under cultivation is flooded for several months. No techniques have been developed to check or control the floods, and shallot beds covered by the flood waters are left uncultivated. Given the size of the plots, the aim of the system is to obtain the best possible result from the small holdings.

Details of early techniques of shallot cultivation and the type of organization that went with it are not known for certain, but since the 1930's a rather intensive system has been in use which requires labor from outside the family. Although wives, children and other dependents do help with the farm work, hired labor, readily available because of the dense population, is used for the more exacting tasks of transportation, watering, and sanding.

As a rule, the plots are divided by narrow gutters into small rectangular beds to allow easy access to the crop during weeding and watering. Because the plants are very tender, reaching only one foot above the ground and planted only few inches apart, walking on the bed can be harmful to the crop and is never allowed. It is in the gutters that the farmer must stand in order to reach the crop. The gutters, which are about one foot wide, also serve as irrigation channels during the dry season and as drainage canals after the rains have flooded the beds. As a further check against the flood waters the sides of each bed are strengthened by a structural framework made of corn stalks and grass.

The size of the beds differs from place to place and from farm to farm. Even on the same farm no uniform size of beds is maintained. Consequently, different and conflicting dimensions have been given by earlier writers. Stein (1929: 152) mentioned ten by eighty-six feet as the standard size of beds; Tettey (1960: 1–5), six by forty; and Grove (1966: 364), six by fifteen. I arrived at an average measurement of four by sixteen feet in 1957 (Nukunya 1957: 12–13). It appears that bed sizes not only differ from place to place but also change from time to time. For instance, the farm in which the 1957 dimensions were taken was found in 1971 to contain beds with an average size of five by eighteen feet.

The shallot crop takes two months to mature, and it is possible to raise three main crops a year if there is no interruption due to floods. In between the seasons corn, groundnuts, and vegetables are planted. The first sowing season which coincides with the start of the traditional calendar[6] lasts from January to March and is known as *fedomi*. The second, known as *fenu*, lasts from April to July and the last, *kele*, runs from September to November. In a given area the beginning of the sowing, which lasts a month, is decided by the leader of the area farmers and announced by the town crier. It is an offense for any farmer to sow his seeds before or after this period. It is important that the crops of a particular area mature at about the same time, otherwise, *yoe*, an insect pest, may spread from matured crops to younger ones, seriously damaging the latter. The pest, a perennial hazard, usually attacks the maturing crops, especially during the dry season.

During the *fedomi* season, which is generally dry, the beds are watered daily for several days before the seeds are planted. At this time and sometimes in the other seasons the farmer depends not only on the irrigation channels which may get dry but also on wells built all over the farm. These wells, built with cement blocks are deep enough to provide a constant supply of water even during the dry season.

Because the farmer irrigates his land whenever necessary, the fluctuation and distribution of rainfall do not exert much influence on the farming calendar. The farmer is also able to cultivate the same piece of land for a long time because he does not depend on the innate fertility of the soil but regularly enriches the basically poor, sandy soil with multifarious combinations of fertilizers. Indeed it is in the system of fertilization that the intensive nature of shallot cultivation is most clearly seen.

A great variety of fertilizers has been introduced, some of which are not even found in the immediate vicinity of Anloga. Principal among them, in rough order of importance, are *nyimi* [cow dung], *lavi* [fish manure], *druimi* [bat droppings], and *yevudu* [chemical fertilizers], also known as *amedahe-du* [poor man's manure].[7] Chemical fertilizers, which

---

[6] The traditional Anlo calendar starts with the first full moon in January and ends with the last in December.

[7] In spite of the low prices at which the fertilizers are sold, many farmers complain that the bulbs for which they have been used rot very easily and therefore cannot be

the government is now encouraging farmers to use instead of the traditional ones, are sold at heavily subsidized prices by the Ministry of Agriculture Extension Office at Anloga and also by local commercial firms.
Lavi, derived from various species of fish, is obtained from the coastal
towns and villages east of Anloga. Common species are *abobi* [anchovy],
deyi [sardinella sp.], *agbatsahe*, mainly *ngogbavi* [*vomer gibbiceps*], and
togo [*tilapia melanopleura*]. All except the last named, a lagoon fish, are
obtained from the sea. For cow dung and bat droppings, however, the
farmer has to travel to Tongu country and to villages across the Keta
Lagoon.

　All of the fertilizers perform specific functions, and they are applied at
different times of the season. The cow dung, always applied before the
seeds are planted, has the dual function of accelerating germination of the
seeds as well as enlarging the bulbs. *Lavi*, which may be scattered on the
beds before sowing or applied soon after germination, is used mainly to
help sustain steady growth while developing the stalk and usually is
applied a few weeks after germination. It is not necessary to apply all in
one season and therefore a series of permutations are used to prevent
unnecessary expenditure and excessive manuring. Thus, whereas cow
dung is used by all every season, *druimi* and chemical fertilizers are not
applied together because they are known to perform largely the same
function. The seasons also affect the type of combinations to be used.
Chemical fertilizers, for instance, are not applied during the *kele* season
because they lead to excessive heat, which is harmful to the crop, but are
instead recommended for *fenu*, the season of heavy rainfall.

　Even before the seeds are planted three different types of hoeing take
place.[8] Other important activities are weeding, watering, and *bomelele*
[breaking the surface]. Two weeks after sowing *lavi* is scattered on the

---

preserved for a long time. As the seed shallots have to be kept for three to six months
before planting, such bulbs do not make good seeds.
[8]　First of all, weeds, and grass are cleared together with any remaining intercrops like
corn and vegetables, all of which are then left to dry on the surface. Clearing of the
beds in this way, known in Ewe as *nugaga* [hoe-weeding], is done with a small hoe
because it does not involve any deep movement of the soil. Actual hoeing (*nunonlo*)
which follows one week later is done with longer and stronger blades. The soil is
inverted to about one foot down; the weeds are cleared and all live roots meticulously
removed, but the dry weeds are well dug in. *Nutotobo* and sowing then follow.
Nutotobo, which is a mild form of deep hoeing, is an artistic exercise requiring plenty
of care and diligence and is undertaken only by the farmer himself or anyone well
versed in the art. The bed is hoed in such a way as to make the surface very smooth
and level, but in a dry season it also has the effect of shuffling the watered surface with
the soil below. In this respect it may be said that shallot farming is in many ways an
art. The neatly cut gutters, the smooth surface of the beds, and the round-walled wells,
all present a picturesque scene to anyone observing the farms.

beds and a stick is used to push it into the soil. Soon afterwards, the weeds which have germinated with the seeds are cleared from the beds to prevent them from choking the young plants and competing with them for the manure. This is repeated if more weeds have grown before the crop begins to mature. And, as we have already seen, during the dry season of *fedomi* and also in the other seasons when the rains fail, watering of the beds becomes necessary. *Bomelele* is performed during the rainy season when there is sign of waterlogging. The topsoil between the plants is loosened by hand. This loosening is also necessary if the surface of the beds becomes hardened up during the dry season due to the alternating effects of watering on the one hand and of heating and evaporation by the sun on the other.

The harvest also brings a new set of activities in its wake. The harvested crop is left to dry on the farm for two or three days, but many farmers now prefer to bring it home the same day for fear of thieves, whose activities have increased in recent years. Failing that, a night watch is arranged with friends and neighbors around the farm. The shallots are then taken home by members of the family, assisted by women hired from the vicinity of the farm. At home, they are left under the sun for about a week for the leaves to be thoroughly dried. The bigger bulbs are carefully selected and tied into bundles for sale at Anloga and Keta markets, from where they are transported to Accra and other parts of the country. The smaller ones are suspended from the ceilings of living rooms and kitchens by cords made with woven palm branches and reeds known as *agbake*, and are kept for future use as seeds.

A bundle of shallots weighs about thirty pounds and may bring between two and eight pounds, depending on the size of the bulbs and the nature of the harvest as a whole in the season. No weights are used, but, by experience, the farmer knows the number of bulbs to tie together to get the correct weight. A government move to introduce a system of weighing is being strongly resisted by the farmers, who believe this will not take into account the size of the bulbs and their appearance[9] in fixing the price. But it is hoped that a system of grading which takes note of these qualities will pave the way for weighing to be introduced.

It has not been easy to arrive at reliable tonnage of shallot products and exports. Ministry of Agriculture figures quoted by Grove (1966: 403)

---

[9]   The size and appearance of the bulbs are the two qualities used in pricing shallots. The bulbs must not only be large and round, but they must also have a rosy-brown rather than light-gray appearance. One of the reasons why chemical fertilizers are not greatly favored is their inability to produce this color in the bulbs.

show that it rose from around 322 tons per annum in 1941 to 1,268 in 1955. These figures were based on returns of ferry depots and customs posts. While all the shallots leaving Anloga have to pass through these posts, no facilities exist for collecting information on tonnage, and it is difficult to understand how the figures were arrived at. Also, because a large proportion of the harvest, as we have seen, is not sold but reserved as future seeds, any figures based solely on the finished product are bound to be misleading. Independent investigation and calculation reveal that the 1970 crop amounted to around 22,000 tons. On this basis the estimated 1,500 acres of land under cultivation will each yield about fifteen tons a year, which corresponds to the annual tonnage per acre the Ministry now gives.

The wealth of the farmers differs a good deal. Although the size of farms is no index to wealth, richer farmers on the whole tend to have larger plots than poorer ones. Figures given by the farmers themselves suggest that rich farmers can make as much as £2,000 gross in a vintage year while the average in an ordinary year for the entire farming community may be put at about £500 gross. But in an industry like shallot farming with heavy overhead expenses, the net income is quite low compared with the gross, sometimes falling below a third of the latter. In extremely bad years even heavy losses are incurred. Taken together, however, the industry is substantially profitable, as can be seen from the life-styles of the farmers.

SHALLOTS AND CONTEMPORARY ANLO SOCIETY

The cash that the industry brings to Anloga farmers has no doubt introduced significant changes both in the landscape and the standard of living. Within the last three decades beautiful story buildings and bungalows, the goal of every ambitious Anlo youth, have replaced the traditional mud huts. Secondary-school education has suddenly erupted with great force to a level unknown anywhere in the Volta Region. When this last point is considered alongside the slow progress education and Christianity made in their initial stages of development, the effect of the shallot culture in this regard can be seen in its true perspective.

Of all the main towns in Anlo, Anloga was the very last to embrace Christianity. From the very beginning the town rejected it because it was seen as a threat to the religious and cultural institutions of the town, which is not only the capital but also the cultural center of Anlo. Thus it was not until 1906 that the Bremen Mission[10] was able to open the first church in the town, over fifty years after Christianity and schools were opened at Keta. It is therefore a remarkable achievement on the part of Anloga that within only thirty years of the establishment of the first primary school there, it should become the first town in the Volta Region to open a secondary school. The Zion College, opened in 1937, owed nothing to the shallot industry for its establishment, but by drawing a large proportion of its students from the area its development and consolidation as an institution of learning was indirectly affected by the newfound wealth of the local farmers. It also shows the seriousness with which the inhabitants took education once the initial obstacles were removed.

Today school education for boys is considered a matter of course, while nearly half the girls of primary school age are at school.[11] And with ten primary and middle schools catering to over three thousand children, the town has clearly become a major center for primary education in the region. The number of secondary schools has now increased to two, both government-assisted, with the local teacher training college making three the number of institutions of higher learning in the town. One remarkable thing about the three institutions is that they all owe their establishment to local rather than governmental or missionary initiative, as is the case in many parts of the country.

Another positive effect of the industry was to arrest a migratory tendency, which was gathering around the 1930's. As a result, contrary to the general trend in the area, the population of Anloga increased steadily from about 3,000 in 1931 to 6,358 in 1948 and 11,000 in 1960. An advance report of the 1970 census puts new figure at 14,000. While emigration is not altogether unknown to the town, there is very little evidence of it, apart from the perennial exodus of school leavers for Accra and other large Ghanaian cities and towns. The reason is that despite the land shortage only those who loathe farming and hard work can complain of unemployment in the town.

Although the majority of inhabitants are farmers and therefore need a reasonable portion of land for their livelihood, the prosperity generated

[10] The Norddeutsche Mission, which was the first missionary group to operate in Anlo, was generally referred to as the Bremen Mission before other related churches joined them to form the Evangelical Presbyterian Church.
[11] Throughout Eweland and Ghana the schooling of girls was not considered important because of the belief that the kitchen, which is their rightful place, did not require classroom education. It was only during the last few decades that the schooling of girls started to increase, but their number still falls short of those of the boys at school.

by the industry's success has led to many subsidiary economic activities which are not dependent on land as such. There are, for instance, the farm hands whom almost every farmer needs during each major stage of the farming cycle. There are also the growing numbers of artisans, masons, and carpenters, needed for the continuous building work going on in the town. Tailors and dressmakers are also enjoy very good patronage. Even private day nurseries have been opened to care for children of working mothers. Indeed, with money around, within certain limits any able-bodied person in town will find something to do. Moreover, although the wages and general income levels of workers in Anloga compare favorably with those in Accra and other big cities, the cost of living is on the whole much cheaper.

It is true that imported goods like sardines, corned beef, milk, sugar, and beverages cost more here than in the cities, but this is more than offset by the ridiculously low cost of accommodation, locally grown foodstuffs, and fish. In the slums of Accra a single room may cost about three pounds and a good meal nearly forty pence. At Anloga a single room costs around one pound for those who have to rent one (and the majority live in family houses, which are rent-free) while ten pence should be sufficient to provide a wholesome meal, perhaps with a lot more to spare. It is therefore no exaggeration to say that shallots have helped to stabilize Anloga society. The inhabitants of many Anlo towns and villages indeed point enviously at the lucky position of Anloga and what shallots have done to the town. If only their own home towns or villages could have a comparable industry that would afford them the opportunity to stay at home!

The town's contact with the outside world has also increased greatly. It is connected with both Accra and Ho, the regional capital, by daily mail services. The sixty-odd self-contained rooms built for the oil prospecting project, now temporarily abandoned,[12] are presently used to augment the catering services of the existing government rest houses. Local foodstuffs, already good in the past due to the abundance of vegetables and fish, have greatly improved with the addition of imported goods like tea, coffee, and milk. There is now a government clinic in the town, but serious cases have to be taken to the government hospital at Keta twelve miles away. However, it is a significant mark of the people's wealth that in the case of serious sickness, they prefer to travel to private

---

[12]   Oil is known to exist off the Anloga sea coast but its quantity has not yet been fully assessed. Exploratory work started in 1964, when dozens of living quarters were built for the workers, but work has been suspended since the overthrow of the Nkrumah regime.

hospitals at Lome, Adidome, or Dzodze, dozens of miles away, to pay large sums of money for services they could well obtain gratis in Keta. In fairness to the farmers, however, it must be mentioned that the Keta hospital which serves the entire Anlo district is always overcrowded and service there is accordingly not always efficient.

Changes in the social structure itself follow the general pattern described elsewhere for the area (Nukunya 1969: 162–208). The major difference here seems to be the presence of over 1,000 postelementary school pupils, which certainly adds a new dimension to local social norms. Although the teacher training college and one of the secondary schools are fully residential and the second secondary school partly so, their extracurricular and outward activities cannot be totally divorced from the town's life. Regular visits to the town by pupils as well as calls by parents, relatives and friends from outside Anloga all add up to make a less homogeneous population. This is also the effect of the presence of tutors and their families, over 90 percent of whom hail from outside the Anloga area. Another significant difference stems from the stability of Anloga population, which makes households built around the nuclear family a more common feature of domestic organization.

Against these developments and changes may be mentioned the major drawback of the area, namely the ravages of the sea and the lagoons which disturb Anloga and, by extension, all the settlements on the seacoast. Although Anloga town itself is quite safe, the damage done elsewhere, usually around Keta, does affect every settlement. The only access to the town by land is from the east through Denu and Keta. But every year in September, when the surf is at its wildest and the lagoon also overflows its banks, the only road linking these places becomes almost impassable and sometimes has to be closed to vehicular traffic. Twice during the last decade, first in 1963 and again in 1968, it became necessary to close the road between Denu and Keta for over a year. To offset this, a road is now under construction which will link Anloga with Dabala and Sogakofe to the north east. When completed it should reduce the dependence on the eastern route and make Anloga and the entire coastal area less dependent on climatic factors.

We see, then, that shallot farming is an indigeneous industry in the real sense of the term. The farmers are predominatly illiterate. But the high productivity achieved and the highly skilled techniques evolved for intensive cultivation of the crop have been acquired through their own efforts. In this way the system as a whole contradicts the argument often made by experts of agricultural development in the tropics that the main obstacle to agriculture in the region is the inability of the illiterate peasant farmer to respond positively to innovations due to his resistance to change. But in Anloga the farmers have not yet been able to master the entire environment.

DISCUSSION

A population faced with limited land resources must devise ways and means of making use of these resources. This leads us to our main problem. Given the physical conditions of the Anloga area, how does one explain the high standard of their farming techniques and the success they have attained so far? This is very pertinent in view of the fact that the terrain in which the shallot industry has been developed is not much different from several areas north of the Keta Lagoon, which have remained relatively undeveloped. This is true especially of the swamps in the neighborhoods of Atiavi and Agbosume. In Atiavi, where the potential land area far exceeds that of the coast both in absolute terms and in relation to population density, cultivation has been limited to sugar cane and some minor crops not comparable in value to shallots. Cultivation techniques have also remained largely rudimentary.

Around Agbosume, where the Anloga farmers used to purchase shallot seeds during the first half of this century, farming as an occupation is of no consequence. There, instead, cloth weaving is the prime occupation and, apart from the coconut plantations and a few hundred acres used for the growing of sweet potatoes, no development of the land in the form of agriculture has taken place. In view of this an explanation of the phenomenal expansion and success of the shallot industry of coastal Anlo is imperative. This is the more so because the three places belong, broadly speaking, to the same cultural area with generally the same ethos.

There are two possible reasons why southern Anlo, especially the Anloga area, should differ in its economic characteristics from the other areas. There is first the high population density which is not shared by the other Anlo areas. Secondly the coastal Anlo's earlier contact with European traders might have prepared them for a more enterprising attitude towards agriculture (Grove and Johansen 1968: 1381).[13] This in turn is related to the emergence of Keta as a major commercial town only a few miles from the shallot farms. If we take for a start the influence of population we inevitably enter an old argument about the relationship between

[13]   Anlo's effective contact with European traders, mainly Danes, started in the early eighteenth century and was for the most part restricted to the coast.

population density and agricultural intensification. Carneiro's (1961) South American material suggests that an increase of population in regions where the area of cultivable land is circumscribed gives the necessary impetus to shift into intensive cultivation. Boserup (1965: 28), using a wider range of data, has asserted that the change towards more intensive systems of land use took place in response to the increase of population within a given area.

In south Anlo there has been a steady increase of population over the last few decades. The population of Anloga, for instance, has increased from 6,358 in 1948 to 11,038 in 1960 and then to 14,032 in 1970. Other settlements have likewise increased in size. Although this is an area of heavy emigration it is clear from the census figures that emigration does not adversely affect population size in absolute terms. This is mainly due to the seasonal nature of Anlo migration, resulting in the overlapping of emigrants and returnees. That the population continues to increase may be explained in several ways. It is likely that those returning at any one time outnumber those leaving, or if the two movements cancel each other out, then the difference is due to natural increase. Either way, the fact remains that the population of the area is on the increase and ways and means would have to be found to feed the new mouths.

It is interesting to note also that the period of the great leap forward for industry (1930–1950) coincided with a population explosion in the area which resulted in mass migrations from neighboring villages to Abidjan, Badagri, and Cotonou. It is also worthy of note that most of the migrations took place outside Anloga, where, unlike the surrounding localities, shallot farming is the only major occupation. For instance, in Woe, five miles to the east, shallot farming and fishing are pursued side by side and as a result it suffered more from migration than Anloga. Yet, just two miles away the large village of Tegbi, where fishing is the predominant occupation, suffered from a mass exodus of fishermen. A comparison of the populations of the three settlements over the last few decades makes the point clearer (see Table 1).

Table 1. Comparison of populations

	Anloga	Woe	Tegbi
1948	6,358	2,977	6,773
1960	11,038	3,450	5,924
1970	14,032	4,060	6,628

Thus it is reasonable to assume that the shallot industry came to rescue the excess population which in turn made necessary the intensification of the industry. As has been mentioned already, the area east of Keta has no agricultural land, and in the west only Anloga and its immediate surroundings have the land for this expansion.

If this explanation is accepted, it will go a long way to explain the second reason, namely, the experience of the coastal Anlo in capitalistic enterprises, for if all the coastal Anlo were credited with this experience, the east would have no land to utilize as does the west. But even here in the east the enterprising nature of coastal Anlo is still evident albeit differently. The emphasis on fishing and the seasonal migrations, the inevitable results of land shortage, have led to the establishment of large fishing companies which operate both locally and in areas of immigration. Though the number of fishing enterpreneurs constitute only a small proportion of the population they form a group large enough to control the entire fishing industry. In terms of the wealth they control and the size of their operations they are by far the biggest capitalists to emerge in the Anlo area, with some fishermen spending well over 23,000 pounds to set up their businesses (Hill 1970: 45). Yet, by the nature of the industry itself and the density of the population, the emergence of these companies has not resulted in any stable population.

The different reactions of the eastern and western halves of the Anlo coast to population pressure pose interesting questions about the relationship between population increase and land use. In the west, especially around Anloga, where there is room for agricultural expansion and intensification, we had the expected result predicted for agricultural communities. But in the east, where cultivation as an occupation is at a minimum, population pressure has taken a different form, resulting instead in migrations and establishment of large fishing companies. Thus it seems that it is only in farming communities that population increase may lead to agricultral intensification.

It is clear that population pressure and an inclination towards farming are not sufficient conditions for agricultural intensification. Another key factor in the Anlo case appears to be the enterprise of the people coupled with their enterpreneurial experiences with the early European traders. One is tempted to conclude that these qualities are essentially limited to the coastal Anlo, for the terrain used by the Anloga farmers for their shallots differ little from that found around Agbosume and Atiavi, where no comparable agricultural developments have taken place. The migrants from Agbosume and Atiavi prefer to migrate to work as laborers in cocoa farms, mining areas and commercial farms to developing their harsh though potentially lucrative agricultural surroundings.

REFERENCES

AMENUMEY, D. E. K.
1964 "The Ewe people and the coming of European rule." Unpublished doctoral dissertation. London.

BENNEH, G.
1971 Land tenure and sabala farming system in the Anlo area of Ghana. *Research Review* 7(2):74–94.

BEATTIE, J. H. M.
1960 *Bunyoro: an African kingdom.* New York: Holt, Rinehart and Winston.

BOSERUP, E.
1965 *The conditions of agricultural growth.* Chicago: Aldine.

CARNEIRO, R. L.
1961 Slash-and-burn cultivation among the Kuikuru and its implications for cultural development in the Amazon basin. *Anthropological Supplement* 2:37–67.

FORTES, M., E. E. EVANS-PRITCHARD
1940 *African political systems.* Oxford.

GHANA
1970 *Population census of Ghana,* volume two.

GROVE, J. M.
1966 Some aspects of the economy of the Volta delta (Ghana). *Bulletin de l'I.F.A.N.* XXVIII Ser. B No. 1–2:381–432.

GROVE, J. M., A. M. JOHANSEN
1968 The historical geography of the Volta delta, Ghana, during the period of Danish influence. *Bulletin de l'I.F.A.N.* XXX Ser. B No. 4:1374–1421.

NETTING, R. MC C.
1968 *Hill farmers of Nigeria.* London, Seattle: University of Washington Press.

NUKUNYA, G. K.
1957 Onion farming by the Keta Lagoon. *Bulletin of the Ghana Geographical Society* 2:12–13.
1969 *Kinship and marriage among the Anlo Ewe.* London School of Economics Monographs on Social Anthropology 37. London: Athlone Press.

RICHARDS, A. I.
1940 "The political system of the Bemba tribe of north-eastern Rhodesia," in *African political systems.* Edited by M. Fortes and E. E. Evans-Pritchard, 83–120.

STEIN, J. T. H.
1929 Agriculture in the Keta-Ada district. Gold Coast Department of Agriculture Paper 16. *Bulletin* 22:152–160.

TETTEY, D. K.
1960 "Shallot industry in South Anlo." Unpublished master's thesis, University of Ghana, Legon.

WESTERMANN, D.
1949 *The African today and tomorrow.* Oxford.

Group-Centered Behavior and Cultural Growth: A Summary of Ecology and Superstructures

M. E. SARMELA

The main lines of sociocultural evolution have been proposed using different terms, which describe either the development of a whole society, the differentiation of organizational structure, or changes in the thinking or mentality of *homo sapiens*.

Sociologists especially have been interested in the differences between "traditional" agrarian society and industrial urban society. Urban society may be characterized by at least the following features: mass production, division of labor, specialization, the mechanization of work and of everyday life, a clock-dominated pace of life, social mobility and heterogeneity, the anonymity of interaction and social intercourse, impersonality and bureaucracy, isolation and lack of personal control between individuals with a correspondingly increased control mechanism upheld by formal organizations. Social competition among individuals has increased continuously with a gain in the number of status symbols (cf. Anderson 1971: 6ff.). From the viewpoint of change in the personality of man, the most significant factor is probably that the network of secondary groups has become extended within urban and agrarian society.

From a social anthropological point of view the primitive societies are KINSHIP (OR FAMILY)-CENTERED. The family/kinship is the most important (or usually the only) reference and status group and is most important to the social security of individuals. The more developed and differentiated societies can be characterized as GROUP-CENTERED.

The term GROUP-CENTERED also describes behavior from a macroethnological perspective and the reference background of the whole individual as we shift to socially differentiated societies. Individuals wish to identify voluntarily and actively with their peer and status groups; solidarity is organic and not mechanical as in a member group like a nuclear or extended family. At the same time the influence of secondary groups on the individual's increasing social integration and on the development of the values and norms which he accepts grow more significant than those of the so-called primary groups. In family-dominated groups the individual's statuses and roles are in a sense determined automatically and there are not many situations which generate competition or the need for comparison. In peer groups the individual has to compete for a level of status; he is drawn into social competition and accordingly feels the need to boost his effectiveness. Behavior becomes more active, more outwardly directed — and a value is placed on results. In peer and interest groups the individual's frame of reference broadens, and it is apparently necessary for these groups to form before new institutions can take root and new technical innovations spread. Special groups create new values, norms, and goals, but they also require of their members solidarity and submission to the discipline of the group.

The cultural growth, that is, technical development, increasing economic capacity, increasing social stratification and complexity, and continuing increase of knowledge and effects at every level of human activity can be described in different ways, e.g. as a "wheel of development." Thus the old rural Finnish-Karelian culture area can be divided into three main regions, whose most evident differences (characteristics of superstructures) are shown in Table 1 (Sarmela 1969).

Table 1.   Superstructure characteristics of three main regions of old Finnish-Karelian culture

Western Finland	Eastern Finland	Karelia
Static agrarian	Dynamic extensive	Static reactive
Furthering integration	Resisting integration	Rejecting integration
Differentiated peer groups, special interest groups	Less differentiated	Not differentiated kinship groups
Group-centered behavior and attitudes	Individual attitudes	External family-centered attitudes
Increased social competition	Little social competition	Little or no social competition
Increased social activity	Social passivity	Social passivity
Increased normativity and pressure for social conformity, group control	Individual or community control	Traditional normativity, extended family control
Increased status symbols	Little interest in status symbols	Few status symbols
Group-oriented ⟵——————————————————⟶ Family-oriented		

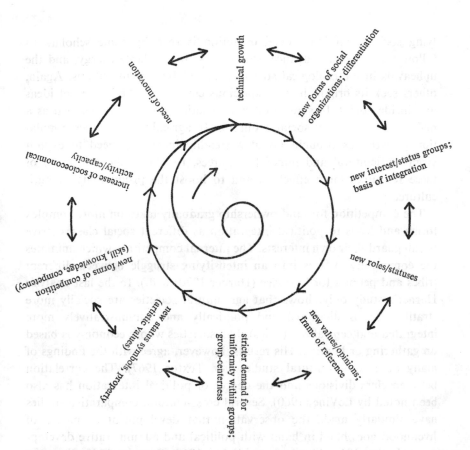

Figure 1. Wheel of development

Group-centeredness is reflected in the development of western Finnish society in its higher stage of economic development, susceptibility to innovation, appearance of ideological and often fanatic, authoritative movements (such as Nazism), appearance of folk art, conformity of ideological and artistic manifestations, e.g. folklore (in increase of moral and normative components and structural conformity of folklore). Compared to the eastern regions western Finland has assumed with increasing frequency the distinctive features of a maximal, specialized, and highly niched ecosystem.

CAUSES AND EFFECTS

It has been easier to describe the changes in the sociocultural structure of societies than it has been to advance theories about the causes underlying social evolution. Social evolution is seen by some scholars to follow technological advance, the increase of available energy, and the upheavals in the ecological structure caused by new inventions. Again, others seek its origins in the capricious currents in the history of ideas and in ideologies. In some studies population pressure is regarded as a major determinant of social evolution. In agricultural societies population growth has brought about a steadily increasing need to exploit virgin agricultural and mineral resources, to render the utilization of these resources more effective, and to boost the productivity of agriculture.

The competition for land ownership gradually takes on more complex forms and leads to political integration as different social classes strive to safeguard their own interests. The internal competition which animates the community evolves into an intensifying struggle between different tribes and peoples for biospace (Harner 1970: 68ff.). In the last analysis Harner's study only shows that agricultural societies are socially more stratified (class divisions) and politically and administratively more integrated and centralized (cities) than societies whose economy is based on gathering or hunting. His results, however, agree with the findings of many other cross-cultural studies (see Textor 1967). The correlation between class divisions and the degree of political integration has also been noted by LeVine (1960). Several cross-cultural comparative studies have similarly made the observation that development of means of livelihood goes hand in hand with political and administrative development (Ember 1963; Murdock and White 1969; Carneiro 1968; Freeman and Winch 1957). An increasingly complex social structure, the differentiation of new groups and social classes, and political and administrative integration and specialization are some of the universal consequences of increased productivity of the ecosystem. Population pressure, however, should not be considered a primary cause of economic and social evolution. An adequate population and a reserve of labor are essential requirements for the maximal development of ecosystems, but nowhere has overpopulation led *ipso facto* to the development of economic or social structures.

Cross-cultural studies also indicate other general trends in development, but the effect on social evolution has up to now been more or less neglected by social anthropologists. Increased economic productivity and complexity of social structure have been accompanied by a growing social strictness and authoritarianism. The attitudes that take shape in productive preindustrial ecosystems are more normative and rigid, sexual mores generally more restrictive, religious dogmas and practice

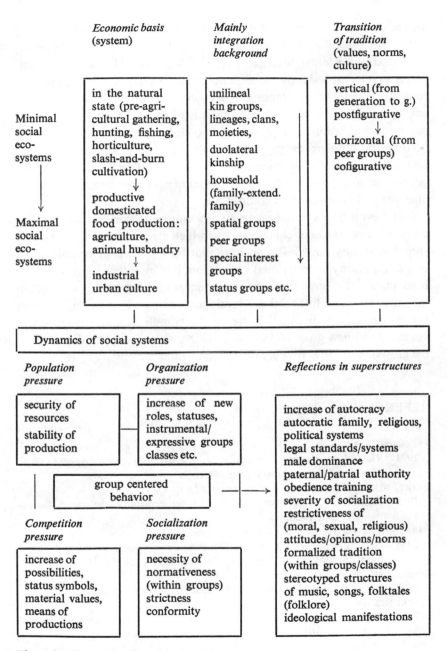

Figure 2. Dynamics of growth process

more severe, and upbringing and education more subordinating than they are in minimal ecosystems. In this respect the studies of Barry et al. are of special interest. Male dominance and parental authority are distinctive traits of agricultural societies, which are reflected, for example, in marriage customs. Stephens (1963: 326ff.) has characterized such family system attitudes by the term autocracy. In its entirety the pressure toward greater social integration has become more severe. The more complex a society is, the more the roles it offers and the tasks it assigns require information and technical knowledge, and the more severe become the pressure exerted on children and youth in their formative stages. Maximal ecosystems require the individual to subordinate himself to the norms of group-centered development (see Sarmela 1972 for discussion of cross-cultural studies).

Social evolution and the tendency of a culture to become complex are cumulative processes or chain reactions which are not set off by one single stimulus: not by population pressure, not by a sufficiency of nutritional resources, not by an individual's invention, nor by a change in economic productivity. The growth of the ecosystem is also affected by changes in the superstructure, by social differentiation and by an increasing pressure toward general competition. These are the stimuli that the values, status symbols, and new goals of the groups bring with them. The dynamics of the growth process is roughly described in Figure 2.

REFERENCES

ANDERSON, NELS
  1971 *The industrial urban community: historical and comparative perspectives.*
        New York: Appleton-Century-Crofts.
BARRY, HERBERT III, IRVIN L. CHILD, MARGARET K. BACON
  1959 Relation of child training to subsistence economy. *American Anthropologist* 61:51–53.
CARNEIRO, ROBERT L.
  1968 Ascertaining, testing, and interpreting sequences of cultural development. *Southwestern Journal of Anthropology* 24:354–374.
COHEN, YEHUDI, *editor*
  1968 *Man in adaptation: the cultural present.* Chicago: Aldine.
EMBER, MELVIN
  1963 The relationship between economic and political development in nonindustrialized societies. *Ethnology* 2:228–248.
FORDE, DARYLL C.
  1964 *Habitat, economy, and society. A geographical introduction to ethnology.* New York: E. P. Dutton. (First published 1934.)
FREEMAN, LINTON D., ROBERT F. WINCH
  1957 Societal complexity: an empirical test of a typology of societies. *American Journal of Sociology* 62:461–466.

HARNER, MICHAEL J.
1970 Population pressure and the social evolution of agriculturalists. *Southwestern Journal of Anthropology* 26:67–86.

HUTCHINSON, G. E.
1965 *The ecological theatre and the evolutionary play.* New Haven: Yale University Press.

LANGE, CHARLES H.
1965 "Cultural change," in *Biennial review of anthropology.* Edited by Bernard Siegel, 262–297. Stanford: Stanford University Press.

LEVINE, ROBERT
1960 The role of the family in authority systems: a cross-cultural application of the stimulus generalization theory. *Behavioral Science* 5:291–296.

MALINOWKI, BRONISLAW
1949 "The dynamics of culture change," in *An inquiry into race relations in Africa.* Edited by Phyllis M. Kaberry. (First published 1945.)

MURDOCK, GEORGE P., DOUGLAS WHITE
1969 Standard cross-cultural sample. *Ethnology* 8:329–369.

MURPHY, ROBERT F.
1967 "Cultural change," in *Biennial review of anthropology.* Edited by Bernard Siegel and Alan Beals, 1–45. Stanford: Stanford University Press.

OPLER, MORRIS E.
1959 Component, assemblage and theme in cultural integration and differentiation. *American Anthropologist* 61:955–964.
1962 Two converging lines of influence in cultural evolution. *American Anthropologist* 64:524–547.
1964 The human being in culture theory. *American Anthropologist* 66:507–528.

SARMELA, MATTI
1969 Reciprocity systems of the rural society in the Finnish-Karelian culture area. *Folklore Fellows Communications* 207. Helsinki.
1970 *Perinneaineiston kvantitatiivisesta tutkimuksesta.* Tietolipas 65. Helsinki: The Finnish Literature Society.
1972 *Johdatus yleiseen kulttuuriantropologiaan.* Ihminen ja yhteisöt cross-cultural -tutkimuksen valossa. Helsinki: The Folklore Institute, University of Helsinki.

SPUHLER, I. N., et al.
1959 *The evolution of man's capacity for culture.* Detroit.

STEPHENS, WILLIAM
1963 *The family in cross-cultural perspective.* New York: Holt, Rinehart, and Winston.

STEWARD, JULIAN
1955 *Theory of culture change.* Urbana: University of Illinois Press.

TAX, SOL, editor
1960 *The evolution of man.* Chicago. University of Chicago Press.

TEXTOR, ROBERT
1967 *A cross-cultural summary.* New Haven: HRAF Press.

WHITE, LESLIE
  1949   *The science of culture. A study of man and civilization.* New York. Farrar, Straus.
  1959   *The evolution of culture: the development of civilization to the fall of Rome.* New York: McGraw Hill.
WOLFE, ALVIN
  1969   Social structural bases of art. *Current Anthropology* 10:3–44.

Ethnocultural Development in External and Internal Isolates

R. F. ITS

The natural setting peculiar to certain isolated areas of the world is the basis for the specific ethnocultural development of human communities there. In most cases, such areas become external isolates where ethnic, cultural, and social processes are somewhat blurred and deviate from the general course of the development of mankind. It should be borne in mind, however, that the population of such isolates, which at present is aboriginal with reference to later arrivals, may itself have come there from other places.

Having broken off from larger ethnic aggregates and finding themselves in specific conditions of isolation which partially or completely preclude the actual ethnoses from communicating with the rest of the world and assimilating mankind's experience, these ethnoses and their cultural traditions continued to be imbued with formerly acquired knowledge and traditions. The latter are most persistent in the spiritual sphere, and account for the obvious gap (or incompatibility) between the material-production potential of these human groups and their ideological and social structures enriched by past experience.

Such ethnoses are generally recognized to include the Indians of California, the natives of Tierra del Fuego, the Australian aborigines, the Bushmen, and a number of groups inhabiting remote and inaccessible mountain regions. The outlying areas of the globe were settled at different periods and as a result of different factors, both objective and subjective. Being relatively or absolutely isolated, the ethnoses in these areas, in most cases, deteriorated in their economic and cultural development, which resulted in the formation of distinctive social structures.

The discovery over the past decades of new isolated ethnoses, and com-

prehensive studies of the peculiar pattern of social and cultural development among those already known, have not infrequently given rise to the
conjecture that conditions of isolation provide a natural laboratory for
studying human history; and that the less opportunity for contact with
the outside world, the more probable it is that the development of an
isolated group is representative of that of civilization as a whole, and is,
in fact, a replica of the road traversed by other peoples in their development. The controversies concerning the division of prehistory into certain
periods, the priority of patriarchy or matriarchy, and the correlation
between family types and clans are largely due to the uncritical adoption
by a number of researchers of this view.

Let us now consider how ethnocultural phenomena pertaining to some
isolated ethnoses relate to their ecology and social history.

The presence of Australoid anthropological types in Southeast and
even in East Asia, and the fact that Australoid features occur in different
groups of Mongoloids indicate, on the one hand, that the Australoids
evolved within the vast area of Southeast Asia, and, on the other hand,
that they may have maintained contacts with Mongoloids over long periods of time, which were not only contacts between different anthropological types, but also contacts between different ethnoses.[1] Regarding the
latter, fairly active ethnocultural contacts continued until they were
broken off due to changes in the geographical environment. Australia is
not part of the zone where anthropogenesis took place; its aborigines are
themselves immigrants from Southeast Asia. Paleogeography shows that
at one time there existed an isthmus between Southeast Asia and Australia; hence, we may surmise that the above-indicated contacts were only
severed from the time the sea level rose 8,000 to 10,000 years ago.

As an aftermath of that cataclysm, groups of pedestrian hunters and
gatherers who had penetrated into the Australian continent long before
the rise of the sea level, found themselves in complete isolation from their
former neighbors. Their lack of sea-faring skills sealed their isolation.

The peculiar type of ecological environment on the Australian continent, and the economic and cultural level which the ancient Australians
had attained by the time they found themselves isolated from the rest of
the world, resulted in the perpetuation, under conditions of isolation, of
the earliest economic and cultural pattern, that of hunting and gathering.
That pattern allows for substantial improvement, but it could not, in the
specific conditions of Australia, grow into another, more progressive
pattern. These hunters could not take up cattle breeding because there

---

[1]   Data on Australians have been taken from V. R. Kabo (1969).

were no bovines to be domesticated. They could not engage in hoe farming without adopting a more or less settled mode of life. It is possible that a sedentary, or partially sedentary, mode of life did exist in Australia in the first millennium after the continent had become isolated (the Australian aborigines of today are still strongly attached to their territories). Judging from paleontological and paleobotanical data, the flora and fauna of that period were sufficiently rich and diverse. Archaeological material testifies to a population growth; there are also indications of the existense of some large groups — the totemic clans and tribe-like ethnic communities of today's Australian aborigines are a reminder of this. But the ancient Australians came up against another calamity, a thermal maximum, which 4,000 to 1,000 years ago destroyed the giant prehistoric animals and changed, beyond recognition, the flora of the continent. The lush plains were turned into deserts, with the lakes and rivers drying up in the summer. The struggle against nature in adapting to the changed conditions must have cost a great many lives.

Under the new conditions, only small populations could survive, for there was not enough food for larger ones. Life became practically nomadic, conditioned by a continuous search for food. The entire material culture was adjusted to this new mode of life. A new type of organization emerged, the local group, which became the basic cell of society. In the spiritual sphere, however, concepts and traditions of the past were retained, which in the course of time became obscure because they no longer corresponded to the existing level of socioeconomic development. Mankind has evolved as a single whole over most of the globe, but in Australia the aborigines faced nature single-handed, and, being divided into small local groups, could not combine their efforts. Minor contacts of the North Coast Australians with Indonesian and Melanesian culture did not affect the way of life of the mass of the aborigines in the hinterland.

In most Australian communities, the level of material culture and production attained previously could only be increased to a limited extent, but not revolutionized. One reason was the low population growth, due not only to the low growth rate resulting from scanty food reserves, but also to the existence of practically isolated demographic units. Thus, a new ethnos or new ethnoses were formed in Australia, which at the time the continent was discovered by Europeans, differed fundamentally in their cultural and physical aspects from other ethnic groups around the world. Later on, these differences were duly explained; yet, for a long time, the reasons for the incompatibility between the complex of the Australian's spiritual perception (petroglyphs, magic rituals, the intricate pattern of social life) and their markedly complex social culture, on the one hand, and primitive, emphatically archaic material life, on the other, were not understood.

The circumstances leading to the isolation of the Indians of California and the Tierra del Fuegans were somewhat different. Both ethnoses are descended from the first migrants to the New World who arrived there from Asia some 30,000 years ago. Like the first settlers in Australia, they had a late Paleolithic cultural level and were relatively small in number. (In contrast to the Eskimos and Aleuts, who came later, the entire Indian population is an anthropological entity, especially in such important genetic features as the blood group "0" and the rhesus factor.) Ecological differences, however, were substantial; from north to south, America reproduced almost all the geographical zones of the Old World. For the first migrants to America, further progress was only a matter of time:

The seeds of early class society and statehood emerged much later in America than in Asia, Africa and Europe; this is largely due to the fact that the Indians' ancestors, initially very small in numbers, had to spend an enormous amount of time and effort to open up their continent (Cheboksarov and Cheboksarova 1971: 61).

Ultimately, somewhat later than in the Old World, America discovered crop raising and domestication of animals and developed, in the more propitious areas, what are known as the pre-Columbian civilizations, which exerted an influence over their neighbors. By the time Europeans arrived in America, it had known the same succession of historical periods and social structures as the rest of the world. However, as the territories with the more favorable natural conditions were peopled by more advanced ethnic groups, the backward tribes were forced to the outlying parts of the New World, which became reserves where an archaic material culture and mode of life was maintained. This is what happened in the case of the California Indians, among them the Yana tribes (Kroeber 1970), who were cut off by the Sierra Nevada and also to the Yamana (Yahgana) tribes which had settled at the extreme point of the New World, on Tierra del Fuego Island, separated from the continent by the ever-stormy Strait of Magellan (Narody Ameriki 1959: 376–390).

The basic tools of both the California Indians and the Tierra del Fuegans were made of stone or wood processed with stone knives. Both used bows and arrows and wooden or bone harpoons. Both were most ingenious in using bark, twigs, and grass to make boats, roofing, hunting weapons, and household articles. Neither knew pottery. Both the Yana and the Yamana engaged in hunting and gathering. The former hunted deer, speared fish in the rivers, and also gathered acorns and herbs; the latter were sea-oriented: they hunted whales and seals and gathered a few edible roots.

The family group, perforce, became the basic economic unit of both the Yana and the Yamana. In the former case, this was due to the break-up of the clan-and-tribal system under the influence of the neighboring tribes. The family group of the Yana included either a married couple and their children or several interrelated married couples, and retained many prehistoric traditions (the men's house, collective gathering of acorns, and collective forms of salmon catching and deer hunting). In the case of the Yamana, the necessity for a constant search for food in the ocean and the fact that a small bark boat could carry only a few persons accounted for the composition of the economic unit: married couples and their children. A tribe would come together only for impor-tant religious ceremonies or when hunting whales.

Unlike the Australians, preservation by the Yana of late Paleolithic traditions in their material culture was due not to the objective ecological conditions, but to factors of social history. After the initial slight retarda-tion in their development, the Yana were under continuous pressure from their neighbors of the Colorado and Sacramento valleys. This lim-ited the area of their habitat, and, in the case of any rapid decline in the population, endangered the very existence of the ethnos. With their mobile boathouses, the Yamana of Tierra del Fuego somewhat resembled the Australians in their struggle to adapt themselves to a changed environ-ment. However, the isolation of the Yamana from the ethnic groups of the continent was neither as early nor as complete as it had been for the Australians. This accounts for a still greater incompatibility between their material life and their spiritual world. It should also be emphasized that the limited size of Tierra del Fuego made it possible for the economically separated family groups of the Yamana, who indubitably presented an ethnic entity, to maintain continuous relations with one another.

The isolation of a substantial section of the Yitsu (the Yi, Nosu or Lolo) of East Asia (Its 1972: 190–217; 245–260; 284–285) took place after the thirteenth century A.D., at an entirely different level of develop-ment and in different geographical and social conditions. They found themselves as an internal isolate in an inaccessible mountain region of Liang Shan, a spur of the Himalayas. The name they habitually used to call themselves is Nosu. In the fourth to first centuries B.C., their ancestors formed the ancient state of Tien and, in the seventh to thirteenth centuries, the medieval state of Nanchao-Tali, which was overrun by the Mongols. After that, some Nosu remained in the Yunnan valleys, while most of them retreated to the Liang Shan Mountains.

Before the Mongol conquest, the Nosu were doubtless an ethnic entity, an ethnic community of the early class period, i.e. a *narodnost* [nationality or people]. Socially this was an early feudal society with rigid caste and class divisions, a hereditary monarchy, a bureaucratic machinery and a military system. It was marked by the existence of a special caste of priests and possessed a pictographic writing system. The economy comprised crop farming (dry farming included maize, buckwheat, and taro, while the flood plains were used for rice growing), livestock breeding (including horse breeding), and commodity and money relations (cowrie shells being used for money). They also had urban-type settlements.

For seven centuries the independent Nosu dwelt high up in the Liang Shan Mountains, and practically nothing was known about their life. The only signs of their existence were their military raids on the neighboring valleys whose population they took prisoner. Only in the mid-1950's, after seven centuries of life in the mountains, did they suddenly become known to the outside world as an archaic society, which a number of researchers described as slave-owning.

The former ethnic unity of the Nosu had been disrupted by the revived tribal organizations, the *tsoshi*, a broad term covering several social phenomena. *Tsoshi* refers to a social institution, an endogamous ethnic community, and the territory of occupation. Each *tsoshi* is divided into four castes or social estates. The highest one is regarded as the true, original Nosu; members of this caste have the right to carry weapons, to possess saddle horses, and are the full-fledged masters and owners of the remaining three castes. The latter come under the joint name of *watsa* [slave or dependent]. These oppressed castes are descended from Miao, Chinese, or Dai prisoners.

The social sphere of the *tsoshi* is dominated by feudal relations of serfdom, with many elements of classical slavery (prisoners and debtors are made slaves, and children born to the members of the third caste are also regarded as slaves at birth). The highest organ of power in the *tsoshi* is the revived people's assembly, in which only the Nosu are represented and which elects the *degu* [chief]. Another feature of the life of the Nosu are unending blood feuds waged by different *tsoshi*.

The economy of the *tsoshi* depends on the low yields of maize, buckwheat and taro grown by the *watsa* with the aid of such primitive wooden implements as the hoe, digging stick, and, in rare cases, the wooden plow. Commodity exchange predominates; dues are always paid in kind. There is preserved the caste of priests who, at present, are the only keepers of the ancient written language.

The Nosu ethnos has gradually merged with those of the oppressed castes. In Liang Shan, as in Montenegro and other mountainous regions, which, owing to external causes, have become asylums for an ethnos or section of an ethnos, history has not merely been arrested, but actually has been turned back. The changes in the material and social life have been so drastic that they have affected the people's former ethnocultural aspect and the trend of their development.

The inhabitants of Australia were isolated as a result of a geological cataclysm. In America and the Liang Shan Mountains the isolation of certain ethnic groups was due to social factors (as has been the case with a number of other internal and external isolates the world over). These ethnic groups, left to face nature single-handed, possessed different shares of mankind's common experience and stood at different levels of human development. This is why of all the ethnic groups under review, only the Liang Shan Nosu have managed to retain their unique way of life and their ethnos (at present they number close to one million) in an unfavorable natural environment (their settlements are more than 2,000 meters above sea level) and complex social setting (among those who have tried to invade "the country of the independent Lolo" over the past 700 years were the Mongols, the Chinese, the Manchus, the Kuomintang, and even units of British and German chasseurs). The Yana and Yamana have been destroyed; they withstood the formidable forces of nature, but were no match for European colonizers. The Australian aborigines formerly numbered several hundred thousand; at present, there are only 40,000 of them. They, too, were helpless when confronted by the colonizers.

All that has been stated above provides enough ground to regard ethnocultural development in internal and external isolates as a multifaceted phenomenon conditioned by geographical environment along with corresponding ecological conditions and by many kinds of outside influences, as well as by conditions inside the isolates themselves (some isolates are at the primitive communal stage, while others are at the class-society level).

It also should be emphasized in this connection, that the world cannot be viewed as a kind of honeycomb, each cell partitioned off from its neighbors and containing a people that has preserved intact all of its unique features and necessarily going through all the successive stages of social development. It is always man who is to blame for artificial isolation, and natural isolation is nearly always his bad luck. In the history of man (and mankind) pure isolation never has been and never can be the trend of development; on the contrary, there would have been no man without society, and there would have been no progress without the communication of one people with another, and without the mutual exchange of experience. A separated humanity could not have resisted the forces of nature.

Hence, the basic trend of social development has been development together, not separately. The examples cited indicate that whenever, owing to tribal alienation or to a forced retreat to a zone of natural isolation, cultural contacts have exerted only a superficial influence over the life of a less-developed people, their ethnocultural and, in particular, social development eventually became crippled and anachronistic.

In other words, all isolates inevitably deviate to a certain degree from the general course of human history. The earlier the stage at which isolation occurs and the more backward historically an isolated ethnos is, the slower its development, the more archaic it appears to the outside observer, and the more often its archaism is believed to be authentic.

This outward, superficial archaism, especially in the sphere of material production, must not be mechanically read into the ethnic and cultural stage of development of a given community; nor should it be mechanically compared to basic trends in the evolution of mankind. Hence, there are no reasons to regard these communities as standard models of this evolution.

REFERENCES

ANONYMOUS
  1959   *Narody Ameriki* [Peoples of America], volume two. Moscow.
CHEBOKSAROV, N. N., I. N. CHEBOKSAROVA
  1971   *Narody, rasy, kul'tury* [Peoples, races, cultures]. Moscow.
ITS, R. F.
  1972   *Etnicheskaja istorija juga Vostochnoi Azii* [Ethnic history of East Asia]. Leningrad.
KABO, V. R.
  1969   *Proiskhozdenie i ranniaia aborigenov Avstralii* [Origin and early history of the aborigines of Australia]. Moscow.
KROEBER, T.
  1970   *Ishi v drnkh mirakh* [Ishi in two worlds]. Moscow.

Social Evolution, Population, and Production

JAMES C. FARIS

1. INTRODUCTION

It is social production that marks the critical disjunction between human society and other animal societies. It is the ability of human society to produce subsistence, rather than control population in order to subsist, that discriminates human society from animal society. Such theoretical arguments can be tested with selected facts of population growth and population dynamics in human history. The theory is speculative, pre-liminary, and, at this point, concerned primarily with the cognitive im-plications, but it establishes the direction for further work.

Social production is that group subsistence activity which involves decisions about differential labor allocations. This means the awareness of alternatives, the ability to value labor, and, consequently, to plan and thus produce activity. Social production cannot be simply reduced to cooperation (though, of course, this is an important and necessary factor) for some animal societies cooperate in hunting (wolves and lions, for example. See Schaller 1972). The critical cognitive factor in social pro-duction is in the recognition or cognizance of labor potential, which could

This paper was initially tested on the participants of a seminar on sociocultural evolution at the University of Connecticut in 1973. It has benefited from and been substantially influenced by discussions with K. Chapdelaine, J. Driscoll, R. Gingerich, A. Marichild, J. O'Brien, B. Roseberry, N. Shapiro, M. Swift, F. Trudel, and D. White. Jennifer Faris, S. Leacock, B. Magubane, P. Newcomer, S. Polgar, K. Sacks, and J. Stauder have also kindly read and commented on an initial draft. Its evolution has been truly a social production.

be described, in fact, as the EMERGENCE of CONSCIOUSNESS — the objectification of work.[1]

This social activity was previously unknown in evolutionary history, and it effectively emancipated society from population control by biosocial means. Population growth could be accommodated rather than controlled. Social production enabled the population growth of producers to play a progressive rather than a limiting role in the future change of society. With the cognizance of the value of labor comes the value of humans as social individuals, as potential producers. It is decisions about allocation to secure greater returns from labor invstement that mark social production, for these enable the group to provide for more members — members whose BEING is now significant. To utilize labor in this manner is to produce.

The objectification of activity (and thus of people as producers) followed on and emerged from actual activity. It was born of struggle between the organization of activity based on biosocial requisites and dictates and the organization of activity which challenged or rejected this. The particular type or form of activity did not change significantly. It will be argued that the qualitative shift from merely hunting and gathering to producing was probably not marked by new types of subsistence activities, but rather by new forms of social relations. It should be clear that the TYPE of activity (hunting and/or gathering) which humans first pursued differed little from the type of activity of many other animals. But organizationally the differences became immense. Tools, techniques, and skills (commonly regarded as FORCES of production) all became social. Cognizance of labor potential, in fact, was undoubtedly required to RELEASE forces of production and enable them to become significant in further social evolution. While the significant differences may not have been initially observable, the consequences led to divisions of labor in which the organization of activity of the participants acquired a significance heretofore unknown. Humans *qua* humans, as producers, potential producers, or as aged producers whose consciousness (knowledge) was still vital, became important.[2] Biosocial mechanisms (see Wynne-Edwards

---

[1]   A common error is to assume objectification implies alienation. Though alienation requires objectification, objectification (consciousness) need not imply alienation. Objectification is necessary, in fact, for knowledge (see Luckacs 1972), and for these tasks in human history it is clearly progressive.

[2]   This (see also 4.2) may not have initially meant completely egalitarian social relations. Women were probably infrequently hunters in societies in which hunting loomed large. In such societies women's production was primarily in reproduction and in processing, and as such, was dependent. Even though with the emergence of social production, reproduction became an important part of production, women may have

1962) for the elimination of excess numbers (such as for making excess members available for natural selection) were no longer relevant — in fact, such mechanisms were literally counterproductive.

To focus on types, methods, or actual forces (tools, techniques, skills) of production as the means by which societies can be classified is to repeat the errors of Morgan (1963), errors all too unfortunately endorsed by Engels (1972).[3] To focus on the forces of production is to focus on the consequences of productive activity, not the cause. Engels, for example, regarded the disjunction between the appropriation of natural products and the production of domestic plants and animals as the distinction between food gathering and food production:

The essential difference between human and animal society is that animals are at most GATHERERS whilst men are PRODUCERS. This single but cardinal distinction alone makes it impossible simply to transfer the laws of animal societies to human societies (1875; emphasis original).

It is not the type of activity, however, but the organization of it that distinguishes animal "gatherers" from human "gatherers." Engels' focus on labor ("The Role Played by Labor in the Transition from Ape to Man" — see Engels 1940) is an amazingly sophisticated discussion for its time (see Trigger 1965) on the biological evolution resulting in *Homo sapiens*. But it led to an unfortunate emphasis on the form or type of activity rather than on the social organization of labor.

The theory of social production put forward in this paper thus focuses on RELATIONS OF PRODUCTION (that is, the actual social relations humans

---

been limited in these early societies by virtue of child-bearing. The enabling conditions which allowed the participation of women in other primary productive activity may have been absent in the work organization characteristic of much of early Pleistocene hunting. In this regard, then, hunting of this type does not constitute the most progressive type of productive activity, and the extent to which it prevailed (over other types such as gathering, see Linton 1970) may be regarded as a measure of the inhibition on further progressive social evolution.

[3] And insufficiently recognized by Leacock (1963; 1972) and Terray (1972) in their discussions of Morgan. Concentration on productive forces rather than productive relations results in the mechanical materialism characteristic of White, Childe, Steward, and Harris (see Faris 1972b). Nevertheless, it should be made clear that the development of the present theory of social production and its use in accounting for much of the anthropological data on population control and social evolution is not a corrective to the work of Marx and Engels, but rather is intended to be an addition and development of their ideas in an area where we now have more information. The contemporaneity of their genius is continually astounding. As Haldane has suggested in his introduction to *Dialectics of Nature* (1940:xii, xiv), "When all criticisms have been made, it is astonishing how Engels anticipated the progress of science in the sixty years which have elapsed since he wrote ... had his remarks on Darwinism been generally known, I for one would have been saved a certain amount of muddled thinking."

enter into to produce) rather than on the METHOD or TYPE of production (e.g. hunting and gathering, agricultural, industrial). Thus, human hunting and gathering (or fishing) types of economies are clearly organized for social production and can be seen to produce in ways that may even approximate (in organization and returns) agricultural harvest (witness the great bison kills of the North American Plains people and the gluts of fishing "harvests" on the Northwest Coast — see Antler and Faris 1973). In this view, small-scale producer-controlled horticulture has much more in common with small-scale fishing than it does with large plantation agricultural systems (which should, in turn, be classified with large-scale mining organization, rather than under the rubric "agricultural societies" — see 2.3 below).

2.   METHODOLOGICAL COMMENT: THE TASKS AND LOGIC OF EVOLUTIONARY THEORY

Before turning to substantive data, it is necessary to consider several methodological implications of a theory of social production, for in arguing for an evolutionary approach to population dynamics, it is important to examine the requirements of adequate processual theory and the methods by which such theory may be tested. The methodology and logic of an adequate science is quite as important as its content and subject matter. The inadequacies of many sociocultural evolutionary theories rest in part in their inabilities to develop sound methods and rules for testing.

2.1   *Processual Concepts and Evolutionary Change*

Only processual and systemic change is relevant to evolutionary theory.[4] It is important at the outset, however, to distinguish between systemic change that is evolutionary and dynamic and systemic change that is not — that is, change that maintains only, that perpetuates homeostasis. An example of this latter type of change might be a furnace governed by a thermostat, or perhaps a self-regulating age organization (see Faris 1972d; Hallpike 1972). In the view adopted here, all evolutionary pro-

---

[4]   That is, capricious or random events are not considered, unless it can be shown how these "accidents" become necessary in social process. Since these can never be "accounted for" in processual theory, social scientists can at best know enough of social dynamics to know what alternatives will not take place should an external random event be introduced.

cesses are of the former type — change is dynamic; it is perpetual, inherent, and generative of new forms. In evolutionary processes there are inherent contradictions giving rise to potentialities in each living system, the resolution of which enables the successor system — a different system characterized by new contraditions and potentialities. Qualitative change is a potential of each system. All living systems are in motion for reasons of internal potentialities, and the locus of change is to be sought in the systems themselves (Faris 1972c).

In evolutionary processes external factors and conditions, of course, play necessary roles, but they can never be sufficient forces. Thus, we must show how specific external condition not just affect change, but how the internal potentialities of the system under consideration (its contradictions) enabled the effect of these particular external conditions.[5] It must be shown how any climactic, environmental, population, or technological situation, for example, articulates which of the potentials and limitations of any social system (see Newcomer 1972a), for they cannot be independent agents determining the course of events (*contra* White 1959; Steward 1955; Whiting 1964). Modern commentators who consider the motive forces in social evolution to be external to the system — to be independent variables — bear a remarkable similarity to Lamarck; consequence is read as cause (see Faris 1972c; Newcomer 1972b).

2.2 *Adaptation and Function*

We must also reexamine the related view that social evolution is the outcome of functional adaptation. Evolution is known from the products of its operation, that is, from the new species, the disjunctions, and qualitative changes which result from its having taken place. The origin of species, then, is the truly significant problem in evolution — how do new forms come into being? This fundamental question is not answered by reference to general statements about the necessary operations for the maintenance of life — such as survival or adaptation. Of course survival and adaptation are necessary for evolution to take place (if evolution did not take place, then the species or society would not persist), but this does not constitute a theory of evolution.

Survival is a statement of persistence only, and adaptation is a description of maintenance processes only. Neither can address the dynamic features of an evolutionary theory, the establishment of new species, each

---

[5] "... external causes are the conditions of change and internal causes are the basis of change ... external causes become operative through internal causes" (Mao Tse-tung 1967:5).

with its own unique laws of development and unique laws of adaptation. Adaptation, like function, is simply an empirical specification of maintenance — NOT change. To view adaptation as the motive force (see Alland 1967) is to treat consequence as cause. To posit adaptation as the motive force is naive, for it says nothing more than that the pro-
    What must be sought is a theory of process that will generate the comes about, except to appeal to external conditions and adaptation to them; for a system that only adapts cannot change in and of itself, it only adjusts when pressured by external agents. In such circumstances, how does one system become another? How is change enabled? What is it that governs the external change agents? For unles the causaliity can be specified, the change can hardly be regarded as processual, and the functional measure of its occurrence is certainly not the job of a theoretical science.

facts of history from elements present in the beginning, not simply look back over history to demonstrate that survival and adaptation have occured in response to a host of external influences.[7]

cess, whatever it is, is working.[6] It cannot suggest how social evolution

2.3   Disjunction and Qualitative Change

A view of evolutionary history which treats every form as a quantitative expression of every other must rely on external determinism, on some

[6]   Dynamic and progressive evolutionary systems can never be maximally adapted in any case, for such overspecialization is dangerous. It leads to stagnation and extinction usually, never to change and advance.

[7]   These processes are normally not observable, ("All science would be superfluous if the outward appearance and the essence of things directly coincided" [Marx 1967, III: 817]), but we deduce them from their effects and their mechanisms. We must look behind reality for explanation, behind behavior for process. Inductive empiricism not only blinds us to such processes, but it effectively denies these processes.
    A process statement simply illustrates the dynamics; it specifies the relationships between the facts observed and the means by which these facts and these relationships (and not others) came about. To explain phenomena, then, scientists must be able to generate these phenomena — to specify the processes by which these phenomena came to be the way they are (and not any other way).
    A scientific explanation is a theory, a statement of the process generating the facts we are attempting to account for. Biological evolution furnishes a good example. No one has ever seen evolution taking place; we see the consequences and perhaps some of the mechanisms, such as natural selection. But the process is an abstract statement which explains how the observable quantitative changes (such as differential reproductive success) result in the qualitative distinctions, the emergence of new forms we call species. In biological evolution a statement of the process can not be just a statement of the incremental and quantitative changes, for this can only describe, but never generate, the data accounted for by evolutionary theory: the origin of species. An excellent treatment of the concepts and methods involved in an adequate theory of social process may be found in Newcomer 1972b. See also Faris 1972c.

type of independent force (environment, population, economy). If all social forms are similar and differ from one another only in degree, some having more or less of something than do others, then anticipation of qualitatively new forms is impossible. This was the mistake of Lamarck, for by accepting an environmental determinism, he was unable to clearly see the significant problem in evolution — the emergence of qualitatively distinct forms, the origin of species.[8]

The emergence of new forms from old, such as the emergence of new species or a new stage in human history, means that new laws of development and new dynamics characterize the form or state. There has been a disjunction with the past — a qualitative change. No new energy or matter comes into being, to be sure, and the seeds of all new forms must be sought in the old. But the transformation of quantitative changes into qualitative changes is what distinguishes evolution from the simple quantitative change whose consequence we call adaptation. The disjunctive form is new in that new contradictions (potentialities) characterize it. External factors affect this new form in different ways than they affect other forms.

Much of post-nineteenth century scientific theory of process — certainly in social science — has been characterized by an emphasis on continuities and similarities (see 3.1 below) rather than on disjunction and change.[9] Of course, Darwin and the early evolutionists had to argue against entrenched religious dogmas about the dissimilarities between animals and humans. But this remained the dominant view in processual analyses long after evolution was an established and accepted fact (see Liebowitz 1969), and its theoretical effect was to cripple research into the implications of the disjunction between animal societies and human society. They were treated as quantitative expressions of each other.

2.4 Classification

It is of critical importance that a science that produces a testable explana-

---

[8] Though he contributed little to its solution, the great genius of Darwin was to clearly specify the problem.

[9] As a result of the prejudices of the nineteenth century, a scientific stress on similarities between human societies became necessary to counter the racist interpretations of alien societies. At the leadership of Boas and his followers, this led to a stifling relativism on the one hand (see White 1947 for an interesting discussion of the incipient evolutionism of these early relativists), or a projection of some form of contemporary social institutions characteristic of developed capitalism on the other (cf. Faris 1972a). Thus, for an example of the latter, we find economic man everywhere maximizing advantage and assigning value in terms of local supply and demand (see Firth 1939) or differential valuation based on culturally specific criteria (Bohannon and Dalton 1962).

tion specify change in systematic natural processes in a way which reflects the qualitative or disjunctive shifts in the development of the system. That is, it is essential that our classifications and taxonomies reflect the essence of development — the qualitative changes that occur in social evolution. In biological evolution the classification into species, each with somewhat different determinants of development and change, is such an example. But biological classification makes sense because we have a theory of its generation, a theory of evolution. Otherwise it could legitimately be argued that a functional environmental classification which would group whales, fish, and submarines, or birds, bats, and airplanes, is as valid as a classification that emphasizes their differences.

Apart from the speculations of nineteenth century materialists, an adequate processual theory in social science has heretofore been lacking. Thus, classifications of human history into stages or epochs hardly reveal any systematic process that generated the particular stages. We have empirical classifications where detailed specifications of reality have substituted for theory — for an explanation of that reality (see Service 1962). We have classifications such as "agricultural society" which group plantation production with small-scale independent horticulture, and not with mining or factory production. We have classifications such as "industrial society" which lump together capitalist and socialist nations, a classification which can in no way reflect the totally different systems of production, distribution, and consumption.

As mentioned previously, one of the more unfortunate mistakes of Engels was in having an adequate theory of social evolution, yet accepting the data of L. H. Morgan as an accurate classification of the stages of human history (Engels 1972). It is not that Engels was wrong about the processual theory, only that he was wrong in accepting an inadequate classification based largely on the forces of production (rather than including social relations of production) to argue for its manifestation.

2.5   *Ontological Implications*

A final methodological point concerns the implications of studying the present to gain clues to the past. Apart from the logic of deductive reasoning, it will be argued below that in understanding the population dynamics and the social organization of the capitalist mode of production, we are in a position to understand more clearly what preceded this epoch. Indeed, it is difficult to see why in fact studying the present to understand the past has not become a fundamental methodological position — as Marx has suggested, "The anatomy of man is a key to the anatomy of the ape" (1970: 145).[10] Explanation involves showing how the potentialities of one system generate its successor, and since "nothing can result at the end of a process that did not occur at its beginning as a prerequisite and condition" (Marx 1971: 78), all the elements of the process must be present from its inception. The present work seeks to trace social production in human history by examining the role of labor and productive relations through their various transformations in the different epochs of human history. An analysis of contemporary capitalism, accordingly, reveals that labor constitutes the source of value in such a system. And it will be argued here that in labor value are found the seeds for the many transformations through history which resulted in the mode of production known as capitalism. Thus, it is not necessary to attempt to find capitalism in Paleolithic society (*contra* Tiger and Fox 1971; see Faris 1972a: 21 for an exposure of this tendency in classical social anthropology), but only to find evidence of the recognition of the potential of labor.

3. ANIMAL SOCIETIES AND HUMAN SOCIETY

As argued above, any consideration of the relationships between the social organization and population dynamics of *Homo sapiens* and that of other animal species must be based upon a clear understanding of social evolution. That is, social similarities and differences established between humans and other animals must be seen as the results of processes which are specifiable, selective pressures which can be documented. It is no longer sufficient simply to describe the social differences in terms of traditional cultural discriminators such as tool making, fire control, or even language. We must discuss how these specific features came into being and how they were significant in altering both society and its numbers, if in fact they did. We must understand the processes and selective pressures which have generated similarities and maintained a continuity of process between human societies and those of other animals, and we must understand those qualitative differences between human societies and those of other animals, for at these latter points processes will be disjunctive and different laws of development and differential dynamics

---

[10] It has been repeatedly pointed out (Burrow 1966; Engels 1940:19, for example) that much of Darwin's inspiration for his thinking on the evolution of species stemmed from observing the competition for survival which characterized the political economy of England in the nineteenth century. Certainly his debt to Spencer for the concept of "the survival of the fittest" is widely known (Hardin 1969:159).

will be at work. It is these points of processual disjunction that we can meaningfully speak of as the dinstinctions between other animal societies and human society.

3.1   *The Continuity Emphasis and the Disjunctive Traditions*

Today, in discussing humans and animals, the dominant and most sanctioned and rewarded view emphasizes the continuity of determinants and the basic similarities of social organization and population dynamics. In fact, knowledge of the population dynamics of animal societies has been taken to be the proof of similar regulations operative in human society (Wynne-Edwards 1962: 21; Sussman 1972: 259). Recent ethological research and field studies of animal social organization are regarded as informative about human society, and the continuities more instructive than the differences (see Kummer 1971; Kortmulder 1968).[11]

However, as noted, many anthropologists have accepted some type of disjunction between human society and animal societies based on one or more traditional cultural discriminators, such as tool making, fire use, or language. It is argued that tool making required the type of mental, physical, and social organization characteristic of humans (Washburn 1961) and thus effectively marks a disjunction; that controlled fire required similar characteristics (Oakley 1961); and that human speech requires species specific innate mechanisms (Chomsky 1968) and supralaryngeal abilities (Lieberman and Crelin 1971). In essence, the symboling behavior (see White 1959) and its physiological requisites are seen to mark the critical disjunction of humans from animals. Apart from the fact that many animal societies exhibit learned symboling behavior (Gardiner and Gardiner 1969), it will be argued below (3.3) that the particular traditional discriminators put forward are at best consequences

---

[11]   This view is carried to its most vulgar extreme in the apologists for various forms of oppression. Aggression and the basis of private property (Ardrey 1961; 1966), imperialism (Tiger and Fox 1971), and sexism (Tiger 1970) are seen as biological manifestations common to humans. While general human problems are accounted for by innate animal behavior in this vulgar view, in the same genre of biological explanation, SPECIFIC human problems (such as the socioeconomic state of black people) require an emphasis on the dissimilarities between HUMAN populations (see Coon 1963). The argument is that black people are in such a condition because they are innately stupider than whites (see Jensen 1969; Eysenck 1971). This general thesis has recently been extended to ALL poor — black and other — by Herrnstein (1971), who argues that ruling classes are those innately superior. These views have been dismissed scientifically many times, but persist as ideological tools for justifying racism, sexism, class oppression, and even imperialist wars.

and concomitants of social production, not causal factors resulting in social production.

3.2 Use and Misuse of V. Wynne-Edwards

We have known for some time that population regulation by social means is an organizational characteristic of a great many animal societies (Wynne-Edwards 1962). Animal societies have no way of producing to accommodate population increase, so their social organizations must regulate population. Population regulation is necessary because any successful species in evolutionary history requires a potential excess of births over deaths. An unchecked population could conceivably increase to the point where the species would be threatened by lack of sufficient feeding resources. This necessitated excess (or potential excess) is managed by means of social conventions which organize the competition for resources (Wynne-Edwards 1965). Spacing and territorial management are, for example, common mechanisms for the control of animal populations (Sussman 1972; Wynne-Edwards 1962), and many other mechanisms for reproductive regulation are also known. Animal social organizations commonly make available excess numbers for natural selection. The various signaling devices necessary for animal dispersion are in aid of resource management, and resource management in animal societies is, in fact, population control.[12]

Human society may be distinguished from these other animal societies precisely because human society has the option of NOT controlling population, but regulating labor (and thereby accommodating population).

---

[12] This requires rejection of Darwin's suggestion (1871: Part III) that many of the various signaling devices (epideictic displays) were mechanisms for sexual selection (Wynne-Edwards 1962:17). From the perspective of this study, however, there has been an unfortunate use of Wynne-Edwards in discussions of competition in human society (see Rappaport 1968). It seems clear that Wynne-Edwards himself misunderstood the implications of his theory for human society. For example, Wynne-Edwards considers that private property is the logical extension of animal territoriality (1962:188–191). He states that the "absence of protection of individual interests [private property] has ... devastating consequences" (1962:189). Wynne-Edwards fails to see that it is ALLOWING individual exploitation that is devastating. It is the group welfare that is important, not individual interest. The genius of his analysis of animal societies simply failed him in looking at humans. In discussing humans, he mistakes possession and management for ownership, and confuses society with its ruling segments, such as the state. He is guilty of the crudest social Darwinism in regarding selection as operating on behalf of those with respect for property interests and law. He also makes the mistake of considering the relatively greater preponderance of patrilineal inheritance forms in human society as a function of male sexual dimorphism (1962:191), and young adult migration as having a primate ecological origin (1962:188).

Human societies no longer had to regulate population because they could not produce, but could now accommodate population.

3.3   Tools and Speech in Human Evolution

It is with social production that the various cultural traits traditionally used to demarcate humans from animals can be understood. Tool use, then, can be seen not only to make possible increased production, but also to be enabled by productive requirements. Innovations, invention, or the diffusion of technological ideas must be seen as necessitated in evolutionary history — as tools or knowledge that enable change to take place, to be sure, but to come into use when the social relations of production demanded them and could utilize them effectively. Thus, some Bushmen have knowledge of agriculture and some agricultural techniques, but simply do not have to engage in agricultural production so long as hunting and gathering will provide for them (Lee and DeVore 1968). Northwest Coast societies such as the Kwakiutl (Ruyle 1973) were state structured, yet were based on essentially hunting and gathering types of production. Certainly, lack of knowledge of agriculture and inadequate technology did not inhibit the adoption of other types of production; the situation simply did not require that these changes be initiated. Other examples are plentiful of the existence of potentially advantageous tools and techniques prior to their emergence as necessary to production. These could be said to approximate mutations in biology which are not selected against, but which will not appear to alter the course of biological evolution until sometime later in the history of the species. Population growth may have been an important factor in bringing about these innovations in specific circumstances as social relations of production changed in quantitative ways to accommodate the growth.

Any discussion of the role of tools must look at just what it was that tools did socially, how labor potential was realized in them as embodied labor. Animals can use tools, even make them, but this is only as individuals and animal tools do not embody labor for the group. In human society, however, tools could mean increased manpower for production, changed land tenure or mobility patterns, and different forms of work organization. The social relevance of tools can be most clearly seen in hunting and gathering societies. Gathering containers, for example, help emancipate societies from fixed territorial commitments and thus enable and permit organizational changes in work. The same is true of tools known as weapons. The hunting advantages of the bow and arrow are clear, but it is also of interest to see how truly social these tools really are.[13] It is here that the primary role of social production becomes clear, for social aspects of tool use are as important in the explanation of their appearance in social evolution as are their technological aspects. While it is obvious that tools facilitated greater control of energy (White 1949), we must ask what the greater control of energy aided. It may have been, for example, required by greater population (see Boserup 1965), which in turn was enabled by the realization of labor potential in social production.

Technological changes may in themselves enable and help bring about qualitative shifts in social production. These shifts not only accommodate population growth, but also establish new laws of population growth and new dynamics of development. The potentialities of each epoch change, and new contradictions come into being. The work of Boserup (1965) is one example of work based on the premise that technological changes are consequences and not causes (see also Carneiro 1967; Harner 1970). Boserup's thesis (limited to agricultural societies and agricultural growth) is that population pressures precipitate changes in technology, social organization, and culture. For Boserup, tools and technology are a function of population pressure, not vice-versa. Boserup sees population as an independent variable rather than as the outcome of social relations of production. Her commitment to this type of determinism is unfortunate,[14] but, as discussed above, any appeal to external agents (independent variables) in the analysis of social change cannot but result in a mechanistic view (see Faris 1972c). There is no doubt that population growth has aided in precipitating many changes in the history of human society, but population dynamics change in each epoch and cannot be understood outside the particular set of social relations of production to which they are subject. To understand population growth (and to see its role in precipitating change) we need to know initially the inherent potentialities of the social system that facilitated, enabled, or required the growth. As noted above, population, ALONG WITH technology, environment — or even climate, is a significant and even necessary factor in social evolution. But it must be shown that these factors can not be sufficient in and of

---

[13] Witness, for example, the exchange of arrow tips that takes place between !Kung Bushmen hunters (Marshall 1965:253). An elaborate series of rules surrounds the distribution of the kill, based on who shot the animal and whose arrow killed it (men commonly use arrows other than their own). The entire exchange of arrows and the rules of meat distribution ensure that everyone gets a share, that arrows are always available, and that production is social.

[14] And is the focus of much discussion in a recent book devoted to a critical examination of Boserup's ideas — see Spooner 1972.

themselves if the social relations of production in societies in question do not enable or require such factors.

Another traditional disjunctive discriminator based on symboling behavior is human speech. The idealist Cartesian thesis, represented by Chomsky (1968), is that human speech capacities are species-specific, innate abilities. This descriptive statement is trivial if true, and completely fails to explain why and how this came about — the requirement any processual (evolutionary) account must demand.[15]

This general tradition has been given support by the dissimilar speech capacities claimed to exist between *Homo sapiens* and classic Neanderthal (*la chapelle aux-saints*) (Lieberman and Crelin 1971). Lieberman and Crelin show that Neanderthal speech could have been but a fraction as efficient as *Homo sapiens* speech in information transmission and, in fact, was qualitatively different. They conclude that "man is human because he can say so" (1971: 221). This conclusion is, however, unrevealing. First, though it may be the case that information is transmitted in Neanderthal speech many times more slowly than in the speech of *Homo sapiens*, this does not mean that other modalities were not available to Neanderthals for symboling and information transmission. Certainly the cultural data for Neanderthals indicate considerable sophistication, and the clear possibility of social production (see Brose and Wolpoff 1971). In fact, early Neanderthal has been considered ancestral to *Homo sapiens* by some anthropologists (Brace 1967).

But the most important criticism is that here, too, no statement of evolutionary process is forthcoming. Speech capacities had to develop for social reasons, it seems patently clear, and it will be in specifying these social relations of production that a solution to the selective pressures on vocal tract morphology will be found. The question that must be asked is what conditions would have enabled, facilitated, and required the emergence of a communication system such as is manifest in *Homo sapiens* speech. And what conditions would have selected against adaptations and mutations other than those that led to the emergence of the system required for *Homo sapiens* speech? When these can be answered, we will then be in a position to understand the reasons for the claimed differences between Neanderthal and *Homo sapiens* speech abilities. The emancipating and liberating change brought about by the transition to social relations

[15]   This criticism, as with others here, does not mean that the views under discussion do not have validity in other types of nonevolutionary explanation. Obviously, Chomsky's ideas of innate mechanisms are framed to answer to the creativity of human language and provide a basis for the analysis of meaningful utterances, not to account for why or how these may have come about. Nevertheless, these ideas have been used as indicators of the disjunction between humans and other animals.

of production which came into being during the Pleistocene facilitated the dramatic shifts of the Paleolithic — in tools, physical morphology, and, if Lieberman and Crelin are correct, in speech abilities. This puts *Homo sapiens* speech, an obvious consequence and concomitant of social production, in its appropriate processual relationship. The demands of social production required more rapid speech and complex information processing (such as is shown to exist in current motor theories of speech production — see Lieberman et al. 1967), and this was met in *Homo sapiens* speech abilities. We cannot assume we have speech by virtue of fortuitous mutation, or as the result of a collection of evolutionary accidents unrelated to the selective pressures brought about by social life. Any concatenation of cause and effect which may be argued to produce the contemporary vocal tract morphology of *Homo sapiens* must rest in a processual explanation premised on the necessities of social evolution. Of course, bipedal posture enabled and required a reduction in prognathism, which helped result in the shape of the supralaryngeal vocal tract in *Homo sapiens* — this point is necessary to any complete explanation of *Homo sapiens* speech. But this cause is not sufficient, for speech modeling requires a complex integrated system of many morphological and neurological components, and to posit biological evolutionary pressures alone is naive. Rather than "man is human because he can say so" (Lieberman and Crelin), "... men in the making arrived at the point where THEY HAD SOMETHING TO SAY to one another" (Engels 1940: 283).

4. POPULATION DYNAMICS AND PRODUCTION IN HUMAN HISTORY

The thesis has been advanced that the disjunction between human society and other animal societies rests in the ability or capacity of human society to produce socially. It has been argued that social production emancipated human society from population control and enabled it to accommodate population growth.

4.1 *Population Regulation*

Regulating population because they cannot produce is a paramount demand on animal societies. Human societies can produce and thereby accommodate population growth. Population growth is a progressive result of the recognition of labor potential. This thesis requires reexamination of the data on mortality and birth-spacing mechanisms, such as infanticide, postpartum sexual restrictions, and various birth control techniques.

We are not so much interested in what factors inhibited population growth but rather in those factors which did not, for they are of most significance from the point of view of evolution. This requires looking at some of the "inhibiting" factors, however, for it will be the argument here that some of the factors traditionally considered to inhibit population growth are in fact properly understood as social means for ultimately promoting progressive population increase.

First, it is necessary to dispel what may be a myth — the high incidence of infanticide during the Paleolithic. This widely held view (see Polgar 1972: 206; Sussman 1972: 259) is represented by Birdsell (in Lee and DeVore 1968: 243) who states that 15 to 50 percent of the children born were of necessity killed. The basis for this estimate is inadequate and speculative. It may be true, however, that natural mortality is sufficient to account for the slow increase in population during this period. Durand argues that "In many cases and perhaps in most cases, improved conditions of mortality may have been the main cause of demographic expansion" (1972: 374; see also Petersen 1969: 351). Instead of limiting population growth, hunting and gathering societies actually encouraged growth. As Polgar observes (1972: 206):

It is hard to imagine, however, that among pre-agricultural people the perception of population pressure would often be consciously translated into the intensification of anti-reproductive practices.

"Encouraging growth" does not simply mean having as many offspring as physiologically possible, for the population dynamics must be understood in terms of the constraints and potentialities of the system of social production. Obviously, in Paleolithic society the health and strength of individuals in the society were of paramount importance so that production could continue. Two or three children in as many years not only decreased a woman's productive contribution, but in those circumstances it also meant the children themselves and their mother were disadvantaged and potentially weak. Thus, a birth spacing mechanism such as a postpartum sexual restriction made good productive sense, as the possibility of a growing, healthy, and efficient PRODUCTIVE population is greater if some attention is focused on the viability (labor potential) of the participants. Infanticide, where it did occur, may have been occasional. But it was not to inhibit growth; rather it was to insure the success of those living. It is not necessarily just numbers that provide the best potential for a growing population, a critical factor is the relative health of the individuals of the society; productive relations in a progressive evolutionary system demand this. Thus, the survival of healthy and strong members was of prime significance. If mortality were the most important factor in the slow rate of population growth during this period, attempts to reduce mortality by selecting for health and strength are even more reasonable; certainly having as many children as possible would do nothing to check mortality or insure a healthy and strong productive force. By careful reproductive planning (which may have occasionally involved infanticides, as well as postpartum sexual restriction, etc.), the productive strength of the society could be best insured — and thereby the growth potential of the group in terms of numbers as well. Weak people, particularly sickly children without productive knowledge (i.e. the healthy aged were more valuable to the group since they possessed this knowledge), could simply not be an asset in such conditions, and in fact constituted a brake on change. They may well have been left or killed (Boserup 1970). This also makes clearer the fear of simultaneous multiple births which occurs widely in the world; simultaneous or very closely spaced multiple children in tenuous circumstances are not an advantage but a possible detriment.

In the view adopted here, contraception, abortion, and postpartum sexual restrictions[16] are all birth-spacing mechanisms serving the same ends as infanticide. In fact, it may be that there is a synchronic or evolutionary order in which one of these practices will appear vis-à-vis any of the others. This must be approached in a more systematic and processually informed way than the usual cross-cultural correlational methods (cf. Saucier 1972; Whiting 1964).

It is in this light that infanticide may be understood best. Although speculation about a high rate of infanticide during the Paleolithic is not warranted by the evidence, it may have occurred. If so, its purpose was to insure a maximally strong, healthy, and productive society — its "cause" could hardly be the various consequences documented. This does NOT say that the effect or consequence of the various birth-spacing mechanisms may not have been consciously or unconsciously to insure adequate resource division (Lee and DeVore 1968), to maintain sexual balance (Balikci 1967), to increase ecosystem stability (Freeman 1971), or to maintain prestige systems (Douglas 1966). It is only that these proposed consequences cannot account for the evolution of the practice. Freeman, for example, correctly points out (1971: 1013) as erroneous the notion

[16]   Saucier (1972:238) is wrong in suggesting that postpartum sexual restriction is not a method of birth spacing (see Polgar 1972:261; Nurge 1972:252).

that "generalized infanticide is carried out irrespective of prevailing circumstances as a strategy of resource management." Further, he states that "Infanticide is a social practice, and causally to invoke blatant environmental determinism should *a priori* raise doubts" (1971: 1013). It is thus particularly unfortunate to observe Freeman retreat to the functionalism and tautology of an explanation in "ecosystem stability" (1971: 1017).

To regard infanticide and other birth-spacing mechanisms as a direct response to some externally derived constraint is mechanical and distinctly Lamarckian. In such a view, sociocultural evolution would be impossible — all human society would still be simply well-adapted Paleolithic groups.

To fully understand birth-spacing mechanisms, however, we need much better data on just when and in what circumstances they occur. Do abortions and infanticides occur more often while another child is still being nursed? Is there abandonment of the practices in times of plenty?[17] What percentage of infanticides involve malformed infants? These are all, of course, empirical questions, but they may shed significant light on the theories suggested herein (see Sussman 1972: 259).

We must seek dynamic relationships in changing societies, not functional relationships in homeostatic systems.[18] With a theory of social production in which the internal potentialities of the system of social relations are transformed to new systems of social relations for production, birth-spacing mechanisms may be seen dynamically, not as inhibitors.

Restated, the argument is that in evolutionary history before the emergence of class structures (i.e. in those societies in which producers still have control over decisions about their production) human societies require strong and healthy members for social production. In general,

[17]   Freeman (1971:1015) quotes an example from the Netsilik in which a father allowed a newborn daughter to live, rather than be killed as had been the fate of some of her sisters. This decision occurred at a fall fishing site, at which the catch was very good. Freeman suggests this decision reflects the father's "mood," when it seems clear the productive successes were an important factor. The difference in interpretation is more than difference in emphasis.

[18]   This is not to imply purposive behavior, conscious striving, and teleology in social evolution. This would imply consciousness not of potential in given circumstances, but of ultimate ends. The arguments of this paper are that the projection of labor potential (the consciousness said to mark the disjunction between humans and other animals) is specific to the circumstances. This, of course, acted primarily to reproduce the initial conditions of the productive process at its end. The dynamic aspect comes in that such production always alters the system somewhat, and potentiality is always changing. Social production is, by definition, change — it is simply that the long term effects may well appear fortuitous in relation to the specific decisions themselves. The arguments herein are decidedly not deterministic.

they attempt to have as many strong and healthy offspring as possible. The various methods of altering maximum reproduction are not thus properly to be understood as population control. They are NOT "keeping family size low" (Polgar 1972: 206), but spacing births, or killing sickly children, or eliminating one or more of multiple births in ways necessary to the health and welfare of AS MANY offspring as possible in the tenuous material circumstances. Reproductive planning for social production is not the same as controlling population for resource management; it is, in fact, quite the opposite. Reproductive planning mechanisms are quality control, having little to do with numbers at all, for by resulting in maximally productive members, the population in fact increased slowly, helping to bring about the later developments discussed elsewhere which we document as social evolution. The recognition of the potential of labor necessitated this reproductive planning.

It should be obvious at this point that any suggestions that warfare in classless societies served to control population (Harris 1972), whether directly or in some indirect manner that had any evolutionary significance, are unacceptable. Part of the demands of production in human history may have required warfare, but warfare did not and could not have evolved in order to control population. Organized competition may function in some peripheral areas to keep population down (see Rappaport 1968), but this is not WHY it exists. As White suggested some time ago (White 1945), it takes evolutionary thinking to really see how inadequate functional thinking is in accounting for social phenomena.

4.2   *The Implications of Producer Control*

The causal importance of the labor potential of healthy producers in the population dynamics of classless societies has been indicated. Cognizance of labor value led to recognition of the value of human beings *qua* humans to the society. This meant that there was some endeavor to maintain each person in as physically capable a state as possible to insure maximum returns[19] for labor, such returns were required to support the children and nonproductive aged. It has been argued that, overall, this resulted in reproductive success as well.

---

[19]   By insuring maximum returns — this is to be understood SOCIALLY, not simply in input/output terms (see Note 30). Production for use cannot be equated with production for exchange. Sahlins (1972) unfortunately focuses on exchange in production, allowing him to quantify the "underproduction" of precapitalist societies. For the implications involved in the distinction between use value and exchange value, and production for use and for exchange, see Marx 1971.

But these population dynamics obtain when producers control decisions about the production. When nonproducers control production (nonproducers who are otherwise physically capable of producing) such as in class-based societies, then too do their production dictates govern the population growth patterns. The slow natural growth that occurred in the Paleolithic was a function of population increase brought about by increasing control of mortality, more efficient resource exploitation, and better work organization.[20] This population increase in turn helped enable (or even necessitate) certain technological innovations, organizational changes, etc., which resulted in qualitatively distinct social forms.

Each progression in this evolutionary development required the same or greater labor inputs (see Sahlins 1972), but in each new epoch it also became possible to produce relatively more with the labor expended. The fact that this occurred is evidence that systematic "population control" could not have been a dominant factor in evolutionary history. Eventually, in such circumstances, it became possible to support nonproductive members of the society who were neither aged nor children, i.e. who were capable of producing but did not.[21] In order to command maintenance, they had to have some control over the production of others, and the emergences of class structures began — a class of producers, and a class of those commanding part of that production without having produced it. However achieved, this was maintained by force and justified by myth and ideology as in legal institutions and concepts, and private property. As producers no longer totally controlled decisions about their labor potential, they also became subject to modes of production whose dynamics introduced new and different population requirements over which they had no effective control. Population is not an abstract entity; it is composed of real people, and the argument of this paper is that it is the class composition of the population which we must understand to understand population dynamics. It is argued that it was the population of producers

[20]   This is not to be interpreted as some type of maximal adaptation to an ecosystem, nor can it be usefully specified in terms of minimax strategic decisions. The decisions and directions of social evolution are necessitated by material conditions and enabled by the potentialities present at any time. This may not appear as maximally adaptive in any systems analysis. For discussion of the error in regarding evolution as adaptation, see 2.2 above and Faris (1972c).

[21]   In an article already overly speculative, an attempt to specify and spell out the origins of inequality will not be attempted (see Note 2). Some features such a theory cannot have are worth outlining, however. It seems clear that theories such as those of Fried (1967) that redistribution results in stratification or those of Sahlins (1958) that surpluses result in stratification are not adequate as formulated (see Newcomer 1972b for a more complete discussion). Nevertheless, Sahlins and Fried are among the few anthropologists of this generation who have focused attention on these problems, and we are in their debt for having done so.

which has the progressive and dynamic role in history. The following examples illustrate this.[22]

4.3 Feudalism: Europe and Africa

The mode of production known as feudalism has been known from many parts of the world, manifest in various forms at various times.[23] The feudal mode of production is characterized by a class of producers, commonly producing on land or some other resource controlled by a small class of aristocrats whose legitimacy is usually sanctioned by mystified birthright, and whose authority is maintained by force of arms. The producers produce for themselves and for the aristocrats in control of the means of production. During the vital and progressive feudal period, production commanded by ruling classes was largely in kind, but later actual rents were demanded as production for use gradually shifted to production for exchange. This shift marks the decline of feudal modes of production, and the rise of the essential requirements for capitalist production.

The social relations of production under feudalism required and enabled a slow increase in population. That is, producing families had to reproduce themselves plus insure subsistence security with numbers of children to help in production and to maintain them in later years. This was accommodated (as well as enabled) by quantitative changes in work organization and in agricultural technology, and by migration of producers into towns. But disease (particularly in Europe) often acted to decimate the urban populations, and mortality was sufficiently high so that town sizes grew very slowly if at all during most of the period.[24]

[22] Interpretations based on contemporary hunting and gathering societies must be attempted with caution. It has been shown that most extant hunting and gathering societies do not exist in any Paleolithic purity, but have been considerably influenced by capitalist expansion in one way or another (see Leacock 1972:24). Similarly, various social practices, such as the reputed female infanticide amongst the Eskimo (Freeman 1971) may well have no evolutionary significance whatsoever, but reflect an institutional arrangement of societies whose existence is no mirror for the progressive Paleolithic societies discussed here.

[23] The following brief survey focuses principally on the populations and economic consequences of feudalism rather than on the struggle between the antagonistic classes which actually generate the epoch and its successor. I do not think this distorts or inaccurately represents feudalism and the transition from feudalism to capitalism. For detailed discussion, see Marx (1965); Sweezy et al. (1950–1953); Davidson (1961; 1969); and Rodney (1971).

[24] Epidemics were most devastating where the greatest concentration of populations occurred. Therefore, despite migration to cities throughout feudal times, the urban populations probably did not grow significantly.

Technological improvements (three-field system, moldboard plow) and increasing exploitation brought about an increase in production rurally which generated a surplus in the hands of the feudal ruling class — to be consumed or hoarded, as there were no productive investment opportunities. In Europe the contradictions in this system were such that it could not continue with the small quantitative adaptations that had heretofore characterized the mode of production. Agricultural technology became as advanced as it could be without research into new areas, research unprovided for and impossible under feudal social relations. And there was little or no possibility for expanding into new European territory with the same mode of production. The population in excess of that required for agricultural maintenance was cast off the land, and having but their labor to sell could only produce for exchange. The accumulations of people and wealth in the emerging cities marked the beginning of a transformation; a qualitative change was occurring as the accumulated wealth and the available labor were harnessed for capitalist production. This necessitated markets, resources (material, capital, and labor), and led to explorations; the mines and plantations of the New World and the labor and markets of Africa yielded the further accumulation of capital for Europe's industrialization. Europe's expansion abroad began as a prop for a decaying feudalism, but was essential for the rise of capitalism.

European feudalism could simply not remain a viable and healthy mode of production. It could not maintain the same social relations, and a change was necessitated as the contradictions became too great. There was insufficient land, too many people, and too much unproductive wealth for the system to survive as it was. Feudalism might have persisted in Europe had the increasing population been able to expand into new lands and maintain the same feudal social relations of production instead of precipitating change. However, without areas into which to move or other innovations to maintain the same social relations of production, Europe's feudalism collapsed and the transformation to capitalism was necessitated.[25]

African feudalism, on the other hand, could probably have remained

[25] There is debate, of course, about the degree to which capitalist production emerged early and helped bring about the demise of feudalism, rather than the demise of feudalism bringing about capitalist production (cf. Sweezy et al. 1950–1953). The uneven development of forces and relations of production, however, make the former appear to be the case, when in fact, the latter must be the process which took place initially. As this occurred first in one place, and thereby influenced developments elsewhere, it is descriptively true that capitalism did later bring about the demise of feudalism in many areas. All societies of successive evolutionary epochs are more inclusive of and dominant over societies still existing with the productive relations of previous epochs.

a viable mode of production for many years had it not been for the influence of a new capitalist Europe (ironically, an interference necessitated by the fact that Europe's feudalism was collapsing). Most of the basic contradictions and potentialities of European feudalism were found in Africa — the accumulation of surplus, the increasing population, and yet there was the same inability of the feudal social relations to accommodate population or to convert surplus to investment capital.[26] But a number of factors in Africa kept feudal modes of production viable and progressive.

First, in response to increasing desiccation, increasing population, increasing militarism, and with the aid of technological advances, the states of the Sudan belt and the proto-Bantu-speaking state organizations moved south and east. There was room for expansion, and these feudal societies (or segments of them splitting off by fission) could expand into areas relatively unoccupied or occupied by nonfeudal groups unable to resist the superior military organization of these feudal states.

Secondly, technological innovations (the adoption, invention, and perfection of several broad crop series — see Murdock 1959) allowed the exploitation of areas previously underutilized. With the appearance of forest-type crops (probably from Asia) the forest belts of West Africa and the Congo basin came to be successfully exploited with feudal modes of production (as well as other nonfeudal productive modes, of course), rather than just exist as impenetrable barriers. Europe lacked this diversity of agriculture. In short, the contradictions in African feudalism were RELIEVED instead of RESOLVED (into a qualitative transformation to capitalism).

Theoretically, once these "solutions" had been fully pursued, however, sharpening the contradictions in African feudal modes of production, new forms would have come into being — probably capitalist. But the fortuitous advantage of a wide range of exploitative strategies, abundant areas in which to implement them, and social organizations capable of fission meant that African feudalism was viable and healthy for a longer period than was the feudalism of Europe. The European penetration of Africa, however, and the great slave trade brought an end to the progressive social evolution of indigenous African societies.

[26] This is *contra* Goody (1963), who argues against the use of the term "feudalism" to describe the state structures of Africa. I do not want to underemphasize the real differences that existed between the social relations of production in Africa and in Europe, for example, in the greater investment in African artisans, the larger African armies, etc. but I think understanding is best achieved by examining similarities, for in this way we can attempt to theorize about the processes which produced the facts we see on the ground — the real job of science.

The contradictions in European feudalism were resolved by the emergence of capitalism — and with this mode of production was required the never-ceasing search for markets, resources, and labor. As noted, the New World provided much of the resource base and Africa the labor necessary for the capital requirements of Europe's industrialism. Africa, moreover, became an important market source for the goods of Europe's industrial production (see Williams 1945). The slave trade decreased the continent's population by as much as one-third (Davidson 1961), and the social evolution of African societies became a function of capitalist modes of production. The viable and progressive feudalism of pre-European Africa was destroyed with the Atlantic slave trade, and this era of chattle slavery under capitalism completely distorted future social evolution on the continent. The point, however, is not that Africa was about to emerge as capitalist when crippled by the slave trade, the point is that African feudalism was at that time still vital; the contradictions were such that feudal relations of production could still be maintained and could be accommodated with solutions unavailable to Europe. Qualitative change was not necessitated. In population terms, expansion and growth WITHOUT changing feudalism, was still possible.

The contradictions of feudal modes of production as manifested in population and economics have been stressed. These contradictions were also manifest in their class base — between producers and those with control over producers. The resolution of this contradiction into capitalism did not change the basis of the system; that is, there was still a fundamentally antagonistic relationship between producers and those having control over producers.[27] The producers, however, increasingly came to sell only their labor and were still subject to the population laws of a mode of production which they did not control.

The population dynamics, then, of feudal modes of production dictated the potential of an ever-increasing population. This was required for the tasks of production, control over which rested in the hands of nonproducers. Large families were required for production, to insure (in the face of high mortality rates) reproduction and for the security of the aged (in a system where rewards for production were in kind, thus inhibiting the aged from providing for themselves). Disease and mortality had traditionally kept the population in check, plus (in Africa and perhaps earlier in European feudalism) expansion into less-developed and less-populated

---

[27] Technically, there were more than two antagonistic classes under feudal modes of production — aristocrats, merchant/artisans, and peasants. Capitalism is the first mode of production which increasingly pits all the producers on one side as a class against all the exploiters on the other side.

areas. Moreover, in Europe "excess" populations were shipped abroad to form settler colonies and remove them as a potential threat to the ruling classes.

But in spite of expansion, colonial ventures, technological innovations, and death, other factors sharpened the contradictions in the feudal epoch of Europe; increasing amounts of wealth remained unproductive. This wealth and the labor force made available by land enclosure movements to dispossess peasants were harnessed to capitalist production. The contradictions of feudal modes of production then find one expression in the facts of increasing wealth and population, neither of which were rationally productive. The only possible resolution of this contradiction was in capitalist modes of production in which both surplus wealth and population could be made productive. In Africa, expansion relieved the basic contradiction, and African feudal modes of production (and consequent population dynamics) remained viable until forever distorted by the penetration of Africa by Europe.

4.4 *Capitalism*

Perhaps the greatest mystification of population dynamics and social evolution has come in the past 150 years. During this time capitalism matured and entered its highest phase, imperialism, and the population growth rate worldwide increased from 0.4 percent per year to 2 percent per year (United Nations 1964). Malthus (1830), in response to the increasing human debris of eighteenth century capitalist production and as an attack on the poor laws, argued that population was outstripping its capacity to feed itself and that the starvation which was certain to result was, in fact, provident. His argument was basically that population expanded geometrically, while agricultural production expanded arithmetically. It was, of course, the proliferation of the underclasses that bothered Malthus primarily, just as it bothers contemporary population growth alarmists (see Huxley 1956; Osborn 1960; Erlich 1968; Hardin 1969).

Today, the composite population growth curves of much of Southeast Asia, most of Latin America and Africa, and the Black and Puerto Rican population of the United States are steep, whereas the population growth curves of Sweden, the Soviet Union, China in the 1970's, and the White middle and upper classes of Britain and the United States are relatively flat (and relatively unthreatening to neo-Malthusians). When the growth curves of ALL areas are combined into a SINGLE world population growth chart, the slope is still steep, and the population is increasing at considerably more than a linear rate. The implications sketched by population control advocates is the familiar Malthusian theme — disaster if the growth curves are not flattened (see Meadows et al. 1972). The composite world population growth chart is deceiving, however, for it disguises the most significant fact — population growth is greatest in underdeveloped parts of the world.

The correlations which ought to be of most interest are between resource distribution and control of production and the growth curves in different parts of the world. The steep curves are positively correlated with underdeveloped societies and oppressed segments of developed societies, and the relatively flat curves are correlated with societies (or segments of societies) in which producers control or have access to the results of production. The steep curves correlate positively with a lack of producer control; they reveal the population dynamics of underdevelopment. This will be argued to be the dynamics of capitalist exploitation.

There is little doubt that world population will continue to increase so long as population growth is necessary to capitalist modes of production. With decreasing mortality brought about by improved medical care[28] in response to demands of the working classes and peasants, it may even rise more steeply. The important fact is that IN SPITE OF population control programs and IN SPITE OF decreasing infant mortality (which allows larger families to be maintained with few children born) and in spite of death in war, no demographic change can alter the dynamics of population growth significantly until the productive system necessitating such dynamics is changed (see Mamdani 1972). This requires attention to the population dynamics of the capitalist mode of production. Hall has summarized this:

As anthropologists we should be aware that the economic system of the West depends upon an increasing population and that in a critical way this system, as Polgar [1972] has pointed out, has ENCOURAGED POPULATION GROWTH (1972: 260, emphasis mine; see also Polgar 1972: 210–211).

Capitalism is a mode of production in which the anarchistic expansion of production is a prime mover. But this expansion is not to accommodate the potential population increase as it may have been in classless societies; on the contrary, it is for the profits of a few. Great quantities of labor are

---

[28] Polgar (1975) suggests mortality declines began before the export of health measures. In any case, medical care contributed to declining mortality. The current world population growth rate is also more impressive when the lives lost in imperialist wars of the twentieth century are added — upwards of seventy-five million people have died as a result of these ventures.

necessary not only for the production itself, but also for keeping wages low with a reserve army of competitors for jobs. This anarchy in production is checked only by the ability of a population to purchase the goods produced, and herein lies an important contradiction in capitalist production, one that the system sooner or later will face.[29] Marx sums up this process of capitalist production:

The labor population therefore produces along with the accumulation of capital produced by it, the means by which itself is made relatively superfluous, is turned into a relative surplus population; and it does this to an always increasing extent. This is a law of population peculiar to the capitalist mode of production; and in fact every specified historic mode of production has its own specific laws of population, historically valid within its limits alone. An abstract law of population exists for plants and animals only, and only insofar as man has not interfered with them (1967, I: 631–632).

Capitalism thus requires an expanding population because it requires an expanding production. But for those NOT producing under capitalism, for those in control of production or having an adequate share of the proceeds of production, population growth curves are relatively flat. The steep growth curves of the working classes are essential primarily because of the demands of capitalist production, and it is only mortality that has kept the growth curves from being even larger than they are. A decrease in mortality, as mentioned above, will not substantially alter the causes for the high birth rate, nor will the basic population dynamics be altered.

Mamdani (1972) illustrates this quite clearly: he shows how and why a major birth control program in India's Punjab (sponsored by the Ford Foundation, Harvard University, and the Indian Government) failed. With care and detail Mamdani demonstrates that people are not poor because they have big families; they have large families because they are poor. The pressure on the land from great numbers of people does not mean farmers thereby control their population; more children mean that more land can be worked, more land can be rented to be worked (from those without sufficient numbers of children) which may result in savings that can be used to purchase more land. More children mean some can migrate to urban areas and send back money from their wage labor. People thereby see the population control program as an attack on their very existence. To be sure it is producers that are involved in decisions about the increase or decrease in family size, but it is the dynamics of

---

[29] A situation already at work in some capitalist countries, such as in South Africa, where the country's consumer products cannot compete successfully in the rest of Africa or in other parts of the world, but whose major population, African, is not paid sufficiently to be able to purchase this production (see Magubane n.d.).

capitalist production that dictates which decision makes rational survival sense to these producers — not being told that large families are not in their interests.

If, however, producers were in control of production, the lessons of history are clear — the population growth curve would flatten considerably.

China over the past twenty years furnishes a good example. The population growth rate of prerevolutionary China resembled that of many parts of the world (see Osborn 1960) underdeveloped as a consequence of capitalism (yet firmly locked into a dependency relation with capitalist powers through imperialism). But following the sequence of revolutions in China (1949, 1966) and the firm establishment of producer control, China has at the present brought its population growth rate to the low level of that of the developed capitalist countries (Sidel 1972).

Producer control eliminates the accrual of surplus labor value by an exploiting class. Planning is possible, and production for exchange no longer a necessary motive factor, as production for use is self-correcting. Vast reservoirs of reserve labor would no longer be necessary to drive wages down, and the anarchistic expansion would no longer be necessary; thus, not only freeing the producers in the developed capitalist nations from the threat to their rate of compensation, but emancipating the underdeveloped nations from the grip of imperialism.

"Overpopulation" is, from this view, not a problem of too many people, but of unequal resource distribution.[30] In fact, one of the true absurdities of capitalist "development" is that in its advanced imperialist phase, many nations of the world are, as NATIONS, ostensibly UNDERPOPULATED. That is, they do not have the necessary population required for an integrated economy, an economy not dependent on imperialist powers. A nation with fewer than fifteen million people, many of whom must be relatively concentrated, can in no way have a modern integrated industrial economy without exploiting the production of foreign labor (as is the case, for example, with capitalist nations such as Sweden and West Germany).[31] This "underpopulation," however, only makes sense when

[30]   It must be emphasized, however, that so long as production remains for profit — for exchange rather than use — a more equitable distribution of wealth cannot, in fact, solve this problem.
[31]   This is not, of course, to argue that all present individual nations must strive to have a population in excess of fifteen million; on the contrary, for regional economic integration across national boundaries would not only efficiently utilize areal populations, but promote international cooperation. As Polgar (1972:210) has stated. "Nowadays the abundance of people is no longer advantageous to anyone for economic reasons." Whether or not the world has sufficient numbers of people for global egalitarian production (for production for use rather than exchange) is a fact that could only be objectively determined in the circumstance.

the history of imperialist expansion and the demands of capitalist production are considered. For the demands of capitalism — of divide and rule, of dependency, and of selective underdevelopment — maintain, require, and bring about the balkanized appearance of Africa, South America, and other less-developed parts of the world, the familiar phenomenon of small nations with but a single export product, constantly at odds with their neighbors, often with an insufficient, but nevertheless underfed, population. Nationalism, then, masks neocolonialism.

The population dynamics of capitalism can be seen in the high population GROWTH RATES (or at least natality rates) of these "underpopulated" nations — which will approximate the growth rates of so-called overpopulated (yet underdeveloped) nations such as India. Only with the elimination of imperialism can these rates by checked and regional economic integration (using the populations of several adjacent small nations) become a reality.

Imperialism fostered the development of small nations with insufficient populations and resources in order to be able to control the production of those people and resources. The only planning under capitalism is for profit maintenance, and thus all development is stifled aside from the monolithic single commodity exports characteristic of many small nations. Should these nations have sufficient people and resources to establish integrated economies, the potentiality of rejecting the imperialist power is much greater, and the profit structure of neocolonialism is possibly threatened.

An example can be seen in Ghana, a country whose economy is severely distorted by imperialist demands. Capitalist developers in Ghana utilize electricity from the Volta River hydroelectric development to smelt aluminium. Although there is ample bauxite available in West Africa, the bauxite for the Ghana smelters comes from Jamaica! The principal reason for this distorted type of production is to insure that an integrated aluminium industry — with Ghanaian ore, electricity, smelting, and finishing — does not develop. For so long as the industry is dependent on other parts of the world — linked by imperialism — there is no threat to the capitalists that the industry could be nationalized or that control could be taken by producers, since Ghanaians do not have all the developed "parts" for the integrated industry. Nor, of course, does Jamaica. Nationalization is conceivable, but only on terms favorable to imperialists. Too much economic power in a single area unprotected by imperialist armies is to be avoided at any cost, for not only would this, if it could be controlled by producers, remove that much labor, resource, and market from imperialists; it would also constitute competition on the free world market. By encouraging shallow nationalism in West Africa, the possibility of uniting the necessary components of an integrated aluminium industry (not to speak of any other components of an integrated industrial economy) is extremely small. ONLY by uniting can the necessary population and resources be brought together. A regional unity or a pan-African unity is the only way of achieving the necessary economic integration for modern free industrial society (see Green and Seidman 1968), and the only way of throwing off the dependency (and the poverty/high population growth rate syndrome) of imperialism.

Thus, capitalist development under imperialism required underdevelopment, and one of the ways this was achieved was to allow the "incorporation" or independence of nations too small to possibly threaten the imperialist nations with an integrated economy. This is a matter of significance in understanding the population demands (and hostility to population control programs) of many smaller nations. Even in larger nations, capitalism in the stage of imperialism can only insure underdevelopment by keeping an integrated economy from arising, by distorting the development of the economies of these nations so that any attempt to emancipate themselves from the network of world capitalism is extremely difficult. Capitalism is not simply a disease. It has severely distorted the body politic of the world, and this makes it much more difficult to stop without a thorough analysis of its nature and consequences.

With the maintenance of capitalism there is little doubt that the world population growth curves will continue to appear essentially as they do. Some apologists have urged enforced population control (Erlich 1968; Hardin 1969) or other less subtle forms of genocide. As Meek has argued:

After all, the advocacy of infanticide or the cessation of medical supplies to "overpopulated" countries is not very far from the advocacy of more widespread and efficient measures to reduce the population. The struggle against Malthusianism is an integral part of the struggle for peace in the world today (1971: 48–49).

So long as capitalism continues as the dominant mode of production in the world,[32] so too will rampant population growth continue in oppressed and underdeveloped areas. With the advent of producer control (which implies permeating many of the "national" barriers now inhibiting inter-

---

[32]   It simply cannot be argued that most populations of the world today, even in more remote regions, are unaffected by capitalism in one way or another (see Faris 1972d). As it became a world force under imperialism, it has successfully permeated or otherwise affected essentially every society in the world. Thus, even in those few societies of the world whose subsistance economies are not capitalist, it may well be that capitalist modes of production govern or affect the population dynamics of those societies.

national cooperation), the existing population will produce for itself, and the population growth will be congruent with the needs of society, i.e. the producers. It may well be (on the strength of the Chinese case) that population increase will no longer be essential or desirable, and in such case, reproduction planning will undoubtedly be encouraged and come into being with no trouble.

It has been the argument throughout that reproduction planning has been practiced in history. Because after the emergence of class structures in history the modes of production are such that control is removed from producers, so too do the producers no longer really control decisions about population planning, but reproduce in terms of the demands of the production system, now controlled by ruling classes. Thus, population programs under capitalism based on moral suasion (or even enforced schemes of some variety) — short of severe genocide — are not going to be adequate and will be likely to be doomed to failure. Reproduction planning is a function of the demands of social production, and this is out of the hands of producers under capitalism. The social relations of production under capitalism dictate the population dynamics, and only when production is once again controlled by producers will reproduction planning be once again their decision. Productive requirements established under planned production in the control of producers may require continued population growth in some areas and not in others. This cannot be predicted in advance. First, the conditions have to be established which enable it to take place. Freedom and planning of any sort is simply impossible until producers can once again emancipate their labor and direct its activity.

5. CONCLUSIONS

A theory of social production and its implications has been sketched. It has been shown that with a dialectical materialist perspective, the fallacies and errors of inductive empiricism in outlining such a theory are avoided; facts may then be accounted for instead of used to "build" theory, change may be seen as inherent instead of introduced and mysteriously external to the system, and the processual character of evolution is the explicit center of focus, rather than the functional and adaptational specification of its consequences.

The argument has concentrated on the importance of a theory of social production in clarifying the disjunction between human society and other animal societies, and on the improved perspective it affords in understanding population dynamics. It is argued that the objectification of labor with the recognition of labor potential in society meant decisions could be made about alternative or differential allocation. This allowed labor to be projected for social use. In terms of population, it enabled human society to emancipate itself from the population control of nature, and allowed population growth to play a progressive role in social evolution. Accordingly, it is argued that postpartum sexual restrictions, infanticide, abortion, and contraception are reproduction planning mechanisms, not population control devices. They came into being to facilitate a productive force, not to inhibit growth. The freedom to plan was the emancipation from biological determinism. This was the essence of progressive production, and clearly demarcated human society from that of animals.

As classes evolved, decisions about differential allocation of labor were no longer in the hands of producers, and the population regulation they had wrested from nature was now surrendered to the production demands of ruling classes as population dynamics became a function of class-based modes of production. This is illustrated in the differential history and population dynamics in the feudalism of Europe and Africa, and it is further traced in the necessities of capitalist production. It is argued that in spite of efforts such as moral persuasion and population planning, reduction of the population growth curves in underdeveloped areas is impossible (see Mamdani 1972) until producers once again control their production. Population planning is, in this view, production planning and can be facilitated only with producer control.

REFERENCES

ALLAND, A.
   1967   *Evolution and human behavior*. New York: Natural History Press.
ANTLER, E., J. FARIS
   1973   "Adaptation to changes in technology and government policy: a new found land." Example, Unpublished paper prepared for the IXth International Congress of Anthropological and Ethnological Sciences. Chicago, Sept. 1973.
ARDREY, R.
   1961   *African genesis*. London: Atheneum.
   1966   *The territorial imperative*. New York: Atheneum.
BALIKCI, A.
   1967   Female infanticide on the Arctic coast. *Man* 2:615–625.
BIRDSELL, J.
   1968   "Some predictions for the Pleistocene based on equilibrium systems among recent hunter-gatherers," in *Man the hunter*. Edited by R. Lee and I. DeVore. Chicago: Aldine.

BOHANNON, P., G. DALTON
1962 *Markets in Africa*. Evanston: Northwestern University Press.
BOSERUP, E.
1965 *The conditions of agricultural growth*. Chicago: Aldine.
1970 *Woman's role in economic development*. New York: St. Martin's.
BRACE, C.
1967 *The stages in human evolution*. Englewood Cliffs: Prentice-Hall.
BROSE, D., M. WOLPOFF
1971 Early Upper Paleolithic man and late Middle Paleolithic tools. *American Anthropologist* 73:1156–1194.
BURROW, J.
1966 *Evolution and society*. Cambridge: Cambridge University Press.
CARNEIRO, R.
1967 On the relationship between size of population and complexity of social organization. *Southwestern Journal of Anthropology* 23:234.
CHOMSKY, N.
1968 *Language and mind*. New York: Harcourt, Brace.
COON, C.
1963 *The origins of races*. New York: Knopf.
DARWIN, C.
1871 *The descent of man*. New York: Random (Modern Library).
DAVIDSON, B.
1961 *The African slave trade*. Boston: Little, Brown.
1969 *Africa in history*. New York: Collier Macmillan.
DOUGLAS, M.
1966 Population control in primitive groups. *British Journal of Sociology* 17:263–273.
DURAND, J.
1972 "The viewpoint of historical demography," in *Population growth: anthropological implications*. Edited by B. Spooner. Cambridge: MIT Press.
ENGELS, F.
1875 "Letter to Lavrov (12 November 1875)," in *Marx and Engels on the population bomb*. Edited by R. Meek. San Francisco: Ramparts Press.
1940 *Dialectics of nature*. New York: International.
1972 *The origin of the family, private property and the state*. New York: International.
ERLICH, P.
1968 *The population bomb*. New York: Ballantine.
EYSENCK, H.
1971 *The I.Q. argument*. New York: Library Press.
FARIS, J.
1972a "Pax Britannica and the Sudan. S. F. Nadel in theory and practice," in *Anthropology and the colonial encounter*." Edited by T. Asad. London: D. Wolton.
1972b "Materialism and theory in anthropology." Paper read at the conference, "Theory on the Fringe." State University of New York, Oswego, New York, 1972.

1972c "Concepts and methodology in social process." Paper read at the American Anthropological Association Annual Meeting, Toronto, Canada, 1972.

1972d "The Southeastern Nuba age organization," in *Sudan ethnography: essays in honor of E. E. Evans-Pritchard.* Edited by W. James and I. Cunnison. London: C. Hurst.

FIRTH, R.
1939   *Primitive Polynesian economy.* London: Routledge and Kegan Paul.

FREEMAN, M.
1971   A social and ecologic analysis of systematic female infanticide among the Netsilik Eskimo. *American Anthropologist* 73:1011–1018.

FRIED, M.
1967   *The evolution of political society.* New York: Random.

GARDINER, R., B. GARDINER
1969   Teaching sign language to a chimpanzee. *Science* 1965:644–672.

GOODY, J.
1971   "Feudalism in Africa?" in *Economic development and social change.* Edited by G. Dalton. New York: Natural History Press.

GREEN, R., A. SEIDMAN
1968   *Unity or poverty?* Baltimore: Penguin.

HALDANE, J.
1940   "Introduction," in *Dialectics of nature* by F. Engels. New York: International.

HALL, R.
1972   "The demographic transition: stage four," in Anthropology and population problems. *Current Anthropology* 13:203–278.

HALLPIKE, C.
1972   *The Konso of Ethiopia.* London: Oxford University Press.

HARDIN, G.
1969   *Population, evolution, and birth control.* San Francisco: Freeman.

HARNER, M.
1970   Population pressure and the social evolution of agriculturalists. *Southwestern Journal of Anthropology* 26:67.

HARRIS, M.
1972   Warfare, old and new. *Natural History* 81:18–20.

HERRNSTEIN, R.
1971   I.Q. *Atlantic Monthly* (September).

HUXLEY, J.
1956   World population. *Scientific American* (March).

JENSEN, A.
1969   How much can we boost IQ and scholarly achievement? *Harvard Educational Review* 39:1–123.

KORTMULDER, K.
1968   An ethnological theory of the incest taboo and exogamy. *Current Anthropology* 9:437–449.

KUMMER, H.
1971   *Primate societies.* Chicago: Aldine.

LEACOCK, E.
1963   "Introduction," in *Ancient society* (L. H. Morgan). New York: World.

1972   "Introduction," in *The origin of the family, private property and the state* by F. Engels. New York: International.

LEE, R., I. DEVORE
1968   *Man the hunter.* Chicago: Aldine.

LIBERMAN, A., *et al.*
1967   "Some observations on a model for speech perception," in *Models for the perception of speech and visual form.* Edited by W. Wathen-Dunn. Cambridge: MIT Press.

LIEBERMAN, P., E. CRELIN
1971   On the speech of neanderthal man. *Linguistic Inquiry* 2:203.

LIEBOWITZ, L.
1969   Dilemma for social evolution: the impact of Darwin. *Journal of Theoretical Biology* 25:255.
n.d.   "Continuities and discontinuities in evolutionary perspective." Unpublished manuscript.

LINTON, S.
1970   "Woman the gatherer: male bias in anthropology." Paper read at the American Anthropological Association Annual Meeting, San Diego, California, 1970.

LUCKACS, G.
1972   Labour as a model of social practice. *New Hungarian Quarterly* 13:5.

MAGUBANE, B.
n.d.   "Political economy of race and class in South Africa." Unpublished manuscript.

MALTHUS, T.
1830   A summary view of the principle of population. Reprinted in *Three Essays on Population* (1940). New York: Mentor.

MAMDANI, M.
1972   *The myth of population control.* New York: Monthly Review Press.

MAO TSE-TUNG
1970   *On contradiction.* Peking: Foreign Languages Publishing House.

MARSHALL, L.
1965   "The !Kung Bushmen of the Kalahari Desert," in *Peoples of Africa.* Edited by J. Gibbs. New York: Holt, Rinehart, and Winston.

MARX, K.
1965   *Pre-capitalist economic formations.* New York: International.
1967   *Capital* (three volumes). New York: International.
1970   *The German ideology.* New York: International.
1971   *The Grundrisse.* New York: Harper.

MEADOWS, D., *et al.*
1972   *The limits of growth.* New York: Universe Books.

MEEK, R.
1971   *Marx and Engels on the population bomb.* San Francisco: Ramparts.

MORGAN, L. H.
1963   *Ancient society.* New York: World.

MURDOCK, G.
1959   *Africa: its people and their culture history.* New York: McGraw-Hill.

NEWCOMER, P.
1972a   The Nuer are Dinka. *Man* 7:1.

1972b "Social process: critical notes toward a methodology of study." Unpublished doctoral dissertation, University of Connecticut.

NURGE, E.
1972 "Comments," in Anthropology and population problems. *Current Anthropology* 13:252.

OAKLEY, K.
1961 "On man's use of fire, with comments on tool making and hunting," in *Social life of early man*. Edited by S. Washburn. Chicago: Aldine.

OSBORN, F.
1958 *Population: an international dilemma*. Princeton: Princeton University Press.
1960 "The need for rational regulation of births in the modern world," in *Three essays on population*. New York: Mentor.

PETERSEN, W.
1969 *Population*. London: Macmillan.

POLGAR, S.
1972 "Population history and population policies from an anthropological perspective," in Anthropology and population problems. *Current Anthropology* 13:203–278.
1975 "Population and environment," in *Horizons of anthropology* (second edition). Edited by S. Tax and L. G. Freeman. Chicago: Aldine.

RAPPAPORT, R.
1968 *Pigs for the ancestors*. New Haven: Yale University Press.

RODNEY, W.
1971 *How Europe underdeveloped Africa*. London: East African Publishing House.

RUYLE, E.
1973 Slavery, surplus and stratification on the Northwest Coast. *Current Anthropology* 14 (4).

SAHLINS, M.
1958 *Social stratification in Polynesia*. Seattle: University of Washington Press.
1972 *Stone Age economics*. Chicago: Aldine.

SAUCIER, J.
1972 "Correlates of the long postpartum taboo: a cross-cultural study," in Anthropology and population problems. *Current Anthropology* 13: 203–278.

SCHALLER, G.
1972 *The Serengeti lion*. Chicago: University of Chicago Press.

SERVICE, E.
1962 *Primitive social organization: an evolutionary perspective*. New York: Random.

SIDEL, R.
1972 *Women and child care in China*. New York: Hill and Wang.

SPOONER, B.
1972 *Population growth: anthropological implications*. Cambridge: MIT Press.

STEWARD, J.
1955 *Theory of culture change*. Urbana: University of Illinois Press.

SUSSMAN, R.
  1972 "Child transport, family size, and increase in human population during the Neolithic," in Anthropology and population problems. *Current Anthropology* 13:203–278.
SWEEZY, P., *et al.*
  1950–1953 *The transition from feudalism to capitalism.* New York: Science and Society.
TERRAY, E.
  1972 *Marxism and primitive society.* New York: Mothly Review Press.
TIGER, L.
  1970 *Men in groups.* New York: Random.
TIGER, L., R. FOX
  1971 *The imperial animal.* New York: Holt, Rinehart, and Winston.
TRIGGER, B.
  1965 Review: the role of labor in the transition from ape to man by F. Engels. *Canadian Review of Sociology and Anthropology* 2.
UNITED NATIONS
  1964 *Provisional report on world population prospects, as assessed in 1963.* New York: United Nations.
WASHBURN, S.
  1961 *Social life of early man.* Chicago: Aldine.
WHITE, L.
  1945 History, evolutionism, and functionalism: Three types of interpretation of culture. *Southwestern Journal of Anthropology* 1:221.
  1947 Evolutionism and anti-evolutionism in American ethnological theory. *Calcutta Review.* 104:147–174.
  1949 "Energy and the evolution of culture," in *The science of culture* by L. White. New York: Farrar, Straus.
  1959 *The evolution of culture.* New York: McGraw-Hill.
WHITING, J.
  1964 "Effects of climate on certain cultural practices," in *Explorations in cultural anthropology.* Edited by W. Goodenough. New York: McGraw-Hill.
WILLIAMS, E.
  1945 *Capitalism and slavery.* Chapel Hill: University of North Carolina Press.
WYNNE-EDWARDS, V.
  1962 *Animal dispersion in relation to social behavior.* New York: Hafner.
  1965 Self-regulating systems in populations of animals. *Science* 147:1543.

Ecosystem Analogies in Cultural Ecology

JOHN W. BENNETT

This article considers some problems arising from the application of biological models of homeostasis and feedback to ecological aspects of social and cultural process — or what anthropologists call "cultural ecology." The position taken is that while such concepts have their uses in social analysis, their emphasis on stability and reversion of the system to previous states tends to obscure the dynamism and adaptive change so characteristic of human societies. It is also argued that ecological theory in the social sciences, and in anthropology in particular, should give greater recognition to these dynamic features of human societies and their use of natural resources, both in the historical or evolutionary context and in the analysis of contemporary situations. By so doing, cultural ecological studies will gain, in terms both theoretical and practical, in socially relevant knowledge.

INTRODUCTION

In the background lies the question of how cultural ecologists can — or should — best utilize concepts derived from the study of plant and animal ecology. These concepts can be used in two general ways when they are transferred from biological to social data: (1) ANALOGICALLY, where the biological concepts and mathematical techniques are used to describe or simulate nonbiological phenomena; and (2) LITERALLY, in which case the actual biological or physical dimensions of the human phenomena would be identified and the same measurements performed on them. An example of the first is Barth's (1956) use of the term "niche" (which usually means in plant-animal ecology the particular use of an environmental range made by a particular species) to refer to the phenomenon of subsistence occupations in human society. We must ask whether these two things are really sufficiently similar to warrant the use of the same term and the generalized meanings and implications associated with it. For example, niche-occupancy among animals or plants is the result of, among other things, adaptive genetic selection, but one would be hard-pressed to find that genetic selection was responsible for the choice of agriculture or herding as an occupation among human groups.

There are few examples of the second case, i.e. plant-animal ecological concepts literally applied to the analysis of human behavior, although in human bioecology and research on adaptability various physiological, genetic, and energy data are collected and interpreted in ways similar to that for non-human species.[1]

The crux of the issue is the exact meaning of the results acquired by using ecological concepts to analyze human behavioral choices and decisions; does this make the behavior "natural," or self-regulating? The "niche" example is relevant here again: the introduction of agriculture into a system of hunting-gathering populations will have biological consequences for the humans and the environment, and other nonhuman species will have to adjust their niche-occupancy accordingly. Something similar would happen if a non-human species with comparable impact were to appear — for example, a grazing ungulate with a heavy impact on the floral environment. However, the appearance of agriculture may have been due to cultural transmission or to questions of power, as when a ruler stabilizes a frontier by resettling farmers on it. Are these cultural aspects of the situation part of "niche-occupancy," or do they suggest that human ecology includes a special form of behavior which requires a different set of concepts to represent a different order of reality?

There is a style of writing in social-science ecology which involves borrowing terms from a standard biological source like Eugene Odum's text (1971), and using these terms to describe and analyze social-behavioral data. In the early years of sociological ecology, writers in the field spoke of the "succession" and "dominance" of socioeconomic groups across the zones of North American cities (e.g., McKenzie 1928), in a conscious borrowing of a concept from plant ecology.

---

[1]   For some available studies of this type, see the following: Lee 1969 (a study of food intake and energy output among Bushmen); Parrack 1969 (estimates of energy levels provided by West Bengal agriculture); Montgomery 1972 (relationship of nutrition and health to social organization in southern India village); May and McClellan 1972 (ecological aspects of nutrition in various southern African regions).

It was proposed that populations in an urban setting distribute themselves in zones across the community according to differences in income, education, and other variables. The process of distribution creates neighborhoods which develop material characteristics (something like natural habitats for plants) appropriate to the group living in them, and therefore, as the original group moves upward and out, the neighborhood is refilled by people of similar character, or by persons for whom the new neighborhood represents a step up or out of something else. These concepts had strong ecosystemic overtones: the city, in this approach, came to be a large system with many subsystems in a state of homeostatic fluctuation and balance. The causes of the process were considered to be beyond the demographic systems under study — impersonal economic forces and the like.

The comparable case for anthropology was the development of the "age-area" idea and its translation into the CULTURE AREA, a concept and a classificatory scheme which dominated a whole generation of ethnologists and spread into other social sciences.[2] This concept also was a borrowing from early plant ecologists, who had found that other things being equal, the older floral species were at the periphery of a geographical area, the newer were in the central portions. When the age-area idea was carried into ethnology, the qualifying factors were ignored, and the impression was given that a lawful regularity in human behavior, below the level of consciousness of the actors involved, had been discovered. Dixon (1928) and others eventually showed that there were more exceptions to the rule than observances, pointing to the fact that historical (situational) circumstances affect the distribution of cultural items in time and space, and only completely ideal conditions will permit such regularities to operate at all. Linton used the telephone in *Study of man* to illustrate the principle of "marginal survival" of older forms like the hand-cranked type, but failed to note that the telephone, with its instant long-distance communication, transforms all spatial relations of objects and ideas based implicitly on slower forms of communication (1936: 329–330).

Another and much later example, this time from evolutionary thought,

[2] Wissler (1926) represents a central statement of culture area theory. Perhaps the VERY earliest was Mason (1895), although the idea was emerging out of several types of intellectual interests and field experience of anthropologists, and there are echoes back into the seventeenth century and foreshadowings in the Greek geographers. The plant ecology material served to crystallize the trend, and the definitive statement of that seems to have been Sapir's (1914), *Time perspective in aboriginal American culture*. The final product, and certainly the last detailed attempt to use culture area theory empirically, was Kroeber's *Cultural and natural areas of native North America* (1939). Kroeber's chief finding was that natural phenomena and cultural patterns coincided only when historical conditions permitted.

can be found in Alland's (1967) and Campbell's (1965) analogies between natural selection in biological and cultural phenomena. Equating cultural and biological traits, they propose (1) that variations MUST occur; that is, selection does not operate unless there are alternatives available, meaning that cultural variation is analogous to mutation in biology — and both can emerge at "random," that is, without reference to specific functions (a challenge to classical functional theory for culture). However, (2) for a variation to survive, mechanisms of continuity and preservation must be available. Thus, certain mechanisms in culture — e.g. symbolic communication or increasing functionality — are analogous to reproduction in biology. A third criterion (3) environmental selection must take place on the basis of consistent criteria in order to display regularity or direction. Because reproductive success is the single end in biology, the situation in culture is much more complex: a given trait must conform to many different systems for strong selection pressures to favor it.

These analogies make logical sense, but the empirical situations represented are widely divergent — the difference between the communication flow in cultural selection and the reproductive flow in biology is sufficient to indicate this divergence. The objectives of analogies at these high levels of generality are sometimes difficult to discern; they titillate the mind and may define very general processes, but they are often ambiguous with respect to the empirical properties of the phenomena represented.

ECOSYSTEM THEORY AND SOCIOCULTURAL DATA

Similar intellectual tendencies are currently exemplified in the attempts to conceive of human society, and of man-nature relations, in terms of ecosystemic functioning.[3] ECOSYSTEM is a concept from plant-animal ecology based on cybernetic principles: the actions, energy production, and consumption of organisms in a particular milieu tend, over a period of time, to complement each other — feed back — so as to permit the system to persist on a sustained-yield basis. Trophic levels or "food chains" repre-

[3]   Ecosystem is commonly advocated as the master concept for a unified science of human ecology, or a general ecology including man (Ripley and Buechner 1970). For other discussions of the concept, see Hall and Fagen (1956); Kalmus (1966); or appropriate sections in any general text in biological ecology. (A first round of attempts at applying homeostatic principles to human behavior occurred in the early 1950's, following publication of Wiener's book on cybernetics (1950). Stagner (1951) presented a proposal to reorganize personality theory around homeostasis; and Bateson (1949); and Ruesch and Bateson (1951), made pioneer attempts to use homeostasis as an interpretive principle for interpersonal behavior, psychiatry, and cultural patterns.)

sent one of these processes: what one organism does not eat is food for another; or, the larger eats the smaller, dies, decomposes, and thereby furnishes another round of sustenance for a third, and so on until the energy is used over and over again without a substantial break or loss.

The concept of ecosystem, and its affiliations with cybernetic theory, features three terms which define closely-related, but significantly different phenomena: steady state, equilibrium, and homeostasis. Social scientists, applying these terms to social and cultural-ecological phenomena, often fail to make the distinctions — a failure related to the fact that many of the applications are analogical, and the dimensions of the systems involved cannot be analyzed with the precise tools used for biological systems. A summary of Buckley's (1967) definitions of these terms follows:

STEADY STATE   The system functions with no apparent change or fluctuation; all subsystems continually reinforce each other. Systems in a steady state are characterized by minimal complexity, and in social systems, reciprocity relations tend to be fixed or ritualized. (Gregory Bateson, in his classic 1949 paper, "Bali: The Value System of a Steady State," described an apparent self-reinforcing set of social behaviors and values to produce a stable culture.)

EQUILIBRIUM or STABILITY   Terms used to describe a particular state of a system when the self-reinforcing characteristics of steady state are visible. However, a system in equilibrium at point x, may not be so at point y. That is, equilibrium need not imply that the system remains stable indefinitely.

HOMEOSTASIS   A process characterized by cycles of equilibrium and disequilibrium; the system moves or fluctuates in response to inducements to change or adapts to new inputs or conditions. Organization and reciprocity in social homeostasis is reasonably complex and capable of change, so long as the same average conditions are maintained over time.

Now, it will be noted that all three concepts lean toward stability — a particularly important point when social systems are the topic. Homeostasis does allow for movement and change, but there is considerable emphasis on a return to a particular state. It is also important to note that all three concepts imply the working of feedback processes to produce a measure of self-regulation or correction; that is, the concepts stress self-containment of systems — the system exists, and receives information from external sources, reacting accordingly in homeostasis, or resisting it, in steady states.

Feedback in cybernetic contexts is usually divided into "negative" and "positive" — terms which have caused considerable confusion when applied to social phenomena. Negative feedback is considered to be a stabilizing function — the messages transmitted back through the system from the output end serve to keep the system operating smoothly. Positive feedback obviously connotes the opposite: the signals result in a change or disturbance — a disruptive function, like the rupture of a valve. These concepts clearly have mechanical sources, and the basic notions of cybernetic feedback were derived from mechanical models and then transferred to biological phenomena.

When applied to social phenomena, feedback requires extensive qualification. In the first place, the most common type of social feedback is reciprocal functioning: two social entities, humans or institutions, communicate back and forth, with their behavior being modified by this communication. The process is much more complex than in mechanical or biological situations, in which the thermostat is the basic model. Secondly, the positive and negative imagery can grossly misrepresent the nature of social change, and result in the imposition of undesirable values. Most human societies REQUIRE "positive" feedback in the sense of corrective change: the positive is not necessarily disruptive but constructive; or, the "disruptive" effects are beneficial to the system because human systems require change in order to modify corruption, redress wrongs, etc. Negative feedback on the other hand, can be, or lead to, social disruption when institutions become obsolescent and static. Actually there are so many possibilities that these feedback concepts are much too simple to handle human affairs in any large sense; their utility may be confined to highly specific, short-term situations.

Moreover, social systems have many indeterminate features: complex relationships among the actors and subsystems, which make prediction of behavior difficult; and hard-to-trace links to external systems, all of which cause dynamic fluctuations and change, making it often a matter of semantic choice to say whether a system is in a state of equilibrium, decline, or restoration. The temporal dimension becomes critical, because the state of the system differs depending on the time of observation. The dynamism of social systems raises the fundamental question of whether anything is gained by using ecosystemic concepts and terminology to describe them, because the available concepts from history and the social sciences often do an adequate job. Proponents of ecosystem analysis respond to this critique by pointing out that the complexities of social systems do not make them any less systemic, and that the concepts can serve to bring together, in a single frame of reference, many disparate observations and can eliminate much distracting detail.

In the ecological context, man's expanding use of nature's resources and his social life have complex reciprocal relationships, and interference with these relationships always tends to disrupt systems and hamper the flow of information back through the channels. The breakdown of feedback, or the growing impedance to feedback as systems, becomes more complex and permits more interference from cognitive appraisals, and constitutes one of the obstacles to attaining a state of sustained natural resource yield, which is one kind of ecosystemic state. Or, the failure to take into account all components of a system in a state of technological change results in progressive damage to the human and natural components.

Perhaps the best case to be made for the use of ecosystemic concepts in human affairs occurs when biological, or natural phenomena generally, are the chief goal of analysis. An example of this principle is available in the research on the sickle cell disease in African and African-derived populations. The findings pertain to the relationship of human subsistence techniques which encourage the breeding of the malarial mosquito, and the frequency of the sickling gene in populations exposed to this mosquito, the link between the two phenomena being found in the fact that the sickle cell disease also confers a certain immunity to malarial infection. Therefore the frequency of the gene builds up in exposed populations practicing agriculture in the tropical forest area. The frequencies of the gene and mosquito populations can reach a steady state, or fluctuate homeostatically, providing a good example of ecosystemic conditions in man-nature relationships. However, the proclivity of human populations to migrate tends to disturb the stability of the system, and makes its properties applicable only to limited historical periods (Livingstone 1958; Weisenfeld 1967).

When ecosystemic concepts are applied to human systems defined mainly in behavioral or institutional terms, the applicability of the concepts is less obvious. Geertz' treatment (1963) of "agricultural involution" in Java (the change of the system toward intensification of its own techniques, rather than evolution to a new type) has been represented to be ecosystemic, but the properties of this system seem adequately described by existing concepts of historical and economic change: the exploitation of the Javanese peasantry by various groups involved in Dutch colonialism, so that fewer alternatives for economic change existed. Here one may make a case for the Javanese agricultural sector as having the general properties of systems, but whether it is ECOsystemic depends on how strictly or how loosely, one wishes to apply these biological concepts.

Geertz (1963: Chapter 2) has also characterized two forms of agriculture common in the tropics — swiddεn (slash-and-burn; shifting cultivation) and wet-rice production, as examples of ecosystems. Here he might seem on solid ground, because he is referring to the biological properties of the floral, edaphic, and hydraulic properties taken as given. Swiddening, in contrast to wet-rice production, is "integrated into, and, when genuinely adaptive, maintains the general structure of the pre-existing natural ecosystem into which it is projected..." (Geertz 1963: 16); whereas rice culture more drastically reorganizes the natural structure. This is well and good, but the phrase "when it is genuinely adaptive" is of course the sleeper; later in the chapter he notes how swiddening, under various social pressures, can become destructive when the interval between cultivation is shortened. He also suggests that the rice system tends to result in human population concentrations, due to its capacity for increasing yield and needs for labor, whereas the swidden system results in a dispersal of population due to its inherently limited yield. These and other conclusions have been subject to criticism: for example, swiddening apparently CAN support large, concentrated populations given the requisite social and political organization (e.g. Dumond's claim [1961] that swiddening in Yucatán supported the Maya cities). The issue illustrates the point that when dealing with human systems like agriculture, an analysis of the "natural" properties of the cultivation as ecosystemic does not tell us what the long-range social-biological potentialities may be. Although swiddening may be closer to nature, wet-rice production has perhaps less degradational potential, because even with the pressures of increasing population and corresponding intensification of production, the system, according to Geertz, is "virtually indestructible." But BOTH systems CAN turn destructive if they are not maintained properly, or if certain social features require them to produce more than the resources can sustain. The key variable is the SOCIAL system — that is, human needs, skills, anxieties, population — all of which are not narrowly determined by particular subsistence systems, but rather, can push these systems to produce at varying rates.

We may consider next one of the more challenging pieces of research in contemporary anthropological ecology: the study of warfare, swine management, and social ritual among the Tsembaga, a particular local settlement, or clan-cluster, of members of the Maring people, a "tribe" of some 7,000 persons occupying a region of about 190 square miles in central New Guinea. While Roy Rappaport has featured "pigs" in his publications on these people (e.g. 1967a and b), the underlying issue seems to be warfare and territorial expansion, a topic of dominant interest in New Guinea ethnology. The curious stylized combat sometimes appears to be no more than ritual confrontation, sometimes genuine mayhem; or invasion and forced resettlement of populations. This "warfare" has been a topic of perennial interest because of its exotic appeal and because it offers, like the potlatch of the Northwest Coast Indians, a kind of caricature of various facets of "civilized" warfare and international relations. The trigger problem in the case of Rappaport's research, therefore, was intracultural, not ecological. His own work, however, came to be an exercise in how an ecological approach might help explain the causes of New Guinea warfare and its territorial implications.

One basic theory of New Guinea warfare, developed in a series of papers by Vayda (c.g. 1960, 1961, 1967, 1971), concerns population increase and decrease and the consequent changes in "man/resource ratios" which might give rise to needs for more territory for gardens and raising pigs, the response being hostile attacks on neighbors. This is an ecological problem because a linkage is hypothesized between population, natural resources, and a particular human activity. The theoretical implications of the problem were developed in a spin-off paper by Vayda and Rappaport (1968) which criticizes anthropologists' prolonged reliance on concepts derived from culture in their ecological studies, and advocates a shift to concepts developed by natural ecologists. Specifically, they cite research into territorial rights; intertribal warfare and raiding; ceremonial feasting; sacred animals; and human sacrifice in various tribal cultures, from the standpoint of how these might maintain "within an adaptive range certain variables (such as size or dispersion) pertaining either to human populations or the faunal and floral populations on which these depend" (Vayda and Rappaport 1968: 495). Consideration of such phenomena would be based on units of *population* and ecosystem, rather than the traditional unit of "cultures."[4]

The basic facts of the case are complex, but a study of Rappaport and Vayda's papers on the Maring yield the following: warfare and its absence among these people seem to fluctuate rhythmically, with intervals of from ten to fifteen years suggested as the pattern in various papers. Periods of peace between groups in potential competition for land appear

---

[4]   Vayda and Rappaport might well argue that their approach is not "cultural ecology" at all, and therefore has no business being considered in this paper. From a narrow or purist point of view, they would probably be correct. However, because their objective appears to be a translation of familiar cultural phenomena into ecological terms, and because this translation adds a dimension of explanation to these cultural phenomena, we choose to include their approach.

to have an element of ritual proscription, insofar as the preparations for thanking the ancestor spirits for guidance and protection in the preceding warfare period consume a considerable period of time. Warfare must not be engaged in while these rituals are under way. Because the rituals involve pig slaughter and feasting, enough time must elapse in order to produce a sufficient supply of animals. These periods of ritual last about as long as the warfare periods — again, from ten to fifteen years. The question is whether the human population, assuming it may be one of the underlying causes of warfare due to the man-resource ratio, also fluctuates accordingly — building up every ten years or so to trigger the chain of insults, rapes, thefts, and other things associated with inter-settlement competition which might result in war; and then, due to adjustments in territorial acquisition, or reduction in overall regional population from driving out a competing settlement, whether the pressures lift and warfare ceases.

Rappaport's and Vayda's attempts to unravel this complex skein appear to differ. Rappaport seems concerned with the systemic features of all aspects of the system, while Vayda focuses specifically on the warfare pattern (raiding; real wars versus "nothing" wars or stylized confrontation; territorial acquisition; territorial invasion versus plain fighting, etc.). Vayda is more interested than Rappaport in the question of why some fights develop into true wars, and others remain at the level of what Rappaport, borrowing a term from natural ecology, calls "epideictic display" (the trading of threats in order to, presumably, make an assessment of true aggressive ability). Rappaport's sweeping objectives are indicated in his summary of his paper (1967a: 28–29).

To repeat an earlier assertion, the operation of ritual among the Tsembaga and other Maring helps to maintain an undegraded environment, limits fighting to frequencies which do not endanger the existence of the regional population, adjusts man-land ratios, facilitates trade, distributes local surpluses of pigs throughout the regional population in the form of pork, and assures people of high-quality protein when they are most in need of it.

That is, he proposes that the recurrent war-and-ritual cycles are somehow adjusted to fluctuations in the populations of pigs and people: when, for example, population pressure produces need for land, the people go to war; then they return and consume pigs. When pig populations increase, destroying the gardens, motivation for consuming pigs arises, but because pigs are to be consumed as the culmination of a warfare episode, there has to be previous warfare to provide the excuse. The consumption of pigs may also relieve "physiological stress" resulting from general excitement or, partly, from disease, and of course incidentally puts everyone back in top condition for the next round of fighting. Thus the ritual cycle[5] is the key not only to warfare, but also to all the other functions mentioned in the previous quotation. Throughout this presentation, Rappaport applies concepts derived from natural ecology: the relationship of pigs to people changes from mutualism to parasitism-competition; the ritual behavior is likened to epigamic and epideictic display; and so on.[6] The applicability of these concepts, and the general proposal that the entire configuration operates as an ecosystemic process or homeostasis is defended on the grounds that the Tsembaga (and the larger unit, the Maring people as a whole) were relatively isolated, and constituted a population in a dynamic self-contained balance with its surround.

If this is the case, then the situation closely resembles that characteristic of animal populations, where changes in one component of the system require adjustments in the others via feedback flow. In animal ecological research, these dimensions and changes are specified with rigorously-

[5] This is a very complex system, and we cannot review it in detail. Succinctly, the culminating, post-warfare ceremonial in this cycle is the *kaiko*, which lasts for approximately one year, and is begun by planting the gardens, which in turn marks the end of combat. The gardens grow until a sufficient number of pigs have accumulated through purchase and breeding, and when this occurs, the *kaiko* proceeds through the harvest of the gardens, and pig slaughter and feasting, involving ritual presentation of pork between men involved in maintaining prestige. The activities of presentation and consuming pork mean that considerable protein is consumed "during periods of stress" (Rappaport 1967a:154) that is, in the presumably tense period of the *kaiko*. The decision to slaughter pigs is made when the consequences of the increasing pig population result in general irritation at their depredations, and fighting, which includes forcing the hamlet settlements farther apart. Rappaport apparently was unable to obtain precise figures concerning the optimal size of pig populations leading to slaughter over a period of years, although he found that over the fifty- to sixty-year period ending in 1963, there were four *kaiko*, meaning twelve to fifteen years between ceremonials. However, he also notes that these durations are not standard for the Tsembaga or other groups. In other words, the cycles are not regular, and the decisions to slaughter are not governed by precise measurements of populations or time.
[6] The proclivity to use concepts from ethology in analogic or quasianalogic fashion is nothing new: McKenzie was doing it in the 1920's. In a series of papers reprinted in a volume of collected papers edited by Hawley (1968), McKenzie explored the concept of DOMINANCE in international relations, urban zoning, and other social groups and segments, leading from an analogy with the physiology of organisms and how this is translated into spatial organization of animal groups — the approach developed later by W. C. Allee and others in their studies of pecking order and dominance-submission relations. An early general reference to the theme of using animal behavioral analogies for human behavior is the volume edited by Redfield (1942) entitled *Levels of integration in biological and social systems*. This book includes papers by Allee, Robert Park, A. L. Kroeber, C. Carpenter (societies of monkeys and apes) and others concerned with the problem. This was really a "first round" of attempts to use ethology to interpret human society; the new ethologists are discussed in Callan (1970) and Alland (1972).

collected quantitative information. It is necessary to know precisely what any organism in the system needs in the way of sustenance; how much it acquires as a result of its foraging or other energy-transforming activities; how much physiological energy is actually generated by these methods; or how much muscular energy is used in the activities performed. The environment that sustains these efforts also must be described in detail, in terms of its energy-producing facility — its "carrying capacity." When organisms in such a milieu are in competition with one another, the point at which competition becomes decisive — involving reduction in the number of one of the organisms through predation or starvation — has to be determined with precision, on the basis of the energy-obtaining and -releasing analyses,[7] because explanations for the behavior of the organism ride on them.

That is, the procedure aims at determining the causes of behavior as they emerge in biological and resource circumstances; the assumption is that the behavior of the organism is not random or willed, but is a necessary emergent from the changing forces in the total milieu. If natural-ecological concepts are transferred to humans, and studies are made of their behavior on the basis of these process assumptions, then along with this goes the assumption that human behavior is likewise largely or wholly emergent from a bioenvironmental matrix of some kind. This, with some qualification, appears to be the fundamental assumption of Rappaport's study. If the human behavior is willed, or purposive, Rappaport's model requires this to be assimilable into the natural process: man wills in response to a perceived environmental factor, but his physiology prompts.

Rappaport's study was the best documented piece of research in cultural ecology at the time of its publication: its ten appendices provide an unmatched assemblage of data on climate, agricultural output, flora, and energy expenditures for the community and its environs.[8] However, these data are not systematically tied into the interpretive analysis of how ritual and other behaviors serve as automatic regulatory mechanisms. That is, the study is not a rigorous, quantitatively-based demonstration of the ecophysiological causes of human behavioral responses to needs. It is, despite its rich data background, fundamentally an analogic operation, in which ecosystemic complexities, and a generalized impression of ecological causation, are plausibly suggested but not worked out in detail.

---

[7]   At the time of writing, work of this kind is just beginning in anthropology.
[8]   Rappaport has recently reworked some of these appendices data in an attempt to portray the energy flow in his New Guinea society (1971b).

That is, Rappaport followed the protocol, but not the analytical operations, of the natural-ecological approach sketched previously.

To whatever extent Rappaport's effort to describe the operation of an automatic feedback system involving environment, animals, flora, and people is a successful one, it is important as a concrete demonstration of the fact that the behavior of men toward each other, as well as toward nature, is part of ecosystems. Rappaport's study is one of the best available portraits of the isolated, small, low-energy system operating more or less in balance with nature (at least during the eleven months of his observation), and it may be that ecosystemic analysis is best applied to societies of this type.

Now, if Rappaport's generalizations are limited to a particular type of society, then the relevance of his findings for the contemporary ecological scene are limited — and certainly Rappaport does not propose otherwise. But the issue needs to be raised all the same, because ecosystemicism is a seductive idea, and others have interpreted studies of tribal ecology as if they had universal significance. The New Guinea people, according to Rappaport, seem to have only a limited awareness of what they are doing, and yet balance with nature emerges. Emergence of such feedback in contemporary society, with its philosophy of continuous growth and constant need for resources, is a remote possibility, other than in very specialized and sheltered circumstances. Balance on a significant scale can be achieved only by political change and conscious planning. Cases like Rappaport's, unless their context is thoroughly understood, can lead to illusions about the capacity of men to work out sustained-yield regimes.

There is, moreover, a factor of time which needs careful consideration. Let us grant that ecological factors and the actions of the Tsembaga did in fact dovetail so as to produce a functioning, largely automatic system of control. However, Rappaport's observations were of relatively short duration — a field period of eleven months — and there is no detailed information available on the time required for this system to emerge, nor how long it might last after the period of observation. On the basis of data from societies of comparable energy levels and sociopolitical tendencies in Africa, there is reason to believe that such systems were quite unstable and likely to give way to depredations on nature and other men on a scale exceeding the previous limits (e.g. Sahlins 1961; Kottak 1972).

The time factor is crucial because various human activities which may be in some kind of balance at a given time period are not usually under simultaneous control, because they can change at different rates and are subject to different forces. This is perhaps less true of tribal and most true of contemporary societies with their many autonomous spheres of action. The writer found an "ecosystemic" balance in the population of Hutterian Brethren in the northern Great Plains during the early 1960's, in which the rate of population increase, the rate of financial savings, the "carrying capacity" (productivity) of the land, the amounts of land available for purchase in the region, and various religious beliefs and social practices all fitted together to result in a conscious, planned process of regular colony division at a population level of about 150 persons (Bennett 1967: Chapter 7). However, setting aside the question of whether this situation is to be defined as ecosystemic, it IS a particular historical phase in the relationships among various endogenous and exogenous variables, and it is subject to change and to recurrent adaptive modifications of any or all of the factors (by 1971, the population level was down to 130 persons, due to rises in operating costs and colony consumption levels).

This case suggests that the question of built-in controls over environmental use is not confined to tribal societies, where they may well be an only half-conscious procedure — the consequence, as Rappaport has implied, of the mutual reinforcing power of many cultural and economic patterns. Such controls can also be entirely purposeful and conscious, in the sense of being planned and maintained as a system of boundary-maintaining regulations, as they are among the Hutterites.

To return to New Guinea, we have understood Rappaport as saying that the feedback states were maintained (or participated in) without conscious awareness of the underlying consequences and causes on the part of the actors. Rappaport's presentation therefore resembles a classic functionalist demonstration: the social activities of warfare, pig rituals, etc., have the function of maintaining populations and gardens in homeostasis. This is reminiscent of Harris' claim (1960) that "functionalism" in social science is comparable to biology's "adaptation," and as all critics of functionalism have noted, an approach of this type tends to neglect change, dynamism, and the purposive factor in behavior. Rappaport might reply that he has not neglected purpose and intention, and knows full well that his people are aware of the specific effects of their actions, if not the long-range balance, but that the processes represented by these actions, whether perceived or unperceived by the actors, nevertheless have these systemic properties. This is the difference between the action level and the process level in cultural ecological analysis. Lacking more details, it is of course impossible really to resolve this question.[9]

---

[9]   There is an additional question concerning this matter of a homeostasis functioning automatically, out of direct awareness of the actors. The behavior itself is, of course, under conscious control, and because most of the behavior appears to be ritual, we are dealing with a high degree of control indeed — control by the sacred — or what

There are, of course, less theoretically-conceived explanations for the New Guinea behavior vis-à-vis swine which do not depend on animal analogies in human behavior, nor on demonstrations of states of subtle ecosystemic balance in ritual behavior and natural phenomena. These New Guinea people appear to have a familiar livestock management problem: raising swine in unconfined spaces, on natural forage. Everywhere in the world people who do this are likely to be confronted with problems of depredation by the animals on flora, and also of cyclical overbreeding, and all must resort to recurrent slaughtering which may or may not feed into market or consumption channels. Families in the Louisiana swamplands used to have annual pig hunts with recreational ("ritual") purposes, involving the consumption of alcoholic beverages and other festivities. The difficulty and inefficiency of swine management in unconfined spaces is due to the individualistic, ranging, voracious behavior of these intelligent animals, who quickly revert to a wild state, and it is no accident that enormous effort in developed agricultures has gone into suitable technology for handling swine in confined, artificial environments.

People who choose to raise pigs in the open thus experience a chronic economic problem: at certain intervals, the cost of raising pigs exceeds the gain. Among other things, they may consider that the opportunity cost of seeking additional land by standard methods of moderate expansion is "cheaper" than other alternatives. But just what alternatives are there? In isolation, possibly none, but in the expanding world of New Guinea, obviously an increasing number. Only history, that acid test of all human affairs, will tell. That ecosystemic processes are probably also at work goes without saying — but the question is, do they help to explain the sociocultural reality of man's use of nature?[10]

Rappaport himself in a later paper calls "sanctity" (1971a). In the secularized, high-energy societies the control systems are regulated by instrumental considerations, or "rationality." The question is, then, if ecosystems in the special sense of sustained-yield principles are to be created, which of these two systems works best, the symbolic-sanctification-automatic control system, or the rational-instrumental-planned? The question is, of course, a spurious one; the difference is not one of choice, but one of level of cultural development. Any attempt to impose sanctified systems of control on our own society would be equivalent to totalitarianism; that is, the political costs might be considered to exceed the ecological gain. But this is, in fact, one of the choices we may have to make.

[10] Vayda has argued (1969), however, that the ecosystem position CAN lead to an analysis of imbalance and dynamism in human ecology, because it does allow for the role of human purposes, at least in a generalized way, and does take fluctuation and change into account. This is possibly so, but the problem is that the systems (like Maring warfare) do not remain in equilibrium long enough to permit a detailed analysis to ascertain their ecosystemic properties.

Scudder's work on Tonga tribalists in Kenya, following completion of the Kariba Dam in their territory (1968; 1972a) provides a contrasting example of systemic analysis in the context of adaptive behavior, rather than systemic determinance. The total system consisted of the following important components (or "subsystems"): the river as a fluctuating resource; the government and its connections with overseas development agencies; the Tonga as a tribal population; Tongan techniques of subsistence as related to climate and soils; Tongan culture and religion; the relationships of Tongans with tribal neighbors. Before the building of the dam and resettlement, Tongan subsistence and the cultural pattern that validated it were in a state of slow evolution toward a particular form well-adapted to the climate and land features. The dam flooded out their home territory, and they were forcibly resettled by the government. It was at this point that Scudder encountered them, and his research then came to focus on just one subsystem: the adaptive strategies developed by the Tongans to cope with the changed conditions. They were required to discover new resources and methods of agricultural production and to cope with the shocks and hazards of a new habitat and a new set of tribal neighbors, all of which required a series of psychological, social, and ritual adjustments. The consumption of new wild vegetable foods required new medicine and curing routines; because some of these were poisonous and many actually have contributed to the increased death rate after resettlement, the accompanying dismay and fear increased mortality, itself requiring adjustments. The analysis is an example of how ideas related to ecosystem theory can dramatize a process called "culture change" in traditional anthropology.

However, Scudder has not yet investigated the effects these new adaptations will have on natural resources over a period of time.[11] Recovery of psychosocial balance — satisfying cognitive and affectual adjustments between men — is often accomplished at the cost of environmental damage (human adaptation at the price of environmental maladaptation).[12] Thus,

[11]   The construction of large dams and water impoundments in tropical regions (Africa, Southeast Asia) has received considerable attention in recent years by a number of disciplines (medical research and epidemiology; natural ecologists; hydraulic engineers; geologists; anthropologists). The work constitutes a model of multidisciplinary ecology in which the role of the cultural ecologist, as partly illustrated by Scudder's work, emerges clearly as one of doing before-and-after studies of behavioral adaptations. For a review of these studies, see Scudder (1972b), in Farvar and Milton (1972).

[12]   Small-scale examples are found in the new communes of the counter-culture movement: the communalists, despite the best of intentions toward nature and the restoration of balanced relations between man and nature, have in some cases been responsible for serious soil erosion, injury to forests, and stream pollution. Intentions

to some extent, the "permanent war economy" of the United States and other nations in the contemporary period represents such an imbalance between one system and another: man-man is kept in reasonable quietude at the cost of man-nature, which appears to be degradational. In many ancient civilizational systems, balance was maintained for certain periods by high infant mortality, or by resource-utilization systems like large water impoundments which functioned effectively for varying periods of time before collapsing.

Still another type of application of ecosystem theory to human affairs is found in the simulation models of institutional systems prepared by biological ecologists (e.g. Holling 1969; H. Odum 1971). Holling's venture is based on the analogies between animal predation and recreational land speculation in the Puget Sound area. The analogies are presented in Table 1.

Table 1.   Analogies between predation and land acquistion[a]

Predation	Land acquisition
Populations (quantity and quality)	
Prey population in generation n	Lots available for sale in market period n
Predator population, generation n	Bidders for lots, market period n
Prey quality (size, etc.)	Land quality
Predator qualities (size, etc.)	Bidders by bidding price
Unsuccessful predators (predator mortality)	Unsuccessful bidders
Alternative prey species	Alternative land qualities and alternative geographical sources of land
Processes	
Attack process (generates number of prey killed in n)	Market process (generates number of lots sold in n)
Prey reproduction (generates number of progeny in n + 1)	Resale process (generates number of developed lots for sale in n + 1)
Predator reproduction (generates number of predator progeny in n + 1)	Population and economic growth (generates demand in n + 1)
Dispersal (generates net number of prey immigrants)	Speculation (generates number of new lots in n + 1)
Motivation (e.g. hunger)	Final selling prices
Competition	Competition (between speculators and bidders)

[a]   Reproduced from Holling's Table 1 (1969:32)

The objective of the ecological studies of predation has been to determine

---

are simply not enough; balance has to be achieved by detailed knowledge of environments and careful adjustment of human needs and wants to the capacity of the environment to support them. (Observations based on a one-month tour of new communes in the Santa Fe and Taos areas, 1971.)

how predatory actions serve to control animal population fluctuation. The processes involved have been found to be complex, due to the large number of variables: rates of searching for prey, hunger patterns, learning attack strategies, diet, topography, cover, age distributions in the animal populations, and so on. The interactions of these variables produce a variety of models of predator-prey populations, each with its own characteristics of stability and fluctuation. Predatory tactics will vary when past circumstances and changing conditions feed back information into the animal population, so as to stabilize the system and "dampen" the population oscillations. Thus reasonable overall stability of population is achieved.

In the land speculation model,

a population and economic growth submodel generates regional population by income and family size each year. This population is converted by a recreational demand submodel into a population of bidders [for lots] according to bidding prices by using a function that relates the proportion of the population desiring land to income, family size, and distance from home. This output of bidders then represents demand. Supply of lots for sale includes unsold lots developed by speculators in the previous market periods as well as developed lots that come up for resale. The amount of this supply is classified in seven categories that define the lots' qualities for cottage development. Both demand (bidders-predators) and supply (number of lots for sale by quality-prey) come together in a complex submodel that mimics the peculiar properties of the real estate market process, and this submodel generates the number of lots sold, the final selling price, the unsold inventory, and the number of unsatisfied bidders. These outputs in turn serve as inputs to a speculation submodel which moves undeveloped land into the next year's market in relation to the size of the market and the rate of price appreciation over the previous three years. Finally, an ecological feedback model simulates the effects of intensity and duration of use, shifting the amounts of land between quality categories in response to regional and local density effects (Holling 1969: 133–134).

The results of these operations generated a model of land speculation which showed properties similar in form to those produced in the studies and simulations of predation and animal populations. Omitting much detail, these properties concerned the way prices responded to changes in population and the supply of lots, and vice versa. Oscillations in these were controlled (damped) in a manner similar to the animal cases: past events tended to control present behavior; that is, the systems achieved stability over time because the "memory" of past events modified present action.

The exercise provides a view of the ecosystem analogy in human affairs which features the application of particular mathematical techniques derived from biological phenomena to the behavior of humans in institutional life. No implication is given that human behavior is somehow like animal behavior; the relationship is purely mechanical, processual. There is no doubt that such applications have intrinsic interest, and serve to illumine the institutional process, but it should be remembered that the result — the portrayal of stability or regular fluctuation — is the result of the particular model, or the particular topic, used for the experiment. Taking land speculation as a whole, it is subject to more, and less predictable, change than the animal case, because all the variables are more dynamic. It is conceivable, of course, that if system simulation of this type ever became official — that is, a phase of governmental control of land and its sale — its regular movements could be maintained by law and other forms of conscious control. In this case we would not be dealing with a "natural" system, open to discovery, but a planned institutional device for controlling and regulating change.

H. Odum's simulations of human processes (1971) in a book-length treatise on system analysis, contain proposals for a theory of cultural ecology on the basis of ecosystem concepts, especially economics, politics, and religion. The following quotation from a section entitled "Wages, Profits, and Savings," illustrates the type of argument:

Savings represent the money flows into storages for work services done and thus provide flexibility and time delays in the reward loop of energy expenditure. An equivalent in the ecosystem is the holding of fruits made in summer for planting in winter. The energy has already been expended in preparing a complex product, but an important material of low-energy value is fed back upstream and has the capability of developing new circuits. With the saving of both money and seeds, what is being used as a loop reinforcement is critical information. In seeds it is in the genes; with money the critical information is already stored as the acceptance of the symbolic nature of currency as a measure of value by the network of people (H. Odum 1971: 191–192).

This exposition is plausible and undoubtedly has heuristic value, but the analogies are fuzzy. Putting savings in the same category with seeds is not an accurate analogy between culture and natural ecosystems, because the saving of seeds by men means that seeds become capital, that is, part of economics. Odum tends to ignore the fact that natural substances are incorporated into human institutions and feedback systems, and the "natural" aspects — the growing of fruit trees — becomes a cultural phenomenon. Both fruit seeds and savings become part of social systems, whatever natural ecosystem they may also be part of. It is necessary to acknowledge, at all times, the existence of characteristic human social systems which may parallel, or control, ecosystems. The more cogent problem is perhaps not whether human affairs are ecosystemic, but rather, the nature of the relationships between natural and social systems.

The important ingredient of human social systems — or "social eco-systems," if you will — is the element of voluntarism: purpose, accomplishment, social control, decisionmaking, and of course cognitive evaluations of these. Human ecosystems are not simple matters of food chains or predator-prey relations, (although they can be shown to be mechanically similar to those), but include conscious objectives and techniques, the buying of time, the "trade-off," and the willingness to borrow from Peter to pay Paul. Because these complex adjustments and exchanges configurate into world-wide systems, it is doubtful if much will be gained in the immediate present by the application of ecosystem concepts based on the proposition of self-regulation, unless such analyses are used for the explicit purpose of constructing control systems. But the seeking of control over the use of resources, and a new framework of choices and priorities which value sustained yield principles more highly, should retain an element of democratic decision and choice, and the role of systems analysis and applications in democratic processes is ambiguous.

Because most examples of the application of ecosystem ideas to human phenomena are cases of analogy, there is a certain relief to find an attempt to use the concepts to clarify the chief DIFFERENCES between human and natural ecology.

E. Odum (1971) distinguishes between human and natural ecosystemic processes in the following manner: the basic process of ecosystem evolution in the natural biosphere is a succession of a regular series of species toward a homeostatic balance (which incidentally links species-succession, a descriptive concept in plant ecology, with ecosystem development, a dynamic concept) in a given habitat. The bioenergetics of the process can be symbolized by "B," or total biomass; "P," or primary production (in plants, photosynthesis); "R," or output (in plants, respiration); — in which case "P/R" is the ratio of production to biomass. In a floral system, when P/R is greater than one, the system is youthful, but as it approaches unity, the system is maturing, and approaching stability or at least homeostasis. So long as P is greater than R, organic matter (B = biomass) will accumulate, so that the P/B ratio decreases. At some point when unity is reached, biomass ceases to accumulate, and a stable system in final stages of succession is reached.

In other words, if plants could reason, they would define efficiency as the state of affairs where there is no further need for additional biomass, and the maintenance of the existing amount as their chief goal of existence. Obviously this is not the human goal — or at least it has not been over the span of human history, and especially at the present. For man the objective is a high P/B efficiency: maximum mass with the lowest amount of energy expended and in the shortest possible length of time. Nature "seeks" a high P/B ratio, not a high P/B efficiency, so the tendency in the human use OF nature is opposite from that IN nature — or in other words, man reverses the law of natural ecosystems: the strategy of "maximum protection" (that is, trying to achieve maximum support of complex biomass structure) often conflicts with man's goal of "maximum production" trying to obtain the highest possible yield (Odum 1971: 262–266). In the homeostatic states to which natural species tend, energy is constantly being retired or rather relegated to the maintenance of balance, rather than, as in the human situation, to increasing production. Man constantly reorganizes energy; he resists entropy.

But man does more; he breaks into succession cycles and prevents nature from attaining these mature states, thus incorporating natural phenomena into culture. The issue here is whether this process is irretrievably dangerous, or whether man, through increasing wisdom and knowledge of nature, can actually find on a conscious, rational basis, his own method of attaining balance: a true sustained yield. If this does come to pass, then man would have become part of "natural" ecosystems in the sense that his will and purpose will have merged with nature instead of opposing it.

The issue, therefore, is not really, or at least wholly, a theoretical one. It is not only a question of whether man's ecological or social action is or is not to be analyzed with existing ecosystem techniques, but also whether man CAN attain a certain kind of ecosystemic state, and HOW he can do it. Obviously short-term homeostatic conditions have been attained in the past, and in these cases ecosystem theory applies. But the logic of culture also works in the opposite direction, as Odum so clearly demonstrates with a great economy of symbols. The issue is not only practical but historical: homeostasis is not a continuous human process, but eventually must be a recurring EVENT in the history of human culture.

However, the ecosystem concept, in the form of a practical recognition of the existence of relationships among organisms and natural substances in particular regions, can play an important role in ecological planning. This has become evident in the issue of pollution in both the developed and emerging nations, where the introduction of new substances and techniques into existing systems of resource use, however stable or unstable these may have been previous to the change, has resulted in a variety of major and minor disasters, most of them avoidable if proper investigation had preceded the innovation (Farvar and Milton 1972). While the omission of adequate study of the whole system can be attributed to scientific atomization and to the Cold War, which induced the big nations to compete with each other in the economic aid field, fault is equally present in the eagerness with which the new nations seized on development as a path to power and rivalry among themselves. Once again, ideological and power issues underlie ecological problems.

The minimal requirement for dealing with the ecosystem situation in human affairs is to ascertain, with the greatest possible accuracy, the WHOLE RANGE of systems which may be involved in a given form of resource use. To show, as have some cultural ecologists, that a particular tribal or peasant society has reached a state of balance with nature, and to attribute this to internal cultural patterns without at least an attempt to discover whether it is not some external factor like a government regulation or market process which permits or encourages this sustained-yield situation, is to commit a crucial error: to confuse historical actuality and the means-end nexus in human behavior with some automatic process at work in nature. Moreover, in cases like these, it is more than possible that the sustained-yield situation in one locality is being maintained at the expense of some other resource complex.

One of the alleged self-regulating systems in human affairs is the "demographic transition," a phrase referring to the fact that the highly-developed industrial societies of Europe, North America, and Japan have tended to display a reduction in fertility as their economies develop, this tendency being based on the trade-off between a reduced number of children and a higher level of family living. The emerging countries of Africa, Asia, and Latin America, on the other hand, just entering the stage of industrialism and a consumer culture, and with public health programs curtailing mortality, have experienced explosive population growth. In order to pay for the support of increasing numbers, these countries must then export raw materials to the developed nations on an increased scale, resulting in a loss of basic resource capital. Thus, the impact of economic aid and the exportation of high consumption aspirations has had a serious demographic and environmental impact on these countries.[13]

To some extent the processes operate as described, and to some extent,

[13]   For accounts of the problems associated with the absence of demographic transition, see the following: Stolnitz (1964); Ehrlich and Ehrlich (1972), various references; Geertz (1963, 1965); Frederiksen (1969). Frederiksen presents diagrammed models of feedback between population and economic policy and practice, suggesting that increasing population as a consequence of attempted economic growth can be avoided. Barry Commoner tends to take this view; Paul Ehrlich disagrees. Hillery (1966) compares Navajo Indians and Kentucky hill people, finding that the former are just entering the transition and the latter beginning to leave it.

then, there may be some tendency for homeostatic conditions to develop around population and level of living as a society matures. However, proponents of the "demographic transition" have tended to neglect the fact that the developed nations displaying it actually maintain fluctuating, sometimes high rates of natural increase — their populations are by no means static, and that there are powerful incentives for further population growth concealed in the labor needs of industry — which is the current situation in Japan. A link between fertility and consumption attitudes is a psychological connection, not a biological one.

Changes in traditional subsistence techniques and economies have also accompanied the exportation of the cultural style of the developed society. Low-energy tribal and peasant populations often intensify their traditional regimes in order to supply more food for the growing population and to obtain a cash income to buy the new gadgets. Swidden agriculturalists in Southeast Asia have taken to shortening the cycle of use and recovery of the burned-over cultivation tracts under such pressures — as well as under the stimulus of foreign agricultural development schemes using maximization models inappropriate to such friable resource constellations (Kunstadter 1972).

EVOLUTIONARY IMPLICATIONS

That the development of culture can also be seen as a historical account of human relationships with the physical environment is a commonplace in anthropology, and the research provides a valuable link between the prehistoric and cultural fields of the discipline. There have been important theoretical accomplishments, but the work as a whole seems largely devoid of significant policy implications. There is an implicit assumption that cultural, especially technological, evolution is a good thing, involving man's progressive control over the environment and affording greater well-being and support of a larger number.

The contemporary demographic and environmental crises clearly suggest otherwise: that cultural-technological evolution, because of its exponential tendencies, has brought the human species close to disaster, and that a new emergent social and mental order is required in order to ensure the survival of the species. Even if we refuse to go along with the extreme doom-sayers, we recognize very serious problems, and realize that an uncritical admiration for growth and development leads to dangerous consequences for the passengers on Space Ship Earth.

Anthropology's failure to include some sort of value frame in its assessment of the course of cultural evolution is in part a consequence of the tendency to scientize — biologize — the cultural process, and to borrow, largely unconsciously, these value-neutral attitudes along with the concept of evolution. From the point of view of the current ecological crisis (not to mention warfare), the use of a biologistic concept of evolution to analyze culture history is nothing short of irresponsible.

In part, the failure to see cultural "evolution" as a consequential process is also based on anthropology's preoccupation with a particular type of society: the relatively isolated, relatively slow to change, low-energy society — a microsystemic community. This type of community, from which most anthropological theory has been derived, has been seen with a certain amount of justification, as an entity in equilibrium with nature. In attempting to apply the theory of this way of life to complex society, anthropologists have tended to ignore the much greater dynamism of the high-energy society, whether it is a matter of the contemporary industrial or the Bronze Age variety. There has been a tendency to see societies as fixed in time, and a failure to acknowledge the inherent dynamism of all human groups; their basic unpredictability; their proclivity to — sooner or later — maximize their use of resources.

Table 2 illustrates the basic factors in cultural history in terms of an oversimplified bipolar typology.

Table 2.   Ideal types of societies based on degree of ecological equilibrium

	Societies in equilibrium with environment	Societies in disequilibrium with environment
Population dynamics	Small, controlled	Large, expanding, weakly controlled
Contact with environment	Direct contact by maximum number of people	Direct contact by minimal number
Range	Restricted to local resources	Resources available from external sources
Sustenance needs	Close to minimal; defined largely by physiological needs	Maximal; defined in large part by cultural wants
Gratification expectations	Low; controlled	High; promise of continued expansion
Technological capacity	Low	High
Feedback loops	Functioning to control resource use	Functioning only to promote resource use

This typology permits us to ask a series of policy-relevant questions about cultural-ecological evolution. For example, is it possible that low-energy technology societies also can experience rapid population growth and pressure on resources even though the latter are listed as character-istics of the high-technology type? The answer is "yes," when we consider this happened in the monsoon Orient, where an improvement in the minimal technology of rice production, plus the effective mobilization of services through cooperative intervillage organization of labor and irriga-tion, provided new food energy, in turn triggering rapid population growth beginning around A.D. 1500. This suggests that social instrument-alities can be as effective as technological in increasing production and transforming of natural resources into energy and goods.

One of the more controversial examples of evolutionary generalizing in cultural ecology and its related fields revolves around this proposition. Wittfogel (1957), argued that "Oriental despotism" arose out of the need for a large-scale bureaucratic organization to control water resources, which led to another sobriquet, "hydraulic society." This thesis was immediately examined by specialists on other preindustrial civilizations, and it has been reworked to show that despotism and bureaucracy can PRECEDE large-scale water and other resource developments, as well as follow it; or that the particular USE of the water — e.g. irrigation versus flood control — is the significant cause of particular social forms.[14]

[14] The term "irrigation civilization" had been used by Steward (1955) before Wittfogel published his major work. Wittfogel appears to return to the earlier Marx-Engels concept of "Asiatic type of society," avoiding the Stalinist distortions of this concept, and it is this "Asiatic type" he calls "Oriental despotism." At the most minute level of research, the approach has produced some interesting studies of the relationship between water resource development and social organization as this results in parallel institutional development in historically unconnected cultures (Beardsley 1964). For some key discussions of the thesis of Wittfogel et al., see the following: McAdams (1960, 1965); Millon (1962); Leach (1959); Sanders (1965). The Leach paper is particularly interesting, because he shows that Wittfogel tends to ignore another major type of Asian "hydraulic society": the Indian-Sinhalese. This type has a great many village-level irrigation works sustained by cooperative labor, and grandiose water impoundments engineered and financed by the king — the latter largely for ornamental purposes and for the watering of the royal gardens and fields. These vast works were not built overnight, and emerged over several centuries on the basis of grants of land to local magnates. Hence these enormous water systems were apparently not accom-panied by the appearance of an authoritarian bureaucracy, and village autonomy was maintained. Sanders, however, for the culture and ecological history of the valley of Teotihuacan, seems to support the generalized Wittfogel hypothesis, stressing the factors of water shortages resulting in crises as population increased, and subsequent social conflict — the two factors stimulating the emergence of large-scale bureaucratic control over water systems and the state. Others concerned with the Valley of Mexico have emphasized different cultural-ecological relationships, in particular, the question of large versus small population centers. It has been proposed that the Classic period was dominated by Teotihuacan, with an absolute monopoly on resources and trade, leading to the decline of smaller centers, while the Aztecs encouraged small settlements,

With respect to the ecosystem notion, the "hydraulic" controversy serves to emphasize the dynamic or developmental aspects of man-nature relations, rather than the stable and balanced. However stable these centralized resource-development systems may have been during their heyday, they all declined, and nearly all led to a civilizational or political decline of major proportions. That is, the large-scale control systems were actually rather precariously balanced, because they depended on a variety of friable arrangements: uncertain water supplies, docile labor, the absence of invaders, and so on. The increasing scale of social and material technology required ever-greater control to keep the system operating. The whole body of accumulating knowledge on the issue testifies to the instability rather than the stability of large-scale man-nature arrangements, and the increasing uncertainties resulting from technological growth.

Or, reinterpreting these events in terms of the several concepts pertaining to self-regulation, we could say that during their heyday, these systems were not stable or equilibratory, but rather the reverse: typical human systems with increasing quotients of "organization" and increasing tendencies to defer the payment of inevitable costs — high P/B efficiency schemes, or positive feedback. Their breakdown, on the other hand, could be defined as a case of a RETURN to pre-existing equilibrious or homeostatic systems with lower levels of organization and with less cost to the related subsystems (negative feedback). Such returns to more primitive systems thus have a dual meaning: in terms of human affairs, or history, they imply social breakdown or instability; in terms of a comprehensive ecological perspective, they represent a reversion to some kind of equilibrium.

This also reaffirms that generalizations about stability and instability in human societies need to consider the factor of time in order to obtain an accurate perspective. The tendency in cultural evolutionary thought to consider states of being at particular points of time as sufficient evidence for process generalization leads to erroneous judgments. The issue is paradoxical because of the great interest in history and change exhibited by these evolutionary approaches.

A position with greater concern for policy would propose that there exists in human behavior a constant potential toward overexploitation of

due to reliance on a dispersed network of economic and trade system. These differing patterns would have quite different implications for resource use, population growth, and social structure: the network system, with its encouragement of smaller centers on the margins of important resource supplies, would tend to develop strong leadership and innovative aggression in the smaller, marginal communities — as in the case of the Aztecs and their many rebellious clients.

resources or pollution of the natural environment, granted that in certain historical circumstances and institutional arrangements, the effects may be minimal or phased out over relatively long periods of time. Man CAN exert a certain control over environmental deterioration by conscious discipline or planning, by ritual regulations, social interaction, or cultural precedents, and/or by very occasional automatic feedback mechanisms operating outside of cognitive awareness. A generalized cultural ecology obviously must include models pertaining to ALL THREE possibilities, although for highly developed pluralistic societies the conscious planning process is the only realistic course.

The solution to the evolutionary dilemma of cultural ecology can be outlined with the use of the criteria on the chart. The basic question is simply:

IS IT POSSIBLE TO COMBINE THE CHARACTERISTICS OF THE EQUILIBRATORY AND DISEQUILIBRATORY TYPES SO AS TO:

1.   Maintain a high technology but reduce the scale of human wants?
2.   Maintain a high technology but reach a stable population growth?
3.   Maintain high standards of living without polluting effects?
4.   Maintain a dynamic and innovative technology but bring it under the control of society?

Many of the current explorations of economists and social planners are directed toward these questions (e.g. Frederiksen 1969), and we are now in an advanced stage of controversy over whether, and how, the apparently contradictory objectives can be reached.

What role might the anthropologist play in this situation? Wilson (1971: 107) visualizes it as follows:

It is the business of the anthropologist to show the Peter Pans who refuse to grow up, who reject the responsibilities of largeness of scale, what tiny societies are like; to show yet again, that the "noble savage" in Arcadia is dream, not reality. To seek a return to smallness of scale is no cure for our present disorders; rather we must examine very closely what aspects of scale necessarily hang together. Can we have the close-knit warmth and emotional security of an isolated village without stifling individuality? Can one enjoy the fruits of science and industrial production without smothering the personal?

These are deceptively simple objectives. They speak in the language of the traditional anthropological preoccupation with the small society, the microsystem, but they also require a serious attempt to struggle with the macroinstitutions of national and world society and show how they affect local systems. However, anthropologists will require extensive training in the institutional social sciences and intensive research experience in macrosystemic societies before they can move vigorously in this direction.

REFERENCES

ALLAND, ALEXANDER
  1967   *Evolution and human behavior.* Garden City: Natural History Press.
  1972   *The human imperative.* New York: Columbia University Press.
BARTH, FREDERIK
  1956   Ecologic relationships of ethnic groups in Swat, Northern Pakistan. *American Anthropologist* 58:2079–2089.
BATESON, GREGORY
  1949   "Bali: the value system of a steady state," in *Social structure: studies presented to A. R. Radcliffe-Brown.* Edited by M. Fortes. New York: Oxford University Press.
BEARDSLEY, RICHARD K.
  1964   "Ecological and social parallels between rice-growing communities of Japan and Spain," in *Symposium on community studies in anthropology.* Edited by V. E. Garfield. Seattle: University of Washington Press (American Ethnological Society).
BENNETT, JOHN W.
  1967   *Hutterian brethren: the agricultural economy and social organization of a communal people.* Stanford: Stanford University Press.
BUCKLEY, WALTER
  1967   *Sociology and modern systems theory.* Englewood Cliffs: Prentice-Hall.
CALLAN, HILARY
  1970   *Ethology and society.* Oxford: Clarendon Press.
CAMPBELL, DONALD T.
  1965   "Variation and selective retention in socio-cultural evolution," in *Social change in developing areas.* Edited by H. R. Barringer, et al. Cambridge: Schenkman.
DIXON, R. B.
  1928   *The building of cultures.* New York: Scribners.
DUMOND, D. E.
  1961   Swidden agriculture and the rise of Maya civilization. *Southwestern Journal of Anthropology* 17:301-316.
EHRLICH, PAUL R., ANNE H. EHRLICH
  1972   *Population, resources, environment: issues in human ecology* (revised edition). San Francisco: W. H. Freeman.
FARVAR, M. TAGHI, JOHN P. MILTON, *editors*
  1972   *The careless technology: ecology and international development.* Garden City: Natural History Press.
FREDERIKSEN, HARALD
  1969   Feedbacks in economic and demographic transition. *Science* 166: 837-847.
GEERTZ, CLIFFORD
  1963   *Agricultural involution: the processes of ecological change in Indonesia.* Berkeley: University of California Press.
  1965   *The social history of an Indonesian town.* Cambridge: Massachusetts Institute of Technology Press.
HALL, A. D., R. E. FAGEN
  1956   Definition of a system. *General Systems Yearbook* 1:18–28.

HARRIS, MARVIN
   1960   Adaptation in biological and cultural science. *Transactions of the New York Academy of Sciences*, Series II, 23 (1):59–65.
HAWLEY, AMOS, *editor*
   1968   *Roderick D. McKenzie on human ecology*. Chicago: University of Chicago Press.
HILLERY, GEORGE A., JR.
   1966   Navajos and Eastern Kentuckians: a comparative study in the cultural consequences of the demographic transition. *American Anthropologist* 68:52–70.
HOLLING, CRAWFORD S.
   1969   "Stability in ecological and social systems," in *Diversity and stability in ecological systems*. Report of Symposium held May 26–28, 1969. Upton, New York: Brookhaven National Laboratory, Biology Department.
KALMUS, H.
   1966   "Control hierarchies," in *Regulation and control of living systems*. Edited by H. Kalmus. New York: John Wylie and Sons.
KOTTAK, CONRAD P.
   1972   Ecological variables in the origin and evolution of African states: the Buganda example. *Comparative Studies in Society and History* 14:351–380.
KROEBER, A. L.
   1939   *Cultural and natural areas of native North America*. University of California Publications in American Archeology and Ethnology 38, University of California at Berkeley.
KUNSTADTER, PETER
   1972   Spirits of change capture the Karen. *National Geographic* 141:267–284.
LEACH, E. R.
   1959   Hydraulic society in Ceylon. *Past and Present* 15:2–26.
LEE, RICHARD B.
   1969   "!Kung Bushman subsistence: an input-output analysis," in *Contributions to anthropology: ecological essays*. Edited by D. Damas. National Museums of Canada Bulletin 230, Anthropological Series 86. Ottawa. (Also published in *Environment and cultural behavior*, 1969. Edited by A. Vayda. New York: Natural History Press.)
LINTON, RALPH
   1936   *The study of man*. New York: Appleton-Century.
LIVINGSTONE, FRANK B.
   1958   Anthropological implications of sickle cell gene distribution in West Africa. *American Anthropologist* 60:533–559.
MASON, O. T.
   1895   Influence of environment upon human industries or arts. *Annual Reports*, pages 639–665. Washington, D.C.: Smithsonian Institution.
MAY, JACQUES M., DONNA L. MCC LELLAN, *editors*
   1972   *The ecology of malnutrition in seven countries of Southern Africa and in Portuguese Guinea*. New York: Hafner.
MCADAMS, ROBERT
   1960   "Early civilizations, subsistence and environment," in *City invincible*.

Edited by C. H. Kraeling and R. McAdams. Chicago: University of Chicago Press.

1965   *Land behind Bagdad: a history of settlement on the Dyala Plains.* Chicago: University of Chicago Press.

MCKENZIE, R. D.

1928   Ecological succession in the Puget Sound region. *Publication of the American Sociological Society* 23:60–80.

MILLON, RENE

1962   "Variations in social responses to the practice of irrigation agriculture," in *Civilizations in desert lands*. Edited by Richard B. Woodbury. University of Utah Anthropological Papers 62. Salt Lake City: University of Utah Press.

MONTGOMERY, EDWARD

1972   "Stratification and nutrition in a population in southern India." Unpublished doctoral dissertation, Columbia University, New York.

ODUM, EUGENE

1969   The strategy of ecosystem development. *Science* 164:262–270.

1971   *Fundamentals of ecology* (third edition). Philadelphia: Saunders. (First published 1953.)

ODUM, HOWARD T.

1971   *Environment, power, and society.* New York: John Wiley and Sons.

PARRACK, DWAIN W.

1969   "An approach to the bioenergetics of West Bengal," in *Environment and cultural behavior*. Edited by A. Vayda. New York: Natural History Press.

RAPPAPORT, ROY A.

1967a   Ritual regulation of environmental relations among a New Guinea people. *Ethnology* 6:17–30.

1967b   *Pigs for the ancestors: ritual in the ecology of a New Guinea people.* New Haven: Yale University Press.

1971a   Ritual, sanctity, and cybernetics. *American Anthropologist* 73:73–76.

1971b   The flow of energy in an agricultural society. *Scientific American* 224: 116–133.

REDFIELD, ROBERT, *editor*

1942   *Levels of integration in biological and social systems.* Lancaster, Pennsylvania: Jaques Cattell.

RIPLEY, S. DILLON, HELMUT K. BUECHNER

1970   "Ecosystem science as a point of synthesis," in *America's changing environment*. Edited by Roger Revelle and Hans II. Landsberg. Boston: Beacon Press.

RUESCH, J., G. BATESON

1951   *Communication, the social matrix of psychiatry.* New York: Norton.

SAHLINS, MARSHALL

1961   The segmentary lineage: an organization of predatory expansion. *American Anthropologist* 63:322–345.

SANDERS, WILLIAM T.

1965   "The cultural ecology of the Teotihuacan Valley." Preliminary report on the results of the Teotihuacan Valley Project, Pennsylvania State University.

SAPIR, E.
1914 *Time perspective in aboriginal American culture.* Ottawa: Canadian Department of Mines.

SCUDDER, THAYER
1968 Social anthropology, man-made lakes and population dislocation in Africa. *Anthropological Quarterly* 41:168–176.
1972a "Ecological bottlenecks and the development of the Kariba Lake Basin," in *The careless technology.* Edited by M. Taghi Farvar and John P. Milton. Garden City: Natural History Press.
1972b Chairman: "Irrigation and water development," in *The careless technology,* section two. Edited by M. Taghi Farvar and John P. Milson. Garden City: Natural History Press.

STAGNER, ROSS
1951 "Homeostasis as a unifying concept in personality theory." *Psychological Review* 58:5–17.

STEWARD, JULIAN H. *editor*
1955 *Irrigation civilizations: a comparative study: a symposium on method and result in cross-cultural regularities.* Social Science Monographs 1. Washington, D.C.: Pan American Union.

STOLNITZ, G.
1964 "The demographic transition," in *Population and the vital revolution.* Edited by Ronald Freedman. Garden City. Anchor Books.

VAYDA, ANDREW P.
1960 *Maori warfare.* Polynesian Society Maori Monographs 2. Wellington.
1961 Expansion and warfare among swidden agriculturalists. *American Anthropologist* 63:346–358.
1967 Research on the functions of primitive war. *Peace Research Society (International) Papers* 7:133–138.
1969 An ecological approach in cultural anthropology. *Bucknell R.* 17 (1).
1971 Phases of the process of war and peace among the Marings of New Guinea. *Oceania* 42:1–24.

VAYDA, ANDREW P., R. A. RAPPAPORT
1968 "Ecology: cultural and non-cultural," in *Introduction to cultural anthropology.* Edited by J. Clifton. Boston: Houghton Mifflin.

WEISENFELD, STEPHEN L.
1967 Sickle cell trait in human biological and cultural evolution. *Science* 157:1134–1140.

WIENER, NORBERT
1950 *The human use of human beings: cybernetics and society.* Boston: Houghton Mifflin. (Second edition, 1954, Garden City: Doubleday.)

WILSON, MONICA
1971 *Religion and the transformation of society: a study in social change in Africa.* New York: Cambridge University Press.

WISSLER, CLARK
1926 *The relation of nature to man in aboriginal America.* New York: Oxford University Press.

WITTFOGEL, KARL
1957 *Oriental despotism: a comparative study of total power.* New Haven: Yale University Press.

Organizational Evolution from Mating Pairs to Trading Nations: Spontaneous and Competitive Striving with Interacting Individuals All Regulating Each Other

F. L. W. RICHARDSON

HUMAN ETHOLOGY AND THE PRIMORDIAL INTERACTIONAL PROCESS

In the following pages we will consider man as though he were only an animal, and thus limited, provide a legitimate biological and behavioral basis for comparison with all other animals. It represents a further attempt to join with others in transforming the natural history of man into a science of human ethology (see Richardson et al. n.d.).

The strategy here is to focus on face-to-face relationships and the sequence of ongoing current happenings in the immediate environment — not on the past, the future, and distant situations, or those not immediately experienced and about which information must be conveyed through language, graphics, or other form. To be consistent, descriptions of relationships will be similarly limited without recourse to linguistic or other symbolic communication and hence without information about the beliefs, rules, values, or other intellectual constructs of the subjects investigated. Instead, the information considered will consist primarily of behavioral-biological interchanges that, however obvious in general, are not often made explicit and are always in detail subtle and complex.

It is here inferred that behavioral exchanges — timing and sequences of actions and inactions, alternating silences and sounds, and the pitch, volume, and tone of the latter — all represent current manifestations of a primordial interactional process similar to that among members of every other mammalian species. It is further inferred that this process is related "generically" (homologous) to the sensory interchanges — visible, audible, olfactory, and tactile — specifically different for each but in general universal for all other animal species.

It is widely recognized and well documented that biological evolution involves and results in both organic and behavioral change, but the former has received far more emphasis than the latter. When considering in particular the behavioral evolution of social relationships, invertebrates such as social insects have, at least until recently, been systematically investigated far more than mammals and, in particular, more than the social progression from lower primates to man. The study of this progression not only has evoked less interest but often has provoked disapproval and active censure.

It is also well documented and widely recognized that the progressive organic and behavioral changes take place precisely because they provide individuals with increasing advantages. This has been widely documented for organic change. It seems natural to apply it also to behavioral change, including social or organizational change, meaning in this instance the increasing interdependence and cooperation among members of the same species. It seems therefore obvious that the progression from the seasonal litters of primitive mammals to "permanent" simian groups evolved just because this gave the latter important competitive advantages, just as the subsequent progression to community organizations gave early man an even greater advantage.

But although increasing group size provides an easily recognizable indication of social or organizational evolution, behavioral-biological developments have brought more significant results, such as the improved capability of a species to control its own population. Thus, by caring for their young, mammals, birds, and some fish, commonly raise only a few compared to the myriads raised by many invertebrates whose unattended progeny provide food for other species. And among many group-living species such as apes and monkeys, an adult female usually raises no more than one offspring a year. A similar change is characteristic of behavioral-social developments in giant insect societies. There is thus for many social species a common evolutionary trend transferring population control away from predator species to the species itself.

In the primordial interactional process — or the behavioral-biological and competitive means by which change evolves — there are a number of fundamental counterforces universal to all animals. One, within each individual, is the inherent and spontaneous generation of energy and consequent actions confronting and counterbalanced by other individuals, all mutually limiting and regulating each other. A second is the periodic display of threatening and hostile actions that repel other individuals on the one hand, balanced on the other, by friendly and companionable interchanges that attract and, so it is inferred, stimulating the latter to unite against strangers and rivals, and to cooperate in joint enterprises.

A third inferred example of counterforces, universal for all animals, is the balance maintained between the advantages a species derives from new developments, offset by a changing degree of disadvantage. Thus humans, and apparently lions (Schaller 1973: 136, 188–189, 362–364), benefit from organizing cooperative undertakings but suffer the disadvantage of considerable hostility and, at least humans kill proportionately more of their own kind than is usual among other species. These disadvantages, however, have been counterbalanced by advantages. Distressingly, if not alarmingly as regards humans, however, the primoridial interactional processes, soon to be described, are becoming progressively disrupted and circumvented as civilizations rush out of control.

PROGRESSIVELY ENLARGING GROUPINGS AND DEVELOPING GREATER SPECIALIZATION AND INTERDEPENDENCE

In describing organizational evolution from primitive mammals to man or the growing interdependence among individuals performing specialized functions, only those behavioral-social developments will be considered that are characteristic of the majority of surviving members. On the basis of the particular behavioral traits common or widespread among closely related surviving species, one may assume that these traits were similarly characteristic for members of the extinct parental species. Thus I infer that the great majority of extinct reptiles from which primitive mammals presumably evolved were relatively lone-living and had no parental attachments to their live young, who upon birth or hatching were well able to fend for themselves.

From such a systematic description, it becomes almost self-evident that as a succession of organisms has over time often become enlarged and more complex (e.g. from small primitive mammals to man), so, also, have similarly organized groupings. In particular, as regards trends starting with small primitive mammals of one hundred million years ago, major social-behavioral developments will be considered as though they had taken place in five successive stages, ending with the industrial nations that dominate the scene today:

STAGE 1. MOTHER AND LITTER, OR TEMPORARY "FAMILY ORGANIZATION"
About one hundred million years ago, there were small insect-eating mammals (not unlike present-day tree shrews) from whom, presumably, the primates later developed (Eisenberg in Richardson et al. f.c.). At an earlier time, other small mammals evolved, the mouse opossums and long-tailed tenrecs being among the closest living species in appearance. If their behavior was similar to that of their contemporary living representatives, these early small mammals lived largely alone except for brief periods when a mother with her litter formed a temporary "family" group. Each animal gathered its own food, which was limited in kind.

STAGE 2. PERMANENT "FAMILY" GROUP, OR BAND ORGANIZATION   Several tens of millions of years ago, monkeys evolved and, to infer from their living relatives, organized long-term "family" groups comprising a membership ranging from a handful to several dozen year-round companions. These family groups often comprised two or more mothers with young and sometimes one or more adult males, the latter usually specialized in guarding and defending against predators and intruders while the female specialized in rearing the young. The members of one family group remained relatively segregated from those in every other. Group members usually refrained from intermingling and instead exhibited an indifference or hostility toward the members of other groups. As in the preceding stage, each individual gathered its own limited variety of food.

STAGE 3. FAMILY-COMMUNITY, OR SIMPLE TRIBAL ORGANIZATION   The family-community type of organization emerged either with early man or a preceding apelike ancestor hundreds of thousands to a few million years ago. The members of one family group, in contrast with the usual practice of simians, regularly intermingled with those in other family groups, thereby forming a community of related families. This multigroup human organization is thus more complex than the usual single group organization of simians. Surviving family communities of this kind generally range from several dozen to a few thousand members.

In contrast, therefore, to the usual simian practice of members in one group remaining continuously within sight or easy calling distance of each other, the members of a human family group were often throughout the day dispersed at considerable distances from each other, usually in search of food. Thus, during the day individuals alternately convened and dispersed, intermingling for a time with one combination of individuals and then with another, but commonly at dusk all members of a family group usually returned to their camp, where they remained in close proximity until dawn. In contrast with the situation in Stages 1 and 2, man or even ape-man before him used a variety of foods (both meat and plant) and added the activities of food preparation and cooking. Different individuals performed specialized functions, but all shared in the eating. Also, from time to time, members from several different families intermingled, and seasonally or yearly a number of families usually came together for community activities.

STAGE 4. FAMILY COMMUNITY AND INSTITUTIONAL ORGANIZATION, OR PRE-INDUSTRIAL STATES   These organizations included chiefdoms and pre-industrial trading and military states developed by the latest species of man several thousand years ago, each state totaling from perhaps ten thousand to several million members. In contrast to a simple tribe, in which members from one to a few communities regularly intermingled, in preindustrial states representatives from sometimes hundreds or thousands of communities intermingled, and also became members of state-wide institutions (priesthood, army, central bureaucracy, or royal court). And in contrast to the periodic and temporary tribal gatherings characteristic of the previously described simple communities of hunting and gathering peoples, there usually came to be a capital city or town serving as a permanent meeting place with centralized institutions.

As within tribes, families and communities formed subunits within states, but to a degree unprecedented in simple tribes, centralized institutions developed and proliferated, serving and regulating the constituent families and communities. Thus in addition to the two-level family-community organization characteristic of simple tribes, institutions comprised a third level in states and hence created a more complex organizational system with greater specialization and increasing interdependence.

STAGE 5. EXPANSION OF INSTITUTIONS AND CITIES AND WEAKENING OF FAMILIES AND COMMUNITIES, OR NATIONAL-GLOBAL ORGANIZATION   The emergence of contemporary industrial-trading nations within the last century or two has resulted in a further enlarging of states and increasing complexity as exemplified by a greater mixing of populations, the superimposition of still more levels of organization, accelerating specialization, and degree of global interdependence possibly exceeding human ability to regulate. Concurrently with a change from a rural-farming to an urban-industrial-trading society, brought about by technological progress, there is a weakening of family-community and intergenerational ties. Thus institutional organization progressively invaded nature's eon-old organization with the consequent disruption of family-community and close intergenerational living — the entire process often referred to euphemistically as "civilized progress."

Accompanying this progressive increase in numbers of individuals belonging to organized groupings has been an increasing specialization and interdependence. But although more individuals became interdependent, the degree of cooperation, at least among human beings, has often in fact lessened.

Thus in Stage 1, a mother, with no other adult to help, had to perform all functions alone in rearing her young. With the emergence of group organization in Stage 2, and for those species that incorporated one or more adult males in family groups, the males usually specialized in guarding and defending against predators and intruders, while the female specialized in rearing the young. With the coming of family-community organization in Stage 3, still more specialized activities emerged, increasing the interdependence of cooperating individuals. Whereas in both previous stages, each individual animal had gathered and eaten its own food (and usually most species narrowly specialized in one kind), man or even ape-man before him complicated the process by including a greater variety of foods and by adding the preparation and cooking as well. Often different individuals specialized in performing different functions but all shared in the eventual eating.

In Stages 4 and 5, with the expansion from local to regional and then to global trade, greater numbers of individuals became interdependent. With technical development accelerating, and in Stage 5, with machine production supplanting handicrafts, the number of different specialized activities rose astronomically as did also the number of interdependent specialists required to perform them. But the degree of cooperation often lessened.

Thus in the line of evolution from small early mammals to modern man, the biological trend toward larger organisms has been paralleled in part by a similar enlarging of organizational groupings. As these organisms have developed more specialized and interdependent subunits, cells, tissues, and organs, so organized groupings have also developed more specialized and interdependent individuals, families, institutions, or other subunits.

EVOLVING INCREASINGLY COMPLEX MEANS FOR
INTERACTING INDIVIDUALS TO
CONTROL AND STIMULATE EACH OTHER

In comparing the evolution of increasingly complex organisms with the organization of their members, similarities are apparent in the evolution not only of more complex forms and greater internal specialization of subunits but also of an increasingly complex means of coordinating and regulating the interdependence of the subunits. Thus, as physiological processes have become progressively more complex for regulating the organs and subunits within an organism (for more efficient preparation to fight or flee, eat and digest, court and mate), so it seems reasonable that progressively greater complexity for regulation should characterize social organization (for more efficiently rearing the young, repelling intruders, and maintaining internal stability). As the process is largely self-regulating within an organism, so it is also within social groups. It also seems natural that both evolutionary developments — anatomic and social — represent different but closely interconnected and parallel responses to a common condition. In the regulatory process, the complex neuroendocrine system provides the organism with an extensive repertory of means for preparing it to cooperate with, contend with, or avoid others.

Simple Observable Distinction Between Contentious and Friendly Relationships

From observing people as an ethologist observes animals, it is apparent that there is a sequence of actions and inactions, sounds and silences that interacting individuals exchange without regard to linguistic meaning.

When ignoring the verbal content of what people say — and even when also ignoring all sound — there are still some simple, useful, and highly revealing discriminations that can be made whether observing animals or human beings.

From the observation of animals in the wild — particularly animals large enough to be seen with the naked eye — by naturalists, zoologists, and now ethologists, both amateur and professional, the following represent some of the simple distinctions that are commonly made:

1. Each time an individual either drives away or repels one or more members of its own species, or is attracted to one or more, such as for courting and mating.

2. The number and duration of occasions when one or more adults nurture, protect, or defend their young.

3.   The occasions, as well as the frequency, and spacing of members, when one makes the "first move" and others follow.

4.   When individuals, on the one hand, regularly and gently touch (or sing or dance) and, on the other, jointly confront, chase, bite, beat, wound, or otherwise attack (or argue with) one or more others.

For convenience, the foregoing considerations may be summarized into interactional discriminations that distinguish friendly from hostile exchanges, whether applied to human beings or other mammals:

1.   Spatial — increasing or decreasing intervening distance or other kinds of spatial ordering, such as one "leading" and others following.

2.   Tactile — gently touching in contrast with beating, biting, jabbing, or otherwise attacking.

3.   Kinesthetic — arrhythmic motions (customary when fighting or arguing) versus rhythmic (when courting, nurturing, grooming, singing or dancing).

These spatial, tactile, and kinesthetic discriminations combine in various ways that are peculiar for each species, and for some species — and man in particular — they often vary from one grouping to another. Also, these discriminations, in the course of evolution from primitive mammals to modern man, have become more complex and thus accompanied and paralleled the organizational trends toward greater size and complexity.

And, although not so well known, numerous investigators in recent decades by combining field, laboratory, and physiological observations have made connections between specific sensory stimuli that automatically trigger given responses from interacting individuals and the associated internal neuroendocrine processes. Thus when known, the specific biochemical, action, vocal, or other stimuli that attract and induce cooperation and the hostile ones that repel will be indicated. Additionally, when known or suspected, the associated physiological processes will be referred to.

These two polar forces — to contend and to cooperate — are universal except for the simplest living beings. To survive, the organism must often drive others away in order to feed and in so doing enforce some measure of separation or segregation. To insure species continuity, the organism must attract and cooperate in mating and in nourishing and rearing the young. For the 200 million years of evolution from the advent of early mammals to the present day, old means of stimulating and controlling cooperation and contending have persisted and new ones have emerged. Thus courting has developed as a prelude to mating, and nurturing the young has followed gestation. And in addition to a victor always chasing his rivals away, he came later to develop the means of conditioning familiar rivals to defer.

Contentious Behavior Essential for Regulating Precedence and Privilege

As ancient probably as life itself, originating a billion or more years ago, and widespread among animals, is the practice of driving away or fleeing from rivals of their own species. No animal can long survive without a defense against rivals and particularly rival members of its own species, who compete for sustenance, mates, and privilege. When 200 million years ago mammals emerged from reptiles, relatively lone-living individuals probably drove away intruding rivals of their own species, as do territorial lizards today. Moreover, the neuroendocrine responses of anger and fear, leading to repulsion and flight, were inherited by early mammals with, according to brain physiologists, the incorporation of a "reptilian" section, still recognizable and functioning in the human brain. With the emergence of primitive mammals and a mother alone rearing her litter (Stage 1), she no doubt drove away other adults of her own species as a means of protecting her young. With more of the young surviving from mothers who were the most fierce and determined in driving away intruding members of their own species, it would seem to be a natural evolutionary development that upon perceiving another adult of their own or a competing species, the neuroendocrine process for inducing anger would thus become more quickly triggered, thereby automatically inducing fiercer threats and a greater willingness to attack than usual.

With the introduction of year-round family groupings including two or more adults (Stage 2), the process of repelling became more complex, with the evolution of the practice of all members of a group jointly driving intruders away. And with the advent of human societies, members from a number of different groups cooperated in driving others away. Then, with the emergence of civilized societies, the repelling groups became enlarged to armies of thousands and eventually millions.

As has been suggested previously, among the special devices used to repel are chemical means. The simplest organisms use chemicals to repel (and attract) individuals of the same or a different species. Even among highly evolved organisms, such as insects and vertebrates, chemicals serve to repel or to induce attack. Honeybees, reacting possibly to a "foreign" smell, attack an intruder from another hive. Bullheads (a freshwater fish) release a substance that reveals to others of their own species their relative rank. Many mammals keep away rivals of their own species by using scent to mark their territories. Some of the most highly evolved organisms, however, such as birds and primates rely almost entirely upon vocal and visual threats to repel rivals. With the advent of man technological means were devised to repel (e.g. spears, arrows, cannons and napalm).

With the formation of stable family groups, systems of ranking developed to establish precedence. Dominance behavior to establish rank is usually not very contentious, for the aim is not to drive another out of sight but simply to force him to stand aside. Such contentious confrontations usually require no more than a few moments of fighting to discover who can force the other to stand aside. After such an initial confrontation, the deferring individual, upon being approached again by the more dominant, will quickly display some symbolic act of deference, such as lowering itself, and thus avoid another contest.

Whereas the members of a simian troop (Stage 2) may all be individually ranked from the highest to the lowest, it is rare among such groupings for a number of individuals to be ranked equally. In contrast, with the appearance of early man and hunting and gathering communities (Stage 3), it became common for members of the same sex and approximate age within a community to have approximately equal status. However, there is commonly a relative "group" ranking for members of each of these sex and age categories. Thus the elders often form a dominant and sometimes united group that, for example, determines a number of matters of general concern to the entire community, whereas young adult males may occasionally direct some of the activities of one or more adolescent boys or maintain order while the entire group moves camp. With the appearance of state societies (Stage 4), it became a common practice, persisting into the present (Stage 5), for entire families, communities, peoples, and institutions to be ranked according to particular classes or castes, whose members are thus graded according to the prerogatives, privileges, rules, and freedoms permitted each grouping. In human societies, symbolic deference, even without a test fight, is also commonplace when the more deferring, for example, stand aside, allowing dominant individuals to proceed first.

Dominance may also be expressed vocally, with one or more dominant individuals silencing others. This behavior has been studied more among birds than among mammals; thus, it is common among male songbirds in the spring preceding mating to claim a territory by singing within it and thus serving as a threat to rival males to stay out. Only those who dare to sing and make themselves evident attract a female and succeed in mating and rearing young. Those individuals who are silent remain on the outskirts of territories and usually do not mate. Somewhat related behavior is characteristic of some monkeys and apes (howler monkeys and gibbons), who engage in much calling and vocalizing, particularly in the early morning. The vocalizing apparently serves to locate other groups and as a territorial claim, and thus often a warning for rivals to keep their distance and hence to maintain group segregation.

In human societies talking with accompanying facial and gestural expressions may be used to attain dominance. Dominant members commonly monopolize conversation, and when challenged keep on talking, sometimes raising their voices until challengers are silenced. The process in conversational dominance is not unlike that in physical dominance between animals, when the conqueror stands over his victim and does nothing while it remains motionless, but should it move or attempt to rise or fight, the dominant member will again force it to submit. Thus dominant individuals have greater freedom to move and vocalize in contrast to the deferring ones, who are more restricted.

In human societies, in addition to repelling and deferring and silencing (which commonly provide means for simultaneously dominating only a few), the recent development of subordination (Stages 4 and 5) has introduced a radical means by indirectly and continuously dominating entire populations. Subordination is defined as a relationship when one or more individuals regularly contribute their services or material things, such as tribute, taxes, and products. Such material donations and services are usually in part compensated for when the superior provides protection against invaders and communal benefits, such as irrigation, roads, supernatural benefits, the settling of disputes, or, a later innovation, money.

Thus, as organized groupings have enlarged and the members have become increasingly specialized, new ways of repelling and limiting the freedom of others have emerged. Over the past one hundred million years, therefore, the repertory of dominance and contentious practices has increased, as have the related physiological processes. Paradoxically, this behavioral-biological process, although basically contentious, provides individuals with means for regulating each other and often for preventing any one individual or grouping from exercising excessive dominance.

Attracting, Pleasing, and Cooperating

An important means introduced by human beings for attracting and maintaining the loyalty of large numbers of subordinate persons is the inducement of monetary and material rewards. In institutional societies the individual leaves his home community to go to a regional or national metropolitan center to become involved in activities with people from many different communities. The importance of these material inducements that institutions provide has received much attention. The field of economics deals systematically with money and the production, distribution, and exchange of material things and services. In addition, the aim of the educational system (particularly in the United States) is to prepare and encourage the student by legitimate means to better himself by accumulating monetary and material things. Psychologists, particularly experimental psychologists in research on learning, further emphasize the importance of material rewards by using food, money, and similar inducements. For human beings, it is also universally recognized that verbal praise and complementary remarks, like money and material rewards, serve to attract.

PRIMORDIAL PLEASURES   What, then, were the needs or inducements that brought individuals together prior to the widespread and relatively recent use of money and material objects? The oldest primordial attraction, almost as old as life itself, is sex. Another as old as the age of mammals is the need to nurse and protect the helpless young. A third is the warmth derived from bodily contact and the apparent pleasure that results from gentle touching.

For most animals, sex, as a means of attracting adult males and females, is expressed in a momentary act performed annually or at least infrequently. Among apes and monkeys, however, the act is performed more frequently, with females usually becoming receptive several times a year. Among human beings the sex act is still more frequent, with a continuous potential receptivity for females, and is usually more prolonged.

Whereas the activity of nursing and feeding the young emerged with birds and mammals (Stage 1), feeding did not develop into a cooperative organized activity with one adult providing sustenance and drink for another, except among some predators including early man. With the development of cooking and the mastering of techniques of fermentation and distilling, feasting became a further means of attracting human beings. And with the emergence of civilized societies (Stage 4), sexual indulgence along with feasting and drinking provided additional inducements for attracting those with sufficient leisure, but at the same time, however, sometimes generated intense hostility, as in the case of the harems and courts of preindustrial states.

Obviously far older than feasting and drinking, gentle touching evolved with the emergence of organized groupings (Stage 2), as a new means for attracting and pleasing adult companions. For members of social species, including both mammals and birds that have evolved organized group-ings, gentle touching, whether, for example, grooming, licking, nuzzling, or preening, has become a widespread if not universal practice. With the coming of man, his loss of body hair, and the much accentuated sensitiv-ity of the human skin, gentle touching developed into stroking and fond-ling among, for example, members of a family, presumably serving to strengthen and maintain their attraction for one another. Not only has gentle touching provided a more sensitive means by which human indi-viduals derive pleasure, but with family members sleeping and touching one another in contrast to many simians, the time devoted to gentle touching may also in the course of primate evolution have become con-siderably prolonged.

RHYTHM AND TONE Additional means for attracting have been intro-duced by human beings. One of these is the use of rhythmic activities; not only do they provide strong sensory stimulation, but they are often combined in rituals with highly complex symbolic representations, appar-ently unique to human beings. Singing and dancing, and all forms of communal rhythm provide a means for uniting different families; these, for example, allay hostilities often latent among persons not in frequent touch as are the members of a single family. In addition to singing and dancing, other rhythmic or tonal expressions include oration, clapping, incantation, stamping, and poetic recitation. Such activities and modes of expression presumably evolved at least hundreds of thousands of years ago and provided a strong sensory means for simultaneously attracting dozens, hundreds, or thousands of individuals, whereas previously de-scribed means, such as sex and grooming, affected usually no more than pairs or a few members within a single group.

Even in plain, everyday conversation, moreover, rhythm and tone are critical in stimulating either pleasurable or displeasing sensations and further complicate thereby the process of contentious and friendly ex-change (Chapple 1970). Language not only provides words and phrases to express feeling and to inform but the rhythm of interacting provides even greater subtlety for the expression of feeling. Thus, as mentioned previously, antagonists competing for talking time regularly interrupt and raise their voices, while often also grimacing with hostility, whereas companionable individuals, with expressions of contentment, commonly synchronize their exchange in soft-spoken tones. But the seeming satis-factions that any one individual derives from synchronous conversing are often outnumbered by an arrhythmic interchange with contestants sparring for talking time, which, as is familiar to all of us, is rarely sensed as satisfying, particularly by those who are unwittingly silenced. And although the displeasure and hostility engendered by arrhythmic conversing may be most manifest in our highly competitive urban-commercial societies, it is by no means absent from the simplest tribal communities.

It is here assumed that competitive arrhythmic and loud talking is commonplace among all peoples. And it is further assumed that physiologically it usually induces displeasing, annoying, and hostile sensations. As human conversing must be hundreds of thousands if not millions of years old, it would seem consistent with evolutionary precedent that some means would have had to evolve to prevent annoyances from becoming hostile, and hostility rising to violence. As will be explained immediately, moreover, competitive talking introduces a new kind of struggle and one for which preexisting animal restraints are largely inadequate.

Among animals of the same species, struggles are usually over tangible things such as food, mates, resting places, and territories. Such struggles are commonly far simpler to resolve than those involving human beings contending to outtalk others. Conflicts among animals cease when the losing animal leaves. This simple process of one individual repelling another probably represents the commonest means by which animal combatants resolve their conflicts. However, resolving a conflict between disputants competing for talking time requires that one talk and the other listen. In such instances no resolution becomes possible should either one leave.

It is thus inherently impossible for disputants to achieve any semblance of consensus if one refuses either to listen or to talk. Similarly, as with combatants, however, a third individual can intercede and sometimes deescalate hostility, often with human beings relieving tension among disputants by occasional interjections of humor. But with pair-conversing so widespread and suitable third parties not always immediately present, one can assume that other means would have had to evolve for discussants to benefit more fully from the enormous potential inherent in exchanging information and stimulating discussion. It therefore seems probable, as intimated previously, that humor, smiling, and laughter represent the major evolutionary development among human beings to limit or prevent displeasure and annoyance from hostile conversing to rise to a level of antagonism precluding rational discussion.

Humor, smiling, and laughter thus can be considered as providing interacting individuals with new means for mutually restraining one another as they keep struggling to gain greater personal advantage. It must be made clear, however, that as annoyances between disputants rise to higher levels of antagonism, both humor and rational discussion will usually cease. Thereafter the disputants will either angrily depart or, losing all mutual restraint, escalate their disagreement and arrhythmic exchange into a shouting and physical combat.

In addition, therefore, to synchronous versus asynchronous rhythms and loudness versus softness of tone that strongly affect an individual's internal states, humor as manifested by laughter, joking, and smiling provides another entirely new development introduced by man. And in contrast to all the aforementioned kinds of sensory stimulation — chemical, auditory, tactile, and visual — laughter and related forms of exhibiting amusement are usually induced by the MEANING of verbal utterances and are thus triggered by intellectual, reasoning, or cognitive processes. As Koestler (1967) so ably points out, discrepancies in meaning or in the use of symbolic expression are perhaps most often responsible for triggering human merriment. This reinforces, therefore, the proposition that laughter, joking, and smiling evolved contemporaneously with language by providing a compensatory means for allaying the hostility latent in verbal exchange and provoked by competitive talking.

COOPERATION   Thus far I have described the evolution of various means for attracting individuals to each other and usually in the process allaying any latent hostility. I have also inferred that the individuals often derive internal sensations of pleasure therefrom. The further inference will now be made that, by attracting and pleasing one another, interacting individuals thereby automatically stimulate each other to cooperate. Among interacting individuals, therefore, mutual pleasure and an urge to cooperate may both derive from similar if not identical physiological processes. The fact that perhaps universally for insects, birds, and mammals gentle tactile exchanges between and among the members within organized groupings are frequent, and usually negligible or nonexistent with outsiders, suggests that tactile stimulation and cooperation are closely connected. Thus the pleasurable physiological sensations from touch may also induce among participants a mutual desire to go to one another's assistance. (Only during the last few decades, however, has research on the human physiology of pleasure and affection begun to appear including, for example, the physiology and pleasurable sensations associated with sex. See Cobb 1958; Masters and Johnson 1965: 512–534.)

On the contrary, the physiology of cooperation, that is, the means whereby one individual is stimulated to lead and another to follow or all members of a group to mobilize to contend jointly against others, is to my knowledge not known at all. However, to evolve any kind of means for selectively attracting organisms that recognize each other as particular individuals probably would require inducing mutually pleasurable sensations in each. If they are to continue to be attracted to each other, means must be evolved for regularly inducing in them pleasurable sensation. From this reasoning the further step is inferred that individuals who derive pleasure from each other are also inclined to cooperate.

DISRUPTING NATURAL COOPERATION AND RIVALRY — DYSFUNCTIONAL CONSEQUENCES OF LANGUAGE, REASON, AND TECHNOLOGY

Imperfect Adjusting

It is well recognized in human affairs that major advances, whether technical, organizational, or other, often create problems, many that are unanticipated. Thus, with all its advantages, the automobile contributed to such problems as urban sprawl and air pollution. Similarly, the introduction of a representative legislature with the potential for helping the poor often resulted in the negation or minimization of this advantage when the rich bribed the legislators.

Prior to such human and often disruptive developments, major advances for any species, such as the ability of a predator to catch and kill its prey, usually show further remarkable adjustments with parallel and innate restraints that prevent such predators from attacking and killing members of their own species. Still there are some long-standing crisis adjustments in nature. For example, overpopulation in nature such as may occur in arctic and desert regions is taken care of by drastic measures, as dramatically demonstrated periodically by moving hordes of lemmings swimming to their death. But although among all animals, the evolution of parallel restraints has prevented rivals from dangerously escalating their hostility, among human beings hostile exchanges have rapidly proliferated while parallel restraints have weakened; thus competitive contending often escalates into violence.

In the transformation from simian to human society, the advent of intelligence, language, and technology provided human beings with means for gaining advantage over rival animals and later over other groupings of their own kind. Many of these advantages were made by circumventing controls ordinarily limiting hostility among members of the same species.

Contending and Provoking Great Hostility

Making a complete break with almost all other animals, early man or possibly ape man before him (Stage 3) through the power of reasoning and technical advances adapted the practices, used previously only by predators to catch and kill their prey, against members of his own species. Thus, through their powers of reasoning, human beings have been able to circumvent their animal instincts, for example, by sneaking up on one of their own kind — a hated rival, and when within range, effortlessly killing him by throwing a spear of shooting an arrow, and if successfully sneaking up to him undetected, stabbing him in his sleep. With animals, instinctive restraints are far stronger than their intelligence, and so they are unable to engage in such practices and, moreover, have no technical means anyway of killing from a distance.

With the emergence of institutional organization and the rapid enlarging of organized groupings into states (Stage 4), mass subordination rapidly spread whereby, for example, the conquerors and their descendants demanded regular payments of tribute or taxes. From that time to this, subordinate peoples have regularly resisted giving donations, for example, by withholding their efforts or hiding their produce or by other kinds of passive-resistance or antiproductivity practices, as these are now commonly called. Thus in addition to early man's escalating violence, civilized human beings have introduced subtle ways of weakening the power of those who dominate them. To balance the newfound means by which a few can dominate many, the latter on a large scale have developed subtle practices and various new means of contending that serve to lessen the gross imbalance in power between a dominating elite and their subordinate masses. Finally, with the evolution of talking, human beings introduced arguing, another new kind of contentious behavior. (Obviously animals, unable to communicate about future plans or past events or to dispute about the supernatural, are spared this form of contending that human language and reasoning have made possible.)

In addition to introducing new ways of contending and increasing violence, language, technology, and reason have, as already implied, made possible also new circumstances and practices that provoke greater hostility or at least inevitably create the potential for greater hostility. When different members of family groups specialized in the daily collection, preparation, and sharing of food (Stage 3), they all became thereby more interdependent. Should a young wife, for example, engage in clandestine meetings with a lover or a husband use food as a bribe to seduce another, then during a period of food shortage the consequent lack of adequate nourishment for all might well induce bickering, and if suspicions were also aroused, and particularly if the in-laws became also involved, this annoyance might escalate to a nearly explosive degree of hostility. As the members of all the vertebrate groupings individually gather their own food, with the exception of some predators, such problems cannot arise.

Human language has additionally made possible a number of means for provoking greater hostility. One way of provoking hostility, common in all human societies "primitive" or "civilized," has been the practice of indoctrinating the young with hate, particularly against traditional enemies. Another related practice is the spreading of derogatory remarks about another, whether true or false, a practice particularly prevalent in institutional societies (Stages 4 and 5). Similarly the conscious use of deceit or duplicity, verbally and behaviorally pretending to be subservient to another, for example, yet conniving to kill or imprison the former, represents another human consequence of language apparently impossible for animals to perform.

Possibly also for simple societies, another consequence of language fostering greater hostility would result when the members of neighboring communities spoke mutually unintelligible languages. The fact that they were unable to converse would strongly tend further to segregate the members of these two communities and hence predispose them to become mutually hostile. Individuals of many simian societies, apparently not possessing mutually unintelligible "languages," more easily move from one group to another so that over the years and decades there would be more intergroup intermingling than among and between primitive human communities, whose members could not converse and presumably would prejudice each other against their unintelligible neighbors.

More provocative of hostility than any of the particular practices described is the subsequent feuding and retaliation that escalate into violence. Thus blood feuds are by no means uncommon, particularly in simple societies, in which each family or community commonly exacts one death at a time. Such one-for-one exchanges sometimes persist over decades and generations. Animals do not, as far as is known, engage in prolonging such reciprocal lethal interchanges for presumably a number of reasons that include a poorer memory. But over short periods of time, one observer at least has recorded a sequence of revengeful fighting incidents among members in a pack of wild African dogs (Van Lawick-Goodall 1971: 97–101). Similar retaliatory practices already mentioned are exchanged in civilized societies between subordinates and superiors often induced by the latter increasing their demands on the former who in turn withhold their efforts. Such antiproductivity practices and passive resistance, widely practiced in every civilized society, weaken the competitive advantages that a dominating elite enjoys, facing them with increasing danger of losing future struggles against skilled and determined rivals.

Disrupting Social-Behavioral Order

The development of technology with the provision to particular groups of decisive advantages as, for example, metal weapons, upset the regulation of contending by the principle of parity of power. For example, mature males of a species were usually of approximately equal strength, stamina, and fighting ability. With only a limited advantage over any specific rival, a dominant individual could not easily force deference on many others. But with a weapons monopoly, dominant individuals could, at least in the short run, subjugate masses. Such hostile dominance was not always offset by means to attract the loyalty of subordinate peoples (such as not discriminating against former enemies and intermingling with them to develop cooperative enterprises).

Although a dominant group may gain a technical advantage as through a weapons monopoly, countermeasures are available to adjust the balance of power. Such means include rebellion (as when King John of England was forced by his nobles to accept the Magna Carta), work stoppages, political demonstrations, and citizens' boycotts. Cartoons are used to expose the foibles of leaders. Conflicts of public and private interests are publicized. Officials are voted out of office. And through education, subordinates are admitted to the ranks of the ruling elite.

Also through technology, groupings have been enlarged far beyond the size that any one individual could know — from a simple tribal community of a few hundred or a thousand members to a state with millions of subjects. Based on preliminary surveys, and with the help of students and others, I have been able to establish tentatively that one person may have friendly exchanges with, and remember, no more than a few thousand other persons. It is thus obviously impossible for dominant persons (leaders) to be acquainted with more than a small percentage of those subordinated. And because among strangers indifference is customary and hostility latent, it would be inevitable that a dominant person would be indifferent or potentially hostile toward the masses of strangers over whom he rules, particularly if former enemies.

Finally, during the past several decades, particularly in advanced industrial societies (Stage 5) community attachments have progressively weakened. In abandoning the family farm and moving to the city, rural people left behind a small, friendly, well-defined community for a looser and larger collection of relative strangers and nodding acquaintances with whom they were less mutually involved and among whom there was usually less willingness to help. And for the many families who change their residence, usually when changing jobs, community attachments are weakened even more.

Not only community ties, but also family ties have weakened. Thus with the moving of nuclear families, generations are often separated. Grandparents may live far away, and children in their late teens may leave home for college or a job. For families living in the suburbs of a metropolitan area, working parents may spend two or three hours a day commuting, thus lessening the time husbands and wives and parents and children devote to one another and reducing the amount of learning that passes from one generation to the next.

Accompanying the weakening of both family and community ties, there has been a tendency for persons to become increasingly segregated by age.[1]

Contemporaneously, indifference and hostility are increasingly manifest by the involvement of youth in crime (including murders and assassinations), in riots, and withdrawal. Within families, it is widely believed, grandparents, parents, and children are more hostile toward one another, and it is further widely sensed that people are less willing to help one another, even sometimes ignoring those in distress. A further proposition is that lack of intimacy and companionship, particularly during infancy and childhood, the lack of sufficient fondling, touching, and parental devotion automatically and unconsciously predisposes persons biologically and behaviorally to be indifferent and hostile toward others.

THE NATURAL MEANS OF MAINTAINING SOCIAL AND ENVIRONMENTAL ORDER

For the billion or more years that life has been on this planet, one

[1] For example, in colleges, youth, having left their families, become segregated in apartments or herded into dormitories and often have little personal contact with either the faculty or families in the community. Upon marriage they often move into an apartment complex with other young married couples. With the birth of a child or upon getting a job or a promotion, they often move again, even when remaining in the same area. And periodically thereafter, with every change of residence, they usually seek out others of their own age and economic status. Throughout their adult lives, the members of different age groups fall into easily recognizable cultural groupings, identified by distinctive coiffures, slang, dress, dance styles, values, and other kinds of symbolic identification.

evolutionary trend has been the development of more complex and effective organisms developing the capability to adapt to a greater variety of environments. For every given species, the underlying behavioral-biological process, widely accepted as having made this possible, has been the competitive struggle among individuals. The individuals influencing most this biological and behavioral development of their species are those who succeed in reproducing the greatest number of surviving descendants. This competitive striving between and among all interacting individuals provides, therefore, the behavioral process underlying biological evolution and progress.

Nature's Competitive Strategy Leading to Biological Evolution and Natural Order

This competitive striving may be conceived as a dual process. On the one hand, there is the reproduction of dynamic organisms spontaneously activated and predisposed to behave in ways that over generations provide the individuals of their species with successively greater competitive advantages. On the other hand, these organisms interact with and compete against other organisms, all thus reciprocally regulating and restraining each other.

All animals are universally activated both to seek greater personal advantage (such as the best food) and, when appropriately stimulated, to mate. Among mammals, in addition, infants are internally activated to suckle and to be attracted to warmth, while for species whose members assemble and segregate into "family" groupings, young and old alike all seem to possess an inner urge or a strong predisposition to touch and be touched. If breeding pairs reproduced over time an ever-enlarging succession of surviving descendants, there would have had to evolve means for regulating and limiting their numbers to prevent the otherwise inevitable overpopulation, mass starvation, exhaustion of all food supplies, and the eventual destruction of habitable environments. Similarly, to prevent myriads of competing organisms from destroying each other, additional means would also have had to evolve to limit hostile contending and thus inhibit combatants, and particularly males of the same species, from disabling and killing each other.

Although competition between members of different species often may be severe, it is usually far less than among members of the same species because the latter compete for precisely the same food, the same resting and hiding places, and all kinds of environmental and specific conditions advantageous to them. Among competing members of the same species, therefore, and with particular reference to mammals, common means have evolved by which these members regulate each other and create a social-behavioral order briefly described and summarized below. In addition, for species segregated into "family" groupings, companions mutually stimulate one another to come to each other's aid and to cooperate in joint enterprises. These competitive and cooperative interchanges may be considered as bringing about three different kinds of social and behavioral order. One is SPATIAL ORDERING, or the geographical distribution of populations. Another is TEMPORAL ORDERING, or regulating the sequence and timing of actions. The third is the GRADIENT OF HOSTILITY AND COOPERATION.

As a result of spatial ordering, populations are geographically distributed throughout an area into LOCAL and semi-independent units. And with the emergence of "family" organization, each local group remained more or less segregated. The multigenerational members, moreover, became a closely interdependent group of companions, each individual usually interacting frequently and cooperating closely with every other.

Temporal ordering is not as immediately obvious. Although all behavior occurs in a sequence, the succession of happenings in the routine living of a group seem often too commonplace to warrant more than passing concern. But there are also a number of occasions when action and interaction sequences are obviously of major importance. Such occasions are commonplace during a crisis, as, for example, when there is insufficient food for all members of a group. During such a situation, members commonly work out their priorities by determining who has precedence over whom, thus establishing that particular individuals follow one another in a given order. Such recurring successions of individuals provide examples of what is meant by temporal ordering or regularities that occur in a sequence. These uniformities in a succession of individuals provide means of determining hierarchies or a ranking by precedence. Thus, for example, during periods of shortage, the stronger regularly eat first and the weakest last. Such priorities provide safeguards for populations under stress. Establishing precedence thus avoids the danger of violence from disorderly scrambles for too little food and the risk of eliminating through starvation an entire population by all sharing equally.

Clearly establishing precedence not only benefits a population faced with an immediate crisis, but sometimes also relieves, as during the beginnings of overpopulation, the future threat of greater and greater overpopulation over a succession of generations. Thus, as practiced by many species of mammals and birds, the stronger and more dominant members, by means not fully comprehended, often inhibit or prevent the weaker and deferring members from breeding. When members of a local population begin to crowd and individuals take to contacting and harassing one another more than usual, such hyperactivity often triggers in members physiological changes (such as overstimulating the adrenal glands), which in turn often result, for example, in a lowered birthrate, a higher number of infant deaths, and sometimes mass dying. Through such means, that have only begun to be appreciated during the past decade or two, it appears that the members of many species in varying degrees themselves maintain control over their future populations. By appropriately timing such interventions, the strong succeed in limiting the numbers of their group to a level commensurate with, if not below, the usual carrying capacity of their localities. This interactional-physiological process, therefore, provides a species with means not only for establishing its own social-behavioral order, but also for preserving the ecological order or the environment, food supply, and all other resources, without which it could not exist.

For additional stressful situations and crises there are many other temporal adjustments or action sequences that lighten the stress and lessen hostile competing. Thus, a dominant animal customarily intervenes in squabbles among subordinate members, and two animals usually cease fighting when one flees, lies helpless, or otherwise defers. Another is the practice of some individuals leaving one group and joining another, providing those discontented in one with the possibility of trying out others. Finally another adjustment or preventive practice has developed among different simian species whose groupings often include two or more adult males. Among these potential rivals, fighting over mates is apparently prevented within a troop by the sexually receptive females accepting all their adult male companions and the latter patiently waiting their turn.

More basic than these common adjustments in regulating competitive striving is the aforementioned universal and inherent condition of approximate equality in fighting ability and size for all adult members of the same species and sex. This equality results in a "balance of power," a parity that prevents one individual from easily beating a rival. Additionally, the wounds and pains sustained by such well-matched combatants must serve not only to shorten an actual fight but presumably also as a strong deterrent discouraging rivals from taking on fights in the first place. Even though a next lower-ranking member might win in a showdown, the traditionally more dominant one may for a while maintain its position. But apparently once the deferring member achieves an obvious superiority, a reversal in ranking becomes imminent. But, as in nearly all confrontations, these periodic and essential readjustments that regulate struggles for precedence usually take place in a matter of moments and without prolonged and violent fighting.

The third and final behavioral regularity is what was referred to above as the gradient of hostility and cooperation. This refers to a practice widespread, if not universal, among mammals and possibly birds, important in regulating degrees of repulsion, attraction, and cooperation, among and between individuals. Generally speaking, my proposition is that for all species and individuals there is an optimum degree of pair and group interaction. Considering pairs only, those that attain this optimum — neither too much nor too little — develop the strongest inclinations to go to each other's assistance and are the least likely to fight. Contrariwise, toward complete strangers there is the strongest tendency to be indifferent or hostile, as there is similarly by individuals that excessively harass one another. (In this latter instance, however, such relationships are usually of short duration with at least one avoiding the other and often moving away.) Finally, intermediate degrees of pair interaction result in intermediate degrees of hostile and companionable interchange.

Although the frequency and duration of contacts predetermines in general the degree of hostile to friendly exchange, the subtleties of voice volume and tone, rhythm, and touch, introduce far more interactional complexity than the simple counting and timing of contacts. And, finally, for a given individual, his well-established gradient of hostile and friendly exchange may rapidly alter, particularly among humans, as, for example, at death, illness, or the introduction of new individuals, whereby is created the potential for new alliances and rivalries.

Destroying the Natural Process of Individuals Stimulating and Restraining Each Other

The competitive striving among organisms has necessarily evolved to create an orderly interdependence. On the one hand, different species are interdependent. All animals gain nourishment feeding either on plants or other species of animal, the prey species often benefiting by the former controlling their numbers. Such interdependencies have over time evolved to create an enduring ecological-environmental order mutually supportive to large numbers of plant and animal organisms.

On the other hand, within a species members are also interdependent not only for reproducing new generations but also to limit each others' strivings and thereby create a behavioral-and-social order characteristic for them. This social-behavioral order, so it appears, evolved to provide every species with its own means of preserving the environmental and ecological order to which it belongs.

Although environmental-social-and-behavioral order appears to have been the usual condition, with occasional catastrophic and destructive interludes, there are still notable exceptions of regularly recurring over-population, mass starvation, and wholesale dying, particularly for species in desert and arctic regions. But for the past many thousands of years, human beings have perhaps been the least self-restrained species by progressively destroying or circumventing this natural order.

My general proposition is that the unique and superior attributes with which human beings are endowed, inherently provided them also with means inimical to themselves and destructive to their environments. This anomalous circumstance is inherent in the very nature of man in that dominant groupings are automatically and inevitably impelled not merely to maintain their advantage but often to keep on striving for greater advantage. Once having become dominant over all other rival animals, and possibly even before, dominant human groupings were inevitably impelled to continue favoring themselves, and as they became more dominant, they naturally took advantage of greater numbers of deferring persons and otherwise permitted practices destructive to their societies, their species, and environments. This process did not however gain momentum until the emergence of multiple chiefdoms and states many thousands of years ago.

By developing three major new advantages — superior language, intelligence, and technology — human beings gained enormous advantages, but in that very process, they simultaneously weakened the natural mechanisms for regulating themselves as a species, their relation to other species, and the environments they shared with the latter. Every major advance has, to a greater or lesser degree, disrupted that mechanism for preserving the natural order and upon which survival depends. Thus, in contrast to animals, natural rivalries are escalated into war, intelligence is used for evil ends, and dominant individuals oppress many. Even language itself, a glory and a necessity for human living, still creates tensions and antagonisms that no animal knows and which human beings, with all their intelligence, often fail to relieve.

In addition to these three principal innovations of language, intelligence, and technology, there is a fourth that has been made possible by the other three, namely the PROGRESSIVE ENLARGING OF HUMAN SOCIETIES. This fourth, similarly, has been both advantageous and disadvantageous, but the process by which it has disrupted the social-environmental order has been through a more complex and indirect chain of causation. Thus technological innovations, such as weapons and intoxicating liquors, can be identified easily as obvious and immediate causes of social disorder, as can also such consequences of human language as deceit and the indoctrination of hate. But the disruptive consequences of progressively enlarging human societies, although familiar in general, are often less specifically and immediately obvious.

The Destructive Process of Progressively Enlarging Human Societies

In the process of gaining greater advantage by enlarging human societies and incorporating necessary adaptations, the advantages also introduced disadvantages that disrupted the natural order. Six of these disruptions will be discussed briefly. Two began causing difficulties in Stage 3 (early man), three others in Stage 4 (early chiefdoms and states), and one in Stage 5 (continental and global societies).

The transformation into Stage 3 — from simian to human societies — involved two organizational innovations rare among or unknown to animals, one enlarging from single to multiple groups, the other having representatives from groups jointly organize common enterprises. By two or more families developing means of cooperating, early man gained a major advantage over all other rival species, but this introduced a wholly new category of relationship, namely acquaintances, intermediate between companions and outsiders, and among whom relationships tended automatically to become intermediate or neutral. But depending on particular circumstances such as festive or competitive occasions, personality differences, and experiences from previous encounters, a relationship, customarily neutral, might veer to either a hostile or a friendly extreme. And with representatives planning and arranging for others, they in time inevitably found themselves in the ambivalent position of providing their constituents with greater advantages or furthering their own self interests. As human societies became enlarged and the number of constituents increased, the latter often competed more actively to influence representatives, increasing thereby temptations that many could not easily resist.

The enlarging from small family-community societies into regional chiefdoms and states was accompanied by three universal developments— group ranking (e.g. social classes), the exchanging of things and services (e.g. trade, employment, taxation), and the emergence of cities together with absentee control of localities. Material and service exchange provided a means for having increasing numbers of strangers and previous "enemies" become interdependent and hence predisposed to cooperate. Among other functions, group ranking by social classes provided these strangers and "enemies" with a simple and immediate means for establishing the relative ranking of each and hence an automatic basis for determining privileges and precedence. Although essential to the process of enlargement, all three have also undermined the social-behavioral order and sometimes the environmental and ecological order as well.

In contrast to a dominance ranking by individuals, which regularly readjusts in response to the maturing, aging, and health of its members, ranking by groups is much more persistent as the dominant group members cooperate closely to maintain or improve their position, while unitedly resisting, if not retaliating with violence against, comparable strivings by subordinates. As part of the process of perpetuating their power, the members of a dominant grouping, such as a ruling elite, often also enforce regulations and customs considered favorable to them. Thus they limit freedoms to entire classes of persons, such as forcing all serfs to continue always in the employ of their masters. Rigidly repressing all open striving by subordinates and thereby preventing a nonviolent process of confrontation, adjustment, and change, inevitably provokes subversive resistance and the risk of eventual violence.

By extending and proliferating the exchange of things and services — whether, for example, through trade, taxation, or employment — vastly greater numbers of individuals became interdependent than ever possible in the small hunting and gathering communities universal for all human beings until around 10,000 years ago. Whereas early man, or some predecessor, first gained great advantage over rival species by a number of family groups cooperating to form a community, so, by exchanging things and services, numerous communities engaged in and extended a new kind of interdependence, enlarging eventually into chiefdoms and states. This interchange gave them enormous competitive advantages over a single independent and segregated community having no cooperative relationship with any other. Notwithstanding this enormous competitive advantage of a chiefdom and state, it is impossible, in any given stage of technology, to coordinate multitudes of individuals as easily as a few, or have unfamiliar persons cooperate as well as companions might.

These two extremes of maximum and minimum cooperation each result from two different kinds of interdependence. Whereas strangers and aliens may in one sense cooperate by exchanging things and services, companions and familiar persons in addition regularly interact, providing thereby the physiological and behavioral means that reciprocally and automatically stimulate them to cooperate for mutual advantage. Whereas the former minimal cooperation is dependent on a largely impersonal interdependence exchanging things and services, the latter maximum cooperation derives in addition from an interactional and personal interdependence. Thus, the expansion from small to large units, although providing great competitive advantages, created a situation impossible for close, uniform cooperation and a situation with the potential for much greater internal dissension.

The extensive networks of trade, and the ruling and taxation of large populations necessitated establishing centers, or capitals, from which rulers, lords, merchants, and sundry important persons could direct their enterprises. This resulted for the first time in continuous concentrations of large human populations crowding in confined urban areas, creating such new problems as disease and the disposal of sewage and garbage. Due primarily to the importation of foreign diseases to which local populations were not immune, epidemics periodically decimated large numbers, particularly following the expansion of long-distance trade.

And from early times, these large concentrations of population required continual importation of basic necessities such as food, water, and wood, unavailable in the immediate locality, particularly in drier, unforested regions where the earlier states were concentrated. In these drier areas, to grow sufficient food for the early enlarging cities, elaborate irrigation systems sometimes including aqueducts had to be built and maintained, with all the highly complex associated problems of engineering, construction, and maintenance.

In these busy burgeoning capitals and centers, the demands for wood were enormous, not only for the building of palaces, villas, ships, town houses, furniture, tools, and the like, but great quantities were required for burning in brick and lime kilns, in forges and furnaces for metal working, and in households for heating and cooking. As a result therefore in the Middle East and China, vast areas have long been denuded of their forests in localities far removed from where the absentee organizers and consumers lived, causing the erosion of soils and the excessive silting of harbors and streams. Such partial destruction of resources inevitably reduces the carrying capacity of these areas to support human, plant, and animal populations. And with particular reference to the desert plains of southern Mesopotamia, the ancient Sumerians, who were probably the first to organize a lively regional trade from a single center, hastened their eventual decline by their initial success in transforming their desert into a garden. Through continual overirrigation and underdrainage, they progressively raised salts to the surface, gradually rendering these areas infertile. Thousands of years later, following World War I, Western irrigation engineers repeated this failure with their initial and extensive canal system planned as a demonstration of how to rehabilitate this former Garden of Eden.

By overconcentrating populations and developing technical proficiency to funnel the necessities for living into these confined urban areas, human beings have disrupted the ecological-environmental order both in the cities and in the surrounding and distant localities. Progressively over the centuries, and particularly in recent decades, ecological and environmental disorder has accelerated alarmingly as human populations expand, cities enlarge, and powerful urban and absentee elites seize control of localities away from the local residents.

And finally for the past century or two, with the proliferation of institutions and the expansion of their activities to a continental and global scale, these institutions have been increasingly drawing recruits away from rural areas and educating, employing, and concentrating them in cities. This sixth and final adaptation furthers the competitive ability of institutions, but, to reiterate briefly, it breaks up families and communities, reducing the intimacy that binds generations and creating the new danger of a lessened interactional interdependence. This in turn leads to a critical interactional deficiency, denying persons (the young and old in particular) the physiological stimulation sufficient for developing and maintaining human health and well-being.

To conclude, as many are aware, this progressive enlarging of human societies has provided immediate advantages that, unless checked, are ultimately disastrous. Considering that over the past many thousands of years, the increase in organizational size has been one millionfold — from hundreds to hundreds of millions — while the enlargment of localities (controlled by hunting and gathering populations) to those ruled by continental nations, although less, has also been considerable. And with the accelerating rate of technical innovation, expanding interdependence, and the like, the human species is set on a self-annihilating course unless soon and drastically redirected.

It is rarely approved as becoming for educated persons to consider the limitations of their reasoning. Few give much thought to the fact that, despite human intellectual progress, their minds are still part of their biological organisms, with all the essential emotional predispositions biologically programmed into their make-up as in all other mammals. Rather than realistically recognizing these emotional limitations, humans when displeased by reality, become highly adept at illusory reasoning through the emotional process of biased and limited thinking. Many, for example, are prone to consider self-seeking as serving, and conversational partners, who approvingly listen, as not only pleasing but intelligent while often viewing less responsive and questioning persons as undesirable and mentally confused.

And to these and many other inborn emotional biases over which humans rarely have full rational control, all persons are also intellectually limited in comprehending complexity. Already, interregional trade has attained too vast an interdependent monetary and material network of global exchange for human beings fully to comprehend. And the changing human needs of these hundreds of millions of materially interdependent global populations, with their shifting rivalries, alliances, and ruling cliques, are not only difficult to keep track of but impossible to foresee and fully control. And, as if this global, material and monetary interdependence were not already too complex for humans to regulate, nearly every technological innovation introduces some new conflict, stress, and disorder. Should the rates of inventions and their use continue to accelerate without compensating adjustments, an accelerating disorder will certainly accelerate the demise of our runaway civilization.

It seems distressingly possible that, not until such a demise, will we launch a determined struggle to decelerate, reverse direction, and recreate a new behavioral-environmental order. However, to design a new and enduring system requires radical changes in degrees of sovereignty, autonomy, centralization-decentralization, and in the size and interdependence of units and sub-units. But whatever the scheme, it can never endure unless it reestablishes a natural, automatic process of individuals mutually stimulating and regulating each other, yet one that human beings are inherently endowed, biologically and behaviorally, to operate and develop.

REFERENCES

ANONYMOUS
   1960   Some clinical changes in behavior accompanying endocrine disorder. *Journal of Nervous Mental Disorders* 130:97–106.
CHAPPLE, E. D.
   1970   *Culture and biological man – explorations in behavioral anthropology.* New York: Holt, Rinehart, and Winston.
COBB, STANLEY
   1958   *Foundations of neuro-psychiatry* (sixth edition). Williams and Wilkins.

KOESTLER, ARTHUR
  1967   *The act of creation.* New York: Macmillan.
MASTERS, W. H., E. JOHNSON
  1965   "The sexual response cycles of the human male and female," in
         Sex and behavior. Edited by F. A. Beach, 512–534. New York: Wiley.
RICHARDSON, F. L. W., *et al.*
  f.c.   "Allegiance and hostility – man's mammalian heritage."
SCHALLER, GEORGE B.
  1973   *The Serengeti lion – a study of predator-prey relations.* Chicago:
         University of Chicago Press.
VAN LAWICK-GOODALL, HUGO
  1971   *Innocent killers.* Boston: Houghton Mifflin.

Biographical Notes

J. Lawrence Angel (1915–) was born in London. He studied classics and physical anthropology at Harvard (A.B. 1936, Ph.D. 1942) with field work in Greece (American School of Classical Studies) and Turkey from 1937 onward. He taught anthropology at the University of California, Berkeley, and at the University of Minnesota and anatomy at the Jefferson Medical College in Philadelphia (1943–1962) before joining the Smithsonian Institution as Curator of Physical Anthropology in culture growth, with side interests in structure-function relations and in forensic applied anthropology.

John W. Bennett (1915–) is Professor of Anthropology at Washington University, St. Louis, and is a member of the Center for the Biology of Natural Systems and the Asian Studies Center of that institution. He received his doctorate in anthropology from the University of Chicago in 1946, and has taught at Ohio State University, the University of Oregon, Waseda University, Japan, and the University of Puerto Rico. He was head of the social research office in the Japan Occupation. He has done research in economic development and social change in Canada, the United States, Japan, Taiwan, India, and Thailand. He has specialized recently in the cultural and economic ecology of modern agrarian peoples. His recent books are *Hutterian brethren* (1967) and *The ecological transition* (1975).

Bennet Bronson (1938–) is Assistant Curator of Asian Archaelogy and Ethnology at the Field Museum of Natural History, Chicago. He studied medieval history at Harvard (B.A. 1960) and anthropology and archaeology at the University of Pennsylvania (Ph.D. 1974). As a research associate of the University Museum of the latter institution he has directed excavations in Thailand, Ceylon, and Indonesia. His special interests include agriculture, ethnobotany, quantitative geography, economic archaeology, and the prehistory and protohistory of Southeast Asia.

MARK N. COHEN (1943–) was born in Philadelphia. He received his B.A. in anthropology from Harvard College in 1965. He undertook graduate study at Columbia University from 1965 to 1971, receiving his Ph.D. in 1971. His special fields of study include human ecology, paleoecology, and the prehistory of Africa and South America. His main research interest has been the development of agricultural economies and most of his field work has centered on the Pacific Coast of South America. He is currently Associate Professor of Anthropology at the State University of New York College at Plattsburgh.

JAMES C. FARIS (1936–) was born in Colorado. He received his B.S. from the University of New Mexico (1958) and his Ph.D. from the University of Cambridge (1965), and has taught at McGill University, the University of Khartoum, and the University of Connecticut, where he is now Associate Professor of Anthropology. He has carried out field research in north Atlantic maritime communities and in the Democratic Republic of Sudan. His publications include the books, *Cat harbour* (1972), *Nuba personal art* (1972), and works on cognition and materialist perspectives in anthropological theory.

MICHAEL J. HARNER (1929–) was born in Washington, D.C. He received his B.A. (1953) and his Ph.D. in anthropology (1963) from the University of California, Berkeley. He has taught at various universities including Columbia, Yale, the University of California, Berkeley, and has served as Assistant Director of the Robert H. Lowie Museum of Anthropology at Berkeley. Since 1970 he has been on the graduate faculty of the New School for Social Research in New York City, where he is at present Professor of Anthropology and Chairman. His anthropological field research has taken place primarily in the Ecuadorian and Peruvian Amazon.

FEKRI A. HASSAN (1943–) is Assistant Professor of Anthropology at Wayne State University, Detroit. Born in Cairo and a resident of the United States since 1968, he holds a B.Sc (1963) and an M.Sc. (1966) in geology from Ain Shams University (Cairo) and an M.A. (1971) and a Ph.D. (1973) in anthropology from Southern Methodist University, Dallas. He participated in archaeological fieldwork in Egypt, Lebanon, Ethiopia, and Algeria, as well as in the United States. His special interests are in the fields of North African and Near Eastern palaeoanthropology, prehistoric demography, geoarchaeology, and the analysis of lithic artifacts with the ultimate aim of providing processual models of culture change in prehistory, especially that of the transition from hunting-gathering to agriculture. Recent publications: *Population growth and cultural evolution* (1974), *Mechanisms of population growth during the Neolithic* (1973).

R. F. ITS (U.S.S.R.). No biographical data available.

G. K. NUKUNYA (1935–) is Senior Research Fellow in Sociology, University of Ghana, Legon. He was born at Woe, in the Volta Region of Ghana. He studied sociology at the then University College of Ghana (1958–1961) and later at the London School of Economics where he obtained his Ph.D. in anthropology with a thesis on kinship and marriage among the Anlo Ewe, his own people. During the last few years his interest has shifted gradually from his original field of kinship studies to economic anthropology, population studies and applied anthropology. His numerous publications include *Kinship and marriage among the Anlo Ewe* (1969) and *Land tenure and inheritance in Anloga* (1973). Among his appointments outside Ghana were Visiting Assistant Professorship at Michigan State University, East Lansing (1967–1968) and Senior Visiting Overseas Scholarship, St John's College, Cambridge, England (1971–1972).

STEVEN POLGAR (1931–) is Professor of Anthropology at the University of North Carolina, Chapel Hill. Born in Budapest, he studied anthropology at the University of Chicago and public health at Harvard. His research includes work in action anthropology with the Mesquakie Indians in Iowa, community development in West Africa, schizophrenics at Walter Reed Army Institute of Research, pregnancy and family planning in poverty areas of California and New York City, and library studies on evolution and ecology. He has been a consultant with the World Health Organization and is currently Visiting Professor at the University of Exeter in England.

KLAVS RANDSBORG (1944–   ) studied prehistoric archaeology at the University of Copenhagen (Mag.Art. 1968), received a university scholarship, and became lecturer at the Institute of Prehistoric Archaeology in 1971. He received his Dr.Phil. in 1972 at the University of Copenhagen and became a senior lecturer. His major interest is in the North European Neolithic and Bronze Ages. He has first and foremost studied problems of culture process, exchange, and social structures.

F. L. W. RICHARDSON (1909–   ) is a Professor at the University of Virginia. He received a dual Ph.D degree in anthropology and geography (Harvard 1941) and was a founder of the Society for Applied Anthropology (1942). For over three decades he has focused primarily on non-verbal exchanges among interacting humans, and for almost two decades he has also concentrated on interactional exchanges among animals — in particular members within and between "family" groupings of mammals. His writings relating humans to animals consist of two popular articles: "Rivalry, revenge, and executive productivity" (1963), and "Managing man's animal nature" (1964). A book *Allegiance and hostility — man's mammalian heritage*, of which he is the editor and principal contributor, is forthcoming.

MATTI ELJAS SARMELA (1937–   ) is Professor of General Ethnology (Cultural Anthropology) and Docent in Social Anthropology at the University of Helsinki and in Cultural Anthropology at the University of Turku. One of initiators in use of statistical methods in ethnology and folkloristics, and of quantitative content analysis of ethnological archive material in Finland, especially interested in cross-cultural studies; fieldwork in Thailand 1972–1973. Books include: *Reciprocity systems of the rural society in the Finnish-Karelian culture area* (1969), *Perinneaineiston kvantitatiivisesta tutkimuksesta* [Quantitative content analysis of ethnological archive material] (1970), *Johdatus yleiseen kulttuuriantropologiaan* [Introduction to comparative anthropology. Man and societies in the light of cross-cultural research] (1972). He has published numerous articles on folkloristics, ethnology, and cultural anthropology and is the editor of *Atlas of Finnish folk culture II*.

Index of Names

Ackerknecht, Erwin H., 175, 176, 179
Acsádi, Gyorgy, 1, 176
Adams, Robert McC., 8, 9, 10, 65, 80
Agokoli, King of Togo, 191
Allan, W., 64, 73
Alland, Alexander, 240, 276, 283
Allee, W. C., 283
Allison, A. C., 179
Amenumey, D. E. K., 203
Amundsen, Darrel W., 177
Anderson, Edgar, 83
Anderson, Nels, 219
Angel, J. Lawrence, 4, 5, 9, 12, 42, 43, 44, 45, 46, 167–190
Antler, E., 238
Ardrey, Robert, 244

Balikci, A., 251
Barrett, J. C., 43
Barry, Herbert, III, 223–224
Barth, Frederik, 273–274
Bartholomew, G. A., 32
Bateson, Gregory, 276; "Bali: The Value System of a Steady State," 277
Baumhoff, M. A., 29, 30, 39
Beardsley, Richard K., 297
Beattie, J. H. M., 201
Bender, Donald R., 11
Benneh, G., 197, 205
Bennett, John W., 4, 14, 15–16, 19, 21, 273–303
Binford, Lewis R., 4–5, 28
Birdsell, Joseph B., 2, 3, 29, 30, 32, 37, 38, 41, 43–44, 81, 86, 87, 250
Blackburn, T., 167

Boas, Franz, 241
Bohannon, Paul, 241
Bonavia, Duccio, 114, 117
Boserup, Ester, 4, 9, 14, 15, 21, 28, 53–54, 62, 81–82, 134, 135–136, 149, 160, 215, 247, 251
Bostanci, E., 167
Bourlière, François, 33, 34
Boyce, A. J., 1
Boye, W., 141
Brace, C., 248
Braidwood, R. J., 90
Brockington, Donald L., 5
Broholm, H. C., 146, 149
Brøndsted, J., 142, 146, 149–150
Broneer, Oscar, 174
Bronson, Bennet, 3, 5, 6, 9, 15, 17, 53–78
Brose, D., 248
Brothwell, Don, 45
Bruce-Chwatt, L. J., 172, 179
Buckley, Walter, 277
Buechner, Helmut K., 276
Burrow, J., 243
Butzer, Karl W., 168, 170, 171, 172, 173

Caffey, John, 179
Callan, Hilary, 283
Campbell, Donald T., 276
Carneiro, Robert L., 9, 11–12, 14, 21, 27, 44, 124, 215, 222, 247
Carpenter, C., 283
Carr-Saunders, A. M., 42
Caskey, John L., 167, 169
Casteel, Richard W., 30, 32
Chang, Kwang-Chih, 7, 8

Chapdelaine, K., 235
Chapple, E. D., 317
Chayanov, A. V., 71
Cheboksarov, N. N., 230
Cheboksarova, I. N., 230
Childe, V. Gordon, 4, 9, 11, 79, 237; *What Happened in History*, 9
Chisolm, N., 71
Chomsky, N., 244, 248
Clark, Colin, 36, 64
Clark, J. G. D., 174
Clement, A. J., 178
Coale, Ansley, 13
Cobb, Stanley, 319
Cochran, Roger, 17
Cockburn, T. Aidan, 45, 171, 181
Cohen, Mark N., 3, 4, 6–7, 9, 14, 21, 54, 79–121
Cohen, Yehudi A., 8
Commoner, Barry, 294
Coon, C., 244
Crelin, E., 244, 248, 249
Cutler, H. C., 103, 108, 117

Dalton, G., 241
Daly, Patricia, 173
Darwin, Charles R., 137, 237, 241, 243, 245
Davidson, B., 255, 258
Deevey, Edward S., Jr., 3, 27, 42, 43
Demeny, Paul, 13
Denton, Goerge H., 171, 175, 183
Descartes, René, 248
Devereux, G., 87
DeVore, Irven, 32, 38, 86–87, 246, 250, 251
Dewey, John F., 170
Diers, Carol J., 177
Dietz, S., 167
Dixon, R. B., 275
Dornstreich, Mark D., 31
Douglas, M., 251
Driscoll, J., 235
Dubos, René, 36
Dumond, Don E., 16, 17, 27, 46, 81, 280
Durand, J., 250

Ehrlich, Anne H., 36, 294
Ehrlich, Paul R., 36, 294
Ember, Melvin, 222
Engel, F., 109, 117
Engels, Friedrich, 137, 237, 242, 243, 249, 297; *Dialectics of Nature*, 237; *Origin of the Family, Private Property, and the State, The*, 128–129; "Role Played by Labor in the Transition from Ape to Man, The," 237
Erlich, P., 259, 264
Evans-Pritchard, E. E., 203
Eysenck, H., 244

Fagen, R. E., 276
Faris, James C., 2–3, 8, 13, 15, 16, 20, 21, 235–271
Faris, Jennifer, 235
Farvar, M. Taghi, 288, 293
Ferembach, D., 167
Ferreyra, Ramón, 94
Firth, R., 241
Flannery, Kent V., 3–4, 5, 7, 8, 31, 80–81, 82, 85, 173
Flemming, Nicholas C., 170
Fortes, M., 203
Found, W. C., 61
Fox, R., 243, 244
Frederiksen, Harald, 294, 299
Freeman, Linton D., 222
Freeman, M., 251–252, 255
French, D. H., 167
French, L. W., 167
Fried, M., 254

Gardiner, B., 244
Gardiner, R., 244
Gearing, Fred O., 8
Geertz, Clifford, 279–280, 294
Gejvall, Nils-Gustaf, 174, 180
Gilbert, B. Miles, 176
Gingerich, R., 235
Gomme, A. W., 177, 182
Goodrich, L. Carrington, 168
Goodspeed, T. H., 95
Goody, J., 257
Gorman, C. F., 60
Gough, M., 167
Green, R., 264
Greulich, William W., 178
Grove, J. M., 206–207, 209–210, 214
Gurçay, H., 167

Haldane, J., 237
Hall, A. D., 276
Hall, R., 260
Hallpike, C., 238
Hardin, G., 243, 259, 264
Harlan, Jack R., 82, 173
Harner, Michael J., 7, 9, 10–11, 14–15, 21, 27, 81, 104, 123–138, 222, 247

Harper, R., 167
Harper, Y., 167
Harris, Marvin, 12, 21, 34–35, 48, 237, 253, 286
Harrison, G. A., 1, 29
Hassan, Fekri A., 2–3, 5, 15, 17, 27–52
Haswell, M., 36, 64
Hawley, Amos, 283
Hegel, Georg W., 12
Heichelheim, F. M., 150
Heiser, Charles B., Jr., 60
Helbaek, Hans, 173
Herrnstein, R., 244
Hillery, George A., Jr., 294
Hilse, D. F., 44
Holland, K., 167
Holling, Crawford S., 289, 290
Homans, G. C., 55
Homer, 181
Hopf, Maria, 174
Howells, William W., 41, 177
Huxley, Aldous: *Brave New World*, 20
Huxley, J., 259

Isaac, Erich, 83
Its, R. F., 9, 227–234

Jacobs, Jane, 173
Jacobsen, Thomas W., 167, 169, 172, 173
Jardé, Auguste, 170, 172
Jenner, Edward, 68
Jensen, J., 244
Johansen, A. M., 214
John, King of England, 323
Johnson, D., 167
Johnson, E., 319
Jolly, A. J., 83
Jones, W. H. S., 179, 183
Justinian I, 175

Kabo, V. R., 228
Kalmus, H., 276
Kaplan, Lawrence, 114, 117
Kelley, David, 114, 117
Keyes, Paul H., 179
Keyfitz, Nathan, 42
Koestler, Arthur, 319
Kortmulder, K., 244
Kottak, Conrad F., 285
Kroeber, Alfred L., 29, 283; *Cultural and Natural Areas of Native North America*, 275
Kroeber, Theodora, 230

Krogman, Wilton M., 176
Krzywicki, L., 38, 42
Kummer, H., 244
Kunstadter, Peter, 295
Kuper, H., 152

Lamarck, Jean Baptiste, 239, 241, 252
Langer, William L., 13
Lanning, Edward P., 84, 91, 95, 96–97, 100–101, 102, 103, 105, 115
Lea, J. S., 167
Leach, E. R., 297
Leacock, E., 237, 255
Leacock, S., 235
Lee, Richard B., 32, 34, 35, 36, 37, 38, 39, 48, 62, 84–85, 86–87, 246, 250, 251, 274
LeVine, Robert, 222
Lieberman, P., 244, 248, 249
Liebowitz, L., 241
Linton, Ralph: *Study of Man, The*, 275
Linton, S., 237
Livingstone, Frank B., 279
Lomborg, E., 144
Luckacs, G., 236

McAdams, Robert, 297
McArthur, M., 36, 48
McCarthy, F., 36, 48
McClellan, Donna L., 274
McCredie, J. R., 167
McDonald, William A., 177, 181, 182
MacDonnell, W. R., 183
McKenzie, R. D., 274, 283
McKern, Thomas W., 176
MacNeish, Richard S., 5, 60, 74, 80, 84, 102, 114, 115, 117
Magubane, B., 235, 261
Maine, Henry, Sir, 8
Mair, Lucy, 8
Malthus, Thomas R., 14, 20–21, 46, 53, 70, 90, 113, 118, 167, 259–260, 264
Mamdani, M., 260, 261, 266
Manglesdorf, P. C., 60
Mao Tse-tung, 239
Marichild, A., 235
Marshall, John F., 1
Marshall, L., 247
Maruyama, Magoroh, 16–17, 19
Marx, Karl, 12, 15, 21, 124, 129, 237, 240, 242–243, 253, 255, 261, 297; *Pre-Capitalist Economic Formations*, 137
Mason, O. T., 275
Masters, W. H., 319

Matthews, M., 167
Maull, Otto, 170, 171, 172
May, Jacques M., 274
Meadows, D., 260
Meek, R., 264
Mellaart, James, 169, 180
Mellink, Machteld, J., 167, 169
Michalopoulos, J. G., 184
Michell, H., 172, 174
Millon, René, 297
Milton, John P., 288, 293
Mintzes, J., 167
Moberg, C.-A., 149
Mongait, A. L., 32
Montelius, Oskar, 140
Montgomery, Edward, 274
Morgan, Lewis Henry, 79, 237, 242
Morgan, W. B., 55
Moseley, John E., 179
Moseley, M. E., 91, 96–97, 106, 108, 109, 110
Moulder, James W., 179
Müller, S., 142, 149, 155
Murdock, George P., 133–134, 222, 257; *Ethnographic Atlas*, 11
Mylonas, George E., 169

Nag, Moni, 1, 42, 43
Naroll, Raoul, 9
Neel, J. V., 84
Nemeskéri, Janos, 1, 176
Netting, Robert McC., 28, 39, 41, 73, 192
Newcomer, P., 235, 239, 240, 254
Newton, Isaac, 14
Nicholson, G., 168, 178
Nieboer, H. J., 133
Nukunya, G. K., 19, 20, 191–217
Nurge, E., 251

O'Brien, J., 235
Odum, Eugene P., 4, 20, 32, 274, 292–293
Odum, Howard T., 289; "Wages, Profits, and Savings," 291
Önder, M., 167
Orans, Martin, 8, 11
Osborn, F., 259, 262

Park, Robert, 283
Parrack, Dwain W., 274
Parsons, M. H., 95
Patterson, Thomas C., 91, 96–97, 100, 102, 103, 106, 108, 109

Payne, S., 167
Peake, H., 65
Pearson, Harry W., 11
Perkins, Dexter, Jr., 173
Petersen, W., 250
Pickersgill, Barbara, 60
Plato, 174
Polanyi, Karl, 7, 12, 13, 125, 136
Polgar, Steven, 1–25, 28, 32, 41–43, 44, 81, 82, 89, 235, 250, 251, 253, 260, 262
Porter, Stephen C., 171, 175, 183
Protonotariou-Deïlakis, E., 167
Putschar, Walter, 176

Raikes, Robert, 170
Randsborg, Klavs, 10, 139–166
Rappaport, Roy A., 245, 253, 280–285, 286–287
Redfield, Robert: *Levels of Integration in Biological and Social Systems*, 283
Reed, Charles A., 90, 173
Ricardo, David, 53
Richards, A. I., 201
Richardson, F. L. W., 2, 14, 19–20, 21, 305–335
Ripley, S. Dillon, 276
Robinson, David M., 169
Robinson, H. S., 167
Rodden, J. M., 167
Rodden, Robert J., 167, 169
Rodney, W., 255
Roseberry, B., 235
Ruesch, J., 276
Ruyle, E., 246

Sacks, K., 235
Sahlins, Marshall D., 3, 8, 12, 21–22, 62, 253, 254, 285
Sanders, William T., 10, 297
Sando, R., 167
Sapir, E.: *Time Perspective in Aboriginal American Culture*, 275
Sargent, R. L., 177
Sarmela, M. E., 9, 20, 219–226
Saucier, J., 251
Sauer, Carl O., 65, 83
Schaller, George B., 235, 307
Schwanitz, Franz, 83
Scudder, Thayer, 288
Seidman, A., 264
Service, E. R., 164, 242
Seymour, Thomas D., 174, 181
Shapiro, N., 235
Shear, T. L., Jr., 167

Sheffer, Charles, 28, 82
Sidel, R., 262
Simpson, Richard H., 177, 181, 182
Slicher van Bath, B. H., 55, 73
Smith, Adam, 11
Smith, C. E., 60
Smith, Philip E. L., 4, 9, 10, 21, 54, 160
Smith, Philip S., 28, 32, 34
Smith, T. C., 73
Sognnaes, Reidar F., 178
Spencer, Herbert, 243
Spooner, Brian, 1, 28, 81, 247
Stagner, Ross, 276
Stalin, Joseph, 297
Stauder, J., 235
Stein, J. T. H., 206
Stéphanos, Clon, 170, 177, 183, 184
Stephens, William, 224
Sternberg, L., 167
Stevenson, Robert F., 1, 10
Steward, J., 237, 239, 297
Stewart, Omer C., 83
Stewart, T. Dale, 167, 176
Stini, William A., 46, 48
Stolnitz, G., 294
Stork, H. E., 95
Sussman, Robert W., 42, 244, 245, 250, 252
Sweezy, P., 255, 256
Swift, M., 235

Tarn, W. M., 183
Taylor, W., 167
Temizer, R., 167
Terray, E., 237
Tettey, D. K., 206
Textor, Robert, 222
Thompson, H., 32, 167
Thoms, H., 178
Tiger, L., 243, 244
Timur, 175
Todd, T. Wingate, 176
Towle, Margaret, 91, 111, 117

Trigger, B., 237
Trotter, Mildred, 178
Trudel, F., 235

Van Lawick-Goodall, Hugo, 322
Vayda, Andrew P., 281–282, 287
Veblen, Thorstein, 126–127
Vita-Vinzi, Claudio, 38, 170, 171, 175

Washburn, S., 244
Watt, Kenneth E. F., 30
Weberbauer, A., 95
Weinberg, Saul S., 173, 177
Weisenfeld, Stephen L., 279
Westermann, D., 199
Westfall, John, 177
Wheat, J. W., 36, 37
Whitaker, T. W., 103, 108, 117
White, D., 222, 235, 237
White, L., 239, 241, 244, 247, 253
White, T. E., 35, 37
Whiting, J., 239, 251
Wiener, Norbert, 276
Willey, Gordon R., 60
Williams, C. K., 167
Williams, E., 257
Wilson, Monica, 299
Winch, Robert F., 222
Winniet (British Governor of Gold Coast), 199
Wiseman, J., 167
Wissler, Clark, 275
Wittfogel, Karl, 297
Wolpoff, M., 248
Woodburn, J. C., 34, 35, 39, 62, 84, 85
Wrigley, E. A., 35, 43, 167
Wright, Gary A., 4, 15
Wynne-Edwards, V., 236–237, 244, 245

Young, T. Cuyler, 4, 9, 10, 21, 54

Zohary, Daniel, 173

Index of Subjects

Abidjan, Ghana, 215
Abor, Ghana, 194
Abortion, 3, 42–44, 46, 266
Acarnania, 169
Accra, Ghana, 199, 209, 211, 212
Achuara, Jivaroan, 128
Adafienu, Ghana, 194
Adaptation, in biology, 286
Adidome, Ghana, 212–213
Aegean islanders, 182
Aegean Sea, 170, 171, 173, 182
Afiadenyigba, Ghana, 194
Aflae, 193, 194
Africa, 9–10, 12, 36, 56, 73, 230, 256–259, 266, 285, 288, 294; East, 64; North, 68, 172, 173, 175, 183; West, 11, 20, 32, 64, 198, 257, 263–264. *See also* South Africa
Agbosume, Ghana, 214, 216
Age-area idea, 275
Aghios Kosmas, 180
Agricultural involution, in Java, 279–280
Agriculture: among Anlo, 191–216; defined, 55–56; and population growth, 82–91, 214–216; and population pressure, 71–118; and population size, 53–76; swidden, 280, 295; transition to, from food gathering; wet-rice production, 280. *See also* Cultivation; Ecological variables
Albanians, 175
Aleut, 230
Alexandria, Egypt, 175
Alps, 170

Amazon River, 11, 124
American Philosophical Society, 167
American School of Classical Studies, Athens, Greece, 167
Amutinu, Ghana, 194
Anatolia, 68, 170, 171, 175, 181, 182
Ancash, Peru, 114, 127
Ancón, Peru, 102; Necropolis, 111
Ancón-Chillón region, Peru, 4, 6, 91–118
Andaman Islanders, 58
Andes, 5
Angaw Lagoon, Ghana, 194, 197, 198
Ankara, 175
Anlo, 20; agriculture among, 191–216, clans among, 200–203; land tenure among, 200–203; women, trading by, among, 199
Anloga, Ghana, 192, 193, 194, 196, 197, 200, 201, 204, 205, 207, 208, 209, 210–214, 215, 216
Antioch, 175
Anyake, Ghana, 194
Arabia, 170
Arabs, Muslim, 175
Aragonese Crusaders, 175
Archaeological Services in Greece, Cyprus, and Turkey, Jefferson Medical College and University Museum, Philadelphia, 167
Arenal complex, Peru, 101–102
Argissa, 173
Armenia, 173
Asia, 36, 230, 294; Central, 64; East, 56, 228, 231; Southeast, 62, 64, 228,

259, 288, 295; Southwest, 15
"Asiatic type of society," 297
Athens, Greece, 174, 183
Atiavi, Ghana, 194, 214, 216
Attica, 174, 180
Australia, 44, 228–229, 230
Australian aborigines, 30, 36, 37–38, 41, 227, 228–230, 231, 233
Avars, 175
Ave, 193
Avu Lagoon, Ghana, 194
Ayacucho region, Peru, 91, 102, 105, 114, 115
Aztec, 68, 134, 297–298

Badagri, Ghana, 215
"Bali: The Value System of a Steady State" (Bateson), 277
Balkans, 170, 171, 175, 181, 182
Band-aggregate. *See* Group size
Band organization. *See* Family group, permanent
Bantu, 257
Bε, 193
Behavior: group-centered, and cultural growth, 219–224; and human speech, 248–249; kinship (or family)-centered, 219
Beldibi, 172–173
Bemba, 201
"Big man," phenomenon, 128
"Big men," 8, 10–11. *See also* Chiefs
Birth control. *See* Abortion; Infanticide
Birth spacing, 250–253
Black Death. *See* Plague
Blacks, in United States, 259
Blekusu, Ghana, 194
Bornholm Island, 145
Brave New World (Huxley), 20
Bremen (Norddeutsche) Mission, Anloga, Ghana, 211
British Archaeological Institute, Ankara, 167
Buem-Krachi, Ghana, 193
Burials: contents of, 140–143; hoards and offerings in, 153–154; and mortuary wealth, 150–153; types of, and social status, 149–150
Bushmen, 34, 37, 227, 274; Dobe, 36; !Kung, 34, 36, 48, 62, 63, 84–85, 86, 247
Byzantium, 68, 169, 175–176, 184

Cachi complex, Peru, 114

California, 30, 39
California Indians, 30, 30, 135, 227, 230–231
Callejón de Huaylas, Peru, 114
Canario complex, Peru, 102–103, 114
Capital, 125–126, 137; among Jívaro, 127–129
Capitalism, 20, 243, 257, 259–265, 266
Caribou Eskimo, 39
Carmel, Mount, 172
Carrying capacity, 284, 286
Çatal Hüyük, 169, 173, 180
Catchment territory, 38–40; defined, 38
Caucasus, 170
Causative theories, 5, 19
Chalandriani, 180
Chiefs, 8, 11, 130–131, 133
Chihua complex, Peru, 114
Chillón River, Peru, 92, 94, 98, 100, 109
China, 35, 135, 259, 262, 265, 332; Han, 168; Sung, 68
Chinese, 232, 233
Chivateros complex, Peru, 100–101
Christianity, 175, 193, 194, 210–211
Chronocentrism, 19
Chuquitanta site, Peru, 109, 110
Clans, among Anlo, 200–203
Climatic change, 4–5, 15, 96, 105
Climatic shock, 5
Cold War, 294
Colonialism, 12–13, 22
Colorado valley, 231
Columbia University, 91; Seminar in Ecological Systems and Cultural Evolution, "Scarcity and Society," 123
Conchas complex, Peru, 109, 114
Congo basin, 257
Constantinople, 175. *See also* Byzantium
Consumption level subsistence, defined, 36
Consumption levels, 36–37, 47–48
Contraception, 183, 266
Copaic basin, 172, 174
Corbina complex, Peru, 103
Corinth, 180
Cotonou, Ghana, 215
Crete, 170, 182
Crusaders, 175
Cultivation: defined, 56–57; pre-agricultural, 74. *See also* Agriculture
Cultural and Natural Areas of Native North America (Kroeber), 275

Cultural change, and population growth, 27, 81-82
Cultural ecology, 273–299
Cultural evolution, 295–299
Cultural growth: and group-centered behavior, 219–224; and isolated eth-noses, 227–234
Culture area, concept of, 275
Culture change, in anthropology, 288
Current Anthropology, 1
Cybernetic theory, 276–278
Cypriotes, 182

Dabala, Ghana, 213
Dahomey, 191, 193
Dai, 232
Danish Islands, 141, 144, 145
Deh Luran, 31
Demographic paradigm, 28
Demographic transition, 294–295
Demographic variables, and population growth, 168–169, 176–177, 182–185
Denmark, 199, 214, Plates, 1, 2; Early Bronze Age in, 139–165; National Museum, 141; State Research Council for the Humanities, 139
Denu, Ghana, 194, 197, 213
Dialectical materialism, 265
Dialectics of Nature (Engels), 237
Diet, 84–85, 112–113, 184; and population pressure, 180–181
Diffusion, 6, 9
Disease. *See* Health variables; Plague
Djursland Peninsula, Jutland, 145, 155, 157–158
Domestication, defined, 56–57
Dorians, 182
Dzelukofe, Ghana, 194
Dzodze, Ghana, 194, 213

Ecological pollution, 293–294
Ecological variables, and population growth, 168, 170–176
Ecology, 14, 19–20, 21; cultural, 273–299
Economic changes, and population growth, 92
Ecosystem: concept of, 276–277; theory, 276–295
Ecuador, 128
Efficiency, defined, 55
Egypt, 68, 173
Elmali plain, 180
El Riego phase, 60, 74

Encanto complex, Peru, 103, 104, 105, 112, 114
England, 12–13, 20, 45, 73, 178, 243, 259
Environmental circumscription, 11–12
Epidemics, 255. *See also* Plague
Equilibrium, defined, 277
Eskimo, 36, 134, 230, 255; Caribou, 39; Netsilik, 252
Ethnographic Atlas (Murdock), 11
Ethnoses, isolated, 227–234
Ethology, human, 305–307
Eurafrica, 169
Europe, 4, 12–13, 31, 33, 129, 150, 171, 173, 174, 181, 184, 255–259, 266, 294; northern, 68; Western, 13, 135, 176
Evangelical Presbyterian Church, 211
Evolution, 15, 19, 20, 21–22; biological, 306, 311, 313, 325–328; cultural 295–299; organizational, 305, 334; social, 27, 238–243, 306, 311
Ewe, 191, 193, 200, 205, 208
Eweland, 191, 211

Family community (simple tribal) organization, 308
Family community and institutional organization (pre-industrial state), 309
Family group, permanent (band organization), 308
Family organization, temporary, 308, 326
FAO. *See* United Nations, Food and Agriculture Organization
Far East, 12, 129
Farming. *See* Agriculture
Fecundity, 42, 183
Feedback, defined, 278
Fertility. *See* Natality
Feudalism, 7–12, 20, 22, 255–259, 266
Feuding, 322
Finnish-Karelian culture area, 220–221
Firearms, 13
Food chains, 276–277
Food gathering, transition from, to agriculture, 3–7
Food storage, 32
Ford Foundation, 261
Formalists, in economic anthropology, 125, 136–137
France, 13
Franchti, 169, 172–173
French Revolution, 20
Functionalism, in social sciences, 286

Gambia, 35
Gaviota phase, Peru, 109
Genieri hoe agriculturists, 35
Germany, West, 262
Ghana, 19, 191–216, 263; Extension Office, 208; Ministry of Agriculture, 192, 209–210
Gishu, 73
Gold Coast (later, Ghana, q.v.), 194, 199
Goths, 175
Graves. *See* Burials
Great Lakes Indians, 58
Greece, 129, 168, 169, 170, 171, 175, 180, 181
Greeks, 182
Group size, local and regional (band-aggregates), 38–41, 48
Guggenheim, J. S., Foundation, 167

Hacilar, 173
Hadza, 34, 39, 62, 63
Harris lines of growth arrest, 178
Harvard Univerity, 91, 261; traveling fellowship, 167
Hasan Mountains, 173
Haya, 64
Health variables, and population growth, 168–170, 174–176, 177–185
Hellenes, 182
Himalayas, 231
Ho, Ghana, 193, 212
Homeostasis, defined, 277
Hominization, 2–3
Horticulture. *See* Agriculture
Hotu, 172
Hrdlička, Aleš, Fund, Smithsonian Institution, 167
Human ethology, 305–307
Huns, 175
Hunting-gathering, 27–49, 81, 83–88, 103–105, 236–238; defined, 33
Hutterian Brethren, 286
"Hydraulic society," 297–298

Ibo, 73
Illurians, 182
Imperialism, 259, 262–264. *See also* Capitalism
Inca, 134
India, 32, 263, 274
Indian Ocean, 12
Indians, United States, 36, 169. *See also* Names of individual tribes
Indian Sinhalese "hydraulic society,"

297
Indonesia, 229
Industrialism, 12–13, 22
Industrial Revolution, 178
Infanticide, 3, 42–44, 46, 183, 250–253, 255, 264, 266
Infiernillo phase, 60
Intensiveness, defined, 55
"Invidious distinction," 126–127
Iroquois, 130
Irrigation civilization, 297
Islam, 175
"Isolated City" model, 71–72
Isolated ethnoses, and cultural growth, 227–234

Jamaica, 263
Japan, 13, 294, 295; Tokugawa, 73
Jasikan, 193
Java, 21; agricultural involution in, 279–280
Javanese Terra, 55
Jaywa complex, Peru, 102
Jefferson Medical College and University Museum, Philadelphia, Archaeological Services in Greece, Cyprus, and Turkey, 167
Jericho, 172–173
Jívaro: capital among, 127–129; kinship systems among, 129–130; labor among, 127–128, 132; population density among, 127; warfare among, 132–133; women, role of, among, 128–129
Jutland, 140, 141–147, 155, 157–158

Kaki Skala, 172
Kalahari Desert, 84, 86
Kara In, 172
Karatas, Lycia, 169, 180, 181
Kariba Dam, Kenya, 288
Karim Shahir, 172
Kazakhstan, 181
Kea, 169, 180
Kentucky hill people, 294
Kenya, 288
Kephala, Kea, 169, 180
Kephallenia, 169
Keta, Ghana, 193, 194, 196, 199, 209, 211, 212–213, 214, 216; Danish fort at, 199
Keta district, Ghana, 192–193
Keta Lagoon, Ghana, 191, 194, 197, 198, 199, 205–206, 208, 214
Ketu, 191

Kinship systems, 130–132; among Jívaro, 129–130
Klamath region, California, 39
Kofyar, 73
Konya Plain, 169, 173
Kpandu, Ghana, 193
Ksar Akil, 172
!Kung Bushmen, 35, 36, 48, 62, 63, 84–85, 86, 247
Kuomintang, 233
Kwakiutl Indians, 61, 246

Labor, 125–126, 132, 134–136, 243, 266; allocation of, 236, 266; defined, 126; among Jívaro, 127–130; and warfare, 132–133
Labor potential, and population growth, 250–255, 266
Labor-saving technology, 134–136
Laconia, 169
Land, 123–126, 130–132, 134–137; defined, 126; among Jívaro, 127–128, 132; and warfare, 132–133
Land quality, and population size, 147–149
Land speculation, 290–291
Land tenure, among Anlo, 203–205
Language, 311, 317–318, 321–322
Latin America, 31, 36, 259, 294
Laureion, 174
Lerna, 173, 180, 181
Leukas, 169
Levant, 170, 175
Levantines, 182
Levels of Integration in Biological and Social Systems (Redfield), 283
Liang Shan Mountains, 231–233
Lima, Peru, 92
Lome, Ghana, 212, 213
Longevity, 180, 184, 185
Louisiana, 287
Louros valley, 172
Lower Barbarism, 128
Lut-s'un, China, 35
Luz complex, Peru, 101–102
Lycia, 169, 180
Lydians, 182

Macedonia, 169
Magellan, Strait of, 230
Magna Carta, 323
Manchus, 233
Marginal survival, principle of, 275
Maring, 280–287

Marquesas, 133–134
Maruyama model of mutual causal processes, 16–19
Maya, 280
Mediterranean, 168, 179; eastern, 4, 42 45, 46, 150, 169, 170, 171, 173, 176, 179, 185
Melanesia, 8, 10, 229
Melos, 173
Mercantilism, 12–13
Mesoamerica, 5, 8, 10
Mesopotamia, 4, 5, 10, 80, 332
"Mesopotamian careers," 8
Messenia, 169
Mexico, 5, 60, 62; Aztec, 68, 134; Valley of, 297–298
Miao, 232
Middle East, 332
Minoans, 182
Mongoloids, 228
Mongols, 68, 175, 231–232, 233
Montenegro, 233
Mortality, 42–46, 250
Mortuary wealth, and social stratification, 150–153
Museo de Historia Natural, Lima, 94
Muslim Arabs, 175
Mycenae, 171, 174, 181, 182

Nanchao-Tali, 231
Natality, 2–3, 6, 42, 181, 184
National-global organization, 309–310
Navajo, 294
Nazism, 221
Nea Nikomedia, 44, 169, 173
Near East, 8, 31, 56, 62, 150, 173, 179
Neolithic Revolution, 53, 54
Netherlands, The, 279
Netsilik Eskimo, 252
New Guinea, 128, 280–285, 286–287
New World, 7, 64, 134, 176, 230, 256, 258
"Niche," Barth's use of term, 273–274
Nigeria, 73, 191, 193
Noefe, 193
Norddeutsche Mission. *See* Bremen Mission
North America, 12, 274, 294; Northwest Coast of, 28–29; 31, 32
North Sea, 147
Northwest Coast Indians, 16, 61, 238, 281. *See also* Kwakiutl; Tlingit
Nosu (Yitsu), 231–233
Notsio, Togo, 191

Nyigbla (Anlo god of war), 201
Nyoro, 201

Oasis theory, 5, 65
Oaxaca, Mexico, 5, 80, 85
Old World, 176, 230
Olympia, 175
Olynthus, 169
Optimum yield, to man, 30–31
Oquendo complex, Peru, 100
Orient. *See* Far East
"Oriental despotism," 297
Origin of the Family, Private Property, and the State, The (Engels), 128
Osmanli Turks, 175
Ottoman Empire, 175–176
Overpopulation. *See* Population pressure
Ovulation, change in, 2

Pacific, 64
Paiute Indians, 58
Pakistan, 32
Palestine, 182
Pamirs, 170
Pampa site, Peru, 108
Permanence, defined, 55
Persia, 68
Peru, 4, 5, 6, 11, 16, 60, 84, 90–118, 134
Petralona, 172
Pigs. *See* Swine management
Piki complex, Peru, 102, 114, 115
Plague, 175, 176
Plains Indians, 238
Playa Hermosa phase, Peru, 109
Pollution, ecological, 293–294
Polygny, 129
Ponape, 133–134
Population composition, 177
Population control, 13, 236, 246–247, 249–253, 260, 264, 266
Population density, 27–49, 135, 176–177, 184, 214–215; among Jívaro, 127; and social stratification, 153–163
Population growth, 13–15, 20–22, 27–49; and agriculture, 82–91, 214–216; and cultural change, 27, 81–82; and demographic variables, 168–169, 176–177, 182–185; and ecological variables, 168, 170–176; and economic changes, 92; and health variables; 168–170, 174–176, 177–185; and labor potential, 250–255, 266; in preindustrial societies, 137; and technological change,

81–82, 104–105, 115–118, 236, 247
Population pressure, 4–5, 9–11, 126; and agriculture, 71–118; and capitalism, 262–263; and diet, 180–181; and slavery, 134; and social evolution, 27, 245–247; and tools, 246–247. *See also* Population density; Population growth
Population pseudo-density, 70–72
Population size, 27–49; and agriculture, 53–76; and land quality, 147–149
Postpartum sexual restrictions, 250, 266
Potato cultivation, 13
Pre-Capitalist Economic Formations (Marx), 137
Preindustrial state, 309
Primary productivity, 29–31
Primordial interactional process, 305–307
Production, African feudal modes of, 257–258
Progress, 19–22
Puerto Ricans, in United States, 259
Puget Sound, 289
Pull factors, 5, 11
Punjab, India, 261
Push factors, 5, 11

Red Zone complex, Peru, 100
Reproduction planning, 265, 266
Resource potentials, 29–33, 47
Resources: defined, 125–126; destruction of, 332–333; imbalance between population and, 105
Rethymno region, 170
"Role Played by Labor in the Transition from Ape to Man" (Engels), 237
Rome, 68, 73, 129, 168, 174–176, 183–184
Rule of the minimum, 32
Russians, Viking, 175

Sacramento valley, California, 231
Saint Paul, Cape, Ghana, 194, 196
Salling peninsula, Jutland, 147
Samoa, 133–134
Santa Fe, New Mexico, 289
Santa Sophia, Constantinople, 175
Scania, Sweden, 141
Scarcity, 123–137
"Scarcity and Society," Columbia University in Ecological Systems and Cultural Evolution, 123
Schleswig-Hostein, 141

Sedentism, 5, 10–11, 65, 90, 107–108
Seljuk Turks, 175
Settlement patterns, 144–145
Sierra Nevada, United States, 230
Slavery, 13, 133–134, 135, 175, 257
Slavs, 175
Smithsonian Institution, Aleš Hrdlička Fund, 167
Social groups: attraction among members of, 316; contending and hostility among, 321–323; contentious and friendly relations among, 311–313; cooperation among, 319–320, 330–332; dominance behavior among, 314–335, 327–328, 331; feuding among, 322; hostility and cooperation among, 326, 328; humor, smiling, and laughter among, 318–319; imperfect adjustment among, 320–321; interdependence among, 328–329, 330–332; kinesthetic activities among, 312, 317–319; language and tone among, 317–318; precedence and privilege among, 313–314; progressively enlarging, 330–334; sex among, 316; social behavior, disrupting of, among, 323; spatial ordering among, 312, 326; sustenance and drink among, 316; temporal ordering among, 326; tactile activity among, 312, 316–317
Social production, 20, 235–238; defined, 235
Social ritual: in Louisiana, 287; among Tsembaga, 280–287
Social stratification: and burials, types of, 149–150; and mortuary wealth, 150–153; and population density, 153–163; and women, 153–163
Societies, human and animal, 243–248, 249, 265–266
Sogakofe, Ghana, 193, 213
South Africa, 261
South America, 11, 12, 56, 60, 215
Spatial ordering, 312, 326
Speech, human, and behavior, 248–249. *See also* Language
Spirit Cave, Thailand, 60
Stability, defined, 277
Steady state, defined, 277
Study of Man, The (Linton), 275
Suberde, 173
Substantivists, in economic anthropology, 125, 136–137
Sudan states, 257

Sumerians, 332–333
Supporting capacity, 11
Surpluses, 5, 8–9, 11–12, 18
Sweden, 141, 259, 262
Swidden agriculture (slash-and-burn; shifting cultivation), 280, 295
Swine management, among Tsembaga, 280–283, 286–287
System analysis, 291

Tahiti, 133–134
Tamaulipas, Mexico, 60, 80
Tanzania, 34
Taos, New Mexico, 289
Technological change, and population growth, 81–82, 104–105, 115–118
Tegbi, Ghana, 194, 205, 215
Tehuacán, Mexico, 5, 60, 74, 80
Tell Mureybat, 173
Temple University, 91
"Tension zones," 4
Teotihuacán, Mexico, 297
Thailand, 60
Third World, 13, 22
Thrace, 173
Thy peninsula, Jutland, 147
Tien, 231
Tierra del Fuego, 227, 230–231
Tikopia, 133–134
Time Perspective in Aboriginal American Culture (Sapir), 275
Timonovka (USSR), 32
Tlingit Indians, 139
Togo, 191, 193, 196
Tonga, 133–134, 288
Tongu, 193, 208
Tools: and population pressure, 246–247; and social relations, 248–249
Trade, of food, 34, 39, 47
Trojan wars, 182
Trophic levels, 277
Troy, 180
Trundholm, Zealand, 154
Tsembaga: social ritual among, 280–287; swine management among, 280–283, 286–287; warfare among, 280–283, 286
Tsinme, Ghana, 201
Turkestan, 173
Turkey, 170
Turks, 175

Ukraine, 172
Underdevelopment, 264

Underpopulation, and capitalism, 262–263

United Nations, 259; Food and Agriculture Organization (FAO), 36

United States, 13, 135, 178, 184, 288–289, 316; blacks in, 259; Indians in, 36, 169 (*see also* names of individual tribes); Puerto Ricans in, 259

United States, National Institutes of Health, 167

University of Connecticut, 235

University of North Carolina, 5

Urban revolution, 9

Venetian Crusaders, 175

Ventanilla Bay, Peru, 94, 100, 102

Viking Russians, 175

Volta region, 193, 210, 211

Volta River, 191, 192, 194, 196, 197, 263

Vulgar materialism, 15

Wadi-en-Natuf, 172–173

"Wages, Profits, and Savings" (Odum), 291

Warfare, 175, 182; among Jívaro, 132–133; and labor, 132–133; and land, 132–133, 135; and population control, 251; and slavery, 133; among Tsembaga, 280–283, 286

Wealth. *See* Mortuary wealth

Wenner-Gren Foundation, 167

West Bengal, India, 274

Wet-rice production agriculture, 280

What Happened in History (Childe), 9

Woe, Ghana, 194, 197, 215

Women: longevity of, 176; role of, among Jívaro, 128–129; and social stratification, 153–163; trading by, among Anlo, 199

World Archaeology, 1

Yamana (Yahgana), 230–231, 233

Yana, 230–231, 233

Yitsu. *See* Nosu

Yoruba, 191

Yucatán, 280

Yunnan valleys, 231

Zarzi, 172

Zealand, 141, 154

Zion College, Anloga, Ghana, 211